Sports Ministry

David Lewis, DMin
Huntington University

David Irby, MAT
Surge International Ministries, Founder and Director

William Galipault, DMin
Southern California Seahorses, Executive Director

Wayne Rasmussen, EdD
The Master's University

HUMAN KINETICS

Library of Congress Cataloging-in-Publication information is available. LCCN 2022034371 (print)

ISBN: 978-1-7182-1021-9 (print)

The web addresses cited in this text were current as of August 2022, unless otherwise noted.

Scriptures taken from the Holy Bible, New International Version®, NIV®. Copyright © 1973, 1978, 1984, 2011 by Biblica, Inc.™ Used by permission of Zondervan. All rights reserved worldwide. www.zondervan.com The "NIV" and "New International Version" are trademarks registered in the United States Patent and Trademark Office by Biblica, Inc.™

Acquisitions Editor: Andrew L. Tyler; **Developmental Editor:** Melissa Feld; **Copyeditor:** Marissa Wold Uhrina; **Proofreader:** Librum Artis Editorial Services; **Indexer:** Ferreira Indexing; **Permissions Manager:** Laurel Mitchell; **Graphic Designer:** Joe Buck; **Cover Designer:** Keri Evans; **Cover Design Specialist:** Susan Rothermel Allen; **Photograph (cover):** Surge International/David Irby; **Photo Asset Manager:** Laura Fitch; **Photo Production Manager:** Jason Allen; **Senior Art Manager:** Kelly Hendren; **Printer:** Color House Graphics

Printed in the United States of America

10 9 8 7 6 5 4 3 2 1

Human Kinetics
1607 N. Market Street
Champaign, IL 61820
USA

United States and International
Website: **US.HumanKinetics.com**
Email: info@hkusa.com
Phone: 1-800-747-4457

Canada
Website: **Canada.HumanKinetics.com**
Email: info@hkcanada.com

E8464

We dedicate this book to Jesus Christ, who shows us what it means to love our neighbor as ourselves, whether that neighbor is down the street or on the other side of the globe. Additionally, we dedicate these pages to the thousands of unsung, unnamed heroes of the sports ministry movement, past and present—whether they faithfully volunteer with church sport leagues, are salt and light in the secular setting of sport, or are part of the multitude of coaches, players, and support personnel who sacrifice time and finances traveling to challenging and sometimes dangerous places to share the love of Christ. Our prayer is that the ideas and examples shared in this book will help encourage and equip the next generation of sports ministers.

CONTENTS

PART III DEVELOPING A VIABLE SPORTS MINISTRY

Sports ministry is a growing field. Numerous sports ministry organizations exist, using a variety of sports, fitness, and forms of recreation. Churches are adding staff and sports ministry programs to facilitate healthy living and social interaction for the purpose of evangelism and discipleship. An increasing number of academic institutions are offering courses and degree programs equipping students in the discipline. Unfortunately, sports ministry academic resource materials have been limited in scope, tasking instructors with developing course content from few curricular options. Recognizing a need for a comprehensive introduction for anyone interested in sports ministry, we have written *Sports Ministry* to provide students and instructors with a foundational resource contained in one volume. Even though sports ministry is a growing field, many people lack familiarity with it. This textbook will provide a solid base of knowledge in theory and practice. With a quality, user-friendly textbook, it is our hope that schools will acknowledge the subject's value and consider adding a course in sports ministry. It complements academic disciplines and preparations for vocational pursuits such as sport and recreation management, youth ministry, missions, church ministry, camping, personal training and fitness, coaching and athletic administration, and so on. The book's content and format will enable an instructor with little sports ministry background to prepare and confidently present the course. For institutions that already have a sports ministry offering, the adoption of this book will strengthen their courses and provide their students with an easy-to-read source of valuable information and encouraging practical insights.

The four authors of *Sports Ministry* each add unique expertise to the textbook. Representing more than a century of cumulative sports ministry and sport management experience, we believe God has equipped us to serve His Kingdom purpose for this role. Combined, we have sport experience at the high school, club, collegiate, and professional levels as players, coaches, and administrators. We have served multiple cross-cultural sports ministry organizations and have developed sport programming within local churches. Several of our own undergraduate sports ministry and management courses have proven beneficial resources in the book's content. Over the

years, we have developed a network within the sports ministry community—a common bond of mutual respect and appreciation, sharing ideas and praying for one another. Several of these practitioners have been referenced in each of our chapters. Because academic course work was unavailable at the time, much of our own sports ministry knowledge and practice have been the result of self-education hit-or-miss efforts. Consequently, we believe formal training will preempt the frustrations we experienced of time-exhaustive trial-and-error endeavors and will better prepare students for their vocational field of service. Advanced formalized sports ministry training will not eliminate all potential pitfalls, but it will provide a better navigating position from which to start.

As followers of Jesus, we have sought to present this book from a Christian worldview, acknowledging the Bible as the revealed Word of God, trusting His counsel for wisdom and direction in the practice of effective sports ministry. We encourage the reader to be like the Bereans of Paul's day who readily listened to what Paul had to say, and "examined the Scriptures every day to see if what Paul said was true" (Acts 17:11 NIV). We encourage you to review the instruction of this book and examine how it aligns itself with the Word of God.

The Scope and Organization of the Book

Theory and the pragmatic practices of sports ministry are common themes throughout the book. Part I begins with a definition of sports ministry and why this form of service is relevant and effective. A brief history of sports ministry follows, reviewing prominent Christian sport figures, the earliest ones known as *Muscular Christians*. In part II, sports ministry practices in America and abroad are studied with a focus on their local and global mission associations. Christian faith considerations are examined as *play* and interpreted in light of the purpose of God's creative order. Various methods of gospel communication within a sport context are explored with examples for practice and implementation. Christian ethical behavior in sport is critiqued, and several specific topics are addressed, with a primary emphasis on the compatibility of faith and sport. The realms of fiscal responsibility, issues related to facility management, and legal matters are reviewed. Part III begins with guidelines for the planning and execution of short-term international trips followed by the practices of sports ministry within local churches. A chapter is devoted to sports ministry organizations. Finally, the book concludes with cultural considerations and the model of servant leadership.

Each chapter includes a Sports Ministry Professional Profile, providing a glimpse into the lives and ministries of individuals and organizations actively engaged in sports ministry. In addition, Sports Ministry in Action sidebars depict a variety of related persons and subjects. The purpose of these is to deepen the understanding of various ministry components and provide a window of tangible applied theory through the lives of sports ministers. A bibliography concludes each chapter, and the examination of its source material should prove beneficial for further study.

The chapters are organized in a suggested sequential pattern; however, the instructor may choose amendments to best meet his or her own teaching preferences and the specific needs of his or her students. For instance, if the class will have a gospel communication assignment, it is best to cover that material early in the semester so students have adequate preparation time. If these assignments also include oral classroom presentations, it will allow

enough time. There is ample course material, so the instructor will need to determine the content that best meets the course objectives.

Instructor Guide and Test Package

The purpose of the instructor guide is to assist the professor with course content and to help spark creative ideas. It is divided by chapter and includes a sample course syllabus, chapter learning objectives, outline and summary, review questions, suggested resources and assignments, and 20 exam questions (formatted as true-false, fill-in-the-blank, and multiple choice). Additional resources provide online links to bolster student understanding. For example, hearing about Eric Liddell's dramatic victory in the 1924 Paris Olympics is enlivened when students can actually watch a video of Liddell crossing the finish line in the 400-meter race.

We hope this book will be not only informative but also transformative—challenging you to view sport from a broadened perspective and to integrate Christian faith into every aspect of your involvement. We encourage you to seek God with the eyes of your heart, serving Him passionately while bringing Jesus to the forefront of your sporting endeavors, honoring Him with who you are and what you do.

ACKNOWLEDGMENTS

The compilation of this textbook has been the product of lifelong journeys, testimonies to God's faithfulness, and the many people He has brought along our paths for the betterment of us all and for the intended glory of His Kingdom. The authors would like to thank the numerous individuals, groups, churches, universities, students, and SMOs who have helped shape our understanding and experiences in sports ministry. We thank Human Kinetics and their professional staff for the opportunity to tackle this project (with special thanks to Drew Tyler and Melissa Feld for their assistance throughout its writing). We thank the contributors of the featured sidebars, stories, and analogies—the wealth of your insights is invaluable, and your collective passion for sports ministry is an encouragement and model to emulate. We acknowledge Eddie Waxer, a humble pioneer of sports ministry who God has worked through to pour into the lives of so many people. We appreciate Kiel McClung for graciously sharing his talents by providing illustrated graphs and charts. We are indebted to Bethany Alcock for the countless hours spent reading each chapter and providing her editorial expertise.

Most importantly, we express our heartfelt gratitude to our families and especially our wives, Lisa Galipault, Susan Irby, Eileen Lewis, and Debby Rasmussen, for their unwavering support, prayers, and encouragement throughout the writing and revisions of this book. You are our unsung heroes, steadfast ministry partners, and blessings from God. Thank you!

PART I

SPORTS MINISTRY PRIMER

The multinational Surge Soccer team on a peace mission, shown here with the Burundian president's team in Ngozi, Burundi.

CHAPTER 1

Introduction to Sports Ministry

Sport has the power to change the world. It has the power to inspire. It has the power to unite people in a way that little else does. It speaks to youth in a language they understand. Sport can create hope where once there was only despair.

Nelson Mandela

LEARNING OBJECTIVES

After studying this chapter, you should be able to do the following:
- Explain the vision and purpose for sports ministry
- Understand significant factors of sport in today's world
- Recognize links between Christianity and sport
- Understand definitions of sport and sports ministry

The headline of *The Guardian* newspaper emphatically sneered, "Football-Mad President Plays on While Burundi Fears the Return of Civil War," and the article went on to say, "In the poorest country in the world, President Pierre Nkurunziza is intent, say opponents, on hanging on to power—and his private stadium" (Howden 2014). In 2013 a pastor from Burundi approached Surge International with this request: "Could you bring a soccer team to my country? We are about to go back to civil war. The presidential elections will happen next year, and we are terrified that the country will split into two and are so afraid of more extreme violence."

President Nkurunziza had led the rebels in the previous civil war, described by many as a "low-tech genocide" (i.e., a lot of atrocities were committed with machetes), and he helped quell the conflict but only after 300,000 casualties. Burundi was on the edge again. In a move considered controversial by the opposition groups and the watching world, President Nkurunziza decided to run for a third term. Within the context of imminent national crisis, 18 soccer players from eight countries answered the call to travel to Burundi for a series of soccer matches, including a match in President Nkurunziza's private stadium that featured his own team, Hallelujah FC; Miniero, a famous Brazilian professional and national team soccer player; and Musa Otieno, the former Kenyan national team captain, who came out of retirement to lead the team. The team also included four Burundian players and two players who had survived the Rwandan genocide despite the loss of most of their family members in the carnage.

The visiting team shared the importance of reconciliation through Christ as the only answer to reunite the country. When Surge International (Surge Soccer) originally committed to the project, it was only after a month of prayer and seeking wise counsel. When Surge made the commitment, it had no money or players for the project, simply a trust that God would provide. Surge began emailing, texting, and phoning associates to share information about the trip to Burundi—the dates, the cost, and the purpose. People responded graciously and sent contributions. Two American college coaches were secured, and they helped recruit U.S. players and assumed the role of players themselves. The U.S. contingent raised support to not only cover their own expenses but also help defray the costs for the international players. Two weeks prior to the trip, the funding was in place—a testimony to God's faithfulness and the call for His followers to seek Him in prayer. The tour was followed by Burundi's national news media, which aired the game with the president's team on national television multiple times. Surge representatives were invited to the presidential palace to dine with the president, his family, and government leaders. A significant highlight of the trip was the training of over 200 pastors in sports ministry, equipping them to promote peace and reconciliation through the grace of God.

In time, the Peace Tournament and a Peace Run were developed, with all the conflicting parties signing a peace agreement in the national stadium. Both events helped each side to understand each other as people who wanted a safe and prosperous country and to find the same common ground in politics that they were finding through sport. Since that time sporadic unrest has occurred, but civil war has been avoided. Additional peace initiatives have been instituted, including a provision for jobs—all because a small group believed that sport (in this case, soccer) could be a unifying force for good.

This remarkable account of peace garnered through sport demonstrates the powerful tool that sport can represent. This chapter provides a brief introduction to sports ministry, defining it and casting its vision within the context of the modern sport culture.

Introducing Sports Ministry

Sports ministry and the many elements of this dynamic movement are continuing to grow and expand. At the heart of sports ministry efforts is the opportunity to build relationships and share the hope of the gospel message of Jesus Christ. Sport has the ability to inspire and empower young people to believe in themselves. Sport also has the power to unite countries and cultures that may not have anything in common other than their love of the game and the love of sport.

To the Church at Philippi, the Apostle Paul writes, "I can do all things through him who strengthens me" (Philippians 4:13 ESV), and to the Church at Colossae he writes, "And whatever you do, in word or deed, do everything in the name of the Lord Jesus, giving thanks to God the Father through him" (Colossians 3:17 ESV). Believers are equipped by God to "do all things through him," and "whatever you do" includes sport. The authority of the **Scriptures** guides all aspects of life and strengthens Christ's followers for the tasks He presents. Sport is used as a relational, bridge-connecting ministry tool as it is rendered "unto Him." Throughout the textbook, key historic figures and current examples will be introduced—individuals who have experienced God's call to make a difference in the world through the powerful platform of sport.

A Vision for Sports Ministry

The field of sports ministry is blessed with visionaries and dreamers, individuals and organizations, that are making a difference in people's lives. They come from all walks of life and represent a variety of sports, and they include athletes who wrestle with their identities as Christian sportspersons and who seek God's counsel about His perspective concerning their sport engagements. Spirit-anointed visions and dreams have led to the organization of successful ministries such as the Fellowship of Christian Athletes (FCA) and Athletes in Action (AIA). The same Spirit has authored the stories of Tom Roy, a world-traveling ambassador for Christ through baseball; Russell Carr, a visionary for sports ministry in Uganda whose influence eventually led to the Disney movie and book *The Queen of Katwe*; Seren Fryatt, a Mercy Ships volunteer in Liberia, who started a national mentorship program through sport; and Dugeree Ganbaatar, a man who lost his arm in a workplace factory accident, subsequently came to a saving knowledge of Christ, and began planting churches in Mongolia through soccer despite never playing the sport as a youth. These stories are journeys of faith and visions actualized.

As one considers his or her own sporting life, the Bible boldly proclaims, "Where there is no vision, the people perish" (Proverbs 29:18 KJV). Author and pastor David Jeremiah expounds upon the importance of the concept of vision: "Without a dream, we float through life without ever catching the current. Many of us fill the majority of our hours with diversions and only a few dreams. But our world is shaped by determined dreamers, by men and women of vision" (Jeremiah 2020, 3).

Why Sports Ministry?

This textbook is written to stimulate thought, prayer, and action. Jesus and his disciples did not live in a bubble, and they certainly did not think inside the box. A criticism of Christianity is that it is too legalistic—just a bunch of rules, a set of dos and don'ts for everyone to follow. This stereotype is not perpetuated in this textbook. Rather, the intention is to introduce how Christian faith and sport can be integrated through examples of Christians in sport, relevant faith-related issues, and sports ministry organizations representing diverse ministry practices. The common theme is not a specific sport, nor is it about color, race, gender, or creed. The shared denominator is a relationship with Jesus Christ and a love for all humankind.

The example and admonition of Jesus is to reach out to people where they congregate. Jesus regularly met people in the marketplace, along the road, in their homes, and in the public square. Major sites where people gather today are athletic arenas and sporting venues. Consequently, sports ministry follows the mandate of Jesus to go where people congregate.

Sport is a major societal influence. It represents a universal language that threads its way through communication barriers and cultural differences. It is a connective, relational bridge—a ready path for the Christian athlete or coach to trod in a language that engages and befriends strangers. Crowds flocked to Jesus as He performed miracles and spoke like no other teacher, authoritatively explaining the Kingdom of God. Sports ministers may not perform miraculous signs like Jesus, but they have drawn crowds through the attraction of something as simple as a ball, paving the way to demonstrate the gospel and to speak about its reconciling love.

Sport provides the Christian participant with an additional form of worship and thanksgiving. If athletic ability is recognized as God given, it is to be cultivated to its fullest extent and offered back to Him as an expression of gratitude. It is easy to recognize how the gifted musician who sings or plays an instrument can honor God through his or her talents. Each note rising heavenward is a note of praise, a sweet fragrance of worship. Similarly, an athlete can offer his or her gifts before God as each skill is displayed and offered heavenward from the court, track, or field. The athletes' gifts differ from those of the musician, yet they are gifts nonetheless if both athlete and musician offer them from the heart. It is not so much the position of the body—the musician's hands playing

---

Scriptures—The Bible is the Word of God. "All Scripture is God-breathed and is useful for teaching, rebuking, correcting and training in righteousness, so that the servant of God may be thoroughly equipped for every good work." (2 Timothy 3:16-17 NIV)

an instrument or the athlete's running, maneuvering, and dribbling. It is the position of the heart that matters. The heart dedicates the body's endeavors as a worshipful expression "unto the Lord." It is time for the church to recognize that worship is not contained solely within the walls of a building. The worship of God is to permeate all of life. If athletes dedicated each practice and each game as expressions of worship to God, it would leave little room for unsportsmanlike conduct or displays of self-promoting adulation.

Sports ministry provides another means for the assimilation of believers within a local church congregation. Congregants typically can assume a number of roles within various ministries, such as choir members, Sunday school teachers, board members, and committee members. Why not add a ministry for the sport minded? How can one's passion for sport be used as a ministry within the church and as an outreach to the community? Closely connected to the assimilation of believers is the development of leadership skills for the church's sports ministry participants.

Sports ministry is a means for the local church to gain visibility within its community. If the church is actively engaged in community sport endeavors, if it has athletic or recreational facilities for community use, and if it intentionally reaches out to the sporting public, the church will be noticed. More specific details about sports ministry and the local church will be highlighted in chapter 12.

Evangelism and discipleship opportunities abound within a sports ministry context. Are followers of Jesus being trained to share their faith in a sport context? Are people taught how to conduct themselves as fans who exhibit behavior consistent with Christian faith? What about the tongue? What are appropriate and inappropriate things to say during athletic competitions? Sport offers numerous teachable moments about pride, sacrifice, personal discipline, teamwork, integrity, winning and losing, motivation, attitude, and so on. This is one of many reasons sports ministry is important and why students should be equipped with a broader scope of missional purpose, outreach, and discipleship.

The Universal Power and Popularity of Sport

From their earliest days, kids kick and throw a ball. It is not long before opportunities abound for more formalized childhood sporting activities. The popularity of sport pervades all sectors of societies worldwide. Whether competing or spectating, there is no denying that sport plays a prominent role in shaping actions and attitudes. According to recent studies on social media influencers on Facebook, Instagram, and Twitter, many of the most followed social media accounts are held by athletes and professional teams, most notably soccer stars. Cristiano Ronaldo of Manchester United and the Portuguese national team has 593 million followers across all three social media platforms. Argentina's superstar, Lionel Messi of Paris Saint-Germain, is second with 375 million followers (on just Facebook and Instagram). He is trailed closely by the Real Madrid soccer team (251.5 million), FC Barcelona (248 million), and Manchester United FC (169 million). The top 10 most followed social media accounts for sports teams are ascribed to professional soccer teams. Seven NBA teams are in the top 30, as well as four cricket teams, two NFL football teams, and one professional baseball team (My Best Ball 2022 and 90 Min 2020). As of 2022, 193 countries belong to the United Nations, while the numbers of countries belonging to FIFA, the world governing body of soccer, is 211 (Russia was suspended in 2022). It is quite extraordinary that the largest political governance organization, the United Nations, is outnumbered by the member nations affiliated with the governing body of a single sport.

Sports are prominent on the list of most watched television shows of all time; take note of the statistical data in figure 1.1. Game seven of the 2016 World Series—won by the Chicago Cubs 8–7 over the Cleveland Indians in extra innings—was watched by 49.3 million people, and over 115 million tuned in to the series (Fox Sports 2016). The 2021 Super Bowl, won by Tom Brady and the Tampa Bay Buccaneers, was watched by close to 100 million people. While those are large numbers of viewers, the 2017 Manchester Derby (pronounced "darby") between Manchester United and Manchester City was broadcast into one billion homes in 189 countries (Jones 2015). Sporting statistics repeatedly affirm the strong popularity and influence of sport worldwide.

Research and studies vary about levels of sport participation and viewership. A lot depends on the criteria used and how it is interpreted. For instance, the analysis provided by Sourav Das and Edeh Chukwuemeka show that the top five most popular sports in the world are soccer, cricket, basketball, hockey (ice and field), and tennis (figure 1.2). The overarching point is that sport is popular worldwide and consequently a tremendous relational bridge for sports ministry to promote the gospel.

SPORTS MINISTRY IN ACTION

Ignite International Uses the Language of Sport to Ignite Generational Cycles of Hope

Inducted into four different sport halls of fame, Ignite founder Judy Fox has said on many occasions, "I don't know that it's right that athletes have the influence they do, but the fact is they have it. Those of us who understand that and walk in that realm have a tremendous opportunity and a significant responsibility to use this platform of influence to make a positive difference" (Ignite International 2021a). With this knowledge came a passion that led Fox to found Ignite International in 2003 with a goal to "use the universal language of sport to ignite generational cycles of hope." Her vision of sharing hope has taken Ignite to more than a dozen nations, predominantly using volleyball and basketball coaches and collegiate athletes. Ignite collaborates with national sport federations, Olympic committees, education and social influencers, and numerous values-based nongovernmental organizations (NGOs). Ignite embraces a nonnegotiable, uncompromising dedication to go where others will not and to reach those whom others do not (Fox 2019).

Judy Fox and Ignite International ignite hope, one life at a time.

Ignite International is multifaceted, with international and domestic programs tackling many of the world's most pressing traumas, including effects of the breakdown of the family unit, abuse, neglect, loss, and having a parent incarcerated or trapped in addiction. Ignite has pioneered numerous firsts:

- First collegiate volleyball team from the United States to go to Nicaragua
- First women's basketball team from the United States to go to Nicaragua
- First athletic teams to reenter Liberia after the civil war
- First women's soccer team to ever visit Liberia
- First athletes to visit Beslan, Russia, after the 2004 terrorist attack
- First volleyball initiative to empower marginalized females in Bethlehem
- First foreigners to provide activity for the Dheisheh Boys' School (Ignite International 2021c)

IGNITE is an acronym:

Integrity: "the state or quality of being undivided" (I say what I am and I am what I say)

Greatness: "markedly superior in character or quality" (I strive for greatness both on and off the court)

Non-Negotiables: "not open to discussion or modification" (my boundaries are set in Truth and do not move)

Influence: "the power to cause an intangible effect" (I embrace the power to affect change . . . I harness the power to better those around me)

Trust: "assured reliance on the character, ability, strength, or truth of someone or something" (I conduct myself worthy of the trust of others)

Excellence: "of the highest quality" (I am excellent in my attitude and my effort) (Ignite International 2021b)

After more than 30 years of affecting lives through sport, Ignite International and Judy Fox remain passionate about serving others, empowering them to move forward in their lives, and equipping them to ignite their world.

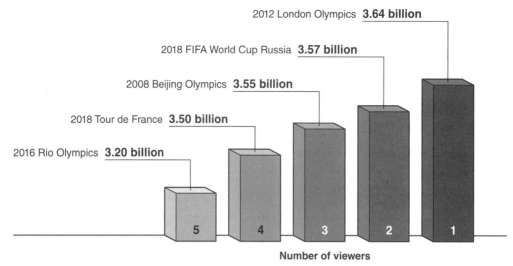

FIGURE 1.1   The most watched sporting events in history.

© Human Kinetics, adapted from illustration by Kiel McClung. Data from Dempsey (2021) and Bada (2018).

Famous statesmen like Tony Blair and the late Reverend Billy Graham, evangelist to the world, recognized the intrinsic power of sport to affect the world.

> *I have always been passionate about sport and its capacity to change people's lives. Sport is often the best anti-crime policy, the best public health policy, the best way to bring people together. (Tony Blair, former prime minister of Great Britain, Reuters Life 2010)*

> *A coach will impact more people in one year than the average person will in an entire lifetime. (Rev. Billy Graham)*

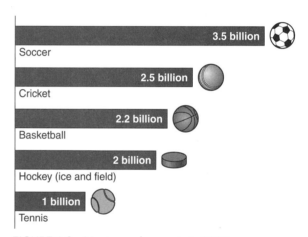

FIGURE 1.2   Most popular sports in 2022.

© Human Kinetics, adapted from illustration by Kiel McClung.

Youth Sports

The interest in sport goes far beyond professional teams and famous sports figures. The opening day of tee ball in Encinitas, California, is like a grand party. Parents, siblings, grandparents, family, and friends crowd the sidelines. The adoring crowd is ready with their smartphones and cameras, recording every move of their children and grandchildren, from putting on their team shirt, hat, and glove to attempting to run to first base—many running toward the pitcher or in other random directions. Smiles, laughter, and cheers are the flavor of the day. Of course, winning and losing are not recognized, there are no standings, and in this case, even if one wanted to keep track of the score it would be too chaotic to do so.

What inspires families to register their four- and five-year-olds for tee ball? Parents understand the importance of physical activity and socialization for their children through sport and group activities. In addition to healthy habits, children learn relational behavioral skills such as cooperation, respect, and sportsmanship. Children should play sports for many compelling reasons, but youth sport also can render a negative influence. It is important for parents to educate themselves on both the positive and negative effects of youth sport. A survey conducted over the span of 30 years by two coaches and athletic administrators found that what young athletes want to hear most from their parents after a sporting event is "I love to watch you play" (Henson 2012).

For those who follow Christ, sport can provide an opportunity to help change the culture of sport from a win-at-all-costs attitude to developing the character and life skills of the players, coaches, and parents

It is almost a rite of passage in the United States for young children to join a sport team at an early age.

(Swanson 2017). Youth sport provides an introduction into the sporting world and can have a lasting influence, shaping one's perspective about sporting activities for the rest of one's life. Whether one's experience has been negative or positive, it can serve as a springboard for a vision for future sports ministry engagements. A godly aspiration is to honor and be pleasing to the Lord within one's sporting life. The Christian athlete is invited to present his or her performance to God as an offering, just as the Apostle Paul urged this sentiment for all believers:

Therefore, I urge you, brothers and sisters, in view of God's mercy, to offer your bodies as a living sacrifice, holy and pleasing to God—this is your true and proper worship. Do not conform to the pattern of this world, but be transformed by the renewing of your mind. Then you will be able to test and approve what God's will is—his good, pleasing and perfect will. (Romans 12:1-2 NIV)

Sport is not to become a consuming idol of one's time, affections, identity, and resources. Rather, it is to be offered before God as a means through which He may more fully transform and shape one's life.

Sport Helps Define the World

Sport is an integral part of the world. Countries and institutions are frequently identified by the sports they play. For example, Brazil is associated with soccer, and the University of Alabama is represented by Crimson Tide football. People find identity in sport. They discover a mutual connecting bond. When the underdog 1980 USA Men's Olympic ice hockey team beat the perennially powerful Soviet team in the semifinals, fans across America proudly claimed, "We beat the Soviets," even though none of them personally donned their skates on the Lake Placid ice. Sport is a means whereby character traits, both good and bad, are revealed and developed. Sport spurs social interaction and augments meaning and purpose.

Sport: Chaos and Peace

A war started after a soccer match in Central America in 1969 (Dee 2014), a civil war was halted after Ivory Coast qualified for the 2006 World Cup, and riots have broken out at soccer matches (too many to cite). Sport was part of a peace initiative during the longest running civil war in African history (2003), and sports ministry to the thousands of refugees who flooded into Europe is ongoing. Sport helps define the world. Sadly, people can literally live and die with their favorite team. A fan's passion is likened to a religious experience in that fervent loyalty and devotion consume them as faithful followers of his or her team (Guiberteau 2020).

Sport for Everyone

In the United States, there are sporting opportunities for everyone—recreation, interscholastic, club, intercol-

A picture is worth a thousand words, as depicted here at Manchester United's Old Trafford Stadium.

legiate, amateur, semi-pro, professional, and esports. With cable television and phone apps, access to a plethora of sport media outlets is available 24 hours per day. Each level of sport provides opportunity for the Spirit-driven believer to have an impact on the world around him or her.

Defining the Term *Sport*

Individuals and societies define **sport** differently. Some definitions are highly inclusive, and others are narrow in scope. Various levels of competitive sport control the airwaves and media outlets. Worldwide sports such as soccer, the Olympic Games, American sports (football, baseball, basketball) typically garner the most attention and tend to dominate the perception of sport definitions. However, definitions differ, and revisions are ongoing. An expansive definition of sport is presented by author and sports minister Bryan Mason:

> *Sport involves four components: 1. Competitive sport at all levels. 2. Physical recreation: Non-competitive activities usually conducted on an informal basis, such as walking/hiking, cycling, and boating. 3. Aesthetic activities, such*

> *as movement and dance. 4. Conditioning activities, engaged in primarily for health reasons and fitness benefits such as aerobics, weight training and exercise to music (Mason 2003, 34).*

According to Paul M. Pedersen and Lucie Thibault, most people associate sport with fun. Yet, to the professional it is related to work, a business, and a source of revenue. Sport can be team or individual oriented. Pedersen and Thibault pose clarifying questions in an attempt to qualify the criteria for defining sport. Should sport classifications include video gaming, drone races, and horse racing? They cite researchers who provide characteristics of sport to include play, organizational rules, competition, physical skills, and institutionalization. Others broadened the definition to include various leisure-type activities (Pedersen and Thibault, 2019, 6-9). Pedersen and Thibault's review of sport definitions concludes that

> *sport does not have to be competitive, nor does it always require specialized equipment or rules; in fact, the broad concept of sport can include activities such as working out, swimming, running, boating, and dancing . . . sport is an all-encompassing concept. It is a collective noun that includes all sport activities (Pedersen and Thibault, 2019, 9).*

---

sport—An all-inclusive term for individual and team competitions, physical recreation, aesthetic activities, conditioning exercises, and nontraditional activities (i.e., esports).

Harnessing the Power of Sports for the Gospel

Sport will always be part of life. As Jay Busbee, writer for *Yahoo! Sports*, contends, "Sports can be a diversion. Sports can be a hobby. And, for a fortunate few, sports can change the world" (Busbee 2013). Who will be among the "the fortunate few" who believe sport can be a tool to help change the world? Is it possible that God could use sport enthusiasts to share the love of Christ with those around them and perhaps throughout the world?

If Jesus has captured the heart, any sport that stirs passions can be used to serve the world for good, whether the sport is team, individual, competitive, or recreational. The followers of Jesus who have a love for sport can use that passion to build relational connections with those around them to share the love of Christ in their neighborhoods, schools, and local and global youth sport clubs. As the Apostle Paul writes,

> *To the Jews I became like a Jew, to win the Jews. To those under the law I became like one under the law (though I myself am not under the law), so as to win those under the law. To those not having the law I became like one not having the law (though I am not free from God's law but am under Christ's law), so as to win those not having the law. To the weak I became weak, to win the weak. I have become all things to all people so that by all possible means I might save some. I do all this for the sake of the gospel, that I may share in its blessings.*

> *Do you not know that in a race all the runners run, but only one gets the prize? Run in such a way as to get the prize. Everyone who competes in the games goes into strict training. They do it to get a crown that will not last, but we do it to get a crown that will last forever. Therefore I do not run like someone running aimlessly; I do not fight like a boxer beating the air. No, I strike a blow to my body and make it my slave so that after I have preached to others, I myself will not be disqualified for the prize. (1 Corinthians 9:20-27 NIV)*

This passage of Scripture presents a key foundation for the practice of sports ministry. Paul encourages his readers to run every step with purpose so they will not be disqualified to win the prize. But first, one must enter the arena and start the race. Paul's example is an exhortation to find common ground with those around them. In Paul's situation, he lived as a Jew in order to identify with Jewish people. He lived like one under the law so that he could be like those living under the law. He became weak to identify with the weak. In all possible ways, he attempted to identify with those to whom he ministered. The principle remains the same today. In the case of sports ministry, common ground is found through sport. The sports-minded can be reached with the gospel through sports ministry methodologies that tap into this inherent bond of sport. To paraphrase the Apostle Paul, one can become a sportsperson to reach the sportspersons around them. Sport can be intentionally embraced so that relationships can be fostered and lives touched. For example, sports ministers have used sport to share Christ's love in communist countries, helped to bring peace in the midst of civil war, run sport camps for churches and sport-themed vacation Bible schools, and helped to mentor students at the university level. The need and opportunities are endless.

Whether one's ambition is to be a successful athlete, an effective coach, or a great parent, true-life examples of sports ministry, past and present, will inspire and equip for godliness. The integration of faith with life is all-encompassing, permeating every aspect of one's life, including participation in sport. Faith is not to be separated from one's involvement in sport. Faith and sport can intimately be joined together. God equips His followers with varying gifts, passions, and abilities. All of them are to be offered back to Him as an offering of thanksgiving and service. The life of a Jesus follower, as an engaged ambassador for Christ through sport, is powerful to influence lives with the message of grace and reconciliation, whether in one's neighborhood, a local park, a gymnasium, a magnificent stadium, or a place along the Amazon River accessible only by a dugout canoe or small plane.

Sports Ministry Defined

A central theme in the definition of sports ministry is to clarify how it is to be practiced. In this growing field, multiple definitions of sports ministry and understandings of how it should be implemented exist, and as such, it is a work in progress availing itself to tweaks and new insights. Here are a few examples:

- "Sports Ministry is merely a vehicle for someone who is in the world of sport (at varied levels) to tell another athlete about their greater love." (Connor 2003, 9)

Interview With a Professional

The Reverend John Boyers
Baptist Minister, Baptist Union of Great Britain
Former Chaplain, Watford Football Club (1976-1992)
Chaplain, Manchester United FC (1992-2018)
Founder, UK Sports Chaplaincy

Courtesy of John Boyers

Long before the Reverend John Boyers (known as the Rev) would become the chaplain for Elton John's Watford FC and eventually for Manchester United, John was a student at Nottingham Institute of Education in England. John had grown up in a religious home in which most of his family were involved in the church. He said he always knew God existed and was responsible for creation—it seemed logical to him—but in truth his faith was built somewhat on superstition. After his beloved Grimsby Town football team lost four matches in a row, he remembers praying that if God would allow Grimsby Town to win their next match, John would try harder in Sunday school. They did win, and he did try harder.

What led you to decide to follow Christ?

At Nottingham Institute of Education, members of the Christian Student Union noticed that I attended church every Sunday, so they asked me if I would like to attend a Bible study. I remember thinking, *That sounds boring*, so I declined. Later they asked me if I would like to attend a prayer meeting. I replied, "Why do you pray? Has someone died?" My interactions with the Christian Student Union were pleasant enough, so when they asked me if I would like to come to a pizza party I decided to go. Over time I clearly saw something different about the faith of the students who came from many different denominations, and my interactions with them eventually propelled me to a personal faith in Christ. I moved from believing there was a God "up there" to seeking to follow Jesus Christ, who, by His Spirit, now was within me. That experience changed my life and my hopes and plans for my future. The new focus was to know God better and to serve Him faithfully, as He desired.

Tell us about your journey to become a minister and eventually a chaplain.

I met my wife, Anne, at the teacher college, and upon graduation, we both went on to teach while aware that a calling to full-time ministry was tugging at my heart. That prompting led me to leave teaching and enroll at London Bible College in northwest London, where I graduated and was ordained as a Baptist minister.

I began my pastoral ministry in Watford, about the time Graham Taylor became manager of Watford FC (and eventually the English national team coach). Graham had a vision to have the club and community more involved with each other. Through comments from Christians studying the Scriptures, praying, and meditating, I felt led to contact Taylor about the idea of chaplaincy for the club.

As I began explaining to Taylor what a chaplain would do, the conversation turned to Grimsby Town. That led me to rattling off the lineup when Taylor played at Grimsby. Our shared history helped lead me to become the team's chaplain and set the stage for me to found UK Sports Chaplaincy and eventually move to Manchester United.

What led you to Manchester United and to start an interdenominational chaplaincy ministry?

While still at Watford, now as senior minister in a local church, I, with the encouragement of Baptist leaders, pioneered SCORE (now UK Sports Chaplaincy) as an interdenominational ministry to develop chaplaincy throughout the UK sporting world.

The following year, Manchester United again asked me to become their chaplain. I felt led to turn down their offer of a full-time position and salary to serve as a volunteer chaplain two days per week. I felt that the Watford model of chaplaincy—a part-time volunteer position—was more likely to be implemented at other clubs.

What are some of the ways that a chaplain serves in the sporting world?

A chaplain is available to serve sportspeople and is open to helping at all levels of the club: from the elite athletes and coaches to part-time cleaners and ground staff. A chaplain must be consistent in involvement, available even for emergencies at all hours. In my role as chaplain, I also saw a need to mentor the academy players. I developed Life Skills, a course helping young players, often away from home, on such important topics as coping with success, coping with failure, prejudice, money, financial matters, and facing life's big challenges.

The Reverend John Boyers is an example of how coming to faith in Christ changed his whole outlook on life. That change led him to believe he should spend his life seeking God's will, not his own, and to look for opportunities to serve. His shared history with Graham Taylor led to John being appointed chaplain for Watford FC. His appointment to Watford FC led him to develop sports chaplaincy not only for the English Premier League but for other levels of football in the United Kingdom and for other sports.

As Rev. John Boyers says, "The role of a sports club chaplain is not an honorary post, not a paid position, and is a real job, not a title; pastorally gifted; able to make non-church people feel at ease; servant-hearted, available, and flexible" (Rev. John Boyers, pers. interview).

- "When . . . sport in ministry is used it refers to a sport-valued approach to ministry. Sport in ministry is integrated in the activity of sport itself. It is the perspective that the demonstration of the gospel in the activity of sport is as valuable as what you say about the gospel." (McCown and Gin 2003, 30)

- "Sports Ministry . . . seeks to serve the purposes of God as He builds His church through the redeeming death of his Son. It provides stimulation to those wishing to use their physical talent for God's glory and the extension of his Kingdom, as well as a motivation towards personal witnessing in the sports arena." (Mason, 2003, 17)

- Through the power of sport, a Jesus follower can use his/her body, mind, and spirit as a platform to minister to the world around them

For the purposes of this textbook the following definition of **sports ministry** is used: a ministry or work built on the relational dimension inherent in sport to share the life-changing message of Jesus Christ, in both word and deed.

SUMMARY

Sports ministry is a growing and evolving field. It originates from the popularity and influences of sport and seeks to engage the world through the shared passion of this common relational connection. Though a variety of definitions of sports ministry exist, the working definition used in this textbook is "a ministry or work built on the relational dimension inherent in sport to share the life-changing message of Jesus Christ, in both word and deed."

Sports ministry can be carried out in local, regional, national, and international settings. It can be fulfilled in churches, through parachurch organizations, multimedia and social media outlets, and so much more.

This book is designed to inspire and challenge you spiritually, intellectually, physically, and emotionally. As you read how ordinary people who have made decisions to follow Christ and are guided by the Holy Spirit have helped change the course of history—in small ways and sometimes in big ways—you should know that you can too! *Sports Ministry* has been written as a book that lives and breathes life—a fresh approach to a Christian's understanding of sport.

---

sports ministry—A ministry or work built on the relational dimension inherent in sport to share the life-changing message of Jesus Christ, in both word and deed.

REVIEW AND DISCUSSION QUESTIONS

1. How prominent is sport in our current world, and how is it expanding globally?

2. What major worldwide sporting events can you think of? What about national, regional, or local events?

3. How do the principles of Colossians 3:17 and 1 Corinthians 9:20-27 relate to the practice of sports ministry?

4. What is a definition of sports ministry that resonates with you?

5. What are some of the goals and outcomes of sports ministry introduced in this chapter?

6. Which sports are you interested in? How could you see yourself ministering through them?

Olympic champion Eric Liddell understood his athletic prowess as a gift from God to be used to bring Him glory.

CHAPTER 2

A History of Sports Ministry

"I believe that God made me for a purpose, but He also made me fast, and when I run, I feel His pleasure."

Eric Liddell, Olympic Champion and Missionary

LEARNING OBJECTIVES

After studying this chapter, you should be able to do the following:
- Trace key historic developments that have led to the contemporary practice of sports ministry
- Identify individuals who are examples of the integration of faith and sport
- Explain the compatibility of sport and Christian faith within a historic context
- Describe Christian influences on the emerging competitive sport scene in America
- Distinguish between sport as a God-given ability and sport as an idolatrous preoccupation
- Discuss examples of sport used as a relational platform for public Christian witness

Led by Harlon Triplett, an informal home-grown weightlifting ministry was organized during the summer of 1975 that combined strength demonstrations with testimonies of Christian faith. Triplett, a senior philosophy major at The King's College (New York), was the reigning 242-pound South Atlantic powerlifting champion. The inspiration for his ministry was spurred on by the example of Paul Anderson, an Olympic champion considered to be the strongest man in the world in the 1950s and '60s. Anderson performed strength exhibitions interspersed with messages about his faith in Jesus. He averaged 500 speaking engagements per year, and all proceeds went to the Paul Anderson Youth Home in Vidalia, Georgia, a home for orphaned and troubled boys. The 1985 edition of the *Guinness Book of World Records* listed his 6,270-pound back lift as "the greatest weight ever raised by a human being" (Bowman 2013, Paul Anderson Youth Home 1988).

Triplett and his college friends led programs at a variety of venues, including stints at the Charles H. Hickey Jr. School (formerly known as the Maryland School for Boys), a division of Maryland's Department of Juvenile Services (Maryland Department of Juvenile Services, n.d.). One evening, during an event at a facility unit, the boys were awed by the weightlifting demonstrations, but they were also intrigued by the testimony of Triplett's Christian faith. Multiple questions were asked, but one in particular stood out. A fifteen-year-old boy asked, "Do I need to give up smoking marijuana before I can ask Jesus into my life?" Triplett paused and insightfully replied, "First, you don't change before you come to Jesus. You come to Him just as you are. If any changes are to be made, He will help you make them. Second, about the marijuana . . . Why don't you ask Jesus to come into your life and then ask Him what you should do about it" (Triplett 1975).

That evening the boys saw more than a weightlifting demonstration. They witnessed a humble, persuasive conviction of faith in Jesus. They saw young men, only a few years older than themselves, exhibiting a confident peace and contentment in life. They heard a message of hope, forgiveness, and love. For several, they saw something that they themselves needed and wanted. Heartstrings were tugged by the presence of Jesus being spoken about and shown by this group of young weightlifters. Several of the boys prayed to receive Jesus into their lives that night. Only eternity will reveal the sincerity of their prayers.

Historically, the principles of sports ministry emerge anecdotally as the world of sport and Christian faith intersect. There were no sports ministry handbooks or how-to guides to follow. Instead, athletes were on their own to determine what it meant to integrate Christian faith into their athletic endeavors. To trace the historic developments of sports ministry it is beneficial to consider the history of sport and the Christian community's evolving perspective of it. This chapter will provide a brief overview of the origins of sport and how it is perceived by the Church, and we will examine muscular Christianity and the emergence of key Christian sport leaders and their influence on the expanding development of organized competitive sport.

Historic Integrations of Faith and Sport

Although survival characterized the central effort of early humans, evidence suggests that physical activities and games have existed throughout history in all cultures. Essential life routines such as hunting and fishing were transformed into challenges and contests. As societies grew, physical activities were linked to military preparations, equipping warriors with skills indispensable for combat (e.g., running, jumping, wrestling, archery, chariot racing, throwing events). The ancient Greeks developed the foundation for the modern Olympic Games by holding competitions held at Olympia accompanied by ritualistic celebrations of their gods. Olympia itself was a shrine dedicated to Zeus. Greek philosophers criticized the games as barbaric and the participants as uneducated, societal misfits (Coakley 2009; Woods 2016). Could their criticisms be a foreshadow of the eventual "dumb jock" stereotype? The games' close association with paganism was disdained as worldly aspirations by the Christian community. The significance and reconciliation of this association will be more fully developed in chapter 7.

The Roman Coliseum

The Romans developed gladiator contests and held these spectacles in the Coliseum. The amenities and seating of the Coliseum were primitive versions of our modern athletic stadiums and arenas, segregating spectators according to social class; special accommodations were reserved for the elites, and the commoners took the "cheap seats." Nearly half the days in the Roman calendar were holidays. Consequently, these events were critical to appease the masses, an idle populace that had a lot of free time. The intention of the ruling class was to entertain the people as a measure of control and to prevent potential insurrection. The games provided a means to rid society of criminals and undesired groups such as Christians. Combatants included man versus man, animal versus animal, and man versus animal. Military demonstrations were reenacted, depicting battle scenes and conquests. A tradition arose wherein the morning competitors were given armor to defend themselves, but those competing during the afternoon entered the arena defenseless, guaranteeing imminent death (Hoffman 2010; Coakley 2009; Woods 2016; Linville 2014; McCown and Gin 2003). The Apostle Paul alludes to this practice when he writes about the apostles being placed at the end of the procession (without armor and thus the certainty of death).

"For it seems to me that God has put us apostles on display at the end of the procession, like those condemned to die in the arena. We have been made a spectacle to the whole universe, to angels as well as to human beings." (1 Corinthians 4:9 NIV)

Scripture's Positive Use of Athletic Imagery

Despite the association of festive religious paganism with the first-century games, the writers of Scripture use athletic imagery as positive metaphors for the Christian faith such as in the following examples:

- The disciplines of the Christian faith are likened to an athlete who goes into strict training. (1 Corinthians 9:25)
- As an athlete competes according to the rules of competition, so the Christian is to live in accordance with the rules of life set forth by God in His word. (2 Timothy 2:5)
- The perseverance of a runner is compared to the perseverance required to live by faith. (Hebrews 12:1)
- The spiritual struggle of the Christian life is compared to a wrestling or boxing match. (Ephesians 6:12)

Some arguments have been made suggesting sport to be incompatible with Christian faith because of sport's associated origins with paganism and idolatrous religions. This question will be addressed in the discussion in chapter 7 about sport and Christian ethical considerations.

How Did the Church Respond to the Emergence of Sport?

Throughout the centuries the Church (the body of worldwide Christian believers as a whole) has fluctuated between condemnation and endorsement of sport in society. Opposition was based on sport participants' perceived inappropriate behaviors that were deemed inconsistent with the Christian lifestyle, primarily gambling, swearing, cheating, and drunkenness. Church leaders accused participants of frequently desecrating the Sabbath through their exploits on the Lord's Day. Objections also arose because of the violent nature of some sports that led to injury and occasional death.

During the Puritan era, sport was considered a distraction that kept men from fulfilling their responsibilities of hard work and the care of their families. Early American colonists shared these Puritan sentiments and had little time for leisure activities due to the harsh living conditions that forced their attention on survival. The Church's initial endorsement of play and games was predominantly due to the support of commoners who found relief from the burdens of their everyday struggles. In time, the participation in play and games was no longer broadly connected to pagan festivals and ritual (Hoffman 2010; Coakley 2009).

The Industrial Revolution Stymies Then Ignites the World of Sport

With the onset of the Industrial Revolution, men flocked to cities to find work. Workdays were long and tiresome, even for child workers, leaving little time for leisurely pursuits. Productivity took priority over play, and public parks and play spaces did not exist. The workforce was discouraged from gathering outside the workplace because it was considered a waste of time, and factory owners feared a challenge to their authority. Workers had little recourse but to work to survive. The 12-hour workday took its toll on workers. Productivity decreased as workers grew weak and ill from poor working and living conditions. As production faltered, management realized their laborers were exhausted from overwork and that healthy workers were more productive than unhealthy ones. Consequently, hours were reduced, child labor laws were enacted, and the pursuit of leisure activities were endorsed. Factory owners began to create access to facilities for calisthenics, physical fitness, and gymnastic-type exercises. By the mid-1800s, organized clubs attracted a growing number of sport enthusiasts among wealthy urbanites and college students from elite schools on the East Coast (Ladd and Mathisen 1999; Coakley 2009; McCown and Ginn 2003; Garner 2003; Watson, Weir, and Friend 2005). In America several key factors occurred simultaneously that greatly influenced the development of organized sport and the influences of Christian faith:

1. The Industrial Revolution expanded urban populations and created the basis for the development of common sport interests.

2. Closely related to the expanding urban populations was the influx of a large immigrant population predominantly from European nations.

3. Sport was becoming more organized as an increasing number of people sought sporting opportunities.

4. The growth of scholastic and collegiate education systems led to the introduction of physical education as a relevant discipline.

5. Muscular Christianity emerged and was eventually embraced by the Christian community.

Muscular Christianity

The term **Muscular Christianity** appeared in a February 1857 edition of *Saturday Review* as a critique of Charles Kingsley's novel *Two Years Ago*. The term had a negative connotation but later would be endorsed by Christians in sport and become a foundation for the practice of sports ministry. Thomas Hughes adopted the term and inserted the concept into his novels *Tom Brown's Schooldays* (1857) and *Tom Brown at Oxford* (1860). Hughes drew a distinction between Muscular Christians and "musclemen": "A man's body is given him to be trained and brought into subjection, and then used for the protection of the weak, the advancement of all righteous causes, and the subduing of the earth which God has given to the children of men" (Ladd and Mathisen 1999,

15). The Muscular Christianity concept brought new meaning to sport in that it linked spiritual growth and the disciplines of Christian faith with sport. American Muscular Christianity believed society could be improved through a vigorous Church with members characterized by a healthy body, mind, and spirit (Watson, Weir, and Friend 2005). In an 1869 edition of the *New York Times*, Muscular Christianity was celebrated as "building muscle, healthy religious principles and moral character" (Ladd and Mathisen 1999, 24). Leading scholars began to realize that education was not limited to the pursuits of the mind but also included the education of the body. Congregationalist pastor Henry Ward Beecher endorsed the role of sports and the importance of health by proclaiming, "If general health is not religion, if it is not Christ, it is John the Baptist; it goes before him" (Ladd and Mathisen 1999, 31).

Sport: A God-Given Ability or a Deterrent to Faith?

During the early days of modern competitive sport, Christian athletes wrestled with the idea of sport as an idolatrous preoccupation that consumed their lives. For some the abandonment of sport was necessary so that its allure would not sabotage their faith. Others embraced sport, accepting it as a God-given ability and recognizing its power as a platform from which to engage the world. Many Christian athletes practiced fundamental principles of sports ministry before it was so named. This next section will survey several examples of prominent Christian athletes and how their faith intersected with their sport participation.

Charles "C.T." Studd: Converted World-Renowned Cricketer

> "Some like to live within the sound of a church or chapel bell; I want to run a rescue shop within a yard of hell."
>
> C.T. Studd

During a revival meeting led by D.L. Moody in 1877, a wealthy English tea planter by the name of Edward Studd came forward to receive Jesus as the Lord of his life. Studd's conversion was dramatic and led

---

Muscular Christianity—A mid-18th-century term that introduced new meaning to sport by linking together spiritual growth and the disciplines of Christian faith with sport.

him to remodel a large room in his house so he could invite merchants and business acquaintances to hear him speak about the life-transforming message of Jesus. Many people came, heard, and were convicted by Studd's preaching. His fervor for the Lord was passionate right up to his sudden death two years after his conversion. A clergyman declared at Edward's funeral, "He did more in two years than most Christians do in twenty" (Grubb 2010, 17). Studd's conversion convinced many of his friends and associates of the authenticity of Christianity. His life had a ripple effect on his colleagues, neighbors, and family, especially on his three sons, Charles (C.T.), George (G.B.), and Kynaston (J.E.K.). The three boys were internationally renowned cricketeers who played for Eton College and Cambridge University. C.T. was considered one of the best all-around players ever to play the game. Regarding his father's faith, C.T. wrote:

I used to think that religion was a Sunday thing, like one's Sunday clothes, to be put away on Monday morning. We boys were brought up to go to church regularly, but, although we had a kind of religion, it didn't amount to much. It was like having a toothache. We were always sorry to have Sunday come, and glad when it was Monday morning. The Sabbath was the dullest day of the whole week, and just because we had got hold of the wrong end of religion. Then all at once I had the good fortune to meet a real live play-the-game Christian. It was my own father. But it did make one's hair stand on end. Everyone in the house had a dog's life of it until they were converted. (Grubb 2010, 19)

The Studd Brothers Meet Christ

One day, a guest preacher staying in the Studd family home cornered C.T. and asked him if he was a Christian. C.T.'s response was evasive and lacked certainty. The preacher pressed the issue, and eventually C.T. yielded and acknowledged his need for conversion. C.T. did not tell his brothers about this encounter, but weeks later it was discovered that each brother was separately encountered by the same young preacher on the same day, and each had a conversion experience. C.T.'s conversion was short lived, and he found himself walking away from the Lord to pursue his own self-indulgent interests. However, God restored him during a Moody revival meeting held at Cambridge University in 1882. Like his father, C.T.'s life was dramatically changed. His love and devotion to God grew (Grubb 2010).

C.T. Chooses Missions Over Cricket

C.T. determined that his days as a cricket player were over, for he had discovered a new purpose and aspiration for his life. He forsook the fame and adulation garnered through cricket and became immersed in the student mission movement. In 1885 C.T. forfeited his international cricket standing to become a missionary, first to China as a member of the **Cambridge Seven**. According to his son-in-law and biographer, Norman Grubb,

C.T. never regretted that he played cricket (although he regretted that he had allowed it to become an idol), for by applying himself to the game he learned lessons of courage, self-denial, and endurance, which, after his life had been fully consecrated to Christ, were used in His service. The man who went all out to be an expert cricket player later went all out to glorify his Savior and extend His Kingdom. (Grubb 2010, 31)

In a letter to his family dated May 26, 1885, C.T. wrote,

I do not say, "Don't play games" or cricket and so forth. By all means play and enjoy them, giving thanks to Jesus for them. Only take care that games do not become an idol to you, as they did to me. What good will it do to anybody in the next world to have been even the best player that ever has been? And then think of the difference between that and winning souls for Jesus. (Grubb 2010, 53)

C.T. Uses Cricket as a Relational Tool

In 1900 the Studd family traveled to India, where C.T. served as a missionary pastor for six years. Though he had forsaken cricket, he soon learned it could be used to build relational connections with soldiers, so he took up the game again, and his skill remained intact. Through cricket he built a relational bridge and held many meetings with men in uniform (Grubb 2010).

C.T.'s Missionary Zeal for Central Africa

C.T. struggled with severe asthma. His overall health had weakened, and he had little money to his name. Yet in 1908 he entertained a stirring from God, a conviction for the people of Central Africa who had not heard about Jesus. He sought the backing of a

---

Cambridge Seven—The group consisted of seven Cambridge University students, including C.T. Studd, who ventured to China as a part of the 1885 student mission movement.

committee of businessmen, who offered their support on condition that C.T. was given a doctor's approval for such a venture. The doctor denied C.T.'s request, and the committee withdrew their funding. Even C.T.'s wife, Priscilla, did not want her husband traveling to the remote region of Africa. She feared for his health, the ravages of malaria fever, and his safety from poisoned arrows. Yet C.T. believed God had prepared him for this purpose. He returned to the committee and informed them, "Gentleman, God has called me to go, and I will go. I will blaze the trail, though my grave may only become a stepping-stone that younger men may follow" (Grubb 2010, 112). At the age of 52, C.T. embarked for Africa. From aboard the ship, C.T. penned a letter of admiration and encouragement to his wife. He concluded the letter by saying, "Good-bye, my darling Priscilla. We began risking all for God and we will end as we began, loving each other utterly and only less than we love Jesus" (Grubb 2010, 125).

After laying a foundation for missionary work in Central Africa, C.T. returned to England to raise support and seek additional workers to join him. In July 1916, he departed England, a land he would never see again. He said goodbye to Priscilla. Over the next 15 years of ministry, he would only see his wife on one occasion for thirteen days. Meantime, Priscilla traveled worldwide in support of the missionary efforts and was regarded as one of the finest missionary speakers in the world (Grubb 2010).

His Grave Paved the Way for Others to Follow

C.T. established a lasting and fruitful ministry in Africa. In hindsight, his words about his grave paving the way for younger missionaries proved prophetic. He endured bouts with malaria, had several heart attacks, and lost most of his teeth. Over the years, he was absent from numerous family occasions, the birth of grandchildren, holiday celebrations, and even the death and burial of his wife, Priscilla, in January 1929. His critics fault his single-mindedness and his unrelenting pursuit of God's direction on him. Shortly before his death, in a critically weakened condition, the only word to be uttered from C.T.'s mouth was *hallelujah*. On July 16, 1931, C.T. whispered his final "hallelujah" and breathed his last (Grubb 2010, 206).

C.T.'s Disassociation With Sport

Using the notoriety he achieved through cricket, C.T. gained access to people and provided a standing with them that he may not otherwise have enjoyed. Yet for himself, sport was so associated with his former misdirected life without Christ that he personally viewed sport more as a hindrance and preferred disassociation from it rather than continued engagement.

Billy Sunday: The Baseball Evangelist

"Listen, I'm against sin. I'll kick it as long as I've got a foot, I'll fight it as long as I've got a fist, I'll butt it as long as I've got a head, and I'll bite it as long as I've got a tooth. And when I'm old, fistless, footless and toothless, I'll gum it till I go home to glory, and it goes home to perdition!"

Billy Sunday

Billy Sunday was born in 1862 in Ames, Iowa, the youngest of four boys. A month after Sunday's birth, his father became ill and died in a Missouri camp while fighting for the Union during the Civil War. His mother remarried but was eventually abandoned by her second husband. The family struggled financially, and the children were separated to live elsewhere. Billy, at the age of 11, and brother Howard (Ed) were sent to the Soldiers' Orphans' Home in Glenwood, Iowa. Sunday's time at the orphanage afforded him the opportunity to learn life skills that would prove beneficial. When Ed turned 16, he aged out of the orphanage, and Billy left with him. Billy relocated to Marshalltown, Iowa, and played on a local baseball team. His speed and ability to chase down fly balls caught the eye of Adrian "Cap" Anson, player and manager for the Chicago White Stockings, now known as the Chicago Cubs (Brown [1914] 1986; Thomas 1961; Knickerbocker, n.d.; Marshalltown Community Television 2019).

Sunday Signs With Chicago

In 1883, at the age of 20, Sunday signed a contract with the White Stockings. He struck out his first 13 plate appearances and was used primarily as a reserve outfielder during his entire five-year tenure with Chicago. Despite seeing limited playing time (appearing in 50 games in 1887—his most during any season with Chicago), Sunday was liked by Anson and by owner, Albert G. Spalding. Spalding (cofounder of Spalding Sporting Goods) had been an outstanding pitcher who eventually was enshrined in Baseball's Hall of Fame. Spalding and Coach Anson developed strict training and behavior guidelines for their players, including abstinence from alcohol

(Brown [1914] 1986; Thomas 1961; Marshalltown Community Television 2019).

Sunday's Disdain for Booze

Many players ignored the team policies, but not Sunday. He complied and consistently worked to improve his game. One season, Spalding hired a detective to follow players, a significant number of whom were penalized for breaking team rules. Sunday was among the players cleared of any accusations. On occasion, Sunday accompanied teammates to the saloons but usually refrained from alcohol because of abuses he had seen from his mother's second husband and from his grandfather (Thomas 1961; Brown [1914] 1986). Late in life, Sunday recalled,

I began to hate booze in my youth, and as the years come and go my hatred for the cursed business and the bootleggers increases . . . I never drank much. I was never drunk but four times in my life. I never drank whisky or beer; I never liked either. I drank wine, and I like wine now, but I have not drunk whisky, beer, or wine since I was converted forty years ago. I used to go to the saloons with the baseball players, and they would drink highballs and gin fizzes and beer; I would take lemonade and sarsaparilla. (Sunday [1932-1933] 2005, 67; Ellis 1936, 499)

The Conversion of Billy Sunday

The most significant thing in Sunday's life during his playing days with Chicago was his conversion to Christ in 1886. While sitting curbside with several of his baseball player friends, a group of singers gathered around singing hymns and imploring listeners to join them inside the **Pacific Garden Rescue Mission** to hear street evangelist Harry Monroe. Sunday heeded the invitation, and his life would no longer remain the same. Sunday continued to play baseball for several years following his conversion to Christ (Martin 2002).

Sunday Leaves Baseball at the Height of His Career

Following the 1890 season, while reaching his prime as a player, Sunday called an end to his professional baseball career. At a slender 5'10" (178 cm) and 160 pounds (73 kg), Sunday was an average batter, finishing with a .248 lifetime batting average in 2,007 plate appearances. He stole 246 bases in 499 games played (Baseball Almanac 2021; Baseball Reference,

n.d.). Though a mediocre player in many ways, Billy was a fan favorite because of his baserunning and acrobatic catches in the outfield.

Sunday Marries Helen "Nell" Thompson

Following his conversion at the Pacific Garden Rescue Mission, Sunday regularly assisted with services at the local YMCA. He was a speaker and often connected with the YMCA on road trips wherever his baseball team played. Of special note was Billy's attendance at the Jefferson Park Presbyterian Church in Chicago, where he met a young woman by the name of Helen "Nell" Thompson. Nell was the daughter of William Thompson, an entrepreneur in the Chicago dairy industry. Initially, Thompson objected to his daughter's acquaintance with a professional baseball player because ballplayers had an unsavory reputation. Nevertheless, Nell continued to see Billy in secret. On September 5, 1888, the two were married and would eventually have four children. Nell was a tremendous help to him, encouraging the refinement of his faith and ministry (Brown [1914] 1986; Thomas 1961).

The YMCA and Evangelist J. Wilbur Chapman

Sunday left baseball to pursue full-time work with the YMCA. He turned down a $5,000 offer to play ball for Cincinnati so he could become the secretary of the religious department of the Chicago YMCA with an annual salary of $1,000. In 1893 Presbyterian evangelist J. Wilbur Chapman secured Billy's services as an advance man for his revival meetings. Chapman provided Sunday with valuable ministry and preaching insights (Martin 2002; Thomas 1961).

The Sawdust Trail Begins in Garner, Iowa

In 1895 Chapman retired temporarily to become pastor of the Bethany Presbyterian Church in Philadelphia. This decision left Sunday uncertain about his future. He considered a return to baseball, but an unexpected invitation was extended for him to conduct a series of evangelistic meetings in Garner, Iowa. He went to Garner with only seven sermons, each of which he preached twice. The services in Garner were the start of Sunday's career as an evangelist and what would become known as the **sawdust trail** (Thomas 1961; Marshalltown Community Television 2019).

Pacific Garden Mission—The Chicago rescue mission where Billy Sunday is purported to have received Christ at the age of 23.

Baseball evangelist Billy Sunday preached in person to more people than anyone else in the history of preaching.

The Baseball Evangelist Draws Unprecedented Crowds

As Sunday's popularity grew, he eventually preached in most major American cities. Wooden tabernacles, seating as many as 16,000 people, were constructed in advance of his revival services. One of his most famous ventures was a 10-week campaign held in New York City, where an estimated 98,000 people came forward responding to his plea to follow Jesus. Sunday's preaching style was flamboyant, reminiscent of his flashy style of play in the outfield. Over the course of his ministry, it is believed that he spoke to more people than anyone else in history (Rodeheaver 1936; Thomas 1961).

Billy Sunday Finishes His Race

Sunday's schedule was relentless, and he frequently preached multiple sermons a day. His health finally paid the price, and he collapsed while preaching in Des Moines, Iowa, in 1933. Sunday's final sermon was delivered on October 27, 1935, at the First Free Methodist Church in Mishawaka, Indiana. He was bedridden and died of a heart attack shortly thereafter on November 6. Billy's tombstone displays a simple verse with an athletic metaphor, "I have fought the good fight, I have finished my course [the race], I have kept the faith" (2 Timothy 4:7). Sunday accentuated the worldliness associated with baseball, but he also used his sporting experience as a relational tool to speak into the lives of millions. Nell Sunday continued in ministry as a speaker and fundraiser for Christian organizations, especially urban rescue missions. She was preceded in death by all four of her children and died in Arizona in 1957. Following two eulogists at her funeral, Bob Jones Jr. stated, "I can hear Ma Sunday now saying, 'That's enough of this foolishness. Let's get down to business and talk about Jesus'" (Jones 1985, 91).

James Naismith: Inventor of Basketball

"I want to leave the world a little bit better than I found it."

James Naismith

James Naismith was born on November 6, 1861, in Ramsey, Ontario. He was the second of three chil-

---

sawdust trail—Billy Sunday's revival meetings were held in large wooden tabernacles. When the tabernacles were constructed, considerable quantities of sawdust were left over and would be spread throughout the tabernacle's walkways. Consequently, when people came forward to receive Christ, they walked on a sawdust trail. The term **sawdust trail** eventually became synonymous with people responding to an evangelist's invitation to receive Christ even if the floor was not paved with sawdust.

dren. Early in his life, Naismith experienced a series of tragic events. Within the span of four months during the summer and fall of 1870, he lost his cherished grandfather, the family sawmill burned down, and both his parents died three weeks apart after contracting typhoid fever. He ultimately was raised by his sister, Annie, and his uncle, Peter (Rains and Carpenter 2009).

A Theology Student Excels at Sport

Naismith entered McGill University in Montreal with the intention of attending the school of theology upon completion of his undergraduate studies. He poured himself into his academic work and found little time for leisure until confronted by a couple older students. They told him, "You spend too much time with your books" and recommended he spend some time in the gymnasium (Rains and Carpenter 2009, 18). Reluctantly, Naismith heeded their advice, and on his visit to the gymnasium, he met Frederick Barnjum, a leading proponent of physical education in Canada. Under Barnjum's direction, McGill was among the first North American universities to offer physical education as part of their academic curriculum. Naismith enjoyed the activities of the gymnasium, and his attendance became routine. On one occasion, he was a spectator at his school's rugby team practice. A player became injured, and the team had no replacement. One of the team's captains approached the group of spectators and asked if a volunteer would step forward as a substitute for the injured player. Naismith volunteered and did an admirable job as a replacement. He was asked to play in the team's next game. He agreed, performed well, and subsequently became a regular member of the team (Rains and Carpenter 2009).

Naismith's participation with the rugby team contradicted what was commonly believed and what he had been taught about sports, that athletics was a tool of the devil. He was also questioned by classmates who knew about his plans to prepare for ministerial studies. How could he justify the coexistence of rugby with ministry? One Sunday, following a rough and physical game of football the day before, he was criticized by students and faculty alike for climbing into a Presbyterian pulpit as the owner of two prominent black eyes. Despite the criticisms, Naismith successfully immersed himself in multiple sports and physical activities. Besides rugby, he played football, soccer, and lacrosse, and he was twice named McGill's best all-around gymnast (Rains and Carpenter 2009).

Naismith Ponders Sport as Ministry

One sporting incident made a lasting impression on Naismith. During a close football game, the lineman positioned next to Naismith became frustrated, lost his temper, and blurted a profanity. Almost instantly he turned and apologized saying, "I beg your pardon, Jim. I forgot you were here" (Rains and Carpenter 2009, 25). Naismith pondered the situation at length. Never had he expressed his view about the use of profanity, and the only reason he could think that his presence deserved an apology was because his teammate saw something different about his character and conduct. Ultimately, Naismith reached the conclusion that the traditional approach to ministry was not the only effective means to reach people: "My attention was directed to the fact that there were other ways of influencing young people than preaching. . . . It was a short step to the conclusion that hard clean athletics could be used to set a high standard of living for the young" (Rains and Carpenter 2009, 26).

Naismith sought the counsel of trusted friends and advisors. He learned about a YMCA training school in Springfield, Massachusetts, that offered a two-year instructional program that combined spiritual and physical development, preparing students to teach at the YMCA, in churches, in schools, and in youth organizations. He believed he would be more valuable and potentially reach more people by working through athletics than by pastoring a single congregation. Many of his friends and his sister, Annie, and uncle, Peter, attempted to persuade him back to the traditional ministry path. Annie told him, "You put your hand to the plough, and then turned back." However, Naismith was convinced of the new direction for his life:

> I felt that there was a new field in which good could be done for mankind as well as in preaching and that some people would be able to do better work in one field than the other. Athletics and gymnastics at that time were looked on as a device of the devil to lead young men astray. I felt, however, that if the devil was making use of them to lead young men, it must have some natural attraction, and that it might be used to lead to a good end as well as to a bad one. (Rains and Carpenter 2009, 28)

Naismith did agree to complete his theology degree before enrolling as a student at the **Springfield YMCA Training School**.

Springfield YMCA Training School—An early American YMCA training center in Springfield, Massachusetts, that taught students how to integrate Christian faith with sport. Notable students and faculty at Springfield include Luther Gulick, James Naismith, Amos Alonzo Stagg, and William Morgan.

Naismith, Gulick, and Stagg

At Springfield, Naismith became close friends and associates with the dean of the physical education department, Dr. Luther Gulick, and a fellow new student by the name of Amos Alonzo Stagg. While at Yale University, Stagg had been an All-American football player and star pitcher on the baseball team. Gulick started a football team, named Stagg as the coach, and selected Naismith to play on the thirteen-member team. Before the opening game, Naismith was impressed by Stagg's pregame prayer because his petition to God did not seek victory on the field, but rather that each man would play his best and represent the true Christian spirit through his conduct. Naismith and Stagg shared the same passionate philosophy for the use of sport to invest in lives (Rains and Carpenter 2009).

A New Indoor Sport

Naismith completed the two-year YMCA training program in one year and was asked to remain as a member of the faculty. Gulick approached Naismith with a twofold assignment. First, he assigned him to the "incorrigible" class, and second, he wanted him to create a new game that could be played indoors during the harsh New England winter months. According to Gulick,

> We need a new game to exercise our students, a competitive game, like football or lacrosse, but it must be a game that can be played indoors. It must be a game requiring skill and sportsmanship, providing exercise for the whole body and yet it must be one which can be played without extreme roughness or damage to players and equipment. (Rains and Carpenter 2009, 32)

The game was to be simple, easy to learn, inexpensive, and with minimal equipment needs. Naismith attempted to modify outdoor games (e.g., football, soccer, lacrosse) for indoor play, but one by one the attempts failed. Eventually, he devised a rudimentary game that would evolve into basketball. He used a soccer ball and nailed peach baskets to the lower railing of the gallery. The railing height happened to be 10 feet (3 m). Had the height of the railing been different, most likely we would have a different height standard for the modern game of basketball. Using just 474 words, Naismith penned 13 rules and asked the school's stenographer to type them up for posting (Naismith 1996; Stark 2021; Rains and Carpenter 2009). To illustrate the significance and popularity of sport, on December 10, 2010, the original typed two-page document of Naismith's rules was sold at a Sotheby's auction for $4.3 million. In comparison, at the same auction, the tattered 1876 flag from the Battle of Little Big Horn sold for $2.2 million, and a copy of the Emancipation Proclamation signed by Abraham Lincoln (one of only 48 known copies) sold for $3.7 million (Catton 2010).

The First Game of Basketball

The first game of basketball was played on December 21, 1891. Naismith arranged nine players on each side and positioned them into a lacrosse formation. The game ended 1–0, with William Chase scoring the only basket. The new game was a hit with the students, and onlookers began stopping by the gymnasium to watch this peculiar sport. A recommendation was made that the game be called "Naismith Ball," but the game's creator suggested an alternative, and it finally became known as "Basket Ball." It remained a two-word name until sportswriters shortened it to one in 1921. Modifications and refinements to the game evolved over time, including reducing the sides to five each, the introduction of dribbling, and the addition of backboards so spectators would not reach over the railing to interfere with shots. The YMCA produced many missionaries who traveled around

While serving as a member of the faculty at the Springfield, Massachusetts YMCA Training Center, James Naismith used a peach basket and soccer ball to create the indoor winter sport of basketball.

the globe, and during their journeys they introduced the game of basketball to other parts of the world (Naismith 1996; Rains and Carpenter 2009).

The Invention of Mintonette (Volleyball)

One of the students influenced by Naismith was William G. Morgan, who graduated in 1894. Upon graduation, Morgan began working at the YMCA in Holyoke, Massachusetts. Inspired by the invention of basketball, he envisioned a game suitable for older businessmen, one that was less strenuous and could easily be played over a lunch break. His invention was dubbed **mintonette**, which would later become known as volleyball. Two major worldwide sports (basketball and volleyball) had their origins in the humble locale of the YMCA (Rains and Carpenter 2009; Mass Moments, n.d.).

Naismith at the University of Kansas

In 1895 Naismith moved to Denver to become the physical education director at the YMCA. He enrolled in the University of Colorado Medical School and graduated in 1898. That same year, the president of the University of Kansas sent a telegram to the president of the University of Chicago asking for a recommendation regarding a new job at Kansas. The request was passed along to Chicago's football coach, Amos Alonzo Stagg. Stagg immediately sent a reply telegram stating, "Recommend James Naismith, inventor of basketball, medical doctor, Presbyterian minister, teetotaler, all-around athlete, non-smoker, and owner of a vocabulary without cuss words. Address Y.M.C.A., Denver, Colorado" (Rains and Carpenter 2009, 71). Soon thereafter, Naismith became the director of gymnasium, campus chaplain, and basketball coach at the University of Kansas. He coached nine seasons and concluded in 1907 with a 55–60 record, and, to date, he is the only coach in Kansas history with a losing career record (Rains and Carpenter 2009).

A Minister in the Gymnasium

Naismith was a man of integrity who was most interested in the moral and physical advancement of young men and women. Foremost, he believed the sport of basketball was intended for exercise and fun. Ironically, he is known to have only personally played the game twice—once as a member of the Springfield faculty team and again in a game at the University of Kansas. He opposed sport participation for financial profit and would have frowned on today's commercialization and inflated professional salaries. He never sought a patent for basketball, though it would have provided him tremendous personal wealth. He valued fair play and sought the availability of athletics and equality for all people, including African Americans who were facing the oppressions of segregation (Rains and Carpenter 2009).

Naismith was a highly educated man with degrees in theology and medicine, though he never formally served as the pastor of a congregation or worked as a physician. (He did serve as university chaplain and physician while at Kansas.) On November 19, 1939, Naismith suffered a severe brain hemorrhage that led to his death nine days later. His funeral was held at the First Presbyterian Church in Lawrence, Kansas, on December 1. The Reverend Theodore H. Aszman eulogized Naismith:

> *He preferred to do his preaching in active living rather than from the pulpit. Building character was basic to Dr. Naismith. He watched the game he invented not as a rabid fan, but as a teacher. He wished to observe the influence of the game on the mind and character of the individual who played it. The testimony to him was to a man, not to an inventor. He truly is one of God's noblemen. (Rains and Carpenter 2009, 193)*

Naismith was a minister in the gymnasium, and the sport he invented continues to be a means to touch countless lives.

Amos Alonzo Stagg: The Grand Old Man of Football

"The boys on sports teams 'are sure to have the most influence' on campus: 'Win the athletes of any college for Christ, and you will have the strongest working element attainable in college life.'"

Amos Alonzo Stagg
(quoted in Lester 1995)

Despite his small stature (5'6" [168 cm]), Amos Alonzo Stagg was an outstanding athlete. As stated in *The Young Men's Journal* (1890), "Of America's distinguished young men none perhaps are more widely known than A. Alonzo Stagg, the robust

---

mintonette—The original name of the game invented by William Morgan that would eventually become known as volleyball.

Christian athlete of Yale College" (Lester 1995, 9-10). Stagg matriculated at Yale in September 1884 with the intention of completing his undergraduate degree and then entering Yale Divinity School to pursue ministerial studies. Initially, he failed to make the football team and subsequently focused attention on baseball. He became Yale's ace pitcher, compiling a six-year win–loss record of 42–8 against Harvard and Princeton. His best performance was against Princeton in 1888, when he struck out 20 batters while allowing only two hits (Lester 1995). He was offered a seasonal contract to play professional baseball, but he held a disdain for the commercialization of sport and declined the offer. He later wrote, "I never did a wiser thing than refusing the $4,200 a season offered me by the New York Nationals in the 80s. . . . If it is money that the college man wants, he ought to be able to make more on a real job than by peddling a physical skill" (Stagg and Stout 1927, 294; Hall 2019, 29).

All-American Football Player and YMCA Representative

In the fall of 1888 Stagg won a starting right end position on Yale's football squad, a team that established an amazing record by outscoring opponents 698–0. He played again in 1889 and was selected to Walter Camp's first All-American football team. During his days at Yale, Stagg was active as YMCA secretary. He made numerous appearances throughout the East representing the YMCA and speaking about his faith in Christ (Lester 1995). Young men were drawn to hear Stagg, curious to listen to an outstanding athlete who turned down a big baseball salary to further his studies for Christian ministry. In October 1888 a reporter wrote in the *Brooklyn Eagle*,

> *He fires hot balls of Truth over home plate. . . . (Stagg) spoke of his own faith in Christ and love for his work and urged others to follow his example in serving God. . . . He believed a man was better every way for being a Christian. . . . He knew that they would feel better satisfied with themselves and the world and have a broader view of life if they became Christians. (Lester 1995, 11)*

Stagg Chooses Athletic Arena Ministry Over Traditional Pulpit Ministry

After one year, Stagg left Yale Divinity School for two astute reasons. First, he surmised that public speak-

ing did not suit him well, and second, he believed he would serve a greater purpose by focusing on ministry within the athletic arena. He would preach his sermons on the field of play rather than from a pulpit. His football players would become his congregation. In preparation for this new direction, Stagg spent two years at the YMCA Training School in Springfield. While there, his coaching career began with an inaugural football team unofficially known as "Stagg's Stubby Christians." He was recognized as a model coach and influencer of young men (Hall 2019).

Stagg's Football Coaching Career at University of Chicago

In the early 1890s Stagg's former Hebrew professor at Yale, William Rainey Harper, took over as the new president of the University of Chicago. Harper had been so impressed by Stagg during his days at Yale that he sought Stagg out and offered him a faculty position to oversee a combined athletic and

Amos Alonzo Stagg believed he would serve a greater purpose through ministry within the arena of sport than from a pulpit.

physical education department. Several days after the offer, Stagg responded, "After much thought and prayer, I feel decided that my life can be best used for my Master's service in the position which you have offered" (Hall 2019, 30). Besides teaching and athletic administration, Stagg would embark on a 41-year football coaching stint at Chicago, amassing a win-loss-tie record of 244–111–27. At the age of 70, Stagg was relieved of his coaching duties at the insistence of the university's president, Dr. Robert Hutchins, in accordance with the school's mandated retirement age policy. Hutchins shared little affinity for college athletics, and Chicago's heralded football program eventually was disbanded during his tenure (Hall 2019; Lester 1995).

College of the Pacific

Stagg and family moved to Stockton, California, where he took over as the head football coach at the College of the Pacific. He helped transform the football program into one that challenged the best West Coast teams. In 1943, with victories over UCLA and California, the Associated Press awarded a national ranking of 19 to Pacific. That season, at the age of 81, Stagg was named the Coach of the Year by the American Football Coaches Association. Three years later, the Pacific administration requested that Stagg step down as head coach and offered him a position as "consultant in athletics." Stagg refused the offer, saying, "I am fully convinced that the pearl of great price for me is to continue my life's purpose of helping young men through the relationship of coaching" (Hall 2019, 128-129).

Stagg's Years as an Assistant Coach and Retirement at Age 98

Stagg ventured east to assist his son in coaching at Pennsylvania's Susquehanna University. He retired as Susquehanna's assistant in 1953 to stay alongside his ill wife. Stagg's initial retirement at age 91 was short lived. One of his former players was the head coach at Stockton College, and he invited Stagg to join Stockton as an assistant coach. He served until his final retirement from football coaching at the age 98 (Hall 2019).

Stagg was inducted into the inaugural class of the National Football Hall of Fame (1951) and was the first recipient to be inducted as both a player and coach. His indelible influence on the sport of football is memorialized by the NCAA Division III's championship game being named the Stagg Bowl and

the winner of the Big Ten receiving the Stagg Trophy. In March 1962, "The Grand Old Man of Football" peacefully passed away in his sleep at the age of 102 (Hall 2019).

Eric Liddell: The Flying Scotsman

"If a thing is worth doing, it is worth doing well."

Eric Liddell

Eric Liddell was born on January 16, 1902, to Scottish missionary parents serving in north China with the London Missionary Society. At the age of seven, Eric and his older brother, Rob (age nine), were enrolled in the School for the Sons of Missionaries near London. Separation from family was a common occurrence endured by missionaries; more of Eric's childhood was spent apart from his parents than the time shared under the same roof. The Liddell brothers grew to become exceptional athletes, competing in rugby, cricket, and track events. By the age of 20, though not sporting the rugged body of a rugby player (5′9″ and 155 lbs [175 cm and 70 kg]), Eric's speed and athleticism propelled him to secure a winger spot on Scotland's national rugby team. Playing in seven international matches during the 1922 and 1923 seasons, his athletic notoriety grew throughout Scotland (McCasland 2001; Ramsey 1987; Keddie 2007).

A Quiet Faith Becomes Public

During the spring of 1923, Eric Liddell had a life-transforming experience. The Glasgow Students' Evangelistic Union (GSEU) was conducting a series of evangelistic meetings in **Armadale**, a coal mining town near Edinburgh where Liddell was studying pure science at the University of Edinburgh. Church of Scotland evangelist David Patrick "D.P." Thomson was placed in charge of coordinating the meetings. Coincidentally, Thomson would eventually become the first biographer of Liddell's life (Keddie 2007). Attendance was low, and D.P. wondered if a prominent Christian athlete speaker would bolster interest in the meetings. Thomson sought Liddell to see if he would consider speaking. Liddell had a genuine faith in Christ, but his faith was quiet, and he had never spoken publicly about it. After a reflective pause, Eric agreed to speak.

Armadale—A Scottish mining town where D.P. Thomson conducted a series of evangelism meetings with dwindling attendances. Thomson sought Eric Liddell to come and speak. Attendance increased significantly, and the event served as a catalyst for Liddell's faith to change from one of quiet reflection to emboldened public witness.

SPORTS MINISTRY IN ACTION

The Father Heart of a Football Coach

Prominent historic personalities are often viewed as surreal and unrelatable. Yet they were real people who faced struggles and the joys and sorrows of everyday life. Amos Alonzo Stagg is no exception. He was a family man, married with children. The relationship with his children is an example that provides insight into the heart of his humanity, a point of connection for those who read about him. Stagg's firstborn, Amos Alonzo Stagg Jr., contracted a severe case of diphtheria when he was seven months old. His prognosis was grim. The senior Stagg relentlessly kept watch over his son and faithfully nursed him back to health. Seven months later, Stagg Sr. embarked on a transatlantic trip to coach runners at the 1900 Paris Olympics. Knowing the uncertainties of crossing the Atlantic, on June 23, Stagg wrote a letter to his then 14-month-old son. Stagg poured out his heart to his son, providing fatherly counsel. He implored young Amos to adhere to eight significant responsibilities:

1. Your father wants his boy to love, protect and care for his mother, giving to her the same kind measure of love and devotion which she has given to you.
2. Your father wants his boy to be sincere, honest, and upright. . . . Hate dishonesty and trickery no matter how big and how great the thing desired may be.
3. Your father wants you to have a proper independence of thought, feeling, and action.
4. Treat everybody with courtesy and as your equal until he proves his untrustworthiness to be so treated.
5. Your father wants you to "abhor evil." No curiosity, no imagination, no conversation, no story, no reading which suggests impurity of life is worthy of your thought or attention.
6. Train yourself to be master of yourself; of your thought and imagination, temper, passion, appetite and of your body. Hold all absolutely under your will. Your father has never used intoxicating liquors, nor tobacco, nor profane language and he wants his boy to be like him in this regard.
7. Your father wants his boy enthusiastic and earnest in all his interests—his sports, his studies, his work . . .
8. Your father wants his son to love God as he is revealed to him, which after all will be the revelation of all that I have said and left unsaid of good to you, my precious boy. (Hall 2019, 60-61)

When Stagg's daughter, Ruthie, came along a few years later, he taught her football just as he taught her brothers and the boys who played on the gridiron for him.

Ruthie, I am a teacher. The most important job I have is to teach you, your brothers, and all the boys who play for me. God gave me football as the way to teach hard work and self-discipline. Those are important lessons for you, so I want you to understand the game. (Hall 2019, 90)

Stagg desired for his children to learn important life lessons that were so entwined with his experience in sport and coaching and to transfer these precepts to everyday living.

Liddell was not a gifted public speaker, yet he spoke with a genuine, heartfelt conviction about his relationship with Jesus. Young men were drawn to the meetings to hear from the rugby internationalist. As much as the listeners were influenced by Liddell, it is suggested that Liddell himself was the greatest benefactor from the Armadale meetings. Newspapers ran stories about his speaking, and regular public speaking invitations would ensue (McCasland 2001; Ramsey 1987; Day of Discovery 2008).

Liddell's Biblical Heart Conviction Prevails

On May 26, 1923, Liddell won the 100-, 220-, and 440-yard (91, 201, and 402 m) races at the annual University of Edinburgh Games. Multiple successful meets followed, and Liddell was destined to represent Scotland as a premier sprinter at the 1924 Paris Olympics. Several months prior to the Games, he learned that several of the sprinting event preliminaries were to be run on Sundays. He held a very strong view about honoring the Sabbath Day and consequently withdrew himself from participating in the Sunday-slated events (100 m, 4 × 100 m relay). His refusal to run on Sunday was not unique. Dozens of British and American athletes had previously chosen to honor the Sabbath by not competing then. An example is American hurdler Forrest Smithson, a theology student who protested the Sunday trial heats by running with a Bible in his hands at the 1908 London Games—and doing so in world-record time. Liddell's refusal to run on a Sunday garnered mixed reviews. Some applauded his convictions while others considered him a traitor to Scotland. "I regret that some are hurt over my decision, but there can be no doubt about the Fourth Commandment," Liddell responded (Ramsey 1987, 57).

Competing in the 200- and 400-Meter Races

Liddell rigorously trained for the 200- and 400-meter races under the watchful eye of athletic trainer Tommy McKerchar. At the Paris Olympics, Liddell came from behind to capture the bronze medal in the 200-meter race. Due to his inexperience and the competitive level of the 400-meter, Eric was not considered a medal contender. He surprised everyone by setting and maintaining an extraordinarily fast pace to win the gold and establish new Olympic and world records (Keddie 2007).

Unprecedented Four-Time Crabbie Cup Winner

Liddell had yet to reach his prime as a runner, but he felt God's call to return to the land of his birth to be a missionary teacher among the people of China. His final race in Scotland was at Hampden Park in Glasgow on June 27, 1925. He won the 100-, 220-, and 440-yard races at the Scottish Amateur Athletics Championship. Wrapping up his competitive Scottish track career, Liddell was a multiple recipient of the Crabbie Cup, awarded annually to Scotland's top track and field athlete. Liddell tied for the honor in 1922 and won it in each of the following three years. No one has ever come close to matching this feat (Ramsey 1987).

Liddell Leaves Fame and Fortune in Favor of the Mission Field

At age 23, Eric embarked for China, where he taught science and administrated athletics at the Tientsin Anglo-Chinese College. He viewed the Min Yuan Sports Field as a facility to train Christians, not simply a place to have games. Eric continued to run periodically and entered the Far Eastern Games at Port Arthur in October 1928. In front of a crowd of 50,000, he won the 200-meter race in 21.8 seconds and the 400-meter in 47.8 seconds. Both times matched the gold medal times at the Amsterdam Olympics despite little serious training, running on a slower track, and racing less-competitive runners (Ramsey 1987). Based on times run during his days in China, it is believed that Liddell would have won multiple medals in both the 1928 and 1932 Olympics (Ramsey 1987).

The Plight of a Missionary Family

Eric married Florence Mackenzie, the daughter of missionaries also serving in China, who was almost 10 years younger than Liddell. They had three daughters. During the autumn of 1940, the armies of Japan invaded China. Life became increasingly dangerous for the missionaries. Consequently, in May 1941, Liddell sent Florence, who was six months pregnant, and their daughters, Patricia and Heather, to Canada. Liddell remained in China, anticipating that their separation would be two years. Soon after their departure, Liddell, along with almost 2,000 others, was sent to an internment camp by the Japanese forces (McCasland 2001).

Living conditions were primitive, but everyone continued to function as normally as possible. Liddell taught science and organized sports and games. With no textbooks, Liddell wrote from memory his own chemistry text titled *The Bones of Inorganic Chemistry: Will These Dry Bones Live*. In time, Liddell's vitality began to wane, and he suffered severe headaches. Growing increasingly weak, he was hospitalized and died from a brain tumor on February 21, 1945, at the age of 43. Due to the war, Florence and the children did not learn of his death until May. Eric never met his youngest daughter, Maureen, who was born in Canada (Day of Discovery 2008; Keddie 2007).

Encouraging Words From One Who Lived Them

In a message presented on September 30, 1931, at St. George's West Church in Edinburgh, Liddell passionately addressed his listeners:

> We are all missionaries. We carry our religion with us, or we allow our religion to carry us. Wherever we go, we either bring people nearer to Christ, or we repel them from Christ. We are working for the great Kingdom of God—the time when all people will turn to Christ as their leader, and we will not be afraid to own Him as such. (Ramsey 1987, 109)

Summarizing Liddell's life is William Struth, former manager of the Glasgow Rangers Football Club:

Eric Liddell's life reminds us to put things in their proper perspective. Sport to him was sport—not the be-all and end-all—and success in it did not prevent him from picking out the things spiritual from the things temporal. His was an example which must have helped others to make a similar choice. (Ramsey 1987, 182; Keddie 2007, 193-194)

Eric Liddell provides a model of one who ran life's race well and finished strong.

Interview With a Professional

Rev. Paul Shea, DMiss

Assistant Pastor, Missions Professor and Missionary

BA, Houghton University

MDiv, Trinity Evangelical Divinity School

DMiss, Trinity Evangelical Divinity School

Courtesy of Paul Shea

After eight years of pastoral ministry, Dr. Shea spent the next 35 years in on-field mission work in Sierra Leone (10 years); studying missions; teaching theology, intercultural studies, and missiology; and engaging in short-term visits in five nations, often with students. His main focus is the growth of global Christianity and motivation and equipping others for global cross-cultural ministry. Dr. Shea is semiretired and active with local church mission outreach.

From your perspective, does the Bible endorse the use of sport as a valid ministry tool?

Christians and the church are called to be like Christ and share him throughout life in word and deed (Colossians 3:17). Sports were obviously known in St. Paul's day, and fitness pleases God but godliness does even more (1 Timothy 4:8). So, I'd say whatever skill or walk of life we are in can and should be employed to share Christ.

Historically, has sport played a role in global missions?

God has used many tools to touch lives—cooking, agriculture, music, teaching of all kinds, medicine, compassion. It's endless, and, of course, that includes sports. I love the humble service of Olympic star Eric Liddell using organized sport activities with teens confined with him in World War II prison camps. They saw Jesus in him. I've been thrilled seeing many creative sports ministries blossom, from team sports to adventure skills and recreation as God opens doors.

What is your vision for the effective use of sports ministry on the mission field?

I've seen sports ministry in missions mature in recent decades. It is one of the best ways I know to establish meaningful contacts and relationships, especially with youth and the unreached. One missionary reported more significant Bible study and discipleship contacts after a sports blitz than years of previous efforts. It is a most effective link to local and lasting ministries and can be a road to establish new churches.

Do you recommend any precautions to take into consideration when employing sports ministry within global missions?

Hero worship, extreme competitiveness, and extravagant expenses must be countered with humility, compassion, and focus on the entire body of Christ, including the disabled, the poor, and marginalized folks. There are pitfalls in the huge and worldly sports world that Christians must counter. No tool in ministry should drown out the sacrificial love and example of Christ.

Is there anything else you would like to add to the discussion about sports ministry on the world scene?

Folks preparing for sports ministry must excel in more than physical prowess—major on your walk with Christ, be a disciple, study the Word and the world around you, learn from others.

Gil Dodds: The Flying Parson

"Track is, has been, and always will be secondary with me. My gospel work comes first."

Gil Dodds

At the age of 13, Gil Dodds had an inauspicious yet providential encounter with former world record holder and American Olympian distance runner Lloyd Hahn. One day, Dodds was throwing stones at passing cars, when suddenly a car braked and out emerged a farmer who chased down the fleet-footed young Dodds and applied his boot to Dodds' "proper place." Dodds was embarrassed that he had been outrun by a farmer until he learned it was Lloyd Hahn. The ironic twist: Hahn would eventually become Dodds' track coach throughout his high school running career and served as his mail correspondent coach during college. Hahn was a strong Christian and not only guided Gil's running but also mentored his Christian faith (Ladd and Mathisen 1999; Larson 1945).

Dodds became the Nebraska High School State Mile Champion and record holder. Upon graduation, he went to his father's alma mater, Ashland College in Ohio, a school not known for athletics and one without a track team. Dodds represented Ashland as an independent runner, funding himself and often hitchhiking to meets. Dodds had a successful collegiate career, winning an NCAA cross country title and being named an All-American miler (Larson 1945).

World Record Indoor Miler

Dodds' specialty was the indoor mile. From 1943 to 1948 he was practically unbeatable, at one point winning 21 consecutive races. He broke the world indoor mile record three times, the final time at Madison Square Garden in 1948 with a time of 4:05.3. He was considered a favorite for the 1948 Olympics, but an injury sidelined his efforts. A highlight of Dodds' career was being awarded the Amateur Athletic Union Sullivan Award, given annually to a United States amateur athlete who best represented the ideals of sportsmanship. Newspapers lauded Dodds' accomplishment: "He [Dodds] exemplifies all the characteristics of a perfect gentleman and sportsman. Modest in victory and gracious in defeat. By precept and example he is a splendid influence on all with whom he comes in contact" (Larson 1945, 56).

A Bible Verse With Every Autograph

Early in life, Dodds, a preacher's kid, knew his calling was to be a minister. As his running fame grew, so did the requests for his autograph. With each signing he included a Scripture reference in the hopes of spreading God's word to the heart of each recipient. The references varied but included passages such as Hebrews 12:1-2, Philippians 4:13, and Isaiah 40:31. He said, "If through my autograph I can inspire a single soul to return to the path of the Lord I will have achieved a greater victory than the breaking of any track record" (Larson 1945, 66-67). Dodds' unique autograph became so widespread that a reporter referred to the practice as "a sermon with every signature." Sergeant Dan Polier, writing in the military newspaper *Yank*, suggested, "Gil Dodds has done more for the American Bible Society than anyone since King James. He signs his name and the autograph seekers dash for the nearest bookstore and buy a Bible" (Larson 1945, 67).

The Credit Belongs to God

Dodds repeatedly credited God with his running talents. His approach to ministry through sport was gentle and flowed earnestly as an outgrowth of his Christ-focused nature. One reporter wrote, "Gil doesn't make himself a pest by constantly talking 'religion.' Rather, he waits for opportunities to witness, and then uses them" (Larson 1945, 68). Dodds was a frequent speaker at youth rallies and filled the Sunday pulpit at numerous churches. After a world record–breaking performance in Chicago, he told reporters that he was more excited about preaching the next day at a church in Goshen, Indiana (Larson 1945). Like Eric Liddell, Dodds refused to compete on Sundays: "Sunday is a different day from the other six. It is a day of rest. Keep it that way! You'll never lose an inch by refusing to compete in events on Sunday" (Larson 1945, 96). One reporter joked, "He wouldn't run on Sunday, not even for a streetcar" (Larson 1945, 80).

The Compatibility of Christian Faith and Sport

Dodds kept his numerous running accomplishments in perspective: "Is my name in the world's record book of sports? I have achieved that satisfaction, but far above all this I praise the Lord that my name is written in the record book of life, through the shed blood of Christ" (Larson 1945, 94). Dodds endorsed the compatibility of Christian faith with sport. He saw it modeled firsthand in the life of Lloyd Hahn, and he experienced it for himself:

From my own personal experience, I tell you this—you can be an athlete and a Christian at the same time. . . . I won't say here that if you become a Christian God will make a world champion miler out of you. But I do say this, that if you accept the Lord Jesus Christ as your personal Savior and yield your life to Him, He will put you just where He wants you to be, and you'll be mighty satisfied with it. (Larson 1945, 95)

When he retired from running, Dodds became a coach and member of the faculty at Wheaton College in Illinois. He died of a brain tumor in February 1977 at the age of 58 (New York Times, 1977).

Jackie Robinson: Baseball's Barrier Breaker

"Someone else might have . . . done a better job, but God and Branch Rickey made it possible for me to be the one, and I just went on in and did the best I knew how."

Jackie Robinson

Jackie Robinson provides an example of applied faith, putting flesh to biblical principle. He grew up in a single-parent household with a mother who held strong Christian convictions. Rather than repaying bigotry and the injustices of segregation with a like-minded, hate-filled approach, Mallie Robinson applied the example and message of Jesus by confronting hatred with love and a kind response: "God watches what you do; you must reap what you sow, so sow well" (Rampersad 1998, 25). A young minister, Rev. Karl Downs of the Scott Methodist Church in Pasadena, also greatly influenced Jackie by making the Bible come alive. Downs befriended the church's youth, participated in sporting activities with them, and knew how to listen. Consequently, Robinson became a Sunday school teacher, and his perspective about church attendance shifted from dutiful compliance to "excitement in belonging" (Mitrovich 2005).

Stellar UCLA Athlete

Robinson followed in the footsteps of his older brother, Mack, and attended Pasadena Junior College. He broke Mack's national junior college broad jump record with a leap of 25'6.5" (7.8 m). (Mack was the 200-meter silver medalist behind Jesse Owens at the 1936 Berlin Olympics.) After Pasadena, Robinson entered UCLA and became the university's first four-sport letter winner, competing in football, basketball, baseball,

and track and field. He was an honorable mention All-American in both football and basketball. Once his athletic eligibility concluded, he withdrew from school to find a job. He was only several months away from completing his degree but felt there was little future for a Black man, even for one with a college diploma (Rampersad 1998).

Military Service and an Honorable Discharge

During the fall of 1941, Robinson played football for the Honolulu Bears and worked construction near Pearl Harbor. He left Honolulu to sail back to California on December 5, two days prior to the Japanese bombing of Pearl Harbor. When America entered the war, Jackie was drafted. He applied for Officers' Candidate School and became a second lieutenant in January 1943. Robinson served several leadership roles and was commended by his battalion commander (Robinson 1995; Rampersad 1998).

Robinson witnessed and experienced multiple instances of racial bigotry and injustice. As morale officer, he was not afraid to stand up for the rights of his men or for himself. On one occasion, Robinson faced court-martial charges for his refusal to sit in the back of a bus. The trial proved that Robinson had done nothing wrong. He was acquitted of all charges, but the experience soured his opinion of the military, and he requested a release from service. He was granted an honorable discharge in November 1944 (Robinson 1995).

Professional Negro Baseball League

With few options available, Robinson became a ballplayer for the Kansas City Monarchs in the professional Negro Baseball League. Travel was grueling, meals were frequently poor, and road trips meant sleeping on the team bus (Rampersad 1998).

Turn the Other Cheek

Branch Rickey, the general manager of the Brooklyn Dodgers, was a man of faith. He had a dual purpose for initiating a meeting with Robinson. Selfishly, he wanted to win ball games, and he also believed that every man, regardless of skin color, should have the opportunity to play baseball. Rickey anticipated the threatening challenges that the first Black player would face to integrate major league baseball (Henry 2017). He knew that Robinson possessed the skills to play, but did he have the character? Rickey asked Robinson, "Have you the guts to play the game no matter what happens?" Robinson responded, "Mr. Rickey, are you looking for a Negro who is afraid to fight back?" Rickey shouted, "I'm looking for a ballplayer with guts enough not to fight back" (Evans and Herzog 2002, 155).

Rickey appealed to Robinson's Christian upbringing, citing Jesus' words from His sermon on the Mount: "If anyone slaps you on the right cheek, turn to them the other cheek also." Robinson would need to faithfully apply the life lessons and words of his mother to overcome hatred with love. It was against human nature to resist the need for retaliation and not to defend oneself against injustices. Robinson would encounter public scorn on the field and as he walked the streets. Likewise, Branch Rickey would be chastised by team owners and league officials.

> *"God is with us in this, Jackie," Mr. Rickey said quietly. "You know your Bible. It is good simple Christianity for us to face realities and to recognize what we are up against. We cannot go out and preach and crusade and bust our heads against a wall. We've got to fight our problems together with tact and commonsense." (Robinson and Long 2013, 3)*

His Demeanor and Play Changed Perspectives

Robinson led the Dodgers minor league affiliate, Montreal, to the 1946 Junior World Series title and had a league-best .349 batting average (Robinson and Long 2013). Not only did he prove himself as a player, but he also proved himself as an honorable man. Montreal's manager, Clay Hopper, was greatly influenced by Robinson. A native of Mississippi, Hopper originally questioned Robinson's humanity because of his skin color. By the season's conclusion, he shook Robinson's hand and said, "You're a great ballplayer and a fine gentleman. It's been wonderful having you on the team" (Evans and Herzog 2002, 159-160; Robinson 1995, 48, 52).

A Champion of the Game

In 1947 Robinson was promoted to the Brooklyn Dodgers and was named Rookie of the Year. He spent 10 seasons with the Dodgers before his retirement at age 38. During his tenure, the Dodgers won six pennants and one World Series. Robinson was on the 1962 ballot for induction into baseball's Hall of Fame. He did not want to receive the honor by virtue of being the first Black major league player. He also wondered if he would be denied the honor because he stood for equality and social justice. He wrote,

> *There are standards and requisites clearly defined for election to the Hall of Fame. I believe they include playing ability, sportsmanship, character, contribution to your team and to baseball in general. If, in the honest opinion of the sportswriters of America, I qualify in accordance with these requisites, then I will feel genuinely happy about it. If I honestly qualify and if I am refused the honor because*

The faith of Jackie Robinson equipped him to demonstrate Christian principles within a hostile and volatile environment.

I fought and argued for the principles in which I believe, so be it. Were it possible to make a swap between violating my convictions and winning this high mark of baseball immortality, I would unquestioningly select adherence to my principles and my integrity. (Robinson and Long 2013, 23)

Robinson was inducted into the Hall of Fame during his first year of eligibility. He serves as an example of a doer of the Word. The convictions of his faith were demonstrated by his actions.

The Pathway to Sports Ministry timeline provides a visual of key dates that have been explored in this chapter (table 2.1).

TABLE 2.1   A Pathway to Sports Ministry: An Integration of Faith and Sport Timeline

1877	Wealthy English tea planter Edward Studd receives Jesus as Lord and Savior during a D.L. Moody revival meeting.
1882	World-renowned cricketer C.T. Studd's life is dramatically changed during a D.L. Moody revival.
1883	Billy Sunday signs to play professional baseball with the Chicago White Stockings.
1885	C.T. Studd forfeits his international cricket standing to become a missionary to China as a member of the Cambridge Seven.
1886	Billy Sunday has a conversion to Christ at the Pacific Garden Rescue Mission in Chicago.
1889	Amos Alonzo Stagg is named to Walter Camp's first All-American football team.
1891	Billy Sunday retires from baseball to serve the YMCA.
1891	James Naismith invents the game of basketball at the Springfield, Massachusetts, YMCA.
1892	Amos Alonzo Stagg begins coaching football at the University of Chicago.
1895	Billy Sunday's sawdust trail begins with evangelistic meetings held in Garner, Iowa.
1895	William Morgan invents the game of volleyball at the Holyoke, Massachusetts, YMCA.
1908	C.T. Studd feels called to minister to the people of Central Africa.
1917	Billy Sunday leads a 10-week revival campaign in New York City, and an estimated 90,000 people come forward to receive Jesus.
1923	Eric Liddell has a life-transforming experience speaking publicly about his faith in the mining town of Armadale, Scotland.
1924	Eric Liddell wins gold and bronze medals at the Paris Olympics.
1925	Eric Liddell is awarded Scotland's Crabbie Award for the fourth consecutive year, a feat unmatched by anyone.
1925	Eric Liddell departs for China to serve as a missionary science teacher and athletic administrator.
1931	C.T. Studd breathes his final "hallelujah," having paved the way for other missionaries to follow with ministry to Central Africa.
1939	Jackie Robinson becomes the first four-sport letter winner at UCLA (football, baseball, basketball, track and field).
1943	Gil Dodds is awarded the Sullivan Award as America's top amateur athlete.
1945	Jackie Robinson signs to play baseball with the Brooklyn Dodgers' affiliate team in Montreal.
1946	Robinson leads Montreal to the Junior World Series title and leads the league with a .349 batting average.
1947	Robinson plays for the Brooklyn Dodgers and is named the league's Rookie of the Year.
1951	Amos Alonzo Stagg is inducted into football's Hall of Fame. He is the first recipient to be named as both a player and a coach.
1962	Jackie Robinson is inducted into baseball's Hall of Fame during his first year of eligibility.

SUMMARY

Historically, Christ-centered athletes have wrestled with the tension between sport as a God-given ability to be cultivated for His glory and sport as an idolatrous preoccupation for the promotion of self. C.T. Studd serves as an example of a world-renowned athlete who needed to step aside from sport because it had consumed his identity. Eric Liddell and Gil Dodds provide examples of Christian athletes who trained hard to perfect their athletic skills yet did not allow sport to usurp the rightful place of Christian faith in their lives. For them, sport was subservient to their faith. When Liddell chose missionary work in China over his budding track career, he was not abandoning sport; he was following God's call to a different direction. The same could be said of Billy Sunday when he exited baseball for the YMCA and ultimately for his ministry as an evangelist. James Naismith and Amos Alonzo Stagg each concluded that traditional ministry was not the only means by which to serve God. They understood that God was present wherever He led them, and they believed they could best serve His purposes by ministering within the athletic arena. Jackie Robinson's faith enabled him to demonstrate Christian principles in a hostile and volatile environment. His example opened a door for changed perspectives and for others to follow. The notoriety of profiled athletes highlights the intrinsic value of sport as a platform from which faith can be shared through word and deed.

REVIEW AND DISCUSSION QUESTIONS

1. Does participation in sport inform Christian faith, or does Christian faith inform participation in sport?
2. Discuss how sport can become an idol.
3. How did the Industrial Revolution initially hinder the emergence of sport but later become a catalyst for its growth?
4. Discuss the differences between musclemen and Muscular Christianity.
5. What five key factors emerged simultaneously in America that greatly influenced the development of organized sport and the influences of Christian faith?
6. Why was it necessary for Jackie Robinson to "turn the other cheek"?
7. How is sport a relational bridge that connects diverse people?
8. Is Christian faith personal but not private?

PART II

CONTEMPORARY
APPROACHES
TO SPORTS MINISTRY

Courtesy of Fellowship of Christian Athletes.

The Fellowship of Christian Athletes (FCA), the vision of founder Don McClanen, has grown to become the largest worldwide sports ministry.

CHAPTER 3

Sports Ministry in the United States

"He is no fool who gives what he cannot keep, to gain that which he cannot lose."

Jim Elliott (1927-1956), martyred missionary

LEARNING OBJECTIVES

After studying this chapter, you should be able to do the following:

- Explain how the field of sports ministry has grown by the grace of God from its humble beginnings to the ministry it is today
- Understand the history of sports ministry in the United States and its significance to sports ministry initiatives in the United States today
- Identify how sports ministry continues to affect a postmodern society and culture, and the special way sports ministry still changes and transforms lives
- Understand and explain the call and responsibility Christians have to take the gospel to America and how sport can be used as a natural way to do so
- Appreciate the special role that chaplaincy plays in sports ministry
- Detail how an understanding of sports ministry, its historical roots, key personalities, and present structures can shape the thinking of those who feel called to this special form of ministering and serving

Known as the innovator of baseball's current affiliated minor league system and for his role in breaking baseball's color barrier when he signed Jackie Robinson to the Brooklyn Dodgers, Branch Rickey was a devout Christian and a key figure in establishing the Fellowship of Christian Athletes (FCA).

Rickey proved to be a catalyst in the realization of what Don McClanen referred to as "God's amazing, miraculous dream." Rickey's assistance has enabled the FCA to become what it is now: the largest Christian sports ministry organization in the world, with over 450 offices and more than 1,000 staff members across the nation, that God uses to bring thousands of people into His Kingdom every year.

Rickey was inducted into FCA's Hall of Champions in 1995. Undeniably, Jackie Robinson received the brunt of prejudicial scorn as the first Black player in major league baseball. Yet Rickey was willing to sacrifice his reputation and face the consequences of standing for justice in the midst of racial inequality. He confronted league owners, fans, and ballplayers. Some members of the press predicted embarrassment and failure. Due to health issues, even his own family expressed concern over the toll his decision could take on his physical well-being (Robinson 1995; Robinson and Long 2013). The important lesson is this: in doing what he did, Branch Rickey demonstrated that he was living a life that was all about "giving up what he could not keep, to gain that which he could not lose."

By the grace of God, and through many people's determination and hard work, the field of sports ministry has grown from its humble beginnings to the thriving ministry it is today. Early advocates believed in the power of sport as a means to share the gospel of Jesus Christ, making disciples, and positively affecting the lives of those they served. These beliefs led to the birth of the earliest forms of sports ministry in the United States. To gain an understanding of sports ministry in the United States, it is best to consider select individuals and organizations using sport to actively engage a variety of populations. The three major organized sports ministries and their methodologies will be explored: the Young Men's Christian Association (YMCA), the FCA, and Athletes in Action (AIA). In addition, several other significant national sports ministry organizations (Pro Athletes Outreach and Missionary Athletes International), sports chaplaincy, the National Christian College Athletic Association (NCCAA), and Christian media initiatives (Faith on the Field and Sports Spectrum) will be examined. This background and these stories will serve to inspire one to consider personal involvement in one or more of these special categories of genuine and effective Christian sports ministries.

Understanding Sports Ministry in the United States

For some, *sports ministry* is a new term. For others, it is the experience that drew them to personal faith in Jesus Christ. For still others, they view sports ministry as their life's calling and vocation. At its core, sports ministry seeks to use the many avenues of sport to glorify God and see lives changed through sharing the gospel message of Jesus Christ. If one were to question the validity of sports ministry as an endeavor in the United States, they need only look at the countless lives that have been transformed by the life-changing message of the gospel presented not from a pulpit but through sport in sporting venues.

In Mark 1:17 Jesus said to Simon and his brother Andrew, "Come, follow me, and I will make you fishers of men" (NIV). They immediately left their nets and followed Him. Later, in verse 22 of the same chapter, it says that the disciples "were astonished at his teaching, for he taught them as one having authority" (NAB). In Matthew 28:18-19 Jesus came and spoke to them after His resurrection: "All authority has been given to Me in heaven and on earth. Go, therefore, and make disciples of all the nations" (NASB). And so accordingly, we are to be witnesses to what Jesus Christ has done for us (Acts 1:8), and we are to make disciples.

Acts 1:8 talks about being His witness to "Jerusalem, and in all Judea and Samaria, and to the end of the earth" (NIV). Chapter 4 will explore sports ministry beyond our Jerusalem, Judea, and even Samaria, to the ends of the earth. In this chapter we will explore sports ministry in our Jerusalem and Judea—the United States—which arguably possesses the most resources and potential for such ministry in a seemingly endless number of sports and sport-related activities.

The Beginnings of Organized Sports Ministry in the United States in the 20th Century

The previous chapter discussed several of the early, and mostly individual, efforts at sports ministry in the United States. This chapter will begin by examining the YMCA, FCA, and AIA. Just as individual athletes wrestled with how to integrate faith and sport, emerging organizations began to equip Christian athletes with sports ministry precepts.

Young Men's Christian Association (YMCA)

When the YMCA originated, it did not have sport or recreational components. With the onset of the Industrial Revolution, young men left the fields and flocked to cities to find employment in factories. Urban areas grew rapidly, and the growth created an environment bustling with saloons, gambling, pickpockets, and prostitutes. Recognizing these unsavory living conditions, and to secure a haven for young factory workers, George Williams gathered a group of men together in London on June 6, 1844, to organize a Christian association for the twofold purpose of prayer and Bible study. The meetings grew, and several years later, the YMCA expanded to North America, with chapters opening in Montreal on November 29 and in Boston on December 29, 1851 (YMCA Richmond 2016; Pure History 2012; Ladd and Mathisen 1999).

By 1854, 397 separate YMCA chapters represented seven nations worldwide. In 1869, four years after the Civil War ended, the number of chapters in the United States blossomed to over 600. By 1885, one-third of American college students were members of the YMCA (Ladd and Mathisen 1999). An original intention of the YMCA was the saving of souls and offering community services such as Christian boarding houses, lectures, and libraries.

The Introduction of Sport and Recreation

As sport clubs emerged, the YMCA also began offering sport and recreational opportunities. By the 1880s the YMCA was constructing their own separate buildings and expanding their sport offerings. The new constructions were equipped with amenities such as gymnasiums, swimming pools, bowling alleys, and auditoriums, and many provided hotel-like accommodations. The YMCA has been instrumental in four key sport and recreational developments:

1. Invention of the indoor sports of basketball and volleyball at the YMCA Training School in Springfield, Massachusetts
2. The first to provide group swimming lessons
3. The earliest to provide public fitness workouts
4. The oldest continuous summer camping program—one of the first known summer camp programs for children, Camp Dudley in New York. Opened in 1885, it is believed to be the oldest running American camp but is no longer owned by the YMCA) (Weeks 2015; Pure History 2012).

A Venue for Evangelism and Christian Expression

The YMCA was pivotally connected to student global missionary efforts and to revivalists (e.g., D.L. Moody, John Mott, Charles Finney, Billy Sunday) and became an active voice in social issues such as prohibition, desegregation, women's suffrage, urban sanitation, poverty, and immigrant assimilation. As the world of competitive sport grew increasingly popular, many chapters instituted **Athletic Sundays** whereby an influential Christian athlete would speak about his or her faith (Hoffman 2010).

The Autonomy of YMCA Chapters

Over the years tensions developed between some YMCA chapters. Many chapters desired to align closely with the biblical moorings of its Christian origins while others embraced the evolving social unity of diverse religions. Consequently, each YMCA chapter develops their own **autonomous polity**. They all share the same motto of "spirit, mind, and body," and most will use sport and recreation as tools to build character, but they may differ in their definition of "spirit."

The YMCA has grown to be one of the largest nonprofit organizations in the United States. It operates approximately 2,600 facilities and has

---

Athletic Sundays—The YMCA programing that featured prominent Christian athletes speaking about their faith at their services.

autonomous polity—In reference to the YMCA, each chapter is self-governing and adopts policy that best fits the needs of its own community.

By permission of Parkview Huntington Family YMCA.

By the 1880s the YMCA expanded programing to include sport and recreational opportunities. Today, facilities frequently include swimming pools, gymnasiums, and fitness centers.

19,000 employees along with an estimated 600,000 volunteers. Nationally, the YMCA serves and enlists 11 million members annually, 4 million of whom are under the age of 18. Their growth and overall track record of successful management gives ample credence to the approach of autonomous polity when it comes to managing their many separate branches.

As for leadership, since 2015 Kevin Washington has served as the president and CEO of the YMCA of the USA organization. After six successful years of leadership, he retired. Kevin first walked into the Christian Street YMCA in his South Philadelphia neighborhood as a 10-year-old to participate in the afterschool program. Years later he would embark on a career with the Y, working his way up through the ranks to the organization's highest position. In his own words, "For the past 43 years I have given the organization everything I have, and were I able to serve 43 more, I still could not repay all that the YMCA has done for me" (PR Newswire 2020). Washington represents yet another fine example of quality and continuity in organizational leadership. In August 2021 the YMCA of the USA named Suzanne McCormick as the next president and CEO. She became the organization's first female leader and brought to the YMCA a strong background and experience in nonprofit leadership (Cridlin 2021).

Fellowship of Christian Athletes (FCA)

Don McClanen, a young Oklahoma basketball coach, had a dream. If prominent athletes could endorse products like shaving cream and cigarettes, why not use the celebrity status of sport figures to talk about and endorse the Lord? In 1954 he wrote a total of 19 letters to professional athletes and sport administrators whom he had read about in articles highlighting their Christian faith. He shared his vision for an organization that would enjoin athletes and coaches alike to influence the nation's youth for Christ. Among those receiving his letter were Otto Graham (Cleveland Browns quarterback), Bob Mathias (Olympic decathlon champion), Louis Zamperini (Olympian who survived a Japanese prison camp during the war), Amos Alonzo Stagg (legendary college football coach), and baseball executive Branch Rickey (general manager of the Pittsburgh Pirates) (Atcheson 1994, 158).

Branch Rickey: A Key Contact

McClanen believed a key contact would be Branch Rickey. After multiple failed attempts to secure an appointment with Rickey, McClanen drove to Pittsburgh with hopes of a cold call meeting with Rickey. His persistence paid off when a 'five-minute' meeting ended up lasting five hours. Rickey caught the vision for McClanen's dream, and he made a statement that Don McClanen would never forget. Mr. Rickey said, "This thing has the potential of changing the youth scene of America within a decade. It is pregnant with potential. It is just ingenious. It is a new thing, where has it been?" Then he asked Don, "Are you independently wealthy?" to which Don answered no and told Branch how he had mortgaged his car to get to Pittsburgh for their meeting. Rickey's response was simple and straightforward, "Well, you are going to need some money. You need $10,000 and I think I know the man who would be willing to give you that $10,000" (Murchison 2008, 19; Atcheson 1994, 163).

With the vision caught, Rickey suggested that McClanen reach out to Pittsburgh businessman, Mike Benedum. He did and soon thereafter, Benedum provided the seed money, and the official charter for the Fellowship of Christian Athletes was rendered on November 10, 1954, in Norman, Oklahoma (Atcheson 1994). Approximately seven months later, on June 7, 1955, Rickey hosted a banquet in Pittsburgh to officially introduce the Fellowship of Christian Athletes (FCA, n.d.). By the grace of God, Don McClanen's idea, his faith, and his perseverance were combined with Branch Rickey's "caught vision" and decisiveness and Mike Benedum's gospel patronage and willful funding. The net result: the FCA was launched and on its way to touching countless lives for Christ through sport.

Featured in Sports Illustrated

Fifteen months after its founding, FCA was featured in a popular new sports magazine, in an article titled "Hero Worship Harnessed: Stars Turn to Evangelism and Score Hit With Admirers at Rally in Denver" (SI Staff 1956). The article focused on FCA's city-wide event held in Denver in which well-known professional athletes canvassed the area, speaking in schools, at luncheons, at the Air Force Academy, and in Sunday school classes. The smallest attendance was 30, and the largest was 2,000. Speakers included baseball players George Kell (Chicago White Sox), Vernon Law (Pittsburgh Pirates), Robin Roberts (Philadelphia Phillies), and Carl Erskine (Brooklyn Dodgers), and football players Dan Towler (Los Angeles Rams) and Adrian Burk (Philadelphia Eagles). One reporter suggested that the athletes were not the most polished public speakers, but they won the hearts of their listeners by the sincerity of their presentation. The

dream laid on the heart of Don McClanen had taken firm root and began its journey to become the world's largest Bible-based sports ministry organization. The Denver FCA rally set the stage for the next vital step in the growth of the organization.

The Single Most Important Event in FCA's History: The First National FCA Camp

Since its humble beginnings in the mid-1950s, the FCA has come a long way to where they are today in their sports ministry endeavors. Shortly after the organization's founding and the successful Denver rally, another key event was to take place. It was in 1956 that this fledgling sports ministry movement held its first National FCA Camp at Estes Park, Colorado. It is significant to note that this weeklong camp was held at the beautiful YMCA of the Rockies retreat and camp facility. This partnership of major sports ministry organizations represented a quality example of cooperative efforts for the greater good and for the propagation of the gospel. This conference has been called by many the single most important event in FCA's long and storied history.

However, there was some doubt as to whether it would successfully launch and even happen at all. In fact, FCA founder and executive director Don McClanen had reserved rooms for 500 people (300 college athletes, 150 high school athletes, and 50 coaches and staff), but when Gary Demarest, the camp's dean, picked up Branch Rickey at the airport, Demarest was worried the camp would be a bust, noting that as of a month prior, only 38 reservations had been made. Branch Rickey's response was classic old-school faith. "Don't forget," Rickey told Demarest on the way from Denver to Estes Park, "Jesus started with twelve." Demarest continued the story: "There were 256 present that night when Mr. Rickey gave the keynote message calling us to boldly witness for Christ and the church. Out of that camp grew the network of citywide programs, chapters, **Huddles** and all the rest that's made FCA national in scope" (Atcheson 1994, 182). Along with his responsibility as the keynote speaker, Rickey was the director of baseball. The rest of the coaches and staff represented significant and successful sporting personalities of the day such as Kansas basketball coaching legend Phog Allen, who served as the director of basketball; Otto Graham of the Cleveland Browns championship team and Doak Walker, 1948 Heisman Trophy winner of Southern Methodist University fame, who served as the football directors; Olympic hero Rafer

---

Huddle—A small-group Bible study for coaches (and athletes) of teams at all levels whether on high school or college campuses or with community club or travel teams.

Johnson, who won a silver medal a few months later in the 1956 Olympics and a gold medal in the 1960 Olympics, and former Baylor football player James Jeffrey, who eventually became the third executive director in FCA history, served as two of the ten Huddle leaders. As for Don McClanen, he willingly stayed and diligently worked behind the scenes as the camp director (FCA, n.d.). His inconspicuous style of directing the camp illustrates an important lesson in servant leadership. Since this first conference, FCA camps and conferences have become a ministry staple, not only in the United States but in countries around the world.

The 1956 first-ever National Camp at Estes Park, Colorado, was truly a watershed moment for the FCA. In this singular event it brought together and engaged an array of athletic levels, from junior and senior high school to college and professional levels, including representation from the Olympic Games. Clergy from Catholic and Protestant denominations, as well as the nation's leading magazines, caught the compelling vision. Even President Dwight D. Eisenhower saluted the FCA for this National Camp. From this event, a surge of ministry activity followed: citywide programs, rallies, school assemblies, banquets, and weekend conferences with prominent athletes and coaches speaking and sharing their testimonies with the goal of reaching youths in the name of Jesus Christ (Atcheson 1994, 195).

So much more could be said about the FCA history, but this summary is a good case study in sports ministry on a couple key levels. The first level is the idea of having a dream and then, through prayer, planning, and much hard work, enabling the dream to become a reality. In the case of Don McClanen, the words of Cardinal Leon Suenens sum up his vision and work quite well when he said, "Happy are those who dream dreams and are willing to pay the price to make them come true" (Inspired Motivation, n.d.). For Don McClanen, his dream of athletes influencing young people's lives for good through a faith-based sports ministry was realized in 1954 with FCA's founding. McClanen followed through on the vision he felt God had laid on his heart, and with God's prompting, he found a way to pay the price to make it a reality. From the outset and throughout the entire arduous process, he relied on God's sustaining power, and the glory was credited to the Lord for the things he and his team were able to achieve. McClanen's original dream of a special sports ministry to young athletes, college athletes, and coaches remains a vibrant and growing reality today. At the time of this writing, FCA was closing in on nearly 70 years of faithfully proclaiming the good news of the gospel of Jesus Christ.

On a second key level, the FCA story is a case study in quality and continuity as far as a vibrant, biblically sound sports ministry is concerned. Where the quality of effort is high and leadership over many years is consistent, good things get accomplished and great results can come to pass. The FCA has been significantly blessed over the years in these two key categories. The numbers are impressive. Annually, over 24,000 young people will attend an FCA sports camp. Throughout the year FCA runs over 21,000 Huddles. FCA now has some form of ministry in over 100 countries worldwide.

The FCA has been led by president and CEO Shane Williamson since January 2017. Williamson became a Christ follower in 1986 while attending an FCA Camp in Black Mountain, North Carolina. He played collegiate football at Wofford College in South Carolina and later enjoyed 12 years of coaching high school football also in the Palmetto State. He joined the FCA staff in 2002 and steadily took on larger roles until taking on his present position. The FCA headquarters are located in Kansas City, Missouri, overlooking Arrowhead Stadium, home of the NFL Kansas City Chiefs, and Kauffman Stadium, home of the MLB Kansas City Royals.

Athletes in Action (AIA)

In 1951 a student ministry organization was birthed on the campus of UCLA by a young seminary student, Bill Bright. The ministry was called Campus Crusade for Christ (now known as Cru). Its goal was to win and disciple college students for Christ. The ministry included social activities, campus lectures, small-group Bible studies, and publishing (Cru, n.d.).

In 1966 Dave Hannah, a draftee of the Los Angeles Rams, initiated a new sport-focused branch of Campus Crusade called Athletes in Action (AIA n.d.a.). In 1968 a wrestling team was formed with top wrestlers from throughout the United States (AIA n.d.a.). This team competed in exhibition matches both domestically and abroad. Starring on the wrestling team were 1976 Olympic gold medalist John Peterson and bronze medalist Gene Davis. Eventually, additional teams were added in basketball, baseball, soccer, track and field, and volleyball. Teams used halftimes and postgame opportunities to share about their faith in Christ with opposing teams and spectators.

In 1977 AIA basketball made national news when the team beat collegiate powers Ohio State, West Virginia, Maryland, UNLV, Syracuse, and San Francisco while compiling an exhibition record of 33–2. They also beat the Russian national team 93–84 (*Athletes in Action vs. Soviet Union Basketball* 1978). According to then UNLV coach Jerry Tarkanian, "They [AIA] beat you up in the first half, pray for you at halftime, then beat you up in the second half" (Cru, n.d.). UCLA grad Ralph Drollinger turned down a $400,000 no-cut contract from the New Jersey Nets to play for AIA. He emphasized that AIA players are different:

The difference between us and many of those we play is that we're doing it for someone other than ourselves. This is demonstrated by the way we play. We have some of the best teamwork I've seen or can imagine, because we're not playing for selfish motivation—personal gain, worldly adulation, and money. As players for God's work, we really try to love each other, our opponents, and the spectators as well. . . . We're convinced that a personal relationship with God is the most important thing in the world. What better way, then, can we love someone else than by sharing that relationship in a loving and affirming manner? (Quebedeaux 1979, 145-146)

Since initially launching as a traveling sports outreach, AIA has grown significantly with staff members on college and university campuses, in professional locker rooms, and in athletic organizations around the world. AIA is led by President Mark Householder, who has been in this role for more than a dozen years and is closing in on four decades of faithful ministry through sport. Mark came to faith in Jesus Christ as a freshman football player through an AIA ministry to athletes at the University of Cincinnati. The national and international headquarters for AIA is located on the Athletes in Action Sports Complex and Retreat Center in Xenia, Ohio. This 250-acre sports complex and retreat center is home to the corporate offices. It is comprised of six sports fields (over 600,000 square feet of artificial turf) and can house 300 athletes and guests at a time for their various sports ministry programs (AIA n.d.a.).

The Values and Goals of Sports Ministry Organizations and Initiatives

Before considering the various methodologies and approaches to sports ministry, it is important to note that these ministries share much in common. Sports ministry organizations may take many different forms of ministry methodologies, but at the end of the day

they share some key overarching values and goals as evidenced by their respective vision, mission, or values statements. Three common values at the top of the list are

1. sharing the gospel of Jesus Christ,
2. making disciples, and
3. serving and supporting those to whom they minister.

Consider the following three mission statements:

- "To put Christian principles into practice through programs that build healthy spirit, mind, and body for all." (Young Men's Christian Association)
- "To see the world transformed by Jesus Christ through the influence of coaches and athletes. To lead every coach and athlete into a growing relationship with Jesus Christ and His church. Our relationships will demonstrate steadfast commitment to Jesus Christ and His Word through Integrity, Serving, Teamwork, and Excellence." (Fellowship of Christian Athletes)
- "We believe whole-heartedly in supporting athletes in both their athletic and spiritual journeys. By serving, training, and sending athletes as influencers into the world we are building spiritual movements everywhere through the platform of sports so that everyone knows someone who truly follows Jesus." (Athletes In Action)

These organizations share a common Christian perspective, viewing life through the lens of Scripture. Consequently, character qualities, attitudes, moral judgments, and personal purpose are shaped by God's directive. Likewise, those who invest time and energy in sports ministry ultimately will be judged by their faithfulness to these same Scripture-based values. In the following pages, we will take a deeper dive into these big three (YMCA, FCA, and AIA). The goal is to acquaint you with those who have faithfully proclaimed the good news of the gospel of Jesus Christ through sport so that you might begin to form your own concepts and beliefs about sports ministry.

Approaches and Methodologies

As previously noted, early on in the mid-20th century the three major **national sports ministry** organizations in the United States were the YMCA, the FCA,

---

national sports ministry—The term used to describe the largest sports ministry organizations that provide gospel-based programs to every state in America using the platform of sport, athletes, and coaches.

and AIA. Of these three major ministry efforts, two have remained true to their original mission, FCA and AIA. The YMCA was very biblically based in its earliest forms but has slowly evolved over the years to embrace autonomous polity, and though they still share a motto of using sport to develop spirit, mind, and body, how this motto is embodied can vary widely from YMCA chapter to chapter. In this section, we will explore examples of the various approaches and methodologies that each of these three major national organizations incorporate into their respective sports ministry efforts.

YMCA

Under the YMCA banner of autonomous polity some chapters, such as the Harris YMCA of Greater Charlotte, North Carolina, remain true to the Y's original founding principles. They are committed to an areas of impact approach that ministers through (1) youth development by empowering young people to reach their full potential, (2) healthy living by improving individual and community well-being, and (3) social responsibility by providing support and inspiring action in their community. As for methodologies, like many branches, Harris YMCA of Greater Charlotte offers a complete portfolio of program offerings for all ages and abilities. Specifically in the sports ministry–related space their program offerings include aquatics, group exercise, preschool learning through play, summer camps, youth sports, adult athletic leagues, diverse abilities programs, fitness training, gymnastics, outdoor activities, and competitive races. They pursue these areas of impact and program offerings from a faith-based experiential approach that honors their Christian mission and places the greater good above self-interest, doing so in an environment where all feel genuinely welcomed, encouraged, and supported (YMCA of Greater Charlotte, n.d.).

FCA

The FCA seeks to unite two passions—faith and athletics—to affect those they minister to for Jesus Christ. Their strategic approach is unique in that they minister first and foremost to and through the coach by ministering to their hearts, marriages, and families. Once this relationship is formed, the FCA comes alongside the coach to minister to fellow coaches, their teams, and athletes who are leaders. The end goal is to achieve the greatest level of influence so that every coach and athlete has a growing relationship

with Jesus Christ and His Church. They genuinely seek to do this with the following four principles always at work in the process:

1. *Integrity (Proverbs 11:3):* We will demonstrate Christ-like wholeness, privately and publicly.
2. *Serving (John 13:1-17):* We will model Jesus' example of serving.
3. *Teamwork (Philippians 2:1-4):* We will express our unity in Christ in all our relationships.
4. *Excellence (Colossians 3:23-24):* We will honor and glorify God in all we do. (FCA, n.d.)

This approach is summed up in three Es:

1. *Engage (1 Thessalonians 2:8):* FCA staff seek to engage in a relational manner with individuals and through different events and environments. They do this by building a genuine level of trust, sharing of themselves and their lives, and ultimately sharing the gospel. Key to the engagement process is connecting with coaches and athletes where they are on their spiritual journey, wherever that may be.
2. *Equip (Ephesians 4:12):* As cultivated relationships bear fruit through coaches and athletes coming to faith in Christ, these individuals are discipled through Christ-centered training, special events, and learning resources, all related to what it means to be a follower of Christ and someone who is daily growing in God's word and learning to apply it in practical ways to their life.
3. *Empower (2 Timothy 2:2):* The end goal is an equipped and mature believer whom FCA can empower to use their time, talents, and treasures to help other coaches and athletes experience the good news of the gospel and then grow in their faith. Further, the FCA desires to develop disciples who will in turn engage, equip, and empower others to come to know Christ and grow in Him. (FCA, n.d.)

The FCA incorporates and uses several specific methodologies and approaches to achieve their vision and mission calling. First, they provide multiple resources for personal spiritual growth. These resources include daily devotions delivered via email, a resource library of sports devotionals, individual and small-group Bible study materials, audio resources with encouraging interviews and

Corporate team prayer is often a regular practice among Christian teams.

teaching, and extensive printed materials and Bibles. Second, the FCA provides training for coaches and community ministries. One of the mainstays since the beginning has been the formation of Huddles. Third, the FCA provides extensive resources both in virtual and printed forms (FCA, n.d.). Additionally, as noted previously, the FCA runs a significant number of summer camp programs. They offer (1) team camps for high school athletic teams, (2) sports camps for individual athletes, (3) power camps for younger kids ages 8 to 12, (4) leadership camps solely devoted to the leaders of today's sports teams and programs, (5) coaches camps to train and mentor future coaches, and (6) partnership camps where FCA partners with third-party camps who use FCA materials (KFA 2017).

The FCA is extremely organized, and their support materials are well conceived and designed. Even with their high level of organizational sophistication, it is all subservient to their simple stated goal of seeking to unite faith and athletics as they minister for Jesus Christ.

AIA

AIA presents a threefold challenge for all college athletes who profess faith in Jesus Christ. On over 200 college and university campuses across the United States, groups of Christian athletes are meeting this challenge. The threefold challenge is this:

1. *Win:* Engage with the culture of sport in your life and understand the importance of knowing Jesus in a real and personal way.
2. *Build:* Grow your relationship with God and others, becoming a leader both on and off the field.
3. *Send:* Practice taking the initiative to share and invest your faith and life into the lives of teammates and others you influence. (AIA n.d.a.)

Another great opportunity for participation in sports ministry through AIA is the program Grow in Your Sport, which provides a great way to personally develop physically, mentally, and spiritually by engaging in various AIA opportunities throughout the year. The following is a sampling of Grow in Your Sport opportunities:

- With a motto of "Strength, Truth, Eternity," AIA baseball is committed to excellence both on and off of the field. AIA baseball teams hone their skills by fielding teams in the following summer collegiate minor leagues: (1) The Chugiak-Eagle River Chinooks in the Alaska Baseball League, (2) The Xenia Scouts in the Great Lakes Summer League, and (3) The Rochester Ridgemen in the New York Collegiate League. Opportunities also exist to compete internationally for travel with AIA baseball.

- In AIA basketball the objective is to create an environment where the players can grow in their faith while sharing the good news of the gospel. The goal is to see Christ followers on every team so that everyone knows someone who truly follows Jesus. For over 25 years AIA has sent high-quality basketball teams around the world with the primary goal of sharing the message of Jesus Christ through the game. An additional benefit is the transformation that takes place in the lives of the AIA team members. They grow in faith, learn to apply biblical principles to competition in many different settings, experience the joy of using basketball to make a difference in the lives of others, and gain invaluable international playing experience.

- Special opportunities are available for the sport of volleyball, with international tours, beach volleyball internships, and pro volleyball Bible studies.

These are just three of many sporting opportunities that AIA offers annually (AIA n.d.a.). Additional sports ministry methodologies used by AIA include (1) ultimate training camps, where athletes go through high-intensity athletic experiences that blend God, life, and sport; (2) college athlete camps; (3) high school athlete camps; and (4) teams and coaches camps. If a sporting activity can involve faith and athletics in unique settings, AIA probably does or has offered the experience.

A few additional special events that AIA offers annually include the following.

- The Super Bowl Breakfast and the presentation of the Bart Starr Award for outstanding character and leadership
- The NBA All-Star Breakfast, which celebrates character, leadership, and faith with the presentation of the Jerry Colangelo and Bobby Jones Awards
- John Wooden's Keys to Life Event held during the NCAA Men's Final Four Weekend. The highlight of this event is the presentation of the Coach Wooden Keys to Life Award to a current or former coach or player who best exemplifies the character traits of the legendary UCLA men's basketball coach.
- The Night of Champions Event, which celebrates the lives of men and women in sport who make a real difference in the lives of others. Each year at this event two new members are inducted into the AIA Hall of Faith. (AIA n.d.a.)

AIA possesses a seemingly endless array of sports ministry opportunities for faith-based Christian athletes to grow in their sport and in their faith and then to share that faith through their sporting endeavors and competitions.

Additional Significant National Sports Ministry Organizations

As mentioned in the chapter introduction, besides the major three, several other significant national sports ministry organizations are worthy of notation: Pro Athletes Outreach and Missionary Athletes International, sports chaplaincy, the National Christian College Athletic Association (NCCAA), and Christian media initiatives (e.g., Faith on the Field and Sports Spectrum).

Pro Athletes Outreach (PAO)

Founded in 1971, PAO has sought to unite professional athletes and couples to grow in their faith as disciples of Jesus Christ and to assist them in positively affecting their spheres of influence. More than ever, today's pro athletes possess a tremendous platform for influencing the world around them. Their lives, both on and off the field of competition, are constantly scrutinized by the media, fans, and the general public. By seeking to foster real spiritual transformation in athletes and couples and by becoming more Christlike, these athletes and their families are better equipped to deal with the pressures associated with their profession. As this is accomplished, they are better prepared to share the gospel through the universal language of sport.

As for their methodologies of ministry, traditionally the primary work of PAO with professional athletes and couples takes place with the National Hockey League (NHL), Major League Baseball (MLB), and the National Football League (NFL) through annual spiritual-equipping conference retreats. A key strategy is PAO's commitment to protecting the privacy of the participants so that they can truly be themselves and enjoy their conference experience (PAO, n.d.).

For over four decades, PAO has consistently grown and is expanding, with new programs including Motor Racing Outreach and Pro Basketball Fellowship; doubtless more are to come. They have also begun a new sports ministry initiative through The Increase, which involves Christian athletes sharing testimonial videos written by the athletes themselves. Included as a part of The Increase initiative is Football Sunday, in essence an outreach tool to be used on Super Bowl Sunday. This video has featured players such as Drew Brees, Anquan Boldin, and Carson Wentz. It has been viewed by more than 2.5 million people around the globe, and it is believed to have resulted in more than 20,000 professions of faith in Jesus Christ (POA, n.d.).

At an early PAO seminar in Dallas in February 1979, quarterback Terry Bradshaw of the Pittsburgh

Steelers and over 100 other professional athletes left their playbooks behind and instead carried their Bibles to the conference for a special time of study and spiritual growth. It was in early events like this that the potential of PAO started to be realized. Professor Howard Hendricks of Dallas Theological Seminary summed this potential up best: "I can't think of a group with greater impact for Jesus Christ than you" (Spoelstra 1979).

Missionary Athletes International (MAI)

The name Missionary Athletes International (MAI) suggests a worldwide-only ministry focus, yet it also has a significant national ministry component. As MAI enters its fourth decade of ministry, it continues to fulfill its stated mission to "glorify God and see lives transformed by sharing the message of Jesus Christ through the global environment of soccer (God Glorified. Lives Changed. Through Soccer)" (Missionary Athletes International, n.d.). The vision for using soccer to reach a lost world led to the inception of MAI by Tim Conrad in La Habra, California, in 1983. The context of its founding began in the spring of 1975 when Biola University hired Conrad as their head men's soccer coach. In God's economy and sovereign way of orchestrating circumstances, Tim Conrad's first assignment was to coach the Biola side in a May trip to Mexico. It was on the dirt fields of those Mexican towns that Coach Conrad realized that a whole village could hear the explanation of how to become a follower of Jesus Christ through a shared game of soccer. For Conrad, this trip and experience was pivotal in the formation of a vision for the effective use of soccer as a ministry tool to communicate the gospel message (Tim Conrad, pers. interview, 2021).

It was a sideline encounter between the Azusa Pacific men's soccer coach David Irby and Coach Conrad that began a relationship that would eventually lead them to work together. During the fall of 1986, Irby joined MAI as its first full-time staff member, and the Orange FC Seahorses soccer team was formed (later to become known as the Southern California Seahorses). In the fall of 1987, after the Seahorses' second season, Brian Davidson, Rick McKinley, and Jon and Dan Ortlip moved to Southern California to join the MAI and Seahorse staff (Dave Irby, pers. interview, 2020).

The 1990s saw a flurry of activity and growth for MAI, starting with the opening of an office in Bolton, England, led by Jon and Ruthie Ortlip. In 1991 Brian and Chris Davidson opened an extension of MAI in Charlotte, North Carolina. MAI's second international office was opened in the Czech Republic in 1993, led by Bill and Lisa Galipault. And finally, a fourth office was opened under the leadership of Rick and Janice McKinley in 1997 in Wheaton, Illinois. As it approaches four decades of ministry, MAI has now consolidated its ministry operations into four divisions located exclusively in the United States. The Southern California Seahorses still play, as well as the Charlotte Eagles and the Chicago Eagles. The newest division, Imago Dei, is located in Chapel Hill, North Carolina.

The driving force behind MAI is its passion for sharing the gospel of Jesus Christ around the world through the sport of soccer. It does this by building genuine relationships through various sport initiatives. MAI's primary approaches to evangelism and discipleship have been through their competitive soccer teams (Seahorses and the two Eagles teams), soccer camps, and short-term international soccer tours. Additionally, MAI provides youth clinics, school programs, inner-city ministries, and training others in sports ministry.

MAI has grown from a few summer soccer camps, an international soccer tour experience, and one highly competitive men's amateur team nearly four decades ago into a sports ministry that affects thousands of lives annually in the United States and around the world. MAI has spread the message of the gospel and discipled many along the way. In 2018 David Urban became the CEO of MAI. Under his leadership MAI is preparing for the challenges and opportunities that lay ahead as it prepares for its fifth decade of sports ministry through soccer. MAI's mission is to glorify God and see lives transformed by sharing the message of Jesus Christ through the global environment of soccer. MAI teams seek to wholeheartedly serve their constituents by pursuing excellence in soccer and by fostering authentic community and spiritual growth. Urban and his leadership team have set out the following values that will guide the organization:

1. *Faith*, rooted in a biblical worldview, guides our decisions and actions. We place a high priority on prayer, submitting our plans to the Lord and seeking His will in all our endeavors. We trust God to provide our needs, and staff members experience this collectively as we raise our own personal financial support. We use the sport of soccer for sharing the gospel in places that may be difficult to access otherwise.

2. *Relationships* establish the community through which we cultivate lives for Christ. We must be involved in relationships so that we can be transformed and have an impact on others. We strive to be a resource to the body of Christ, and in order to

---

SPORTS MINISTRY IN ACTION

Tom Roy: The Gospel and America's National Pastime

America's national pastime has been a consistent part of Tom Roy's career and ministry. He signed a professional baseball contract with the San Francisco Giants and later served 15 years as a major league scout, including associate international scouting responsibilities with the Atlanta Braves, San Diego Padres, and Philadelphia Phillies. He is a former chaplain and Bible study teacher for the Chicago White Sox, has coached collegiately, and for 28 years served as the NCCAA chaplain. Roy is the author of *Released: A Story of God's Power Released in Pro Baseball* and is the founder of Unlimited Potential Inc. (UPI), a baseball-specific sports ministry.

Roy volunteered to coach a baseball clinic for the Billy Graham Evangelistic Association as a part of the 1979 Milwaukee crusade. Graham routinely used sports and athletic celebrities as a part of his crusade weeks. UPI was birthed a year later while Tom was working in the admissions office and serving as the head baseball coach at Grace College in Winona Lake, Indiana. He spent the summer months traveling throughout the United States organizing UPI baseball clinics while speaking evangelistically. The organization worked closely with local churches and frequently used hometown or visiting team Major League Baseball (MLB) players to help with the clinics. It also partnered with Baseball Chapel, which conducted services and introduced them to MLB players.

A memorable highlight for Roy was in the mid-1980s when he was coaching at Huntington College (now Huntington University). Hank Aaron was scheduled to speak at Huntington, and Tom picked him up at the airport. Tom was so overwhelmed to be seated next to his childhood hero that he became lost while driving to the hotel. Aaron eventually asked if Tom knew where he was going, and he had to admit they were lost. The additional travel time led to a conversation about the gospel. According to Tom, Aaron was deeply stirred to the core of his heart, and the two of them spent the following days speaking further about the message of Christ. Besides Hank Aaron, Tom, too, was awed by the power of the gospel.

Tom Roy serves as an example of a ballplayer and coach who uses America's national pastime as an opportunity to develop his own faith and to impart it to others. (Tom Roy, pers. interview 2022; NCCAA, n.d.b.; Shepherd Coach Network, n.d.)

---

do so, we develop partnerships with other believers, increasing our effectiveness.

3. *Submission* places ministry first, soccer second. We desire to see God glorified over our ambitions. We submit our love of the sport of soccer, our pride, and our ambitions to the cross. We seek to develop sports ministers who are "Christians who play soccer" rather than "soccer players who are Christians."

4. *Transformation* is the outcome we seek. We want to see "lives changed" through the transforming power of the gospel applied through Sports Ministry Training (SMT). This happens through developing an authentic relationship with Christ and applying it on and off the field of play. The transformation starts in our hearts, is demonstrated in our actions, and bears fruit as we serve others.

5. *Love* motivates everything we do. We cannot give away what we do not have. Because we have received the perfect love of the Father, we can now give it away to others. Once we have experienced the love of God, the natural response is to tell others about it. The result of being connected to the very source of love is a selfless, sacrificial, servant-minded approach to ministry. God's love compels, motivates, and urges us to be practical expressions of His love through the environment of soccer (Missionary Athletes International n.d.).

Sports Chaplaincy

The practice of **sports chaplaincy** exists in a wide variety of sporting environments and cultures and can be expressed in many ways. The models shown in figure

---

sports chaplaincy—Broadly defined as the provision of pastoral care which meets the spiritual needs of athletes, coaches, and others who work or participate in sport.

3.1 help frame the provision of sports chaplaincy and are not intended to divide nor rank in importance. It is likely that any one form of chaplaincy possesses elements of models. That said, there are many differing expressions of this practice that exist in a wide variety of sporting environments and cultures. In the context of sports ministry, sports chaplains provide this care to athletes, coaches, administrators, support staff, and, by extension, family members and friends. Sports chaplains provide spiritual guidance and ongoing tangible support after practice sessions, before contests, and during times of crisis, large and small.

AIA and Sports Chaplaincy

Since the early 1970s, AIA has been involved in sports chaplaincy ministry by providing the NFL with chaplains who serve on a full-time basis as volunteers for league teams. The chaplains work to meet the spiritual needs of coaches, players, team executives, and their spouses. This is accomplished through weekly Bible studies (studies are available for players, coaches, and couples), one-on-one mentoring, equipping sessions, chapel services, and outreaches around the world. AIA also provides many chaplains for Major League Soccer teams (AIA n.d.a.).

Each year, in cooperation with team chaplains, AIA serves pro athletes through the following opportunities:

- Pro Bowl Outreach (January)
- Super Bowl Breakfast (Super Bowl Week)
- Senior Bowl Breakfast (February)
- Combine Bible Studies (February)
- NFL Owners Meetings Outreach (March)
- Mission trips to Panama, Costa Rica, and Brazil (March)
- Uncommon Award (April)
- Iron Man Golf Tournament (June)
- Athletes in Action Golf Classic (July)

FIGURE 3.1   MODELS OF SPORTS CHAPLAINCY

1. Embedded Chaplain

This chaplain has an official appointment from the club or sporting environment. He or she will have a consistent presence and a recognized position and role. The primary objective is to foster a ministry of presence and the building of relationships over time.

2. Sports Mentor

This form of chaplaincy tends to be invited by an individual sportsperson rather than an organization. The focus is the spiritual development of the Christian athlete. These mentors tend to be strong in biblical-based teaching and discipleship.

3. Chapel-Based Chaplain

This model is prevalent in baseball. Chaplains will provide chapel often to whole teams and visiting teams on a regular basis. The chaplains are then encouraged to build relationship with players and athletes outside of that time.

4. Formal Chaplain

This type of sports chaplain is similar to an embedded chaplain in that he or she has an official function at the club. However, most of his or her engagement is on a formal basis, conducting services for the club or sporting environment.

5. Tour Chaplain

A tour chaplain operates in sports such as golf, tennis, cycling, and surfing for which there is rarely one venue to meet competitors, but the chaplain is required to tour with them. These chaplains tend to build strong connections with a relational approach and often support competitors with one-on-one meetings and Bible study groups.

Reprinted by permission of CEDE Sports.

Cede Sports and Sports Chaplaincy

Cede Sports uses the international language of sport to mobilize the gospel-centered work of churches and sports chaplains around the world. Since its founding in 1996, it has worked with thousands of churches and chaplains in more than 100 countries. Cede Sports creates the infrastructure and support to empower the day-to-day work of Cede Partners and Cede Network. Its ministry is encapsulated in the word *cede*, which means to relinquish or yield control. Cede Sports works to see God glorified and others succeed (Cede n.d.).

The National Christian College Athletic Association (NCCAA)

Founded in 1968, the mission of the **National Christian College Athletic Association (NCCAA)** is to be an association of Christ-centered collegiate institutions with the mission to use athletic competition as an integral component of education, evangelism, and encouragement. The NCCAA serves member schools, of which there are nearly 100, by setting association standards, developing communication resources, providing regional and national competitions, and reaching out to local communities and around the world. It is committed to equipping student-athletes and coaches to make a positive impact for Christ. Part of the commitment to making a positive impact for Christ is evidenced in the example of the sports ministry opportunities that the NCCAA facilitates every year shown in table 3.1.

Another facet of ministry at the NCCAA is the *Game Plan 4 LIFE* devotionals that are produced and sent out on a regular basis to member institutions. These devotionals are created by athletic personnel and are designed to encourage and edify fellow athletes, coaches, and administrators.

TABLE 3.1   National Championship Christian Service Projects From 2021-2022

Sport	Service project
Men's and women's golf	$1000 and 400lbs of food donated to Grace Community Food Bank
Men's and women's cross country	173 household items donated to God's Resort in Joplin, MO
DII men's and women's soccer	1500 CSP hours and $500 donated for Thanksgiving meals
DI men's and women's soccer	380 toys, 800 pairs of socks, and $1500 donated to Living Hope Ministries
DII women's volleyball	164 toys and 260 pairs of socks donated to Living Hope Ministries
DI women's volleyball	180 hours served at various ministries in Point Lookout, MO
Indoor track and field	$900 donated to Feed the Ville
DI men's and women's basketball	$250 and 720lbs of food donated to Combined Community Services
DII Men's and Women's Basketball	70lbs of hygiene items donated to the homeless
Outdoor track and field	$1200 donated to Eden's Glory
Men's and women's tennis	140 hours of service providing youth clinics to the local community
Softball	140 hours of service providing clinics at local schools
Baseball	90 hours of service providing a youth clinic to the local community
Victory Bowl	300 hours served at Lakeview Camp cleaning the building and grounds
Men's Volleyball Invitational	75 hours of service visiting front line workers

Courtesy of National Christian College Athletics Association (NCCAA).

NCCAA—The National Christian College Athletic Association, founded in 1968, is an association of Christ-centered collegiate institutions with the mission is to use athletic competition as an integral component of education, evangelization, and encouragement (NCCAA, n.d.a.).

Interview With a Professional

Dan Wood

Executive Director, National Christian College Athletic Association (NCCAA)

BS physical education/kinesiology, Southern Wesleyan University

Right out of college, Dan Wood became the head men's soccer coach for Limestone College. After three seasons of coaching, he changed careers and worked his way up to regional manager of ten Wendy's fast-food franchises. Though quite successful, his heart was still in coaching. Dan returned to soccer coaching when asked to coach the Bartlesville Wesleyan men's soccer team (now Oklahoma Wesleyan University). After five seasons with Bartlesville, he assumed the role of head men's soccer coach at Indiana Wesleyan University, where he also taught kinesiology and sports science. He remained at IWU for five years before being hired as the vice president for the DataFund Links program, a facilitator of high-end golf tournaments. It was during this time that Dan was asked to join the board of the NCCAA. Two years into his board service, in 2000, his fellow board members prodded him to become the chief executive officer of the NCCAA. He accepted, and for over two decades he has brought leadership and passion to intercollegiate athletics. More than just sports, this organization seeks to glorify God by furthering the gospel message through love, integrity, faith, and excellence. He has written for a variety of publications on subjects ranging from student-athlete recruitment to population diversity at faith-based institutions. As a survivor of cancer, Dan sees every day as a gift to be shared with others.

What characteristics and qualities must a person possess to be successful as a leader in sports ministry?

The leader must possess a strong personal relationship with Christ and be led by the Holy Spirit. Beyond this, it is important to be adaptable and quick in these changing times, and not be bureaucratic. It is wise to be incredibly patient and humble, a leader who lets those around them express themselves. One should always be relational, outgoing, and gregarious with a strong work ethic.

How does your faith in Jesus Christ influence and guide your leadership style?

In my estimation, Jesus Christ was the greatest coach who ever lived. He engaged with his disciples, who then, in turn, went out and changed the world. I try to learn from Christ's example daily and grow in my faith and understanding. My faith is therefore critical to my approach to leadership in every way. Put another way, I see the Great Commission as every Christian's calling. As a result, I live and lead accordingly.

What are the future opportunities you see for the NCCAA sports ministry?

Our NCCAA team wants to grow our missional impact every year. We want to continue to steward our organization by seeking Christ first. We also see great opportunities for partnering with other sports ministries.

What are some of the challenges you see facing future sports ministry efforts?

Perhaps the greatest challenge is sharing the gospel through sports ministry in a world that is increasingly postmodern and post-Christian—a world that is essentially secular. As for opportunities, the need for hope is very significant in a world that is struggling to find hope and peace. It is our belief that sport and intercollegiate athletics continue to be a great platform for reaching people for Christ and discipling them, and for offering them hope and peace.

The NCCAA also facilitates a vibrant prayer network that is important both in the life of the organization and its member institutions as well as the sports ministries it supports. The NCCAA Prayer Network has over 1,000 prayer warriors who pray for the requests and rejoice in the praise reports.

One final special annual initiative is the NCCAA Sports Ministries Award. The purpose of this award is to recognize member institutions having significant spiritual outreach through the use of athletic ministries. An example of a recent recipient of the Sports Ministries Award was Columbia International University (CIU). The CIU Rams teams went on mission trips and served in various ministries. Baseball, softball, and women's volleyball teams served on international mission trips or had individual team members participate in trips. Baseball, basketball, cross country, golf, soccer, softball, track and field, and volleyball teams served in ministries such as sports camps, mentoring in local schools, and refugee ministry.

Sports Ministry Media Initiatives

The growth of social media platforms has enabled sports ministry organizations to expand their networking capabilities and to deliver resources to interested constituents. These platforms created additional roles and employment opportunities within the field of sports ministry. Two successful examples of these initiatives are *Faith on the Field* and Sports Spectrum.

Faith on the Field *Podcast and Radio Programming*

Hosted by national media personality Rob Maaddi and his wife, former reality TV star Remy Maaddi, *Faith on the Field* is a one-of-a-kind, multiplatform, weekly sports talk radio show that has become a must-listen for Christian athletes, sports fans, and anyone who wants to hear a positive, uplifting program about athletes and their faith in Jesus Christ. All episodes are available for free 24-7 via several delivery modes and are easily accessed on their website www.faithonthefieldshow.com and most podcast platforms after first airing on radio stations across the United States. On their weekly podcast, Rob and Remy talk about the impact of faith in Jesus Christ on the sports world while also talking about important issues of the day with the aim to inspire hope, encourage listeners to faith, and challenge them toward positive action. They produce numerous episodes that feature interviews with prominent Christians in an array professional sports. *Faith on the Field* originally launched on 610 ESPN Philadelphia in 2017. The show now airs weekly on 97.5 The Fanatic in Philadelphia along with additional radio stations in Charlotte, Atlanta, Orlando, Las Vegas, and Los Angeles (Faith on the Field, n.d.).

Sports Spectrum

Sports Spectrum, a ministry of Pro Athletes Outreach, promotes itself as the place "Where Sports and Faith Connect." Sports Spectrum delivers compelling stories of athletes and their faith journeys in a number of formats such as their quarterly magazine, podcasts, online devotionals, videos, and newsletters. They provide current faith-focused stories with content suitable for all ages. The magazine uses a positive format to explain how Christian faith plays a role in the lives of some of the country's top athletes, who live to be defined by God, not by their sport.

Sports Spectrum was originally founded in 1985 as a magazine called *SportsFocus*. Simultaneous to the launch of the magazine, Sports Spectrum produced a show that aired on ESPN hosted by Julius Erving (Dr. J), a legend in the day with the Philadelphia 76ers. The goal and underlying message of the show, according to Erving, "was to spread the Gospel." Everyone associated with the program were born-again Christians. Both the magazine and the show provided opportunities for Christian athletes to talk about sports, their faith, and the importance of living righteously. One of their promotional lines was, "If you want to know the 'what happened,' read the sports page; for the 'whys,' read *SportsFocus*." To this end, a key strategy for both the magazine and the show is to deliver inspirational stories about athletes and their faith. For example, every year during the week prior to the Super Bowl, Sports Spectrum reporters conduct video interviews, asking NFL players like Zach Ertz questions such as, "How important is it for you to use your platform to glorify God?"

Sports Spectrum also provides professional Christian athletes with a special media platform to address an age-old gripe they have with traditional sports media. Frequently, when players share their personal faith or express thanks to God, their sentiments are deleted from the article or broadcast. Sports Spectrum operates differently. As Steve Stenstrom, president of Pro Athletes Outreach (PAO), puts it, "We like to say that we're putting Jesus back in the conversation." This is clearly an important media initiative in sports ministry with significant access to mainstream American professional sports and professional athletes (Curtis 2018).

SUMMARY

Sports ministry in the United States takes many forms with countless different methodologies and approaches, yet at its core, all sports ministries share the common goal of using these many avenues of sport to glorify God and see lives changed in great ways through the good news of the gospel of Jesus Christ. The gospel message, presented not from a pulpit but through sport in sporting venues, has been a game changer for ministry in a postmodern society and culture. In this chapter we covered five unique categories of sports ministry. First, large national sports ministry efforts cover essentially every region of the United States. Second, other national sports ministry organizations are not as large but still significant. Third, attention was given to the unique and special roles played by sports chaplains. Fourth, we discussed the special ministry of the National Christian College Athletic Association (NCCAA) and the special work they do with and through intercollegiate athletics. Lastly, the emerging world of sports ministry media initiatives was considered. There is so much vibrant sports ministry activity that the reader has countless opportunities to consider as to where he or she might get involved and, in doing so, make a real difference in the lives of others. Investing in sports ministry experiences pays rich dividends both in the near term as well as in life eternal.

A closing summary statement of what was covered in this chapter is captured in the words of AIA basketball player Ralph Drollinger, "As players for God's work, we really try to love each other, our opponents, and the spectators as well . . . we're convinced that a personal relationship with God is the most important thing in the world" (*Athletes in Action vs. Soviet Union Basketball* 1978).

REVIEW AND DISCUSSION QUESTIONS

1. In your estimation, how have sports ministries changed over the past 75 years?
2. What are the major core values of sports ministries?
3. What kind of competencies do you think are required to be effective in sports ministry?
4. In what ways are sports ministries similar to one another, and in what ways do they differ?
5. What style of sports ministry described in this chapter could you see yourself getting involved with either during or after college?
6. What kinds of career opportunities exist for sports ministry in the United States?
7. What do you believe are the key challenges and opportunities presently facing sports ministry in the United States?
8. How do you think sports ministry in the United States will change over the next decade?

Sports ministry is a global endeavor to reach the nations with the gospel.

CHAPTER 4

International Sports Ministry

"We must be global Christians with a global vision because our God is a global God."

John Stott (1921-2011), English preacher, author, and theologian

LEARNING OBJECTIVES

After studying this chapter, you should be able to do the following:
- Understand the reasons why Christians should be doing sports ministry internationally
- Observe how and where international sports ministry are developed
- Recognize the importance of partnerships in international sports ministry
- Appreciate the strengths and weaknesses of varied lengths of international service
- Acknowledge the fact that people considered the "ends of the earth" are now living in neighborhoods throughout the United States

"We were behind by 16 points in the third quarter, and Coach ordered us to into a pressing man-to-man defense. Although exhausted we did it, and Bud (Schaeffer) was the key to our winning." (One Challenge 2015)

In 1952 Bud Schaeffer was a 25-year-old graduate of Wheaton College, where he had been an All-American basketball player and earned a degree in biblical studies. He was chosen to be part of the first basketball missions tour sponsored by Orient Crusades (now One Challenge) in response to an invitation from Madame Chiang Kai-shek, wife of the president of the Republic of China (Taiwan). She had asked for a basketball team to come and share Christ with her people, and that's what they did! After eight weeks on the ground in Taiwan, missionary Dick Hillis wrote to supporters in the United States, "Through them [the team] over one quarter million have heard the gospel . . . in the 160 meetings and 79 basketball games." Earlier in the trip he had written, "Yes, it is a new thing to use a basketball team for evangelism—but God is blessing" (Ladd and Mathisen 1999).

Bud Schaeffer followed up this trip with another outreach to the Philippines. In 1955 he moved there with his family, and they spent 12 years pioneering the use of sport to reach and disciple people for Christ. Schaeffer later returned to the States and directed One Challenge, the growing ministry, then known as Venture for Victory and now known as Sports Ambassadors, for 16 years. His influence caused many others to catch the vision for sports ministry, resulting in several new and diverse ministry groups (One Challenge 2015).

This chapter will begin by looking at some of the theological background for international and cross-cultural sports ministry before describing what international sports ministry looks like and how it has been done. It will also dig into the rationale for engaging in sports ministry in another country or a different culture that might have a great financial, time, or human cost.

Why Minister Internationally?

There are a multitude of reasons not to minister internationally. It requires a person to leave the comforts and familiarity of home to travel to or relocate, often as a couple or family, to a place with a different language and dissimilar culture. The cost of doing so is high, the sacrifices are many, and success is not guaranteed. So why do people take precious vacation time to go on a short-term basketball mission trip? Why would a college graduate spend his or her first two years out of college ministering in a refugee camp, using sports to build relationships? What causes a family with young children to pull up roots and spend six years in another culture helping churches learn how to use sports camps as a way of serving and reaching out to their communities?

A Mandate

Much can be said about taking care of one's own, looking out for one's community, blooming where one is planted. Certainly, this principle is portrayed in Scripture. In the Gospel of Mark, the man whom Jesus freed from demonic oppression begged to go with Jesus as he left the region. Jesus' response: "Go home to your own people and tell them how much the Lord has done for you, and how he has had mercy on you" (5:19 NIV). The man went home, and his story was heralded there and subsequently throughout the world.

Jesus was explicit with his followers that their ministry was to go beyond their current setting and understanding. Before his ascension, in his final face-to-face communication with his disciples, Jesus articulated a mission known as the **Great Commission**. Jesus exhorted,

All authority in heaven and on earth has been given to me. Therefore go and make disciples of all nations, baptizing them in the name of the Father and of the Son and of the Holy Spirit, and teaching them to obey everything I have commanded you. And surely, I am with you always, to the very end of the age. (Matthew 28:18-20 NIV)

Great Commission—Jesus' directive to his disciples to make disciples of all nations. (Matthew 28:19-20)

Dovetailing with this admonition is another directive he gave his disciples in Acts 1:8: "But you will receive power when the Holy Spirit comes on you; and you will be my witnesses in Jerusalem, and in all Judea and Samaria, and to the ends of the earth" (NIV). Jesus gave them a mission and promised to enable them to fulfill the task. The equipping power, he said, will come from the Holy Spirit. Whatever talent, knowledge, or experience one may have, it is not enough without the Spirit's help. But with the Spirit's influence, the more talent, knowledge, and experience, the greater possibilities there are for success.

The scope and direction of the ministry, which is the focus of this chapter, is presented in the picture of concentric circles: Jerusalem, Judea, Samaria, and the ends of the earth (figure 4.1). Though all the disciples were not born or raised there, Jerusalem is presented as their hometown—the center whence this expanding mission commenced. It is filled with people like themselves and their family members. Moving outward from the city's starting point, Jesus highlights "all of Judea." While increasing the area of the mission to a region rather than a single city, the people to whom the gospel witness will be delivered continue to be of the same culture as the disciples.

There is a significant distinction with the next circle, Samaria, which is different in ethnicity and religion. A region north of Judea, Samaria was home to a people who were a Jewish/Gentile mix. Many centuries earlier, when the area was overrun and controlled by Assyrians, large numbers of Jewish residents were relocated, but a remnant remained and began to intermarry with the Assyrians. This mix of ethnicities caused Jews to cease interaction with the Samaritans, considering them unclean. While the Samaritans continued to worship God in much the same way as their Jewish counterparts in Judea, they drew the ire of the Jews by rejecting the temple in Jerusalem and constructing their own.

Jesus' mission to go beyond the boundaries of Jewish culture was a huge shock and hurdle for the disciples. During his three-year ministry, Jesus demolished this relational barrier by engaging Samaritans, including the woman at the well (John 4). Subsequently, Peter, the leader of the early church, received a vision and experienced an encounter with a Roman centurion (Acts 10) that prompted his confession, "I now realize how true it is that God does not show favoritism but accepts from every nation the one who fears him and does what is right" (Acts 10:34-35 NIV). The eyes of the Church were opened, expanding its vision and understanding of the mission before it.

From the inclusion of Samaritans and Romans within the church, the step to the last circle of ministry is simply a matter of location. With the gap between Jews and non-Jews (Gentiles) bridged, the "ends of the earth" as a goal for spreading the good news of God's forgiveness becomes a no-brainer. If God loves the world and offers salvation to all people, then all people need to hear the gospel. God wants Christians to be faithful witnesses wherever they are. If one is not faithful where he or she is, why would he or she assume to be faithful in another country or with people from a different culture? One should beware of following a call to share the gospel in another country or among people of a different culture if not currently sharing the gospel with the people in his or her own neighborhood.

When a small group of sports missionaries were planning to move to the Czech Republic, one of their goals was to plant a church among the people they believed would be coming to Christ through their ministry. Planting a church was seen as the pinnacle of success for a missionary. In retrospect, while it is easy to envision the goal of planting a church and is a commendable and biblical endeavor, it may not have been God's goal for them. Incidentally, none of the group had planted nor pastored a church before. Ultimately, in the six years there as a team, God did not use the group to plant and lead a church. They were, however, able to witness for Christ on the various teams they played on, in the neighborhoods where they lived, and among the people with whom they interacted. The team helped churches run children's sport camps, where the gospel was presented

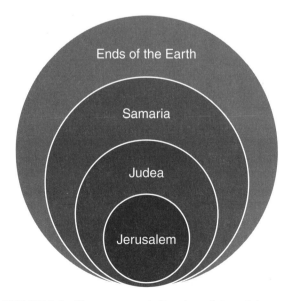

FIGURE 4.1 The scope and direction of the ministry.
© Human Kinetics, adapted from illustration by Kiel McClung.

to their communities. They also hosted several conferences for Czech Christian athletes, providing instruction about the integration of faith and sport, a new concept for the Czech church. The group's ministry practices were things they had done at home, things in which they were already proficient before relocating internationally.

What Is Needed?

"From everyone who has been given much, much will be demanded; and from the one who has been entrusted with much, much more will be asked" (Luke 12:48 NIV). Does the U.S. Church have what it takes to reach the world? To be sure, the United States is not the only missionary-sending country, but it is the largest. Of the nearly 400,000 missionaries on the field in 2010, the United States sent 127,000, with Brazil being the next largest sender with 34,000 (Steffan 2013). While the U.S. Church is not solely responsible for reaching the lost around the world, it is uniquely equipped for the mission. To accomplish a global task requires sufficient means. It can hardly be argued that the United States is short on resources when it comes to faith, sports, and finances. It is the confluence of these three that make the United States a mission-sending powerhouse.

The percentage of Americans who identify as Christian continues to decline, but the numbers show a still sizable Christian population in the United States, with 63% claiming to be Christian (43% Protestant, 20% Catholic) (Pew Research Center 2019). The United States has more people identifying as Christian (210 million) than any other country. It should not be a surprise that Christians can be found in every aspect of society, from business to government, medicine to education, the arts to sport.

Not only is the United States rich in the number of people of faith, it also has an abundance of sporting opportunities and participants. Developing countries often have limited sport options a person may pursue. The United States has a seemingly unending variety of sport and recreation opportunities made available through schools, communities, and privately owned organizations. American Christians with experience or expertise in what would be considered a niche sport (i.e., cricket) have open doors and points of commonality with people in countries like India, Pakistan, and Nepal where that is the most popular sport.

With a 2019 gross domestic product (GDP) of over $21 trillion—the world's largest—individuals in the United States are in a position to be generous with their charitable giving (World Bank n.d.); the U.S. Church is particularly well resourced. The statistics indicate that Americans are indeed generous, more so than any other country's population. In a 2016 study Americans gave a collective 1.44% of GDP, nearly double the next two largest givers, New Zealand (.79%) and Canada (.77%) (Charities Aid Foundation 2016). Religious institutions, including churches, denominations, and mission organizations, have perennially been the largest beneficiaries of charitable giving (NP Source 2018). Chapter 9 will discuss ministry funding, both domestic and international, in greater detail.

A Bridge (to Relationships)

In many cultures, the days when street corner preachers drew crowds of people are long past. A stranger knocking at the door wanting to talk about religion is seldom welcomed inside. In an age of fake news and every scam imaginable, most people are guarded when encountering visitors they do not know, even if they share similarities. It can be difficult to share Christ with people if a relationship has not already been established. However, people will listen to those they know and trust.

While sharing the gospel in one's home country can be difficult, the process in a cross-cultural setting is even more challenging. Bethany Duval, writing for the mission organization TEAM, identifies lessons she has learned from interviewing missionaries. Developing relationships is key to sharing the gospel, and building them takes time, especially in places where a new language must be learned and a different culture comprehended (Duval 2017). Another avenue important to missionaries is finding the culture's open doors through which relational common ground can be found, which enables the gospel to be shared.

Sport and recreation activity opens doors that circumvent cultural barriers. It provides a base of commonality among the ministry team and those with whom they minister. The team sport environment is especially suited to relationship building because it requires a group of individuals to work together to accomplish a shared goal. It necessitates a level of trust in one another and compels team members to know and support each other. Conflicts and jealousies might arise within a team, but even then, the understanding is that if these challenges can be resolved, it will ultimately make the team better. Whether it is a volleyball team or a hiking club, these are places of belonging that offer opportunities to know and to become known. The resulting team dynamics quicken and deepen relationships, and it is within the context of these relationships that the gospel can be shared

Cross-cultural barriers can be minimized by making relational friendships developed through the common bond of sport.

most effectively (Quatro 2009). Relationship is a central process in evangelism and discipleship. This principle is illustrated in the following statement:

> *The manner in which many of us became Christian was by looking over someone else's shoulder, emulating some admired older Christian, saying yes to and taking up a way of life that was made real and accessible through the witness of someone else. So, although books, films, and lectures may play a part in confirmation, they will all be subservient to the main task of putting young Christians in proximity with exemplary older Christians, "mentors," we shall call them, who will invite these younger Christians to look over their shoulders as they both attempt to be Christian. (Hauerwas and Willimon 2014)*

Help Indigenous Sports Ministries Reach Their Own People

To move halfway around the world and insert oneself into another culture to share Christ is not an easy assignment. It can take years to learn the language and understand the history and culture to build relationships that lead to conveying gospel truths in a way that can be understood. God has frequently called and equipped people to be effective in this task. It is also a costly route with respect to the finances, time, and human resources needed to be successful. Is there a better or quicker way of reaching a specific people group? Common sense implies that the person or people best suited to reach a specific culture or people group is someone from within that group itself. Starting and growing **indigenous sports ministries** is a strategic imperative.

Who better to reach a Croatian water polo player for the Kingdom than a Christian Croatian water polo player? No cultural or language barrier need to be overcome, and he or she is invested in the sport and knows the system. Hopefully, the Croatian Christian athlete already has a burden and desire to share Christ with his or her teammates and coaches. Perhaps he or she just needs some help, encouragement, and support from someone who has already done it. He or she might recognize a better way than an organization's method. If a sports missionary can come alongside Christian athletes in these countries, train, and release them, he or she will effectively multiply the ministry rather than simply duplicating his or her own efforts, which can be commendable in its own right.

An optional ministry approach is to select a country and a relevant sport within that culture, and commission sports missionaries to begin outreach. This method is not uncommon and has often resulted in vibrant ministry over the long haul. Perhaps the more strategic way of launching ministry is to invest

---

indigenous sports ministries—Unlike a franchise or a chapter of an existing ministry, these are autonomous sports ministry organizations run and directed by people native to the country where they operate.

Interview With a Professional

Seren Fryatt
Founder and Director of L.A.C.E.S.

Life And Change Experienced thru Sports (L.A.C.E.S.) is a 501(c)(3) organization that "leverages the power of sport to mentor at-risk children" in Liberia, West Africa, with recently expanded work in neighboring Sierra Leone.

Can you share a little bit about your journey and why Liberia became your focus?

Growing up in a Christian family in Muncie, Indiana, I began playing soccer when I was eight years old. I played through my college years and graduated with a degree in athletic training. I was serious about soccer and competition, so one of the ways that I connected with success was through wins and losses. I didn't see it at the time, but my coach, Alan Alderson, was trying to go beyond developing us as players; he was trying to develop us as people.

After graduating, I worked as an athletic trainer, but I didn't feel fulfilled. So I decided to quit and spend some time volunteering. I had heard of Mercy Ships, which is an organization that turned ships into hospitals to provide surgeries, health care, and community development programs around the world, so I applied to be a volunteer. Initially, I was turned down because I have a medical condition that causes me to have absence seizures. But a year later, the woman who originally called to turn me down called me again and said that she had been advocating for me, and she offered me a volunteer position, which I accepted on the spot. That's how I ended up living on a ship in Liberia and participating in a discipleship training school.

How did the Mercy Ships experience become L.A.C.E.S.?

After a few weeks I was able to get off the ship, and while playing some pickup soccer, a coach for one of the country's women's professional teams saw me and recruited me to play. With my team I was able to travel to different parts of Liberia, and while traveling, I saw the devastation caused by the 14-year civil war the country had recently come through. The women I played with had very hard lives off the field, but when we played, I saw the joy that the game gave them.

But there were times when my competitive spirit would come out, and it drove me crazy when my teammates showed a lack of commitment to the team. I went to the coach and asked him why he allowed this kind of behavior. He responded that the team was not about winning and losing and that they were not there to win championships. All these women had endured 14 years of their country going through war, destruction, and loss. For them, soccer was their brief moment of happiness in otherwise difficult lives. What he said flipped the switch for me. I saw the power of sport and what it was doing for these women.

I later encountered children, many of whom were homeless, some of whom may even have been child soldiers, but all of them had loss and trauma in their lives. When these young boys and girls got to the soccer field there was fun, enthusiasm, and their imaginations and spirits were captured. Through this environment, I saw that we could invest in them and teach them things that went well beyond the game, just because they would show up to play. As I reflected on the efforts of Coach Alderson, it all made sense. While I didn't catch what he was doing during my college days, his teaching influenced the development of L.A.C.E.S. and has impacted thousands of kids over the years!

After my time with Mercy Ships, I returned home, but my passion for Liberia didn't go away, and at the time, I couldn't find an organization that was doing what I envisioned. I was challenged by a friend to start something on my own. There were a hundred reasons in my mind why I couldn't do it, but in the end, it was a lack of faith that God could do something like this through me. Then I realized it was God who was doing this and that He wanted to use me in the process. My friends helped me put together a business plan, understand nonprofit finances, and taught me how to raise funds. Before long we had enough to run the program for a year, and we started in 2007.

How did you get it started on the ground, and what does the program look like day to day?

The people I knew in the soccer community and the contacts I had working with a nongovernmental organization there in Liberia gave me the support I needed to get established and hire leaders that continue to work with L.A.C.E.S. 14 years later! The ministry on the ground in Liberia is run 100% by Liberians, and because it is a sustainable model, it has run over a decade without me engaged in the day-to-day operations.

When we began to expand into Sierra Leone, we had the Liberian leaders do the training because their experience and deep knowledge of the program is what was needed to continue empowering communities.

L.A.C.E.S. staff must live in the neighborhoods where they work so that they can visit kids in their homes. All staff must be active in a local church. L.A.C.E.S. is not affiliated with any single denomination and will work with anyone they feel doctrinally compatible with. L.A.C.E.S. is a mentorship-based sports program for at-risk youth that teaches values such as self-esteem, discipline, and respect. These values are presented in a biblical context, examining how they are reflected in the life of Jesus Christ. We then apply the principles learned to show how these traits can be manifested in the lives of each player. Staff are the living gospel as they mentor, coach, feed (part of the program), and train (there is a leadership component as well) the youth on the teams (Seren Fryatt, pers. interview, 2021).

One of the program's players, Samson, ran away from home to live on the street because he felt that the street was a more stable environment than his home. Along with some friends, he washes pans and does other odd jobs to provide himself with food and essentials. L.A.C.E.S. provides the only three meals he is guaranteed each week. Before joining the program, he would also steal things, but through a chance to play soccer in a safe place, mentoring, meals, and having people who care about him, he is now living with hope for a better future (Sneed 2019).

---

effort, time, and money to equip, train, and support indigenous sports ministries.

At least two attitudes can limit or undermine the maximization or expansion of international efforts. First, missionaries (speaking from an American perspective) might see themselves as the experts and perhaps unconsciously see the Christians in the people group they are serving as unable to do or less capable of doing sports ministry. This attitude can limit the growth of sports ministry in the country to only what the missionaries themselves could manage. Second, some ministries tend to take what they know from their own organization and attempt to re-create it in their new country and cultural setting. This attitude tends to produce an appearance of building their own kingdom rather than God's. The patriarchal nature of this attitude is manifested when indigenous workers begin to look and sound like the organization's staff. Ministry performed the organization's way is thereby valued rather than adapting to a new or different approach that might be better culturally suited to this particular people group.

Where Sports Ministries Have Gone

The first-century Church experienced tremendous persecution, causing its people to scatter throughout the Roman Empire. As they fled, they began spreading the teachings of Jesus and consequently grew in their understanding that the salvation of Jesus was for everyone and not limited solely for the Jewish people. Features of the Roman Empire such as the system of roads and trade routes, the mix of cultures, and the common Greek language aided the early Christians in their efforts to reach both Jews and Gentiles throughout the known world (Loizides 2008).

Ministering internationally through sport shares some similarities with the early Church. The growing ease of international travel led to a renewed commitment to reaching the world for Christ, as evidenced in the late 1700s in England and the expanding British Empire throughout the 19th century to its peak in the early 20th century. Not insignificant is the rise of international sport (a common 'language') from an 1844 cricket match between the United States and Canada, to the modern Olympic movement begun in 1894, and through the proliferation of regional and world competitions in dozens of sports (Srinivas 2018).

Sports ministry as a developing discipline among young men had become prevalent in the latter part of the 19th century in both England and the United States through the Muscular Christianity movement (as examined in chapter 2). During the mid-20th century, sport was more fully developed as a tool for evangelism and taken internationally by both men and women to reach people of other cultures.

A Defining Moment

Christian athletes such as Billy Sunday, Eric Liddell, and Gil Dodds are examples of those who used their sporting prowess and fame as a means of securing an audience for the gospel to be communicated, not only to those who were already part of the Church, but also for those who had not yet heard or accepted it. Their notoriety proved to be effective, and revivalists such as Dwight L. Moody and Billy Graham began inviting athletes to share their faith stories from the platform of their crusades. When the revivalists traveled internationally, athletes often accompanied them. In 1949 Dodds was in Scandinavia with Youth for Christ (YFC), and the following year he went to Korea and Japan.

A defining moment for international sports ministry was the team that traveled to Taiwan in 1952, as highlighted at the beginning of the chapter. Dick Hillis, the former YFC leader in Taiwan, had started a new organization known as Formosa Crusades in 1950, currently One Challenge (One Challenge, n.d.). It was through Hillis that the request came for an evangelistic basketball team to minister in the schools and military bases where preachers and missionaries were unable to gain access. The sports ministry arm of One Challenge, now known as Sports Ambassadors, continues to use traveling sport teams to share the gospel and support churches around the world. Early on they sent resident missionaries (e.g., Bud Schaeffer) to help churches use sport as part of their ministry within their communities. Sports ministries have gone around the globe opening doors to countries that are traditionally closed to missionary work. While first expressions of international sports ministry might have come predominantly from the United States, Christ followers around the world are using sport to minister cross-culturally.

Examples of International Sports Ministry

The basketball team that shared the gospel in Taiwan in 1952 provided an example for other organizations to replicate. Athletes in Action (AIA), a ministry of Cru (formerly Campus Crusade for Christ), began in 1966 as a traveling sports ministry within the United States. The ministry career of Carl Dambman provides a picture of how international ministry has changed and adapted over the years. In 1975 Dambman joined the AIA traveling wrestling team, which competed in tournaments and shared the gospel with about 100,000 people each year throughout the eastern United States. After using this large-group evangelism style in the United States, Dambman, with a team of wrestlers, moved to Austria and later Germany to begin outreach to wrestlers in Eastern Europe and the Soviet Union. This was typically a clandestine, one-on-one ministry, locating individual wrestlers or finding teams that they could train alongside and develop relationships. Many of those with whom they ministered had never had a Bible or talked with a Christian, because they had grown up within a system of institutionalized atheism. Much different than speaking to large crowds at major events, this type of ministry was more difficult, and for years it yielded little fruit. They also worked with other sports and various groups from Europe and North America, including AIA Ireland (football and rugby), Charlotte and Chicago Eagles (soccer), and Christian college teams (various sports).

The team received enough positive response to keep pressing ahead, and the ministry took a giant leap forward with the fall of the Iron Curtain in the late 1980s and early 1990s. Dambman moved his family to Moscow, where they lived for 20 years. He continued to reach and disciple high-level athletes, helping them learn how to use their prominent profiles to share the gospel. He also worked to develop sports ministry partnerships throughout Russia and Eurasia, training leaders and churches about the use of sport in ministry. In the late 1980s Dambman and his team worked with Christians in Sport UK and Sportler Ruft Sportler (German sports ministry, roughly translated as "sportsmen calling sportsmen") to start the European Christian Sport Union, a group that held training conferences for sports ministry workers.

Dambman has also been at the forefront of sports chaplaincy work, ministering at 18 Olympics (nine as an official chaplain). He continues to serve as an instructor and mentor at the International Sports

Dambman (standing third from left) and fellow chaplains at the Athens Summer Olympics in 2004.

Leadership School in South Africa and the EurAsia Sports Ministry School for Russian-speaking leaders (Cru, n.d.). Opportunities to expand God's Kingdom through sport have led Dambman to 90 countries over his ministry career.

Sport is a cultural force in almost every country, and there are likely few places that sports ministers have not gone. Whether a country is considered closed to missionaries, sport opens doors for Christian athletes to compete and encourage the building of relationships through which the message of Jesus can be communicated. Countless organizations and individuals have been involved with international sports ministry using a variety of methodologies. Their work has encompassed evangelism as well as church planting, with a ministry focus ranging from street children to elite professionals, in locations from church parking lots to Olympic villages.

How Ministries Choose Where to Go

Ministries do not use one single formula to select the location of their ministry. Each organization may have a different set of parameters to determine where they will go. With this in mind, consider the following factor: all ministries would affirm that they pray for God's guidance. When individuals or organizations pray for direction, they are not necessarily seeking the audible voice of God or a vision to illuminate their path, though both concepts are manifest in the biblical record (Philip and the Ethiopian eunuch in Acts 8:26-31; Paul's vision of the man from Macedonia in Acts 16:6-10). These manifestations do not suggest that God directs everyone in a like manner. James 1:5 provides assurance: "If any of you lacks wisdom, you should ask God, who gives generously to all without finding fault, and it will be given to you" (NIV). Romans 12:1-2 declares that believers are to worship God truly with their bodies and minds: "Then you will be able to test and approve what God's will is—his good, pleasing and perfect will" (NIV). Prayer, when done in a spirit of willingness to know God's will and a commitment to follow His guidance, positions the believer to a place where he or she will be better prepared to hear, or sense, God's direction.

Most often prayer is adjoined to research and situational evaluation. Mission organizations use a variety of value statements or considerations to determine where to venture. One such consideration is the need of **unreached people groups**. Within Reach Global is an organization whose vision is "Reaching unreached people groups in the 10/40 Window with the Gospel of Jesus Christ" (Within Reach Global n.d.a.) (Within Reach Global, n.d.a.).

The 10/40 Window refers to a geographical area of the northern hemisphere, between latitude 10 degrees

---

unreached people groups—Communities that share common language and culture but have little access to Christian resources through which they can hear the gospel.

and 40 degrees, from the western end of Africa to the eastern end of Asia. This area contains between four and five billion people, the majority being Animist, Hindu, Muslim, and Buddhist. In this geographical area are people groups that are considered unreached, so the gospel must come from outside the group in order for them to have the opportunity to hear and understand it (Within Reach Global n.d.b.). This area represents the greatest spiritual need for workers to be sent. These statistics and descriptions of unreached people groups are generally accepted throughout most mission organizations and church denominations.

A separate consideration is the sport in which an individual or organization has the most proficiency. Basketball or soccer, the two largest, allows engagement with people in the vast majority of countries worldwide. If the area of expertise is hurling, curling, surfing, or polo, the field of potential ministry is severely reduced. The other side of the coin, however, is that the scarcity of a sport may open unique doors within those limited places because of one's expertise if those communities need Christian witness. Countries with a desire to compete globally in sports such as soccer and basketball historically have been open to outside groups or personnel coming to help develop a particular sport. If this type of need combines with spiritual needs, those with the expertise to fill both are well suited to minister in these locations.

At times it is an event rather than a country or people group that becomes a place of ministry. **Global events ministry** has become a major focus of various organizations. Examples of mobilizing multiple organizations for major sporting events include the 1994 World Cup of Soccer (Sports Outreach Los Angeles) held in the United States; the Sydney Olympics in 2000 (International Sports Coalition); and the 2018 Winter Olympics in South Korea, where a coalition of 144 local congregations of various denominations (The United Churches of Korea) helped organize ministry opportunities and housing for approximately 3,000 missionaries. These three support ministries sought to organize local church outreaches at individual competition sites and through the production of evangelistic print and video materials for distribution to fans. In these cases, it is the location and timing of the event that determines where and when the ministry must go, and it is routine that these locations will differ each year or cycle (Mulkey 2018).

As described earlier in the chapter, the best person to raise up indigenous ministries in a particular people group is someone from that group. Perhaps the second best person would be someone from that ethnic background coming in from outside. The size and diversity of the U.S. population are such that many Christians originate from outside the United States. They, or perhaps their parents, immigrated to the United States, and while they may be born or naturalized citizens, they still might be very connected to the language and culture of their former or native homeland. Often a desire to be a missionary is accompanied by a desire to reach people who share the same ethnic heritage. Cultural affinity, then, is another factor for individuals or organizations to consider when deciding where to establish work.

A final value-related example of choosing a ministry location is in response to an invitation by someone from within that country, whether an individual, church, or missionary requesting assistance from someone who has the level of expertise that those in-country do not have. This invitation prompts a partnership to learn the language and gain a cultural understanding to best reach their neighbors.

Identifying With Whom to Work Internationally

Seldom do sports ministers or organizations go into a country or people group and begin work without knowing someone or some group already there. The norm would be for them to respond to an invitation, as noted earlier, or to establish a working relationship with individuals, churches, or organizations. The benefits and potential drawbacks of whom one chooses to work with will likely be different from country to country, so one's homework must be done and priorities set.

Here are three general points to consider:

1. Whoever the sports minister works with—an individual, denomination, or organization—should share similar doctrine. Care must be taken to ensure alignment is not being made that contradicts one's core theological beliefs. Plenty of fringe groups and cults say some of the right things but do not agree with basic nonnegotiable tenets of biblical faith.

2. Both sides of the partnership should share a similar vision of what can or should be accomplished together. Do they view everyone as a helping hand to what they are already doing, or are they looking for direction or training? Do they have a vision to develop ongoing, indigenous sports ministry, or are

---

global events ministry—A coordinated, multiorganization effort aimed at using a singular event such as the Olympics or Super Bowl to provide a wide range of ministry outreach strategies.

they looking for assistance with sports ministry that will help them get people into the church? It is important that the vision be compatible (at least compatible enough) that both sides of the partnership feel that their priorities are being accomplished.

3. Sports ministers must be honest about what they can and cannot provide. If the church or denomination desires sports ministry training for nationals but the sports minister only has two spiritually mature yet inexperienced volleyball players, he or she must provide an accurate assessment of their capabilities. Being forthright with partners also includes financial expectations. Will the ministry group cover all costs for their staff while they are in-country, or are they expecting contributions from the in-country church or organization? Does the church or organization expect the ministry group to cover all costs for translators or other related assistance?

These are points of discussion that need to be made clear from the outset, otherwise they can become points of contention later.

Individuals considering work with a specific church or denomination must answer a few questions, besides doctrinal issues, before entering any kind of **partnering agreement**. What are the possible benefits and drawbacks of the partnership? For example, partnership with a denomination might provide ministry opportunities in other parts of the country where this denomination has established churches or small groups of believers. A potential drawback might be the reputation of the denomination. One denomination may not be comfortable associating with another one, thereby limiting potential people connections. Another question to raise is, What is the denomination's general view of sport? For example, a pastor might desire to use sport in ministry, but he or she is a rebel within a denomination that does not endorse sports ministry, thus limiting potential work. If the vision is to equip an indigenous sports ministry to grow and flourish, seek a **champion**, a person or people who share the vision and commitment to reach others for Christ through sport and who preferably have sport and ministry abilities and experience. This person (or people) would be the focus of much time and effort to develop their leadership potential for this emerging ministry. Ideally, they would be capable of training others and growing the ministry without needing future missionaries.

International Ministry in Terms of Length of Service

Varieties of sports ministry, when done internationally, can be identified in several ways. They can be identified by the general objective such as evangelism, discipleship, or church planting. Another distinction is the method or means by which the ministry is carried out—for example, rugby matches, sports camps, basketball academy. An additional identifier is the length of time a person will be involved. The following terms and concepts are not directly linked to sports ministry but are common among mission agencies, NGOs, and churches to help prospective participants understand the duration of the commitment.

Short-Term Missions

One designation used to represent a relatively brief term of service is *short-term missions* or a *short-term mission trip*. These ordinarily last from one week to three months and can have one or a combination of purposes. First, a short-term sport team can accomplish things that those on the ground in the receiving country could not do on their own. This might include playing a series of games against local opponents near the work of the receiving ministry. These games often provide opportunity for the local church or ministry to gather large numbers of people to hear the gospel (perhaps at halftime or after a game) or receive print materials. A visiting U.S. team competing locally will raise the profile of the church or ministry in the eyes of the community. In addition to playing games, these teams might assist with work projects, either for the receiving church or ministry or for the adjacent neighborhood. Volunteer labor is always appreciated by those who would have otherwise had to do it themselves. Teams have the ability to run sport camps and clinics for children. Locals are highly appreciative when people (even strangers) take an interest in their children and provide meaningful experiences for them. Churches and ministries often do not have the number of personnel or expertise needed to run a week of sport camp, so the team provides beneficial outreach and service. One criticism of these teams is their lack of cross-cultural sensitivies and that they operate from a purely American perspective, which can be offensive and counterproductive. While the

partnering agreement—Sometimes referred to as a *memorandum of understanding*, it is a written document drawn up to indicate expectations and obligations of organizations that are agreeing to work together.

champion—An indigenous Christian with sport and ministry skills or experience with a vision to reach her or his country's athletes for Christ.

criticism may be legitimate, quality prefield training and diligent in-country supervision can minimize these problems.

Sports Friends is a branch of the international mission organization SIM, which has ongoing work in 70 countries. The fourfold strategy of Sports Friends is to (1) share the vision of churches using sport as part of their ministry to their communities; (2) train leaders to start sports ministry in a church or church-planting context; (3) equip coaches who can reach, disciple, and mentor youth; and (4) develop leaders that can coordinate, train, and expand sports ministry to other churches or areas (Sports Friends, n.d.). While short-term sport teams are frequently used, Sports Friends' strategic imperatives in training coaches and leaders more often requires spiritually and athletically mature and experienced mentors. It might be a small team of coaches training national coaches or a group of pastors traveling to speak with national pastors and leaders about the power of sports ministry to reach people for Christ.

Second, because of the brief duration of a short-term trip, the focus tends to be on the life change of the participants themselves rather than on the on-site ministry goals. Whether the goal (stated or unstated) is that the short-term missionaries develop a deeper Christian worldview, enhance a vision for missions, or have a fresh encounter with God, it is regularly recognized as an outcome of the experience. A goal of short-term sport teams is quite often articulated by both the sending and receiving organizations as a way of introducing people, most often young adults, to mission work. It also allows the organizations to meet and develop relationships with potential missionary recruits. A real-life mission field encounter and interaction with missionaries and indigenous leaders can be used by God to give short-term workers a vision of what God might call them to do in relation to long-term missions. Plenty of anecdotal evidence supports the fact that short-term mission experiences have resulted in participants becoming long-term missionaries. Yet the question remains—How many of those were committed to missions before taking a short-term trip to learn more? Research is limited about short-term mission experience leading to longer or full-time missionary service. One study showed that 50 percent of those who returned from a short-term mission trip became more interested in pursuing full-time mission work during the year after their short-term experience. But this study did not follow up on whether those who expressed increased interest actually took the next steps toward full-time service (Friesen 2004). Regardless, experiencing an on-site mission broadens the perspective of the participant beyond the level of their pretrip exposure.

A third goal of sending short-term teams from a church or mission agency perspective is that those returning from a short-term mission experience will be more invested in the church's mission program or agency in regard to prayer and finances. The theory is that once a person has gone into the cross-cultural ministry setting, experienced the needs, and seen how the missionaries and local Christians operate, that person will be more motivated to pray for and financially support the work of missions in general. Anecdotal evidence shows an increase in giving, but two reviewed studies show that a statistically significant increase in missions giving after a short-term mission experience is not supported by data (Probasco 2013) and (Priest et al. 2006).

There is no lack of opinions about short-term missions. Some think these trips should not even be identified as missions but as "vision" or "exposure" trips, because missions is a vocation and a two-week vocation is an oxymoron (Greenfield 2015). Others criticize these trips as a waste of money, a drain on the receiving missionaries and churches, and glorified vacations (Bremner 2013). Certainly, some short-term trips are guilty as charged while others accomplish great things on the ground and produce lasting fruit in the lives of those who participate. A plurality of those writing on the subject agree that pretrip training and posttrip follow-up are key to ensuring that the trips are beneficial for those receiving the teams and that long-term fruit in the lives of those who return home is lasting and not left to rot. Short-term mission trips provide churches, missionaries, and mission agencies opportunities to envision, train, challenge, and use the strengths of people in fulfillment of the Great Commission. Only eternity will adequately judge the research studies and anecdotal experiences concerning the validity of short-term missions.

Stint Missions

One way to overcome the weaknesses of short-term trips is to lengthen the experience. This next length of service is as a *stint* and indicates a commitment of four months to two years. The stint process is stronger than the short-term trip from conception because it requires a higher level of commitment. The average short-term trip is less than two weeks and is often placed during a break in a school schedule (e.g., fall break, Christmas break, spring break). It is not usually difficult to arrange for time off, and, depending on the destination, the finances needed—whether paid for outright or fundraised—are more easily managed. For a person planning an international mission stint, the requirements are much greater than a short-term trip. Taking a year or more off work or

SPORTS MINISTRY IN ACTION

Bill Crossan's Heart for International Ministry

In 1992 Bill Crossan was looking for an international ministry experience with Athletes in Action. As a collegiate distance runner he desired to travel to the Barcelona Olympics to meet Olympic athletes and share the gospel with them. One AIA staff member who was setting up the various summer outreaches convinced him that spending eight weeks in the Czech Republic building relationships was a better fit for his personality than trying to meet and obtain a minute or two with Olympic athletes at the entrance of the Olympic Village. That eight-week, short-term trip was followed by a two-year stint with AIA in the Czech Republic, where he continued to develop relationships through camps and distance running with a Czech club. Returning to his Atlanta home in 1995, he still had a desire to serve in international sports ministry, though he was not sure where. Just prior to the 1996 Atlanta Olympics, Bill received a call from his Czech running coach, who told him that the Czech Olympic team needed a place to hold training camp before the

Courtesy of Bill Crossan.

competitions started and asked if Bill could secure accommodations. He immediately called a friend who was a former AIA staff member and was coaching at LaGrange Community College at the time. Within three hours, Bill was able to inform the Czech Olympic Federation that all 197 members of the team had housing for training camp. During the Olympics, AIA coordinated housing for coaches who were not able to stay in the Olympic Village. People from Bill's church arranged homestays for 16 Czech coaches, and Bill spent those competition weeks in a van driving them to various venues in Atlanta. This humble service opened hearts toward Bill and his message. The experience convinced Bill and Adrianne, whom he married a few weeks after the Olympics, that the Czech Republic would be their ministry destination. After a few summers of taking short-term teams to the Czech Republic, the couple moved there with an initial three to five-year resident missionary commitment, which turned into more than 20 years.

Bill's ministry changed as God opened doors and led in unexpected ways. Bill approached a basketball club about a chaplain role, and the owner told him that nobody wanted to talk about Jesus, but since he was an American, he could help the club with its marketing. Having no marketing experience, Bill declined the offer. His heartfelt desire was for the evangelization and discipleship of athletes. Later he reconsidered the offer and discovered that even with no background, he knew more about marketing than they did. He found himself at the club two or three days a week having all kinds of spiritual conversations with the general manager, coaches, and owner. This direction in ministry prompted Bill to pursue a master's degree in sport management, which expanded his opportunities to other basketball clubs. Eventually, he completed a PhD. His doctoral project served the needs of the Czech Basketball Federation, which created even more opportunities. Now he teaches part-time at the Sports University, where he interacts with undergraduate through master's level students. Some of his graduates have gone on to work in various sport federations and with professional clubs.

A couple things Bill believes were keys to the success they have had are that (1) AIA insisted that he and his wife both learn the language from the outset of their time in the Czech Republic, and (2) they were open to modifying the method of ministry while maintaining the message. Throughout their time, Bill and Adrianne built deep and lasting relationships with Czech people and have seen many come to faith and actively minister to the sport world within their own sphere of influence (Bill Crossan, pers. interview, 2021).

school is considerably more difficult to navigate than a two-week trip. So, too, is the amount of financing and support necessary to meet one's needs while in-country. Housing, food, and transportation, among other things, add up quickly, and when those costs are extended over time, the commitment to providing or raising funds becomes a tall order. The increased demands of this longer period of service tend to weed out those who are merely interested from those who believe that God is leading them in this direction and possibly beyond.

Though these logistical hurdles are bigger than a short-term trip, so are the experiential benefits. Being embedded in a culture over the course of a year or two gives a person opportunity to learn some of the language and come to understand aspects of the sport culture (and culture at large) that a short visit cannot provide. Making friends and observing what people value and celebrate can help create or solidify a desire to minister long term among a people group.

Spending a longer time in service gives the stint missionary additional time to become better relationally acquainted with the sending organization and with the in-country host ministry. He or she can gauge how well the organization supports its field missionaries and better understand their dynamics and core values. The sending organization and the in-country group (missionaries or church) are better able to instruct and mentor the stint missionary as he or she works alongside them. This exposure enables them to evaluate the stint missionary's suitability for ministry within this people group and his or her level of spiritual maturity and adaptability.

Resident Missions

In addition to short-term trips and stint missions, a third designation used by many mission organizations is resident missions. This description identifies those who commit to international ministry for two or more years. Globalization has accelerated the process of missionaries assimilating into other cultures. The movement of people around the world and the multiethnic structure of many countries make it easier for missionaries to take up residence and become part of the culture.

Two years may not sound like a long period of time compared to the missionaries of the 18th and 19th centuries who said goodbye to family and friends, never to see them again, as they left the West for the Far East, the Pacific Islands, and other remote locations. No longer do missionaries pack their belongings in coffins and buy a one-way ticket to the place they plan to spend the remainder of their lives sharing the gospel. A. W. Milne sailed to the New Hebrides in the South Pacific in 1785. He knew that the headhunters of those islands had killed all the missionaries who had come before him. He ended up ministering there for 35, years and when he died, the locals buried him in the center of town under the inscription, "When he came there was no light. When he left there was no darkness" (Batterson 2013).

The ease, speed, and relatively low cost of international travel have, among other factors, changed the way that much of the global Church views missions. The blinding speed at which technology has advanced has taught impatience with things that take time. Television shows resolve decades-old cold case crimes in about 40 minutes, and movies portray heroes preventing world destruction in about two hours. Big things, important things, often take time and are not accomplished overnight. Reaching the baseball community in Cuba with the gospel will take time. Evangelizing and discipling field hockey players in Australia does not happen in a single conference or over the course of a single season. These transformations take time, often a very long time. But the openness of the modern world has made it possible for missionaries to have an impact, even in a shorter window of time, making a three- to five-year missionary residency a more regular occurrence.

This shorter version of resident missionary service mirrors what is happening in general with careers in America. A U.S. Bureau of Labor Statistics Longitudinal Survey of nearly 10,000 men and women over a period of 37 years shows that between ages 18 and 52, the average person will change jobs more than 12 times, with half of those changes coming between ages 18 and 24 (Bureau of Labor Statistics 2019). It is estimated that the average person will make five to seven career changes within his or her working lifetime (Vardhman 2020). It should come as no surprise that missionary commitments are reflective of these trends, so much so that a three-year or longer commitment is viewed as long term.

R. T. Kendall quotes Jonathan Edwards, 18th-century American preacher and theologian who famously said, "The task of every generation is to discover in which direction the Sovereign Redeemer is moving, then move in that direction" (Kendall 2003, 73). This principle can be applied to modern-day ministries. It is evident that great benefits come from short-term and stint international mission experiences. However, because the nature of ministry is relational, the residential missionary, committed over a longer period of time, has the advantage of broader and deeper opportunities to speak into the lives of people they serve.

Ministering to Internationals in the Neighborhood

Having discussed the merits and methods of international ministry, might it also be accomplished without ever applying for a passport? In 2017 nearly 50 million people living in the United States were born in other countries. More than 12 million residents were from Mexico, one million or more were from another nine countries, and 10,000 or more were from an additional 128 countries (Pew Research Center 2018).

Increasingly, American Christians are reaching out to these immigrants, who are often found congregating in communities or geographical areas in close proximity to Christian churches. In addition, international students, migrant and temporary workers, refugees, and foreign tourists can be reached. It is

---

SPORTS MINISTRY IN ACTION

International Sports Ministry in Chicago

Cody Snouffer has worked with the Chicago Eagles, a soccer ministry of Missionary Athletes International, since 2012. In an interview, he shared about his ministry. In West Chicago and the surrounding county, where he lives with his family, approximately 125 first languages are spoken. To reach kids in the area's apartment complexes, they decided to help their staff coaches relocate to several of these apartment complexes and organize soccer teams. They soon found themselves working not only with the Hispanic majority, but also with children from Burma, Ethio-

Snouffer (*right*) and one of his multiethnic teams.

pia, Sudan, Poland, Ukraine, Iraq, and Iran, as well as African American and Caucasian American-born kids. The coaches who live in the neighborhoods are assisted by volunteers to run small micro leagues (4v4 rather than 11v11) and more competitive club teams for ages 10 to 19. The programs are run at the nearest schools, within walking distance of these families. This model began when Snouffer and his wife, Jennifer, moved into an apartment that shared a property line with an elementary school. Initially, he asked the school janitor for permission to play soccer on the field with kids from the complex. About nine months later, the school asked to meet with the coaches. Coincidentally, the fourth and fifth grade students, who had numerous writing assignments, were writing stories that included their Eagles coaches, and the school administrators wanted to find out who these guys were. The teachers had noticed a change in this group of boys, as evidenced by their improved schoolwork, and concluded that the Eagles' soccer program was in part responsible. Snouffer shared the strategy and vision they had for the neighborhood and school, and the result was continued permission from the school administration to use the property. This exchange led to the identification of other complexes near schools and additional coaches taking adjacent apartments to start leagues and teams. School officials collaborated, and the programs were encouraged by administrators who had witnessed the benefits.

A spiritual curriculum was developed for the coaches to use with their teams. Since the majority of coaches live in the same neighborhood as their players, off-field interactions regularly occur. For the older club teams, in addition to the spiritual curriculum, an optional Bible study is offered and held in the home of one of the coaches or players. The program now includes the potential for older players to experience an international trip to play and minister in another culture. Several players have come through the program and now are helping coach and minister to the younger kids (Cody Snouffer, pers. interview, 2021).

important to realize that these communities are varied and cannot be stereotyped. As with any community, the question to be asked is, How can they best be served? Physically close in proximity yet culturally diverse, they correspond to the Samaritans as in the admonition of Acts 1:8, as mentioned earlier. Too often Americans are guilty of shunning these immigrant populations because they appear different, yet they are mothers, fathers, sisters, brothers, sons, daughters—neighbors to be welcomed and embraced. When encountering the Samaritan woman at Jacob's well on the outskirts of Sychar, Jesus told his disciples, "Open your eyes and look at the fields! They are ripe for harvest" (John 4:35 NIV). His words emphatically resound to the Church in America today. God has brought these people within earshot of local churches so that they can be served, loved, and introduced to the Savior.

SUMMARY

Jesus' command to His disciples to "make disciples of all nations" continues to apply to His present-day followers. In His infinite wisdom, Jesus did not give a detailed account of what it meant to disciple and teach the nations. The Church is free to be creative with the methods used to disciple as long as the message aligns to what Jesus taught. Sports ministry has been employed around the globe to bring the good news of salvation through Christ to the nations.

While the United States may be uniquely positioned to send sports ministers because of its human and financial resources, international sports ministry is not exclusively an American enterprise. Thriving indigenous sports ministries exist in every corner of the world, with numerous countries sending their own missionaries abroad. From the early evangelistic teams to international coalitions of ministries, the breadth and scope of sports ministry continues to expand.

The benefits and challenges of international sports ministry were examined. Also, the role that length of service can play in developing relationships and being effective was discussed. Lastly, it has become evident that going to other nations is not always needed because the United States is becoming increasingly diverse.

REVIEW AND DISCUSSION QUESTIONS

1. Does the Great Commission apply to you? In what way(s) have you worked to fulfill it?
2. What resources are needed to carry out international sports ministry?
3. In what way can sports open doors to the culture of a country?
4. What is considered important when deciding where to minister internationally?
5. If you have taken part in international sports ministry, was it short term, stint, or resident? Which do you see as most effective?
6. Why should raising up indigenous sports ministries be a primary focus of international sports ministry efforts?
7. How does partnering with the right or wrong people or organization affect your international ministry?
8. Whether you feel that you could carry it out or not, describe an opportunity to reach the nations through sports in your immediate vicinity.

Courtesy of Joanne Green, Huntington University Sports.

How does faith influence one's participation and view of sport?

CHAPTER 5

Faith Considerations

"Sport is an activity that involves more than the movement of the body; it demands the use of intelligence and the disciplining of the will. It reveals, in other words, the wonderful structure of the human person created by God as a spiritual being, a unity of body and spirit . . . You are true athletes when you prepare yourselves not only by training your bodies but also by constantly engaging the spiritual dimensions of your person for a harmonious development of all your talents."

Pope John Paul II (Gill 2020)

LEARNING OBJECTIVES

After studying this chapter, you should be able to do the following:
- Understand the concept of play as a part of what it means to be created in the image of God
- Describe how play and competitive sport are both similar and different
- Recognize both the positive and negative aspects of competition as it relates to faith
- Articulate biblical faith principles that can affect the Christian's participation in sport
- Identify aspects of sport that make it an ideal place for evangelistic and discipleship ministry

The Academy Award–winning movie *Chariots of Fire* depicts a contrast between play and competitive sport. This contrast is embodied in the two highlighted Olympic sprinters: Eric Liddell and Harold Abrahams. Liddell said, "I believe that God made me for a purpose. But He also made me fast, and when I run, I feel His pleasure." Abrahams said, "I'm forever in pursuit and I don't even know what I'm chasing. . . . And now in an hour's time I will be out there again. I will raise my eyes and look down that corridor; four feet wide, with 10 lonely seconds to justify my whole existence. But will I?" (Hudson 1981).

Abrahams relentlessly hones his craft for competition to prove himself equal to or better than others and is unable to feel joy or contentment, even when he wins.

> *Liddell, on the other hand, feels God's pleasure when he runs. As his pulse races and his skin drips, his muscles cycling perfectly between tense and relaxed, he feels the splendor that girds creation. He's exercising in the literal sense: "exercising" his body, exploring its capabilities, with innocent pleasure. We see this every day on playgrounds as children sprint and skip and climb with shrieks of delight. (Grimm 2012)*

A common mistake made by many people, including people of faith, is a compartmentalization of life. Public and private life are disconnected—for example, work life from recreation, spiritual life from temporal life. The early Church grew in the context of a Platonic dualism, separating the sacred and the secular. Though the Bible does not support this secular/sacred divide, Christians often still look at things this way, compromising with culture's version of truth. Thus, a Christian displaying decidedly un-Christian behavior on the field of sport might justify his or her actions because "this isn't church and that's how the game is played." In reality, a person's life is unified and one's faith and belief system influence every aspect of who he or she is and what he or she does. This chapter will consider how faith influences viewpoints, including one's participation in sport.

Designed for Play

A brief description of the creation of humanity and what will be called **true play** will help explain why people are drawn to sport, often with great intensity. God fashioned mankind as the pinnacle of His creation (Genesis 1-2), in His image and likeness (Genesis 1:26). God is spirit and without a physical body. Theologians describe human resemblance to God's image and likeness by referring to the fact that humans are spiritual, emotional, and relational beings with the ability to think, reason, and choose.

From His imagination, God created the vastness of the universe as well as the intricacies of earth—the enormously varied numbers of complex plants and animals in all shapes, sizes, and colors. Adam and Eve were placed into a garden paradise, and each were given a charge. Adam was given the task of working in and taking care of the garden. God also entrusted the naming of animals to him (Genesis 2:15-20). Together, the man and the woman were tasked to "be fruitful and increase in number; fill the earth and subdue it" (Genesis 1:28 NIV).

The culmination of God's amazing creation and the description of people being made in God's likeness is also seen in humanity's ability to be creative. A combination of God-given imagination and individual talents are used to create experiences and things of great beauty or complexity, experiences or things that may or may not be useful but bring joy. We are drawn to these activities by virtue of being created in the image of the Creator.

It is this combination of imagination and creativity that leads to the discussion of true play. Johan Huizinga, a Dutch historian and cultural theorist, authored the book *Homo Ludens: A Study of the Play-Element in Culture* in 1938. His purpose was to relate the basics of play to different aspects of culture such as language, civilizing functions, law, war, knowledge, poetry, philosophy, and art. Although he did not write from a Christian perspective, what he has to say is instructive for Christians considering sport. He begins with a description rather than a definition of play.

1. Play is enjoyment (fun). Enjoyment is an essential characteristic of play, or what has been referred to earlier as "true play." This "fun-element" characterizes the essence of play for everyone (Huizinga 2014, 3-7). Play, in this sense, is not for the sake of pleasing parents, impressing someone, obtaining a college scholarship, becoming healthier, making

---

true play—Play that is generally thought to be an unstructured activity, entire to itself and for its own sake (Ellis 2014, 3).

a living, and so on. True, basic play is simply for the enjoyment of it.

2. Play is voluntary. If one is forced or coerced to participate, then it is not true play (Huizinga 2014, 8).

3. Play is separate from ordinary life. It takes the player away from reality and puts him or her in a separate:

   a. *Place:* A field, court, pool, track, and so on. The living room carpet becomes imaginary volcanic lava, and if anyone touches it, he or she is eliminated. The backyard becomes an imaginary football stadium, baseball field, golf course, or battleground. Imagination has no limits.

   b. *Time:* The game begins, and the game ends. The time of the game may not correspond to the time of nonparticipants. Two halves, three periods, nine innings, three attempts—these are all measurements of time that are unique to sport. For play, it could last a few seconds or all afternoon.

When it starts, it starts, and when it ends, it is over.

   c. *Set of rules:* The rules are determined and agreed upon by those participating. Whether children are playing cops and robbers or having a tea party, the roles and rules are accepted. The rules in this type of play are confined to the current place and time and can change as the game progresses.

   d. *Reality:* When one plays, the fantasy of the game eclipses the true reality of life. The player becomes lost in the game and consumed by the imagined reality. The children playing restaurant are swept up in their roles as the cook, waiter, or patron (Huizinga 2014, 9-10).

4. "Play is non-seriousness" (Huizinga 2014, 5). Play in this context is not necessary for daily life needs. It does not produce and is completely dispensable. It is not serious business, providing food to eat, protection from

God's creative intention for play is to be an expression of joy.

the elements, and so on. However, one can be serious about play. When children or adults are playing, they are frequently serious about their participation. If the local youth soccer league ceased to function, or the university's volleyball program were dropped, the world would continue with little effect, except on the participants in that particular game. People are quick to respond, "It's just a game," and in the sense of nonseriousness, they are correct. Because play is unnecessary does not, however, denote that it is meaningless. Play is unnecessary yet meaningful (Harvey 2014, 71).

5. Play is uncertain (Huizinga 2014, 10-11). The results of play are not predetermined. Because anything can happen, players experience a sense of freedom, adventure, and possibility.

6. Play promotes the formation of social groups (Huizinga 2014, 12-13). Playing creates bonds among people. For this reason, colleges have activities for incoming students; church youth groups have crazy game nights; and Fortune 500 companies take employees to a ropes course or escape room. The groups enter the play activity as individuals but emerge from it as a team.

Play is not limited to what is understood to be sport or recreational pursuits. The components Huizinga conveys are manifest in other areas of culture. When done for the purpose of joy, music (composing or performing), dance, literature, sculpting, painting, and other creative and imaginative pursuits can be considered true play. They are enjoyable, voluntarily engaged-in activities that are separate from normal life, non-serious, and free and that promote the formation of social groups. As people are motivated to play, they are emulating the actions of the one in whose image they have been created. Humans could live in a world without art, literature, sport, or music, but life is much richer with them.

Regardless of the circumstances, joy is God's intention for humankind. Whether rich or poor, healthy or sick, awareness of God's presence and being thankful are keys to joy. In Ecclesiastes 8:15, the teacher writes, "So I commend the enjoyment of life, because there is nothing better for a person under the sun than to eat and drink and be glad. Then joy will accompany them in their toil all the days of the life God has given them under the sun" (NIV). Paul speaks about the joy of contentment: "I have learned the secret of being content in any and every situation, whether well fed or hungry, whether living in plenty or in want. I can do all this through him who gives me strength" (Philippians 4:12-13 NIV). Paul further

instructs believers, "And whatever you do, whether in word or deed, do it all in the name of the Lord Jesus, giving thanks to God the Father through him" (Colossians 3:17 NIV). Is God evident and His joy experienced in sport participation?

Defining Play

A precise definition of play is difficult. Huizinga's attempt is lengthy:

> *Summing up the formal characteristics of play, we might call it a free activity standing quite consciously outside "ordinary" life as being "not serious," but at the same time absorbing the player intensely and utterly. It is an activity connected with no material interest, and no profit can be gained by it. It proceeds within its own proper boundaries of time and space according to fixed rules and in an orderly manner. It promotes the formation of social groupings which tend to surround themselves with secrecy and to stress their difference from the common world by disguise or other means. (Huizinga 2014, 13)*

Oxford theologian Robert Ellis provides perhaps the most succinct definition as seen at the beginning of the chapter: "Play is generally thought to be an unstructured activity, entire to itself and for its own sake" (Ellis 2014, 3). The idea of play is separate from games and sport, which are more structured.

Huizinga does not approach play from a Christian perspective, nor does he identify a physiological or psychological reason why humans and animals (who also have a healthy sense of play) engage in playful activity. Huizinga writes, "If we call the active principle that makes up the essence of play, 'instinct', we explain nothing; if we call it 'mind' or 'will,' we say too much. However we may regard it, the very fact that play has a meaning implies a non-materialistic quality in the nature of the thing itself" (Huizinga 2014, 1). While Huizinga credits nature with supplying the impetus to play, Christians believe God is responsible for His creation's desire to play. Specifically for humanity, play is an expression of imagination and creativity. It is this God-given appetite for play that will prove to be the connection with sport.

From Play to Sport

Considering the modern world of competitive sport, from tee ball to the World Series, it is possible to confuse sport with the concept of true play because of their many similarities. Unlike play, as a God-given inclination, sport is the product of humanity's attempt to organize and enhance play. Introducing competition to play adds a measure of meaning and heightened emotion and excitement. The extra level of meaning tends to increase performance and intensity similar to the way goods and services are improved and become less expensive in an environment of competition (Erdozain 2011, lecture 4).

Robert Ellis identifies four main differences between play and sport while acknowledging others might exist.

1. Modern sport is a form of bureaucratized play. In play, rules are local and can change during the play session. Cops and robbers played in one locale or country might look quite different from the same game played in another region. Play's informal, participant-governed activity differs from institutionalized rules enacted by clubs, leagues, and national and international associations.

2. Sport, unlike play, has an *agon* element or quality. The word is Greek (from which comes the English word *agony*) and means a contest or struggle. The *agon* aspect of sport pits one person or team against another with the goal of determining who is the best. While an athlete might enjoy the activity itself, there is now a goal beyond simple joy, which is to demonstrate one's superiority by winning.

3. Another distinction of sport compared to play is that it "is an embodied contest of physical and mental exertion" (Ellis 2014, 128). This element not only distinguishes sport from play but also from games, such as chess or cards, involving mental exertion but with little physical effort expended. Competition amplifies the struggle when physical and mental demands are combined.

4. A fourth aspect of sport is that it incorporates a substantial amount of skill that can be enhanced by training and practice. Focused work and effort can produce improved skills, leading to a better chance of success.

Ellis summarizes, "Sport gathers up elements of the definition of play and adds to it that it is a bureaucratized embodied contest involving mental and physical exertion and with a significant element of refinable skill" (Ellis 2014, 129).

Comparing True Play to Sport

Here is a list of differences between true play and sport:

True play: One plays simply for the enjoyment.

Sport: Sport can incorporate a playful spirit but has a goal (i.e., winning) and a host of other reasons why one competes (e.g., to compare oneself with others, to prove oneself, to gain recognition, to please someone, to obtain a scholarship, to learn life lessons, to enhance a resume).

Sport is the product of humanity's attempt to organize and enhance play.

True play: True play is voluntary.

Sport: For some, sport is voluntary. For many children, it begins with parents enrolling them in a sport (different from a child deciding on his or her own to go outside and play). As children mature, many continue participating for a variety of reasons. Higher levels of sport increase the temptation to compete for more self-focused reasons such as pride, adulation, or other accolades. External rewards and internal motivations replace the enjoyment of simply participating.

True play: True play provides a separation from ordinary life (place, time, rules, reality).

Sport: Locations are intentional physical spaces (e.g., court, stadium, field, pool, track) rather than an imagined place. The time element is still separate from real time, but instead of being free to begin and end when it suits those playing, sport time (or number of attempts) is predetermined, constricting and limiting those participating. The random and fluid rules of informal play, agreed upon by players in sport, become rigid and codified. The participants must adhere to these rules even if they do not agree with them. These rules also carry enumerated penalties that are assessed by appointed officials if participants are judged to have broken the rules. One thing that remains similar in the comparison of play and sport is the idea of the immediate experience as a different reality than normal life, of becoming lost in the game. The experience becomes the participant's world for the duration of the contest, and they are fully invested in that reality.

True play: True play is nonserious and superfluous, and it does not produce anything. Players can be serious in their play, but the outcome of play is not consequential.

Sport: When goals other than enjoyment enter the picture through competition, the amateur might have an increased seriousness in his or her approach to the game because of the desire to win and prove him- or herself superior. In addition, other outcomes might be associated with winning or losing such as social standing, scholarship considerations, or the approval of a parent. For the professional athlete, the seriousness is elevated further because competition is a source of personal income, profit for the organization, and associated jobs. Sport remains nonserious in the sense that life would continue if sport were to disappear, but the seriousness for the participant is magnified, resulting in potential decreased enjoyment of the experience because of one's inability to continually succeed. As with

play, sport "is radically unnecessary but internally meaningful" (Harvey 2014, 69).

True play: Nothing is certain, results are not predetermined, and anything is possible, creating a sense of freedom and anticipation for participants.

Sport: Similar to play, individuals or teams are not guaranteed to win or lose. Like play, competition offers freedom and hope. In sport, this freedom applies to the spectator as well as the participant. Fans realize that their team may be the underdog, but on any given day they could rise and be victorious. This hope is a powerful connection between play and sport.

True play: True play promotes the formation of social groups.

Sport: Sport also promotes the formation of social groups. With team sports, the bond within the team or organization can be very strong. Sport brings together communities of people, which in part provides rationale for cities to offer attractive incentives for professional sport teams to play there. Universities spend large sums of money to have athletic programs as a means to promote solidarity among their student population.

Some sports ministers and organizations might mistakenly promote the idea that God created sport, and since everything in creation is good because God created it that way, sport is good. This theory further states that He created sport perfect, but people have corrupted it. Therefore, the Christian's task is to find his or her way back to the perfect state of sport as God intended.

The real connection, however, between God and sport is true play, which He designed as a part of human expression. From the foundation of play, it was humanity's attempts to organize and elevate play that has resulted in the creation of competitive sport. As the image bearers of the Creator, humans possess the desire to play. Thus, competitive sport has captured the hearts of people around the globe because it contains an element, though corrupted, of true play.

The Problem of Competition

This section provides a foundation for competition as it relates to play and the introduction of contested sport. Chapter 7 will build on this foundation, addressing ethical considerations and specifically competition's compatibility with faith. True play is for enjoyment only; while competitive sport is different than this kind of play, it is possible to engage in competitive sport with a play-spirit. Competitive sport

SPORTS MINISTRY IN ACTION

SRS: In Sport. For People. With God.

SRS is a sports ministry located in Altenkirchen, Germany, a ministry reaching far beyond the country's borders. Founded in 1971 by German and European Motocross champion Helmfried Riecker, SRS's staff of approximately 50, along with 800 volunteers, evangelize and disciple through a variety of methods including sports teams, camps, and retreats.

The SRS purpose statement reads, "SRS International exists to envision, launch, build and develop ministry in and through sport in countries that have little or no sports ministry in partnership with different agencies, churches, and individuals." SRS has partnered with more than 30 countries to develop sports ministry. It sends individuals or teams to train and assist emerging sports ministers, provide training materials, offer training conferences (in person and online), and help with fundraising and administrative support (SRS 2020).

Daniel Mannweiler is the current head of the ministry. His first exposure to SRS came when he was six years old and heard about Helmfried Riecker. He pleaded with his mother to see and hear this man speak. It was the first time Daniel heard about combining faith and sport; the two were not enemies as many had believed.

Daniel and his wife, Kathrin, competed professionally throughout the world in the triathlon. They spent six years in Stellenbosch, South Africa, helping with ministry projects for children in the townships, working with high-level European athletes who came there to train, and organizing Christian sports camps. Many of the athletes were not believers, yet most participated in all the spiritual aspects of the camps. They continued working with SRS on their return to Germany, and in 2022 Daniel was asked to take over the ministry's leadership.

Daniel's message to churches and athletes about sports ministry is this:

Often pastors will ask me if I can connect them with a famous Christian sportsperson to speak at their church. Sometimes I can, but I first encourage them to be raising up athletes from their church. Many times when a young Christian is gifted in sport, they are not able to be part of all the programs the church offers. Churches must be able to support and encourage Christian athletes in creative ways so that their giftedness in sport does not become separated from their faith. When I speak with Christian athletes about the possibilities of sports ministry, I always ask them to listen to what is in their heart and to ask them what their desire is, and what they believe Jesus' desire is for them. (Daniel Mannweiler, pers. interview, 2022)

Throughout its history SRS has a been a world leader and innovator in sports ministry.

can offer positive outcomes for one's efforts. Almost universally, the sporting experience is touted as aiding personal development and teaching teamwork, perseverance, respect, responsibility, and hard work. Sport can be a means to teach all these things when **personal development** is the focus of the sporting experience by those organizing, facilitating, and participating in the sport experience. Quality character attributes do not happen automatically, and if winning is the primary focus, personal development is too often neglected and sometimes undermined completely.

It is the incorporation of the *agon* element, in the organization of play into sport, that makes competition difficult for people of faith as well as for those seeking to use sport as an instrument to instill positive character formation in young people.

Ideally, competition takes place with the play-spirit intact. Most youth league sports profess allegiance to something akin to the Olympic ideal: "The goal of the Olympic Movement is to contribute to building a peaceful and better world by educating youth through sport practiced without discrimination of any kind and in the Olympic spirit, which requires mutual understanding with a spirit of friendship, solidarity and fair play" (International Olympic Committee, n.d.). The desire is for sport to be an enjoyable activity that contributes to the health and character development of all participants. This stated view is similar to the one adopted by the colleges and universities of the National Collegiate Athletic Association (NCAA): "The NCAA is a member-led organization focused on cultivating an environment

personal development—Within a sport context, personal development is a philosophy that prioritizes character development over winning.

that emphasizes academics, fairness and well-being across college sports." (National Collegiate Athletic Association, n.d.)

Such virtuous aspirations run up against two major barriers in their pursuit. The first is the fallen human nature of men and women. In the Genesis creation account, God had a regular presence in the garden with Adam and Eve until they broke trust with God in an effort to become equal with Him. As a result, their descendants share the same propensity for self-rule (and ruling the lives of others) rather than submitting themselves in obedience to the authority of God; they have abandoned Him to follow their own misguided decrees. Paul describes this apostasy in the New Testament as "the flesh." He remarks, "The acts of the flesh are obvious: sexual immorality, impurity and debauchery; idolatry and witchcraft; hatred, discord, jealousy, fits of rage, selfish ambition, dissensions, factions and envy; drunkenness, orgies, and the like" (Galatians 5:19-21 NIV).

The second is competition itself. When Paul references, "Everyone who competes in the games" (1 Corinthians 9:25 NIV), "compete" is the Greek word *agonizomai* from the root *agon* discussed earlier. The other six times this is used in the New Testament, the NIV translates it three times as "fight," and once each as "contend," "wrestle," and "make every effort." If sport is viewed purely from the perspective of compe-tition, winning becomes the greatest good. It is para-mount among any other possible good that might be produced. Because competition is between individuals or teams, victory over the other person or team tends to assume the highest value. As the saying goes, "If it doesn't matter who wins or loses, then why do they keep score?" (Morrison 2021). The zero-sum nature of sport (for me to win, you must lose) incentivizes all sorts of corruption. Recognizing the human condition after the fall, competition is understood by many as intrinsically problematic, the logical outcome and source of nearly all the ills of sports (i.e., violence, cheating, performance-enhancing drugs, and bitter rivalries) (Hoffman 2010, 144-165). If winning is the greatest good, an athlete might be tempted to view his or her opponent as an enemy, an obstacle to his or her success, someone to be dominated or controlled. Consequently, gamesmanship, cheating, and physical or psychological intimidation are often considered part of the game. Fans contribute to an athlete's or team's success by cheering for them to play their best, taunting the opponents in hopes of knocking them off their game, and berating officials, pressuring them to make favorable calls for their own team or against the opposition. Commenting about sport, C.S. Lewis stated that he did not "allow to games any of the moral and almost mystical virtues which schoolmasters claim for them; they seem to

CASE STUDY

When Values Collide

The mission statement summary of Major League Baseball's (MLB) Houston Astros is, "Our Values, Vision, and Mission: Trust, Integrity, and Excellence are at the foundation of everything we do" (Major League Baseball, n.d.). The Astros won their first World Series in 2017, but it was later discovered that throughout the season they had been stealing signs to gain an advantage over other teams. It seems that integrity lost out to winning in the competition of values. MLB investigated and found it to be an almost entirely player-led problem. In 2020 MLB suspended the team's general, assistant, and team managers for one year, having vowed to hold management accountable. The general manager and team manager subsequently were fired by the Astros. The team was stripped of draft picks and fined $5 million. None of the players were disciplined, and the franchise retained its status as 2017 World Series Champions (Axisa 2020).

Discussion Questions

1. What happens when the lines of integrity are crossed by an individual or within a team or sport's organization?

2. Members of the Astros management were penalized. Should the guilty players have been penalized as well? Do you believe the verdict to be fair? Why or why not?

3. How does the poor judgment of a few members taint the image of an entire organization?

4. What has been your experience concerning a breach of integrity in a sport context?

me to lead to ambition, jealousy, and embittered partisan feeling, quite as often as to anything else" (Lewis 1955, 129-130).

The Potential of Competition

The influence of fallen human nature leads to a multitude of temptations for players, coaches, and fans that are inconsistent with the practices of Christian faith. Do competitive sports offer redemptive possibilities? Is it possible for participants and spectators alike to act with mutual respect for opponents? Is fair play an outdated idea? Can individuals compete with the spirit of true play and enjoy the experience, win or lose?

Competition is everywhere in the world. This fact does not suggest that competition is virtuous, but it does require the Church to wrestle with its reality. Competition is a daily occurrence, whether auditioning for a spot in the school band, preparing a résumé for an upcoming job interview, or producing a better and cheaper product than a rival company. Sometimes, a person might not know who he or she is competing against; the competitive experience is not personal or relational. It is feasible for a business to sell the most product while other companies still thrive, albeit at a lower level. Competitive sport is a manufactured contest outside of real life that attempts to make each encounter a win-or-lose situation. Competitive sport does, however, involve real-life impulses, thoughts, and feelings. The level or type of sport, as in the following discussion, might aggravate or alleviate negative attitudes or actions that accompany participation. Competitive sport is relational and often intense, especially in face-to-face or full-contact sports (see figure 5.1). It is true that competition can entice a player to entertain negative thoughts and actions. Consequently, competition is a venue for players to learn how to overcome these temptations.

Individual and Team Sports

Figure 5.1 categorizes sports to help Christian athletes assess the appropriateness of participation and the eventual ministry potential of specific individual or team sports. In the case of individual sports (figure 5.1a), athletes are isolated in many respects. They have no teammates to rely on. They arguably experience more pressure as they share the credit or blame with no one else. Ministering to the individual athlete can be easier because more attention can be given to

them than to multiple members of an entire team.

Team sports (figure 5.1b) require a level of coordination and cooperation with teammates in order to compete at peak level. There are relational dynamics within team sports that are not present when an athlete competes as an individual. This factor will figure significantly in the analysis of whether sport is a suitable place for ministry.

Side-by-Side and Face-to-Face Sports

A second category is a comparison of side-by-side or face-to-face sports (see figure 5.1, a and b). Side-by-side sports occur when individuals or teams compete on their own without an opponent actively playing against them. Bowling, golf, skiing, track and field, and swimming are among side-by-side competitive sports. Each person or team has its own ball or lane while competing for the best scores or times. The focus is on what the individual or team can do to maximize its performance; it is not so much about what the opponent is doing.

In face-to-face competition the individual or team is playing against another person or team but with only one ball, puck, or field that each tries to control. In face-to-face competitive sports, the individual or team needs to consider their own play as well as the play of its opponent. The relational level of competition increases from side-by-side sports. One opponent or team actively attempts to force its will or obstruct the actions of the adversary or team. The challenge is not limited to how well the individual or team can perform. It has become interpersonal, because the individual or team faces an opponent who is trying to thwart their efforts. Striving to do one's best while also trying to prevent the opponent from doing their best raises the level of interpersonal intensity. This type of competition increases the potential for corruption but advances the level of potential growth in athletes as well.

Levels of Contact in Sports

A third category is contact in sport. In this group, games like basketball and soccer permit incidental contact with opponents, but this contact is not central to the sport itself. Likewise, baseball and softball have minimal incidental physical contact. Some other sports listed in figure 5.1b, such as ice hockey, lacrosse, and touch or flag football, exhibit greater physical contact, yet the primary objective is to score more goals or points than the opponents.

Individual Sports

	Full contact	Contact	Noncontact
Competitive side-by-side			Weightlifting
			Swimming
			Running
			Canoeing or kayaking
			Track and field
			Bowling
			Golf
			Ski slalom or downhill
Competitive face-to-face	Boxing		Tennis
	Wrestling		Table tennis
	Mixed martial arts		Badminton
			Racquetball
			Squash

a

Team Sports

	Full contact	Contact	Noncontact
Competitive side-by-side			Crew
			Swimming relays
			Track and field relays
Competitive face-to-face	Football (tackle)	Soccer	Tennis doubles
	Rugby	Basketball	Table tennis doubles
		Ice hockey	Volleyball
		Field hockey	Badminton doubles
		Lacrosse	
		Water polo	
		Football (touch or flag)	
		Baseball	
		Ultimate	
		Team handball	

b

FIGURE 5.1 Competition is the focus of these figures; therefore recreational activities have been omitted: (a) individual sports and (b) team sports.

© Human Kinetics, adapted from illustration by Kiel McClung.

This physical contact is more frequent—perhaps more forceful—elevating the intensity of the game. Rule restrictions limit the amount or type of contact between players, with some form of penalty assessed to those who violate the restrictions.

The final category is full-contact sport, which appears in parts *a* and *b* of figure 5.1. In these sports, physical contact is fundamental. Boxing, martial arts, and wrestling are scored by physical blows, takedowns, or incapacitating the opponent. Mixed martial arts (MMA) "combines wrestling and striking martial arts into one complete discipline, including techniques from Thai-boxing, judo, Brazilian jiu jitsu and boxing" (International Mixed Martial Arts

Federation, n.d.). Due to the nature of football and rugby, they have been included on the list because physical contact is an integral part of these sports. The line of scrimmage in football is a physical struggle, and many plays end with the tackle of the ball carrier. Rugby is similar but without the padding. While trying to outscore the opponent, the physical nature of these games is why they are included in the full-contact category. The difference between contact and full-contact is the degree and severity of the contact.

Face-to-face contact and full-contact sports increase the temptation to physically intimidate, dominate, or do bodily harm to opponents. Hockey,

Competitive sport is naturally interpersonal and is intended to bring out the best in participants.

soccer, and basketball have their enforcers. In professional hockey, the officials occasionally allow players to drop their gloves and fight for a short period of time before breaking them up and penalizing both players. In recent years, reports of football bounty scandals (i.e., rewarding players for intentionally sidelining opponents) have surfaced, from youth levels to the NFL. The goal of professional boxing (as opposed to the much more controlled Olympic boxing), mixed martial arts, and to some extent wrestling is to bring the opponent to submission. The object is to pin, knock out, score enough points, incapacitate the opponent, or inflict enough pain to cause them to quit, submit, or tap out.

On a personal level an athlete might be comfortable with the incidental contact in sports such as basketball or baseball but find it hard to justify the brutality of MMA, boxing, or even football because of the temptation (or expectation) to physically dominate or intimidate opposing players. Further detail is provided in the Assessing Sport Participation section.

Team sports require a greater level of coordination and cooperation to compete at a maximum level. They provide more relational aspects while competing against other teams and within the team itself. This relational concept can figure significantly in the analysis of a sport's suitability as a viable ministry option. This is discussed further in the Assessing Sport as a Place for Ministry section.

The Bible and Sport

Earlier in the chapter, play was described as a combination of God-given imagination and individual talents to create experiences of beauty and complexity and that may or may not be useful but bring joy. Humans have taken the play impulse, organized it, and made it competitive. Thus, an environment of competitive sport elicits questions for the Christian: Is participation in competitive sport compatible with faith, and is competitive sport a suitable place for ministry?

The Apostle Paul and Sport

There is neither endorsement nor rejection of sport in Scripture. Although the Apostle Paul, in his New Testament writings, used some athletic imagery or terminology in communicating the gospel, he did not speak directly to the issue of how the Church and its people should or should not engage sport. His use of athletic illustrations or terms has led some in the modern sports ministry movement to conclude that Paul was affirming and endorsing sport as good. Victor Pfitzner argues that much of the vocabulary of sport used in Paul's day had long since lost any concrete connection to actual athletic context (Pfitzner 1967, 31). Contemporary examples of sport vocabulary are numerous and come from a variety of sports. Baseball phrases commonly used today include such expressions as "Let's make sure we have all our bases covered," "That [result] was a home run (or a grand

Interview With a Professional

Courtesy of Josh Merrill.

Josh Merrill, Shepherd Church
Sports Pastor at Shepherd Church in Porter Ranch, California
Executive Director of Eternity Sports

Although he grew up in a church setting, it was sport that captured Josh Merrill's heart and imagination. A three-sport standout athlete in high school (football, basketball, baseball), he turned down Division I football offers and chose basketball as his college sport. He walked away from the Lord to pursue the life of a professional athlete. The prospect of playing professional basketball after college led him to play in the NBA summer leagues, and for several years he played professional basketball in different countries. After his first international season he had a reawakening of his faith. After a few more international seasons and a deepening of his faith the question became, "What's next?" This led to Shepherd Church.

What was it like starting sports ministry at a church that had none? Did you feel up to the task having had no sports ministry training yourself?

The opportunity to start sports ministry at Shepherd Church was clearly God's direction, as it was meant to be. I got connected to a sports ministry pastor in another state, and that was helpful, but I was really learning as I went along. At first, I didn't have 40 hours a week of work to do, but before long there weren't enough hours in the day or days in the week to get everything done! So we began to hire staff and recruit volunteers as the ministry expanded. Eventually, I completed a graduate degree, a master of arts in Christian ministry.

Why do you think that sport is a great place for ministry?

I love sports! For a lot of athletes it's the way that we connect with other people. Athletes tend to view all of life through a sport's lens, and that makes it easy for us to relate to one another. I think sport is the most nonthreatening way to get someone to be involved with anything church-related or to come onto the church campus. It's an easy invitation for Christians to say to their friends, "Come play softball or join my basketball team for this season." Sports accelerates friendships. It is a bonding activity that helps connect people, and it is through those relationships that we can share our faith.

What does sports ministry look like at Shepherd Church?

We want Shepherd Sports to be the front door of the church, an outreach to the community. We organize and provide a quality sports experience that allows visitors to rub shoulders with people in the church and encounter the gospel through praying before and after games, listening to a devotional, or doing a Bible study. It's not easy to connect with people in church, especially in big churches like ours, being in an hour service once a week. Through our sports programs people who are new to the faith or new to the church meet and develop relationships quickly. When they come into the church service, they have a group of friends and acquaintances, so they feel part of the church body.

Do you only provide competitive programs for adults?

No, we also run youth leagues, clinics, and academies in various sports and even have a basketball club system. Through these we are able to minister to kids through coach-led devotions at practices and create ministry touches with the entire family. In addition, we also offer recreation and fitness groups that are led by people in the church who have a passion for things like mountain biking, golf, fitness training, and triathlon training.

How has the sports program affected the church body?

Our programs are almost fully run by volunteers. If we have 320 kids in our youth basketball league, our five staff members are trying to resource and help 32 volunteer coaches, a number of volunteer referees, and scorekeepers. We supply our coaches with a series of devotionals to use with their teams during practice, and we make sure there is a 10-minute time during the practice where there is no one on the floor, no basketballs bouncing, so they can do the devotional with their teams. For many of our church members this is an ideal way for them to be introduced to serving. They are learning how to "be the church".

Let's talk about Eternity Sports. What is it, and how are you involved?

Eternity Sports grew out of the Sports Outreach Los Angeles (SOLA) organization, my good friend Steve Quatro, and a vision God had given me to equip churches to use sports and inspiring Christian athletes and coaches to boldly play and coach for God's glory. The culture of high-level competitive sports is not friendly to Christianity; in fact it is hostile toward people of faith. This culture has influence all the way down into youth sports as it demands allegiance to sport and to self. Having been adversely affected by sports culture and seeing how it suppresses faith, I wanted to organize and resource athletes and churches so that we could redeem the culture of sports for the Kingdom. We have put out the Playing for Eternity challenge and are praying for one million athletes and coaches to accept the challenge. We are continuing to produce new resources for faith-driven athletes and have developed a docuseries where we interview and connect with professional athletes as they navigate their faith in today's culture. All of this to share the hope of Jesus through those that love and play for God's Kingdom (Josh Merrill, pers. interview, 2022).

---

slam)," "I struck out," "It's time to step up to the plate," "Taking one for the team," an idea or person being "out in left field," a problem being referred to as "a curve ball," "playing hardball," "I'll go to bat for you," "Keep your eye on the ball," and "Heads up." In some cases these phrases are used by people who may not even associate them with the sport of baseball but understand the meaning. Thus, some scholars believe Paul used these words or phrases because they were commonly used in debate rhetoric rather than his familiarity with and support of sport (Ellis 2014, 132).

There were occasions when the Apostle Paul used clear athletic imagery.

Do you not know that in a race all the runners run, but only one gets the prize? Run in such a way as to get the prize. Everyone who competes in the games goes into strict training. They do it to get a crown that will not last, but we do it to get a crown that will last forever. Therefore, I do not run like someone running aimlessly; I do not fight like a boxer beating the air. No, I strike a blow to my body and make it my slave so that after I have preached to others, I myself will not be disqualified for the prize. (1 Corinthians 9:24-27 NIV)

These verses emphasize spiritual realities: living the spiritual life (running the race) and running in a faithful manner (strict training) for an eternal crown or prize (life with Christ for eternity), with great focus and self-discipline (the spiritual disciplines of the Christian life).

Even if Paul was familiar with the terminology and practice of sport, his use of the imagery of athletes, as well as farmers and soldiers, is solely for the purpose of helping his readers understand spiritual truth and not to approve of or teach anything about sport, farming, or war (Weir, n.d.).

The Bible lacks direct pronouncements or commandments concerning sport. How are the Church and individual Christians to determine the appropriateness of participation or its use for ministry? Unlike other historic church leaders, John Calvin (1509-1564) evaluated sport and games from a biblical perspective. He may have been characterized as a stern, self-disciplined workaholic, but his theology "assigned vocational and avocational pursuits to a sphere of life called the *adiaphora*, 'the things indifferent,' in which the Christian's conscience was to hold sway; discernment was to be guided by general principles gleaned from the Scriptures" (Hoffman 2010, 75). He accepted some forms of play because the mere pleasure of playing was deemed a valuable end in itself rather than having life-sustaining useful purposes: "In the acceptance of the present life we must remember that it is given us not only to use but to enjoy. It is obviously the natural order of things that we should indulge in taking pleasure from those things which God has given us liberally to enjoy" (Calvin n.d.). Sport or play was to be balanced, without overindulgence or rigorous asceticism. The Christian's desire to glorify God and his or her mindfulness of eternity were to overcome any temptation levied by sport.

Assessing Sport Participation

All sports are not the same. One can say that he or she is solidly in favor of sport (general) while not approving of certain sports (specific). In this section, sport will be used in a general sense. In the next section, Assessing Sport as a Place for Ministry, more distinction will be made between sports. The question is how biblical principles can guide decisions about whether to participate in sport. These principles are stated using a sampling of relevant Scriptures and a self-examination question.

1. The Mastery Principle

> "'I have the right to do anything,' you say—but not everything is beneficial. 'I have the right to do anything'—but I will not be mastered by anything" (1 Corinthians 6:12 NIV).
>
> "Then Jesus said to his disciples, 'Whoever wants to be my disciple must deny themselves and take up their cross and follow me'" (Matthew 16:24 NIV).
>
> "Therefore I do not run like someone running aimlessly; I do not fight like a boxer beating the air. No, I strike a blow to my body and make it my slave so that after I have preached to others, I myself will not be disqualified for the prize" (1 Corinthians 9:26-27 NIV).

Whether it be cultural norms, contemporary philosophy, or physical desires, all must be subject to God's wisdom and the teachings of Scripture. Consider this self-examination question for the athlete: Can I participate in this sport, continuing to be the person I know myself to be in Christ, or does my participation cause me to think and act contrary to biblical teaching and how I would normally think or act?

2. The Temple Principle

> "Do you not know that your bodies are temples of the Holy Spirit, who is in you, whom you have received from God? You are not your own; you were bought at a price. Therefore honor God with your bodies" (1 Corinthians 6:19-20 NIV).
>
> "Do not offer the parts of your body to sin as an instrument of wickedness, but rather offer yourselves to God as those who have been brought from death to life; and offer every part of yourself to him as an instrument of righteousness" (Romans 6:13 NIV).
>
> "For physical training is of some value, but godliness has value for all things, holding promise for both the present life and the life to come" (1 Timothy 4:8 NIV).

While the soul is more important than the body, the believer needs to care for the body and make sure he or she uses it for good rather than evil. Here is another self-examination question for the athlete: My body is God's temple; God's Spirit lives in me. My body belongs to Him, and I am to use it in His service. In my sporting experience, am I honoring and serving God with my body?

3. The Benefit Principle

> "'I have the right to do anything,' you say—but not everything is beneficial. 'I have the right to do anything'—but not everything is constructive" (1 Corinthians 10:23 NIV).
>
> "Do not let any unwholesome talk come out of your mouths, but only what is helpful for building others up according to their needs, that it may benefit those who listen" (Ephesians 4:29 NIV).
>
> "But to you who are listening I say: Love your enemies, do good to those who hate you, bless those who curse you, pray for those who mistreat you" (Luke 6:27-28 NIV).

The relationships gained through sport allow the Christian athlete to grow, not only in his or her own faith, but to help others find and grow in faith. Another question is this: Is my sporting involvement beneficial or constructive for me and the lives of people around me? Am I helping myself and others grow toward Jesus or away from Him by my participation?

4. The Glory Principle

> "So whether you eat or drink or whatever you do, do it all for the glory of God" (1 Corinthians 10:31 NIV).
>
> "Yet he [Abraham] did not waver through unbelief regarding the promise of God, but was strengthened in his faith and gave glory to God, being fully persuaded that God had power to do what he had promised" (Romans 4:20-21 NIV).
>
> "And whatever you do, whether in word or deed, do it all in the name of the Lord Jesus, giving thanks to God the Father through him" (Colossians 3:17 NIV).

By training and competing, with God in mind, in a way that reflects and pleases Him, God's glory is recognized by the Christian athlete and can be recognized by those around him or her. The Christian athlete should ask him- or herself, In my play, is my motivation to bring God glory or is it to bring myself glory? Do I recognize and appreciate God's presence in my sport experience? Do my actions take away from God's glory?

5. The Fruit Principle

> "But the fruit of the Spirit is love, joy, peace, forbearance, kindness, goodness, faithfulness, gentleness, and self-control" (Galatians 5:22-23 NIV).
>
> "For this very reason, make every effort to add to your faith goodness; and to goodness, knowledge; and to knowledge, self-control; and to self-control, perseverance; and to perseverance, godliness; and to godliness, mutual affection; and to mutual affection, love. For if you possess these qualities in increasing measure, they will keep you from being ineffective and unproductive in your knowledge of our Lord Jesus Christ" (2 Peter 1:5-8 NIV).
>
> "Therefore, as God's chosen people, holy and dearly loved, clothe yourselves with compassion, kindness, humility, gentleness and patience" (Colossians 3:12 NIV).

A self-examination question is, By taking part in my sport, am I growing in and displaying the fruit principles, or is that fruit being undermined in my life because of my participation?

6. The Love Principle

> "'Teacher, which is the greatest commandment in the Law?' Jesus replied: '"Love the Lord your God with all your heart and with all your soul and with all your mind." This is the first and greatest commandment. And the second is like it: "Love your neighbor as yourself"'" (Matthew 22:36-39 NIV).
>
> "A new command I give you: Love one another. As I have loved you, so you must love one another" (John 13:34 NIV).
>
> "We love because he first loved us" (1 John 4:19 NIV).

Here is a final question: Am I successfully carrying out the greatest commandment to love God and love others in my sporting activities?

These principles connect to the experience of joy previously discussed. If one understands one's sport participation as a gift from God and connects with Him through these principles, sport can be joyful, regardless of the circumstances encountered (e.g., wins or losses, peak performance, or injury).

Assessing Sport as a Place for Ministry

Another question to consider is whether sport is a suitable place to share the gospel message or to disciple believers. Does sport have inherent qualities that can assist and accelerate the process of spiritual formation?

Sport as Community

The majority of the New Testament letters were addressed to churches, small groups of believers scattered throughout Asia Minor between Jerusalem and Rome. It was in and through these communities that people came to faith and grew in their relationship with Jesus; believers had a place to belong, be known, be encouraged, grow, learn, and be held accountable. God gifted some within those churches "to equip his people for works of service, so that the body of Christ may be built up until we all reach unity in the faith and in the knowledge of the Son of God and become mature, attaining to the whole measure of the fullness of Christ" (Ephesians 4:12-13 NIV). Among the many instructions given through the New Testament writers, "one another" appears approximately 60 times including, "love one another" (1 Peter 4:8 Berean Study Bible), "encourage one another" (1 Thessalonians 5:11 NIV), and "forgive one another" (Colossians 3:13 NIV).

Sport is a relational bridge builder, and play (as well as sport) promotes the formation of social groups. C.S. Lewis confessed his dislike for doing things with a bat and ball, but while he saw the dark side of sport, he regretted it, saying, "Yet not to like them is a misfortune, because it cuts you off from companionship with many excellent people who can be approached in no other way" (Lewis 1955, 129-130). The relationships formed within these social groups are powerful and can influence one's viewpoints. People might seek help from strangers, but most often they pursue advice or assistance from someone with whom they have an established relationship. Good relationships provide comfort and trust, two key qualities for evangelism and discipleship efforts. For this reason, a church or sports ministry might prefer choosing a relationship-building sport or activity for their ministry setting.

However, sports fans understand that sport can divide and alienate people just as readily as it brings them together. Within a team, competition for a particular position or playing time can create a wedge. Competing communities can stir friction between fans and players. The divisions can intensify and even result in violent behavior. Rivalries exist across the spectrum of youth, high school, club, professional, and national team sports. Examples include Alabama–Auburn (college football), Brazil–Argentina (soccer), LA Dodgers–San Francisco Giants (baseball), India–Pakistan (cricket), Green Bay Packers–Chicago Bears (football), and the Boston

Bruins–Montreal Canadians (hockey). Coaches have been known to characterize opposing teams in militaristic terms and reference them as enemies to be conquered. These characterizations encourage an aggressive mentality that can lead to inappropriate conduct during the competition.

Despite the divisive possibilities that come with sport, positive relationships can develop within sport. Teammates can develop strong relationships because they share common experiences while working together to compete successfully. The player–coach relationship is a unique dynamic, with the coach wielding a great deal of influence. While the coach has more power in the relationship, this does not mean that a player cannot influence a coach. The quality of this relationship depends on a mutual level of trust. A player is less likely to respond to a coach who is demeaning and hypocritical. Additionally, multidirectional relationships exist with fans, team personnel, officials, and opponents.

The word *community*, when considered within a team context denotes a relatively small circle of people. Ministry tends to be most effective within small groups. Jesus modeled the usefulness of this approach. He did not ignore the throngs of people and on numerous occasions spoke and ministered to gatherings of thousands. Yet it was with the intimacy of small groups where Jesus instructed His closest disciples. He chose 12 men with whom He strategically devoted Himself and over the course of three years prepared them to lead His church. He lived among them, taught them, and daily demonstrated His teachings for their benefit. He thoroughly trained them, so they were equipped to apply the life lessons He had taught them. Within the 12 He selected a subgroup of three—Peter, James, and John. They were the ones who accompanied Him along the mountainside and witnessed His transfiguration (Luke 9:23-36). They were the three with Jesus when He raised Jairus' daughter from the dead (Mark 5:21-43). On the night of His betrayal, it was Peter, James, and John He selected to join Him as He agonized in prayer in the Garden of Gethsemane (Matthew 26:36-56).

The community aspect of team sports makes them a favorable environment for ministry. A church or ministry wanting to affect a large number of people might organize a youth league with a number of teams. Each team (community) would provide a small-group atmosphere where the coach has the opportunity to know and relate to each player, and the players relate to and learn from one another. The

overall community of the league also gives opportunities for ministry with the families of participants.

This is not to say that individual sports are not a place for ministry. With individual sports a coach might be able to go deeper in relationship because he or she is only dealing with one player. The coach knows the individual athlete better than he or she would be able to know each player in a team sport setting.

Sport as Laboratory

A laboratory is a place of discovery, experimentation, observation, testing, proving, and manufacturing. The sport environment of practices, games, travel, and all the adjoining social interactions provides ample opportunities to teach and learn spiritual lessons. If one is intentional and diligent, sport can become a laboratory where participants can develop character qualities such as self-control, patience, and faithfulness. Along with game tactics and technical skill development, coaches have the opportunity to pour themselves into the lives of their players, teaching life lessons and helping them to grow physically, socially, and spiritually. Besides the essential physical disciplines of training, nutrition, and rest, coaches can assist their athletes in practicing **spiritual disciplines**.

Dallas Willard's Golden Triangle illustrates how Christians can grow spiritually. Each side of the triangle is essential and works in conjunction with the other two: "Interaction with God's Spirit in and around us," practice of "spiritual disciplines," and "the faithful acceptance of everyday problems" describe how one can "put on the new self" (Colossians 3:9-10) (Willard 2006, 26-31).

The third side of Willard's triangle, the faithful acceptance of everyday problems, is where the laboratory of sport can be particularly helpful. Everyday life has its share of obstacles and temptations, but the norm is to try to avoid that which is unpleasant, evade confrontation, and escape conflict. The Scriptures state that these unpleasant circumstances will test the faith of the individual (or group), producing perseverance, godly wisdom, and the development of spiritual maturity (James 1:2-5). In the sport environment, especially in face-to-face contact sports, trials and tests are normal, even magnified, in both training and game situations. Coaches use natural and devised teachable moments to challenge players to cope with an array of circumstances. Coaches routinely stop action during training to evaluate progress, make

---

spiritual disciplines—Behaviors or exercises that draw individuals to God, allowing Him to grow them to spiritual maturity. Examples of spiritual disciplines include prayer, reading Scripture, worship, giving, submission, fasting, and confession. These practices are common among believers but might be expressed differently from one individual to another.

corrections, and explain concepts to the entire team. They provide halftime and postgame analysis and evaluations to determine the team's plan of action. A coach or sports minister can use teachable moments to apply spiritual principles. For example, if the team has been studying James 1:2-5, the trials and temptations can be viewed as opportunities for **spiritual formation**. The coach or sports minister can reinforce these concepts in training and game situations as part of real-time feedback or half-time or postgame talk.

Willard places significant emphasis on the physical body's role in discipleship and spiritual formation. The body becomes a tool for spiritual growth rather than a hindrance.

> *Our part in this transformation, in addition to constant faith and hope in Christ, is purposeful, strategic use of our bodies in ways that will retrain them, replacing the "motions of sin in our members" with the motions of Christ. This is how we take up our cross daily. It is how we submit our bodies, as a living sacrifice, how we offer the parts of our body to him as "instruments of righteousness" (Romans 6:13). (Willard 2006, 85)*

The sheer physicality of the sport setting lends itself to spiritual formation. Willard's writing is especially revealing:

> *Let me be as clear as possible. When we speak of spiritual formation we are speaking of the formation of the human spirit. And the spirit is the will or the heart and by extension, the character. And that, in practice, lives mainly in our bodies. The one reason why the idea of spiritual transformation through being merely preached at and taught doesn't work is because it does not involve the body in the process of transformation. One of the ironies of spiritual formation is that every "spiritual" discipline is a bodily behavior. We have to involve the body in spiritual formation because that's where we live and what we live from. . . . Spiritual formation is never merely inward. (Willard, n.d.)*

The laboratory of sport challenges the Christian to overcome the temptations to act in an un-Christlike manner. If a person can do this in the heat of competition, especially in those of face-to-face contact sports, he or she should be able to face similar temptation in life away from sport. Through ongoing faith in Christ and effort on his or her part in the laboratory of sport, the Christian can grow in faith and help the non-Christian get a picture of how Christ can change a life. Paul W. Powell, Baptist pastor, seminary dean and prolific writer, is thought to have written this: "God is more concerned about our character than our comfort. His goal is not to pamper us, but to perfect us spiritually."

Sport as the Enemy of the Status Quo

The environment of competitive sport is one of constant improvement. If a player is not improving, he or she will be left behind as others surpass him or her. Likewise, improvement and growth in discipleship and spiritual formation can be expected, even demanded.

Many church members fail to recognize the need for spiritual formation. Others recognize the need but fail to act. Pollster George Barna observes, "Unfortunately, my research reveals that a majority of believers who figure out where the journey goes, and what it takes to maximize the opportunity God grants us by completing the journey to wholeness, instead choose to settle for a less complete and fulfilling life" (Barna 2011). Willard agrees, using an athletic illustration: "A baseball player who expects to excel in the game without adequate exercise of his body is no more ridiculous than the Christian who hopes to be able to act in the manner of Christ when put to the test without the appropriate exercise in godly living" (Willard 1988, 4-5).

Athletes need a vision for transformation. The vision can come from experiences of success and failure, strength and weakness, training and competition, and challenges from players and coaches. A vision enables an athlete and coach to recognize potential. Once potential is recognized, actualization can become a reality through a commitment to the process of development. Various drills, exercises, and repetitions perfect skill development. A good coach guides the process, making corrections and providing encouragement along the way.

Spiritual progress is synonymous with **sanctification**. Vision, commitment, and implementation are all needed for spiritual formation, but the ultimate fulfillment relies on this work of the Holy Spirit (i.e., Romans 15:16; 1 Corinthians 6:11). Sanctification is an act of grace. The individual has a part to play under the guidance of the Holy Spirit (2 Peter 1:3-8;

---

spiritual formation—An ongoing process whereby believers intentionally cooperate with the Holy Spirit to conform their thoughts, values, and actions to those of Christ.

sanctification—A work of the Holy Spirit; a freedom from the constraints of sin; a process of becoming holy and pure.

Colossians 3:5, 8, 12). Willard explains how grace and effort combine in the process of spiritual formation: "Grace is opposed to earning, not effort. In fact, nothing inspires and enhances effort like the experience of grace" (Willard 2006, 80).

Biblical transformation and the sanctifying work of the Holy Spirit encompasses every aspect of a believer's life. Motives, behaviors, attitudes, and speech all come under His scrutiny. Faith in Jesus is not compartmentalized; it is not confined to a church building. A follower of Jesus is always His follower—whenever and wherever, including the athletic arena. The integration of faith with sport can influence the treatment of a teammate, a coach, an official, another competitor, a spectator, and so on. If the Christian athlete or coach can effectively live out the Christ-life in the sport setting (Christian or secular), it will add weight to the words that he or she shares about what it means to be a Christ-follower.

SUMMARY

Eric Liddell, created in the image of God, recognized running as a gift to be cultivated and enjoyed, whether running on the beach, training for competition, racing in a village, or competing on the world stage of the Olympics. His faith assured him that he did not need to prove himself worthy of people's admiration or of God's love and acceptance. He was competitive and wanted to win every race; however, his joy was not in the winning but in the running, as was seen at the beginning of the chapter: "But He also made me fast, and when I run, I feel his pleasure." Liddell exemplifies carrying the play-spirit' into competitive sport. Harold Abrahams might have enjoyed simple non-competitive running (we are not told), but he described himself as an addicted runner who used running as a defensive weapon against his critics. Winning was essential, but even winning did not result in anything beyond a transient sense of joy.

For those who wish to minister to others in the sport environment, there must be a clear understanding of the integration of faith and sport. Faith—what one believes about God and their relationship with Him as found in the Bible—must inform whether, why, and how Christians participate in sport. The Kingdom of God is prioritized above the allure of sport. The arena of sport offers opportunities to come to faith in Jesus Christ and to be sanctified by the work of the Holy Spirit. Spiritual formation is the primary focus of those who participate and organize sport with ministry in mind.

REVIEW AND DISCUSSION QUESTIONS

1. Explain what it means to play using Huizinga's six characteristics.
2. Compare play to sport, and list some of the differences.
3. Discuss the problems and potential of competition in relation to sports ministry.
4. What are some of the biblical principles that can help the Christian determine if he or she should participate in competitive sport?
5. Describe the characteristics of competitive sport where evangelistic and discipleship ministries can thrive, and identify characteristics of potential problems that may be encountered by a sports minister.
6. From what you have read in this chapter, which sports do you think would be the best fit for a church sports ministry program?

Postgame evangelism in Brazil with Portuguese translation.

CHAPTER 6

Gospel Communication

"We have good news to communicate. So if evangelism is to take place, there must be communication—a true communication between ancient revelation and modern culture. This means that our message must be at the same time, faithful [to Scripture] and contemporary."

John Stott, Anglican minister, author, and theologian

LEARNING OBJECTIVES

After studying this chapter, you should be able to do the following:
- Understand the commissioning and equipping authority of Jesus to share one's faith
- Explain key components essential for effective gospel communication
- Construct one's own personal faith journey by following the example of the three-part outline of the Apostle Paul's story
- Discuss biblical concepts and applications that connect sport-related objects for use in teaching life lessons
- Construct a devotional message by following a four-part outline method
- Acknowledge the complete dependence on God for ministry effectiveness that transforms lives

During a short-term collegiate women's soccer trip to the Czech Republic, players wore faith bracelets that provided a succinct way to present the gospel. Simply explained, these bracelets represented heaven; signified sin; salvation through the shed blood of Jesus; a cleansed heart; and spiritual growth. Whether it is a bracelet, necklace, cards, or a paneled ball, the use of such visuals to initiate discussion and expound on the central message of the gospel has been a widely used evangelism method proven to be effective.

During a match ministry occasion, a player spoke to members of the opposing team and spectators about her faith in Jesus. Upon completion, she invited interested listeners to join the team at a local pizzeria. Whether it was genuine interest in her message or the opportunity for free pizza, a group of people responded positively to her invitation. While there, one young Czech woman engaged a team member in conversation. She was intrigued by the message about faith in Jesus. She herself was unchurched, but something about this women's team and the message she heard resonated with her. The player used her colors of faith bracelet to explain the fundamental message of the gospel, and the young woman posed thoughtful questions throughout the explanation. When the time came for the team to depart, the young woman was told the time and location where the team would eat breakfast the next morning. Her desire was to see the team prior to their departure to a new city. When morning arrived, the young woman was seated at a table awaiting the team. She was joined by three other young Czech women. The three new women had traveled throughout the night by train at the invitation of their friend so that they, too, could "hear words about Jesus." Pointing to the colors of faith bracelet, she asked the soccer player to explain the bracelet's meaning to her three friends. Once again, the central message of the gospel was shared, with many questions asked along the way. Ultimately, no decisions were made that day by the four women. Yet they clearly heard and understood the salvation message. The soccer team left for their next destination but continued to pray for the women, trusting that God would stir their hearts to receive Jesus for themselves.

Gospel presentations conclude with the full spectrum of responses, from rejection to heartfelt reception and everything in between. Ministry teams are commissioned to faithfully communicate the gospel. The receptivity of the message is left in the hands of God. He alone can stir a wayward heart. The emphasis of this chapter is gospel communication—how the gospel and its influence can be communicated by Christians in sport. Only a sampling of key methodologies will be examined.

Gospel Communication

Jesus commissions and empowers His followers to proclaim the gospel message (Matthew 28:18-20; Acts 1:8). Throughout the centuries, faithful believers have trumpeted this good news of salvation. Yet in the modern era, the idea of one's faith being a private matter is frequently heralded. This concept contradicts the mandate of Jesus and the bold example of His early disciples. Prior to His ascension, Jesus told His disciples that they "will be my witnesses" (Acts 1:8 NIV), and when told by the religious leaders to no longer speak the name of Jesus, Peter and John asserted, "Which is right in God's eyes: to listen to you, or to him. As for us, we cannot help speaking about what we have seen and heard" (Acts 4:19-20

NIV). Christian faith is indeed personal, but it is never private. Recall Jesus' words to His disciples imploring them to let their light shine for all the world to see and to never let it be hidden under a bowl (Matthew 5:14-16).

Steve Connor asserts that "evangelism is arguably the most written about and least practiced subject in Christendom: like the fishing club that meets every week and talks about fishing but never actually fishes, or the chap that stirs the paint but never takes it out of the pot" (Connor 2003, 54). Connor continues:

Evangelism: the word is derived from the Greek verb euangelizomai, to announce or proclaim good news. We have great news to share, and we should love to tell the story. The message is not ours but God's: this message must be clear, and our method must be strategic. Communicating these truths is a "commission"—a direct order from God to all Christians, no one is exempt. A non-proclaiming Christian is a contradiction in terms. . . . You may ask: What does this have to do with sports ministry? We need to understand that ministry is first and foremost about God: introducing and cultivating personal salvation through and in obedience to Jesus Christ (Connor 2003, 55).

Heart-shaped gospel colors are used as an evangelistic tool during a sports ministry team visit to an elementary school in Costa Rica.

Proclaiming Jesus is much more than a mandate. It is a passionate, stirring desire that cannot be silenced. The prophet Jeremiah and the Apostle Paul both attested to the validity that the word of God within them could not be contained:

His word is in my heart like a fire, a fire shut up in my bones. I am weary of holding it in; indeed I cannot. (Jeremiah 20:9 NIV)

I am compelled to preach. Woe to me if I do not preach the gospel! (1 Corinthians 9:16 NIV)

The same Jesus who was prophesied by the prophets and preached by the apostles is the same Jesus proclaimed by modern sports ministers. The stirring of the heart from centuries past is the same stirring today.

Four Key Evangelism Sites

Sports ministry most frequently uses these four sites of evangelism:

1. *Individual:* one on one
2. *Small group:* team or huddle group
3. *Large group:* league, banquet, special event
4. *Mass group:* crusade or rally

The *message* of the gospel is unchanging and centuries old. However, the *method* of gospel proclamation is subject to change and modification. **Gospel communication methodology** is the strategy used to convey or transmit the good news of faith in Jesus Christ. The methodology and message content should fluctuate depending on the occasion and audience. For instance, the message emphasis to a church congregation should differ from one given in a public setting. The size of the audience should influence what method to use. A discussion among four friends at the kitchen table should differ from the method employed in a 5,000-seat arena. The location can also dictate methodology. Is the occasion indoors or outside? Is the message presented in one language, or is translation necessary? These are a few of the factors when considering the most appropriate methodology.

Two Keys to Effective Gospel Communication

Two key elements of effective gospel communication are (1) what is seen and (2) what is heard. This concept is **incarnational living**. People must see the authentic living out of the gospel—biblical concepts being practically applied to daily life. It is one thing

---

gospel communication methodology—The strategy used to convey or transmit the good news of faith in Jesus Christ.

incarnational living—The ongoing process of practicing the admonitions of the gospel, biblical concepts being practically applied to daily life.

to talk about forgiveness and another to visually see grudges put aside and forgiveness practiced. To hear about love and to definitively witness its demonstration. To advocate community service and to actually accompany one's neighbors into the trenches. As the epistle of James admonishes, "Do not merely listen to the word, and so deceive yourselves. Do what it says" (James 1:22 NIV). The words of Jesus poignantly express, "Why do you call me 'Lord, Lord' and do not do what I say?" (Luke 6:46 NIV). The message of the Bible is clear: God's word must not merely be talked about or only believed; it is to be obeyed through application. The sincere conviction of one's belief is demonstrated by the subsequent actions one exhibits. Consequently, will the gospel be demonstrated through the lives of sports ministers? Will observers see Jesus in the people who are talking about Him and claim to be His representatives? Will ministry recipients be treated with genuine Christlike care and concern? Will service be offered in an others-centered approach? Will the lives of Christian athletes compel people to want what they have? Will the gospel be communicated by what is seen?

The second component of gospel communication is what is heard. How is the message disseminated? What methods of communication are to be employed? A powerful method to convey the gospel is the use of story. Biblical story encapsulates the presence of God. It enables the hearer to envision the reality of God's intervention within human experience. The Bible is filled with stories of God's interaction with His creation, and His people's interaction with Him and with one another.

Biblical Narrative

Narrative is a powerful communication tool. Both the Old and New Testaments include numerous instances of **biblical narrative**. Ever since childhood Sunday school classes have been held, Old Testament stories have been retold—Noah and the ark (Genesis 6-9); the adoption of Moses by Pharoah's daughter (Exodus 2); Israel's deliverance at the Red Sea (Exodus 14); David's confrontation with the Philistine giant, Goliath (1 Samuel 17); Daniel in the den of lions (Daniel 6); and Shadrach, Meshach, and Abednego rescued from the flames of a fiery furnace (Daniel 3). Likewise, the New Testament reiterates narratives such as the story of Jesus' birth (Luke 2); the restoration of Bartimaeus' sight (Mark 10:46-52); the salvation of a greedy tax collector named Zacchaeus (Luke 19); the trial, crucifixion, and resurrection of Jesus (Luke 23-24); the outpouring of the Holy Spirit on the day of Pentecost (Acts 2); and the salvation of Saul on the road to Damascus (Acts 9). Stories help to figuratively apply flesh to spiritual principles. Many of the life lessons revealed through biblical narrative can be used in a sports ministry setting. These stories can serve as analogies for modern sport lessons: David and Goliath were engaged in a competitive scenario; athletic determination mirrors the abiding trust of Shadrach, Meshach, and Abednego; and a "never quit" mentality shadows the perseverance of Jesus—all transferable principles. The lasting endurance of stories testifies to the power of narrative as an effective tool for sports ministry communication.

Parables

Closely associated with biblical narrative are **biblical parables**. Jesus was a master teacher, and his parables were analogous stories that enhanced His message. The parables were reflective, causing listeners, including His closest disciples, to question their meaning. Examples of His parables include the sower and the seed (Matthew 13), the ten virgins (Matthew 25), the unforgiving servant (Matthew 18), the lost son (Luke 15), and the good Samaritan (Luke 10).

Three common gospel communication methods that correspond to biblical narrative and parables are (1) personal story, (2) object lessons, and (3) devotional messages. These three approaches are widely used within sports ministries.

Personal Story

Each individual's life can be represented as a personal story shaped by God as He continually adds chapters to the lives of His followers. Personal story is a broad heading encompassing one's life in its entirety. A type of personal story is one's **faith journey**. The content of a faith journey will depend on the occasion, audience, and designated amount of speaking time. It is

---

biblical narratives—Stories, often historic, that reveal the character of God and the redemptive plan for His creation. They comprise nearly half the content of the Bible.

biblical parables—Real-life or fictitious stories or allegories used to convey truth and life lessons. They typically use common objects, scenes from daily life, circumstances, and individuals to illustrate intended precepts.

faith journey—A personal account of what God has done and continues to do in one's life, most often emphasizing how one has come to know Christ and the transforming results of that decision.

Interview With a Professional

Miriam Mendes Reiche

Missionary in Japan serving with Conexão Voluntários em Campo

Bachelor's degree in education from University of Rio de Janeiro State, Brazil

Miriam Reiche has been involved with Sports Ministry since 2007, serving in Brazil and other countries of South, Central, and North America; South Africa; the Middle East; Europe; and Asia. Her ministry is mainly focused on sports ministry leadership development, discipleship, and mentoring. Reiche's mission is serving, training, equipping, and mentoring people to be and do what God wants them to be and do so that they can be used by Him to transform lives and communities.

What prompted you to become involved in sports ministry?

I have always loved sports and Christ. But I didn't know I could use my passion for sports to share my faith and love for Christ. Then in 2007, during the Pan American Games in Rio de Janeiro, my church hosted the Chicago Eagles men's and women's soccer teams, and I had the chance to learn from Pastor Rick McKinley about sports ministry. Two months later three other young people and I started a sports ministry project in a local community near the church to which I belonged at the time. I always say that community was my first mission field. After coordinating this project for six years, I passed the baton to another leader and started to dedicate myself more to training sports ministry leaders in Brazil and other nations.

Who have been your sports ministry role models?

My first role model was Pastor Rick McKinley, who was the director of the Chicago Eagles ministry. His integrity, servant heart, generosity, compassion, and love for God and for people inspired me. Pastor Jonson Tadeu and Pastor Marcos Grava, whom I met in 2010 during my first experience in sports ministry outside of Brazil, became role models too. They played a very important role in developing the sports ministry in Brazil. Pastor Jonson inspires me with his passion for sports and for people. He truly cares about and loves people. Pastor Marcos inspires me with his love for the nations, his integrity in everything he does, and his willingness to share his faith with nonbelievers. I had the privilege to spend lots of time and serve on different occasions with these three men of God and testify how they lead like Jesus.

How do you maintain your own personal fervor for the Lord while ministering to others?

In addition to my daily devotion, I set aside moments once a week to study the Scriptures, to worship God, to go to a place surrounded by natural beauty to contemplate Him and hear His voice. That is, I try to put spiritual disciplines into practice in my life because I need it to maintain a healthy faith, ministry, and relationship with God and people. The book *Celebration of the Disciplines* by Richard Foster helped me a lot in this process of building a life of devotion to God. And as a missionary, I love to read biographies of missionaries who inspire and encourage me.

Why do you believe sport to be an effective ministry tool?

I believe it because I have lived and experienced it since 2007. I have seen God using sport language and sport people in many different and powerful ways in such different contexts. I personally have experienced God using sport to bring salvation, deliverance, healing, and purpose to lives, and to the restoration of people, marriages, and more. Sport is possibly one of the easiest and simplest languages to connect people's hearts and needs to the gospel message.

How do you communicate the gospel within a sports ministry context?

First, through your life and witness—playing, living, acting, and reacting according to the Christian's manual, which is the Bible. Be a "little Christ" in the world of sport. Second, be sensitive and mindful, and make the most of the opportunities God gives you to share your faith, especially your personal testimony, your history with God, what you have learned from Him, your

> continued

journey with Jesus. Sport is a challenging context for faith because it exposes who we really are. However, for this reason, a good testimony is a concise and clear proclamation of the gospel message of Jesus.

What principles do you consider to be most important when communicating the gospel in a cross-cultural setting?

When I think about communicating the gospel in another culture, I always think about the Lord Jesus, especially in the Bible verses of Philippians 2:5-8. Jesus is the greatest example of someone who came to communicate His message in a completely different cultural context from his own. I learn the following principles from Jesus: self-denial, humility, servant and teachable heart, compassion, love, and obedience.

What advice do you give to anyone interested in pursuing a sports ministry vocation?

I think each of us must be and do what God created us to be and do. Finding out and living this God-given purpose is a blessing that everyone should enjoy. So first I would recommend this person to find his or her life purpose. In this process of seeking, take the chance to experience sports ministry in different contexts, know sports ministry leaders, talk to them, read about sports ministry. By so doing, you can confirm if this ministry is for you; what your role is in this ministry; and where you fit according to the gifts, talents, skills, knowledge, and experiences God has given you. Finally, if you don't start where you are, you'll never know how far God can take you.

Is there anything else you would like to share about the communication of the gospel within a sports ministry setting?

The more I study, work, experiment with, and learn about sports ministry, the more I realize the need to be simple with Jesus. Just live like Jesus in the sport world and communicate the gospel message as simply as possible—as He did. Feel compassion and love for people because compassion drives us to share. Love is the fuel and the right motivation for us to continue effectively sharing the gospel of Jesus regardless of context and circumstance.

---

beneficial to practice sharing one's faith journey in a concise and compelling manner. When a faith journey is shared, in essence, the speaker is saying, "If God has worked in my life, He can also work in your life." It enables the listener to catch a glimpse of what it means to be a Christian and how he or she also can become one. If the hearer is already a believer, the faith journey can be a word of encouragement that heightens the mutual bond that is shared together as followers of Jesus.

The Example of the Apostle Paul

A biblical example of a faith journey is Paul's testimony of his conversion as presented before King Agrippa in Acts 26. The context of Paul's occasion is his imprisonment in Caesarea. As a Roman citizen, Paul was awaiting transfer to Rome to stand trial for accusations of Jewish law violations as alleged by the Sanhedrin. King Agrippa and Bernice had traveled to Caesarea to visit the governor, Porcius Festus. During their visit, they heard about Paul's case and requested an audience with him. Acts 26 details Paul's defense

before Agrippa and the high-ranking officials of the city. His testimony adopts a three-point outline about his conversion to the Christian faith: (1) life before his conversion, (2) the conversion details, and (3) life after his conversion. Paul's account can serve as a model for training purposes as one constructs one's own faith journey.

Paul's Example: Before His Conversion   Paul chronicled his life beginning with his upbringing. His purpose was to build a connecting bridge of communication with his listeners. He wanted them to personally identify with his story so that they might consider their own stories. He appealed to his listener's knowledge about himself, citing, "The Jewish people all know the way I have lived ever since I was a child. . . . They have known me for a long time and can testify, if they are willing" (Acts 26:4-5 NIV). He continues by exclaiming that he lived according to the strictest sect of Judaism as a Pharisee. He was convinced that those who claimed allegiance to Jesus were grossly misguided and deserved imprisonment— even death. He obtained authority and commission

A postgame faith journey is shared with the help of a translator to a Costa Rican team.

from the chief priests to track down followers of Jesus. He was obsessed with ridding the world of Christians, even traveling to foreign cities in the hope of forcing them to blaspheme and disavow Jesus. When Christians were put to death, Paul voted for their execution. His listeners knew the truth about what he was sharing. They knew Paul's background and his role as a passionate, highly educated Pharisee. By connecting with their shared knowledge, Paul drew his listeners into his own story so that they were prepared to hear about his conversion.

As individuals prepare their own faith journeys, it is important for them to think about common connecting bridges that they might adopt as they speak to their audiences. What "before" components will best enable their hearers to identify with them? How can they best begin their message to captivate the attention of their listeners? Can they identify common themes that would fit the sport-minded culture? Several topical possibilities include a personal story related to the love of sport, striving for excellence, personal pride, winning and losing, being a team member, contentment and dissatisfaction, sport, and personal identity. Would any lead-in rhetorical questions engage the audience and encourage personal reflection?

Paul's Example: The Conversion Experience

The second component of Paul's faith journey is his conversion experience. Paul (formerly known as Saul) was intent to destroy the Christian faith and was persuaded to obtain the commission of the chief priests to embark on a journey to foreign cities. It was during one of these excursions that Paul was miraculously encountered along a road to Damascus. A blinding light from heaven illuminated Paul's path, causing him and his companions to fall to the ground. A voice resounded, "Saul, Saul, why do you persecute me?" (26:14 NIV). With fearful bewilderment, Paul asked who it was that was speaking to him. Jesus identified himself and told Paul that his life would no longer be the same. Rather than persecuting the followers of Jesus, Paul would begin preaching the very name he had attempted to silence. He would be sent to both his own people (the Jewish nation) and to the Gentiles to open blind eyes and proclaim freedom from the domain of Satan and the forgiveness of sins attainable through Jesus.

Paul's conversion is a dramatic story of tremendous transformation. As individuals consider their own conversion experience, their story may be quite different from Paul's. Yet the same Jesus who encountered Paul on the road to Damascus is the same Jesus who meets people today. How can they best describe their own encounter with Jesus? What were the circumstances that led them to acknowledge that Jesus is Savior and Lord? By explaining their own story, each speaker will enable listeners to hear how they, too, can experience Jesus for themselves.

Paul's Example: After His Conversion

The third part of Paul's story is the aftereffect of his conversion. Paul contended that he was obedient to the vision from heaven. He preached repentance in the name of Jesus to those in Damascus, Jerusalem, and Judea. He spoke to Jew and Gentile alike. Because of his preaching, his life was threatened, and he was seized by the Jewish authorities. It was for this reason that he now stood before Agrippa, trusting the faithfulness of God to sustain him as he proclaimed the suffering and resurrection of the Christ. Hearing about the resurrection, Festus abruptly interrupted Paul, protesting loudly that Paul's tremendous learning had caused him to go mad. Yet Paul appealed to Agrippa's understanding since the king was familiar with what Paul was saying:

> "King Agrippa, do you believe the prophets? I know you do." Then Agrippa said to Paul, "Do you think that in such a short time you can persuade me to be a Christian?" Paul replied, "Short time or long—I pray to God that not only you but all who are listening to me today may become what I am, except for these chains." (Acts 26:27-29 NIV)

Paul's defense concluded with Agrippa's rejection of the message. Paul had ushered his audience to the very doorstep of the Kingdom of God, inviting them to encounter Jesus as he had done. Agrippa and the others could have had their own Damascus road experience with Jesus but instead chose to walk away. This occasion contrasts with the recorded response of the crowd on the day of Pentecost when Peter boldly proclaimed repentance in the name of Jesus (Acts 2). Peter's listeners were deeply convicted by his message, and about 3,000 were convinced, placed their faith in Jesus, and were baptized (2:41). Faithful proclamation of the gospel is the responsibility of Christ followers, whether thousands or no one embraces the appeal to come to Jesus.

As individuals reflect on Paul's "after," they can consider the influences that their conversion has had on the direction of their own lives. What has a relationship with Jesus done, and what does it continue to do? What transformational changes have been experienced? What difference does Jesus make? Has their character been affected? What about their speech? Do they have a different outlook on life? And what about their motivations and desires?

Similar to Paul's example, assessment will need to be made if it is an appropriate time and occasion to offer an invitation to the listeners to respond to the faith journey. Would they, too, like to place their trust in Jesus? The response could follow the pattern of Peter's crowd on the day of Pentecost when hearts were pierced and newfound faith was birthed. Yet the invitation can also fall on deaf hearts, rendering no apparent conviction as evidenced at Paul's defense

before King Agrippa. Whether conversions are bountiful or nonexistent, the objective of sports ministry is to proclaim the gospel faithfully, ultimately trusting the Holy Spirit to penetrate and soften hard hearts to the life-changing love of Jesus. When testifying about God and His word, it is powerful and not to be underestimated. The Scriptures declare the sustaining influence of God's word:

> "For my thoughts are not your thoughts, neither are your ways my ways," declares the LORD. "As the heavens are higher than the earth, so are my ways higher than your ways and my thoughts than your thoughts. As the rain and the snow come down from heaven, and do not return to it without watering the earth and making it bud and flourish, so that it yields seed for the sower and bread for the eater, so is my word that goes out from my mouth: It will not return to me empty, but will accomplish what I desire and achieve the purpose for which I sent it." (Isaiah 55:8-11 NIV)

Do not be discouraged if your faith journey elicits little response. Even the Apostle Paul's faith journey beset rejection. Gospel seeds planted on one occasion may bear fruit at another time. Evangelistic results are encouraging, but God seeks faithfulness more than results. After all, it is His work to convict the heart; sports ministry adherents serve as instruments in His hands.

Key Points When Preparing a Faith Journey

The focus of Paul's faith journey was his conversion—in his case, a life opposed to Jesus transformed into a staunch representative and ardent follower of the Lord. He became known by Christians as "the man who formerly persecuted us is now preaching the faith he once tried to destroy" (Galatians 1:23 NIV). And as a result, they praised God because of Paul. As sports ministers prepare their individual faith journeys, they should keep in mind several things:

1. One's faith journey is uniquely one's own. No two faith journeys are exactly alike. Each will have identifiable similarities since the same Jesus authors each story, but each will also have characteristic nuances. Embrace the story God chooses to write in your life. It is the one He is giving you.

2. Sharing one's faith journey does not mean that everything has been figured out and perfected. It is an ongoing journey that confronts the ups and downs of life. Listeners will identify

SPORTS MINISTRY IN ACTION

Sample Faith Journey: Jen Mattison, Collegiate Soccer Player, Discovers an Answer

Jennifer Rickert

The following is a transcribed account of Jen Mattison sharing her faith journey at a school assembly program in Australia. Jen had traveled to the Sydney area as a member of the Houghton University women's soccer team; they had partnered with Missionary Athletes International (Charlotte) and Athletes in Action (Australia) for a short-term international sports ministry trip during the spring of 1998. Mattison was a team captain and three-time All-Conference, All-Region, and NAIA All-American Honorable Mention soccer player at Houghton (1996-1998). During her senior year she was the president of her campus' chapter of the Fellowship of Christian Athletes (FCA). The video of her faith journey presentation has been widely used as a classroom example instructing students about the construction of a concise faith journey message.

For most of my life I've never known what it was like to live in a functioning two-parent household. My mom's first marriage ended in divorce when I was five. She remarried when I was eight, but eventually that ended in divorce also the summer before my senior year, which is like your year 12. I wish I could say that was a happy 10 years, but unfortunately, I can't because my father was an alcoholic. So I spent most of those years trying to understand why a can of beer was more important to him than I was. I was at that age in school where doing what you're not supposed to was cool—like going out on weekends drinking and smoking. I had to ask myself, "Was being cool enough to forget all the anger that I had at home? To forget crying myself to sleep every night because I didn't have anybody to talk to about my problems and to tell me it was okay?" Every day I'd ask myself, "Why me, why me?" It didn't end there because my friends couldn't understand why I wouldn't just go out drinking with them. So most of the time they would forget about me—not even call me because they knew I wouldn't go with them. Most of high school I felt very alone and was often by myself.

The one thing I had to keep me going and to help me cope with everything going on at school and at home was soccer. I started playing when I was 10. By the time I got to high school, I knew I never wanted to stop playing soccer. There was one little problem—we didn't have a high school soccer team at my school. My friends and parents talked with the school, and they started a soccer program. In seventh grade, I became the starting center forward for our team. As the years went on, I enjoyed soccer, but things at home grew worse. As I said earlier, before my senior year, my parents got divorced. At the same time, I had to start considering what college I would go to. I thought it would be easy because I had good grades and there were a lot of college soccer coaches calling me and wanting me to come play for them. As it turned out, it was more difficult because I was looking for a school that didn't allow drinking. None of the schools who were looking at me fit this category. After a while I thought I would just have to go with it so I could play soccer.

One of my teachers in high school suggested that I go to Houghton University. Even though I only lived 45 minutes away, I had really never heard of it before. He said, "They have everything you are looking for—they have a great soccer team; they don't allow drinking or smoking." It was close to home, which I could be happy at now, because my father was gone. They had a great Christian atmosphere. Everything about it really sounded great, but I really wasn't sure about the Christian part. I wasn't a Christian. I had gone to church a few times but was really clueless when it came to "God stuff." And I was worried about not fitting in, and I was sick about not fitting in. I decided to go there, and as it turns out, it was the second-best decision of my life. I made better friends there in the first year than I had all through high school. No one cared that I didn't want to drink. Everyone

> continued

seemed to care about me as a person. And I really didn't know why, but I found out that it was because they knew who Jesus was. They began talking to me about who Jesus was. They said He cares about me. I don't ever have to feel alone because He's there for me. He has a plan for me. And that's when I finally had an answer to my question, "Why me?" Because it was a part of God's plan that I wasn't even aware of. So on September 22, 1995, at the age of 18, I made the best decision of my life. And it was this: I prayed to God and asked Him to come into my heart, to be a part of my life.

Even though life is still tough, I don't have to go through it alone because He is there for me. He is faithful, and He is the only one who was faithful to me. I wanted to share this with you because life can be tough, and you don't have to go through it alone. God wants to have a relationship with you. He wants to be there for you, and He wants to be your friend.

readily with the speaker who honestly shares about life's struggles. Even the Apostle Paul concluded that he had not yet been made perfect but was pressing forward to what Jesus had in store for him (Philippians 3:12-14).

3. Do not inordinately bask in the "before" section. The purpose of the "before" is to build a relational connecting bridge as an introduction to the content that is most important. Emphasis must be placed on what God has done and continues to do in your life. Bring Jesus to the forefront of your story.

4. Use concise clarity, and refrain from **Christianese**. Examples might include expressions such as, "When I was saved" or "I was born again," and theological terms such as *justified*, *sanctified*, and *redeemed*. If words of Christianese are used, they should be explained thoroughly.

5. Select an identifiable central theme that threads its way throughout your story.

6. Because audiences will vary, be prepared to share a different component of your story depending on the perceived needs of your listeners.

Object Lessons

By studying the teaching examples of Jesus, sports ministers can develop similar methods to convey instructional messages. One of the teaching tools that Jesus employed was the use of object lessons—physical representations that illustrate spiritual truths. As mentioned previously, His parables are classic examples:

1. Various types of soil and their suitability for the fruitful germination of seed correlates with the types of human hearts and their receptivity to the gospel. (Luke 8:4-15)

2. The herding of sheep and goats portrays the gathering of the nations for judgment; the sheep represent the chosen, and the goats represent the lost. (Matthew 25:31-46)

3. The parable of the prodigal son teaches multiple lessons, including the gracious mercy of the loving Father, forgiveness, and restoration for the wayward, and it describes the joyous celebration that accompanies repentance. (Luke 15:11-32)

Jesus used *people as object lessons*:

1. The widow who gave out of her poverty is commended for her generosity. (Luke 21:1-4)

2. Jesus elevated children as examples of the kind of faith to be practiced by his followers. (Luke 18:15-17)

3. The healed Samaritan leper was affirmed for his gratitude in contrast to the nine others, who failed to return and give thanks to Jesus. (Luke 17:11-19)

Jesus used his *circumstances* as a basis for teaching:

1. He taught about faith and doubt through Peter's failed attempt to walk on water. (Matthew 14:25-33)

2. Jesus demonstrated his power and taught the disciples about His authority as He calmed the raging storm. (Luke 8:22-25)

3. Zacchaeus' interaction with Jesus represents a life transformed and demonstrates the Lord's forgiveness and restoration. (Luke 19:1-10)

Christianese—A slang term for the terminology that a churched audience would understand but is not relatable to the non-churched.

Closely related to object lessons are significant *biblical symbols* that convey spiritual realities:

1. At the Lord's Supper, the bread and cup represent the body and blood of Jesus. (Luke 22:19-22)

2. The Holy Spirit is likened to a descending dove as Jesus was baptized. (Luke 3:22)

3. The hope of redemption is depicted through a barren, blood-stained, wooden cross that bore the sacrificed Savior. (Colossians 1:20)

Overall, the Scriptures and the teaching methods of Jesus routinely use the objects of ordinary life to illustrate spiritual lessons.

Five Recommendations When Getting Started

The construction of effective object lessons takes practice, and the following recommendations provide helpful guidance. Do not give up, learn from mistakes, and grow in this skill.

1. *Keep the instruction about the Scripture text central.* The object is a means to bring further understanding of and reflection on the text itself. Allow the object to assist understanding, but be careful that it does not become the center of attention and overshadow the message of Scripture itself. Weave the Scripture text into the lesson. Avoid simply reading the Scripture with the assumption that the listener will be able to connect the object with the message. Verbally explain the Scripture within the narrative of the object itself.

2. *Develop a clearly defined objective statement or lesson aim.* The lesson aim should be derived from the Scripture text. What is the intent of the passage being used, and how can it be applied to the lives of the listeners?

3. *Think creatively and prayerfully.* How can the Scripture text be made visual, and its meaning enhanced for the listener through the object? What object would best fit the intended audience? Keep in mind that small children might be the intended audience of an object lesson. Young children think concretely and might not have developed enough cognitively to relate a physical object to an abstract concept. Nonetheless, it is still valuable to provide them the attention and significance of gathering together for such lessons. The process of the lesson occasion might be the greatest beneficial connection with them rather than the lesson itself. If older children or adults are present, they might become the ones best served through the lesson.

4. *Consider what comes first in lesson development: the Scripture text or the object to be used for its explanation?* Typically, the Scripture text comes first. Once the message of the text is understood, an object is sought to present the message more clearly. However, as one begins to think in object lessons, the two will almost begin to blend together; that is, objects will become a reminder of Scripture lessons, and Scripture lessons will spur the thoughts of relevant objects.

5. *Read object lessons.* Just as a preacher listens to and reads the sermons of others to hone his or her own preaching skills and gain insights, so too should an individual do with object lessons. Such reviews might spawn new ideas and concepts stemming from the same object or bring to mind contrasting or different objects that can be used.

Object Lesson Modifications

Object lessons are designed to facilitate thinking and association. They might be used as designed but most likely will need to be modified or adapted to best fit the teaching objective and occasion. Consider these factors:

- *The audience:* Who is the target audience? How will the audience be engaged in order to effectively relate to them?

  1. What considerations need to be made about *audience size*?

     a. *Visibility:* Can everyone see the object or demonstration clearly? What adjustments are needed to best enhance the visibility of the presentation?

     b. *Volume:* Can everyone adequately hear? Will voice amplification be needed?

  2. *Age appropriateness:* What is the age of the listeners? Will questions or language need to be reframed to make it more listener friendly?

  3. *Gender specificity:* Will the object lesson or story need to be adapted to best fit a particular gender?

  4. *Cultural sensitivity:* Will the object lesson fit the culture? Some language and illustrations may be familiar in one's own

culture but not understood in a different cultural setting. It is also important to demonstrate respect for cultural differences and traditions while simultaneously adhering to the gospel. Chapter 14 will more fully address the subject of cultural sensitivity.

5. *Spiritual identity and maturity:* Will terminology need to be rephrased or explained to enhance listener understanding? For example, a non-Christian audience might not comprehend terms that are commonly understood by a Christian group. Do any cultural factors need to be considered when assessing spiritual identity and maturity?

- *Setting:* What space, facilities, and resources are available? How will the object lesson need to be revised in order to best fit the setting? Some demonstrations might be great for the outdoors but are impractical when taken inside, and vice versa. Can the lesson be modified?

- *Time limits:* How much time is available? Time limits will determine the extent to which audience participation will be afforded.

- *Making it your own:* Personalize the object lessons by illustrating them with individual stories and examples. Adapt them to one's own ministry setting and context. Revise questions and objectives to serve the intended purpose. Use inclusive personal pronouns that engage both speaker and listener: *us*, *we*, and *our* instead of *you*, *they*, and *them*. The message of the lesson is for the intended benefit of everyone—the speaker included.

Questions and Observations

Additionally, consider these questions and observations relative to composition and delivery:

- An object can be used multiple times for different lesson aims.

- Is the object appropriately tied to the lesson and Scripture text? Avoid stretching things in an attempt to make them connect superficially.

- Will the audience participate? Audience participation helps engage the listeners and personalizes the lesson. Following the teaching example of Jesus, He frequently involved his listeners: "Throw your net on the right side of the boat and you will find some [fish]." (These were Jesus' postresurrection words as spoken to his disciples in John 21:6—reminiscent of a similar preresurrection event recorded in Luke 5:4.)

- Are the questions rhetorical (i.e., questions not intended for a response but merely thought provoking)? Or will the questions probe the audience for a response, either individually or as a group? Reflect on this story of Jesus: A woman accused of adultery was brought before Him in an attempt to entrap Him. Jesus silenced the accusers, and one by one they left as he reframed their question with the thought-provoking statement, "Let any one of you who is without sin be the first to throw a stone at her" (John 8:7 NIV). In reference to a question about the payment of taxes, Jesus requested to see a denarius. He asked, "'Whose image is this? And whose inscription?' 'Caesar's,' they replied. Then he said to them, 'So give back to Caesar what is Caesar's, and to God what is God's" (Matthew 22:20-21 NIV).

- If participatory questions are used or if members of the audience participate in a demonstration, be prepared for and welcome spontaneity. Object lessons and their ensuing questions frequently spawn the unexpected, either within the demonstration itself or with unintended ideas that emerge. Learn to flow with these detours and quickly discern if they can be helpful for your overall objective, and if you can even expound on it. Be careful to avoid unnecessary sidetracks that lead the lesson in an unintended direction.

Below are two sample object lessons. Observe the formatting and how the object augments the overall lesson aim.

Devotional Message

A **devotional message** can be constructed using a simple four-part outline:

1. *Hook:* The purpose of the hook is to build an attention-getting connection with the audience. It can take the form of, among other things, a story, a video clip, rhetorical or interactive questions, a demonstration, or an object. A good hook will lend itself naturally to the message objective and not become overshadowing.

---

devotional message—A word of instruction and exhortation, similar to a sermon but abbreviated in length, typically 5 to 10 minutes.

SAMPLE OBJECT LESSON 1
Title: The Clock Is Ticking

Theme

Preparation for the second coming of Christ

Text

For the Lord himself will come down from heaven, with a loud command, with the voice of the archangel and with the trumpet call of God, and the dead in Christ will rise first. After that, we who are still alive and are left will be caught up together with them in the clouds to meet the Lord in the air. And so, we will be with the Lord forever. Therefore encourage one another with these words. (1 Thessalonians 4:16-18 NIV) He who testifies to these things says, "Yes, I am coming soon." Amen. Come, Lord Jesus. (Revelation 22:20 NIV)

Scripture Commentary

Jesus bodily came to earth in order to die by crucifixion and be resurrected on the third day. Upon His ascension to heaven, His disciples were comforted by the knowledge that He would return (Acts 1:11). The return of Jesus is described as sudden and with the authority of a loud command from on high. His reappearance is associated with the joyful gathering of His followers to Himself so that they will be with Him forever. Consequently, His people are to be encouraged to endure the trials and difficulties that will come their way, knowing that these struggles are temporal and will eventually be swallowed up by the eternal.

Object

An air horn (can be borrowed from a local school or recreation team)

Mila/iStock/Getty Images

Lesson Aim

Be encouraged and encourage others with the good news that Jesus has promised to return. One's life should be lived in preparation for His second coming.

Lesson Description

Have you experienced the excitement of a close sporting event—one that keeps you on the edge of your seat, heart wildly pounding as the clock ticks down? *(Receive responses or recap the excitement of a recent well-known event such as the Super Bowl, World Series, Stanley Cup, World Cup, or a local school game.)* The excitement of a big game has everyone on their feet, emotions high with anticipation. As the minutes wind down to seconds, the crowd shouts the final countdown: "10, 9, 8, 7 . . ." *(If appropriate, ask for the audience's participation. Have them stand and instruct them to join in the countdown at the appropriate time. Then in your best enthusiastic sports broadcaster's voice, say the following.)* The crowd is in a frenzy! Everyone is on their feet! The final seconds on the clock are winding down! 10, 9, 8, 7, 6, 5, 4, 3, 2, 1." *(Sound the air horn.)* The game is over! Fans burst onto the field! Tears of relief and joy overflow! Hugs and high fives abound! *(Ask everyone to retake their seats.)* When the sound of the horn is heard, it means the game is over. There is no more time for another play. There is no more time for one additional opportunity—one final chance. When the clock ticks down and the horn sounds, the game is over! It is done! It is finished!

The Bible speaks about a ticking clock. *(Read the text from 1 Thessalonians 4:16-18.)* A time has been established when Jesus will come again. Heaven's clock quietly and steadily ticks away, drawing closer and closer to the day of His return. The air horn loudly sounded when the game was over. Likewise, the heavenly trumpet call of God will suddenly resound and proclaim the coming of Jesus. Just as the fans of the winning team joyfully anticipated the conclusion of the game, so do the followers of Jesus joyfully anticipate His return. His victory is a victory for His followers. His arrival ushers His people to Himself and to the eternal home He has prepared for them.

> continued

SAMPLE OBJECT LESSON 1   > continued

Conclusion

Jesus desires that His second coming be joyfully anticipated. His followers prepare themselves for His return by living in a manner that is pleasing and acceptable to Him. He wants His word to be obediently lived and boldly proclaimed, telling others about Him so that they, too, can know Him and look forward to His return. Do we hear the faint yet mounting crescendo in the distance? Do we hear the whispered voices of the heavenly hosts? *(Say the following in a whispered voice that increases in volume with each number.)* "10, 9, 8, 7, 6, 5 . . ." Revelation 22:20 says, "He who testifies to these things says, 'Yes, I am coming soon.' Amen. Come, Lord Jesus" (NIV). Are we ready to welcome Him? The heavenly clock is ticking. *(If appropriate, an evangelistic invitation can be made, helping the listeners know that they, too, can be made ready for Jesus' return by receiving Him as Lord and Savior.)*

SAMPLE OBJECT LESSON 2

Title: Filled to Fulfill

Theme

Salvation, Jesus entering a life

Text

Yet to all who did receive him, to those who believed in his name, he gave the right to become children of God, children born not of natural descent, nor of human decision or a husband's will, but born of God. (John 1:12-13 NIV)

Scripture Commentary

Jesus identified Himself with humanity by taking on human flesh. His presence is likened to light shining in the midst of a darkened world. He came for His own, but they refused Him. Yet those who do acknowledge and receive Him are given a new birth—born not by the will and desire of their parents but born of God. As recipients of God's birth, they are called children of God. Through His Spirit, He lives within them (Romans 8:14-17), equipping and empowering them to be His witnesses (Acts 1:8) and to take on the character of His presence (Galatians 5:22-23).

Object

A baseball glove and ball

Photodisc/Getty Images

Lesson Aim

Each person is created by God to be filled and transformed by His presence and to fulfill the purpose and plan He has for them when He is received into their lives.

Lesson Description

Begin by examining the baseball glove, displaying how it has everything it needs to perform its function. It has a pocket, finger and thumb accommodations, the correct linings, materials, and so on. Place the glove 5 to 15 feet (1.5-4.6 m) away from you. Toss the ball to the glove. The ball will not be caught. Try a second attempt. Same result. What's missing? Despite the fact that the glove is perfectly designed to fulfill its intended purpose, it has a missing vital need. The glove needs a hand inserted into it—to guide it, direct it, enable it to perform according to its specified design. Put the glove on your hand, toss the ball in the air, and catch the ball. With the hand inserted, the glove can function and fulfill its intended purpose.

This physical illustration demonstrates a spiritual lesson. As human beings, we are created by God, and He has designed each person with the capacity to know Him and to fulfill the purposes of His intentions. Just as the manufacturer designed the glove to be filled with a hand, God has designed each person to be filled with His presence. As the Scriptures declare, to all who receive Him (filled with His presence), He gives the right to become His children (fulfilling their intended design).

Conclusion

How are we doing? Is something missing? Are we living life like a glove without a hand inserted to guide and direct—discontented and unable to fulfill our purpose? Or are we living life like a glove with a hand fully filling the pocket, experiencing the satisfaction of accomplishing God's intended purpose for us? According to His word, if we receive Him, He will call us His own and we will experience the contentment of fitting into His plans.

Modification

The object in this lesson can be changed to accommodate soccer by using a soccer shoe in place of a glove and a using a foot image instead of a hand.

2. *Book:* The book is the cited Scripture passage (or passages). Determine if the passage will be read in its entirety or paraphrased within the lesson.

3. *Look:* The look reviews the Scripture and its context in light of the message's objective. It also allows the speaker to interact with the text through personal or borrowed story. The book and look are integrated and represent the meat of the message.

4. *Took:* The took seeks to tie the lesson together to life application. What does the lesson intend for everyone to learn? What is the action point of the heart (conviction and motivation), the hands (what will be done), the feet (where to go), and the voice (what will be said)?

The following sample devotional message is similar to one presented at a postgame contest during a sports ministry trip to Russia. Throughout the trip, the airwaves were filled with songs from the same Russian musical artist. Whether riding in a taxi, eating at a restaurant, or hearing music emanating from merchant shops, the same songs were continually repeated. When the translator was finally asked to identify the singer, he responded, "Alla Pugacheva—she is very popular." Her popularity was noted and would prove to be a resourceful point of connection with Russian audiences—an effective hook. The sample devotional message has been formatted to model the four-part lesson outline.

Prayerful Dependence on God

The communication of the gospel is a spiritual exercise and is dependent on the Spirit of God to speak to the heart of the listener. A message can be eloquently delivered, and illustrations cleverly conceived, but unless God moves to convict and convince, the words may fall on spiritually deaf ears. This realization does not negate the communicator's responsibility to diligently prepare lessons; it simply adds the foundational component that there is a dependence upon God to stir the heart of the listener. Prayer acknowledges this dependence. From concept to preparations, delivery, and response, all components of gospel communication need the revealing and convicting work of God. There is no multistep methodology guaranteeing successful communication. The transforming communication of the gospel is more than a disbursement of information, more than an intellectual understanding of precepts—though these things are included. Gospel transformation penetrates the deepest levels of the soul and necessitates the prayerful preparation of God's intercession. Regardless of the methods employed, sports ministry teams are fully dependent on the illuminating work of the Holy Spirit to enlighten the hearts and minds of all people.

SAMPLE DEVOTIONAL LESSON
Title: Do You Know Alla Pugacheva?

Hook

"How many of you know the name Alla Pugacheva?" The translator relayed the question from English to Russian. The listeners responded with an enthusiastic reply. "Of course, we all know Alla Pugacheva."

"What does she do for a living?" Again, the question was translated, then followed by the responses, "She sings," "She's on radio and recordings," "She's very popular."

"What songs does she sing?" The crowd blurted out a chorus of titles with obvious familiarity.

"How much money does she make?" The people responded, "Lots of money—she's very wealthy."

It was quite evident that this group of Russian men and women knew their national celebrity, Alla Pugacheva. Then the question was asked, "How many of you could phone Alla Pugacheva right now and invite yourself over to her home just to spend some time together?" The translation of the question was met with a burst of laughter, then answers such as these: "She would have nothing to do with us, Who are we? Why would she want to visit with any of us?" "She wouldn't even take our phone call. We are not her friends."

There was a difference between knowing about Alla Pugacheva (her name, her occupation, her wealth—the facts) and having a personal relationship (a friendship) with her. In a similar manner, there is a difference between knowing about God and having a personal, intimate relationship with Him. Many people know some of the Sunday school stories about God and people of the Bible: Christmas is the celebration of the birth of Jesus; Easter focuses on the crucifixion and resurrection; David slew the giant Goliath; Noah built the ark; Adam and Eve were the first people created. Factual knowledge differs from the deeper understanding of salvation as espoused by Scripture. God calls us to intimacy with Himself. Such knowledge is more than factual; it is a living, growing *relationship* with our Creator.

Book (Acts 9:1-18; 26:1-32): The Apostle Paul: Truth Confronts Religiosity

Prior to his conversion, the Apostle Paul had a religious knowledge of God but in reality, did not know Him. Paul was well educated, a Pharisee among Pharisees, a zealous proponent of his shortsighted and erroneous doctrine. He deceptively believed that he knew the God of Israel and was justified to challenge the Christian faith. He vigorously persecuted the Church and heartily approved the imprisonment and subsequent martyrdom of Christian leaders. His miraculous conversion on the road to Damascus freed him from living a lie. The eyes of his heart were opened to the truth, and Jesus became his Lord, Savior, and friend. Paul's life was transformed. His spiritual blindness was turned to sight. Truth swallowed deception. Empty religiosity was replaced with an authentic relationship with God. Paul's knowledge of God penetrated the very core of his being. He became a bold preacher and teacher of the One whom he had previously attempted to silence. He considered his former life as rubbish in comparison to the surpassing greatness of knowing Christ Jesus. As recorded in his letter to the church at Philippi: "What is more, I consider everything a loss because of the surpassing worth of knowing Christ Jesus my Lord, for whose sake I have lost all things. I consider them garbage, that I may gain Christ" (Philippians 3:8 NIV). He welcomed as an honor the sufferings for the cause of Christ because the truth had seized his heart. His knowledge of God had become intimate, relational, and real.

God has revealed His nature as relational. Humanity has been created in His image and shares this *relational* quality. Relationship was established in the Garden of Eden. Adam and Eve were to relate to God personally and intimately and also to one another. When the first couple sinned, a consequence of their transgression was a broken relationship. God confronted a hidden Adam, "Have you eaten from the tree that I commanded you not to eat from?" (Genesis 3:11 NIV). Adam exhibited the brokenness of his relationship with Eve by pointing the finger of blame and exclaiming, "The woman . . . gave me some fruit from the tree, and I ate it" (verse 12). Yet it was not only Adam's relationship with Eve that was severed but also his relationship with God. Adam's corruption ultimately led him to blame God for his own failure: "The woman *you* put here with me—she gave me some fruit from the tree, and I ate it" (Genesis 3:12, emphasis mine).

Look: A Form of Religion Versus Authentic Faith

How many of us can relate to Paul and to the numerous other folks who at one time claimed the knowledge of God while lacking the evident fruit of intimacy with Him? How many of us have grown up in religious homes, well acquainted with many of the Bible stories and regularly attending church and Sunday school? How many of us have attended catechism classes, been examined by church officials for confirmation qualification, actively attended youth group meetings and other church-related functions? Knowing about God and believing oneself to be a Christian? Yet has the knowledge only been a formal non-life-changing empty shell, adhering to a form of religion, based on human effort and not on the convicting and indwelling work of the Holy Spirit? Like Paul, have we had a conversion experience with Jesus that has changed our lives and continues to transform us? Do we now understand that the knowledge of salvation, as recorded in Scripture, is firmly grounded in an intimate relationship with God? It is a life of surrender—yielding all that we are in loving, obedient submission to His will. The deepest longing of every human heart is to reestablish the severed relationship between God and ourselves. We were created for the purpose of intimate fellowship with Him. Sin has broken this bond, and the relationship can only be mended through the redemptive work of Jesus Christ. While we were yet sinners (broken, alien, and separated from God), Christ died for us (Romans 5:8). His transforming work on our behalf enables us to die to self (Galatians 2:20) and to emerge as a new creation in Christ Jesus (2 Corinthians 5:17). We are recipients of His Holy Spirit (1 Corinthians 6:19), and our hearts cry out with expressions of restored intimacy, "Abba, Father" (Romans 8:15-16).

Took: The Fruit of Godly Knowledge (Relationship)

In the Gospels, Jesus conveyed a warning to discern the waywardness of false teaching. He illustrates His concern by comparing false prophets with the fruit of a tree. Good trees produce good fruit while bad ones produce rotten fruit. Lives are discerned by the fruit they bear. Those born of the Spirit have an authentic knowledge of God, and the holy fruit of His presence will be manifest in their lives. When a personal and intimate relationship with God is entered through Jesus Christ, one's character and attitude begin to take on the resemblance of His nature. Because God is holy and pure, the qualities of His abiding presence are to be exhibited within His followers. To know Him is to become increasingly like Him.

It is a tragic realization to know that many people lead a life of self-deception, not discerning the distinction between knowing the facts about God and having an abiding relationship with Him, like the Russian audience who only knew *about* Alla Pugacheva but did not have an active relationship with her. God extends His arms of embrace to each of us, welcoming us into a life of relationship with Him. To receive His embrace is to forsake our sin and to be purified with the provision of His holiness. We are each invited to come, enter, and eat at the table of His presence! So, come!

The Evangecube, like an object lesson, is one of many visual evangelism tools used when presenting the gospel.

SUMMARY

Gospel communication is mandated and empowered by Jesus. Numerous tools and methods are available to effectively share the gospel. This chapter has highlighted several key methodologies: personal story, object lessons, and devotional messages. The importance of incarnational living has been emphasized once again. The gospel message is not only to be heard but is to be seen, as evidenced through the lives of Christ's followers. Communication methods might readily be conceived and skillfully crafted, and the message passionately delivered, but only the Holy Spirit can work in the midst of a lesson to reveal the intended truth that convicts hearts. Consequently, prayer is essential. Gospel communication is a ministry of dependence—dependence on God to soften hard hearts and to open the blind eyes of the soul.

REVIEW AND DISCUSSION QUESTIONS

1. Why are stories such powerful communication tools?

2. What is one of your favorite biblical narratives, and why is it a favorite?

3. Objects, demonstrations, personal stories, and the hook can all be effectively used as connecting points with an audience. Why must the speaker be cautious about these connectors overshadowing the message?

4. Is there a distinction between an object used in an object lesson and a hook used to begin a devotional message? Explain.

5. Explain the importance of prayer as a spiritual discipline as it relates to gospel communication.

6. How does your faith journey compare and contrast to that of the Apostle Paul? To that of Jen Mattison?

7. What might inhibit a Christian athlete from publicly sharing his or her faith journey?

8. Is the Great Commission of Jesus a command, a recommendation, or a suggestion, and how does He conclude His commission as recorded in Matthew 28:18-20?

The integration of faith and sport, the sacred and the secular.

CHAPTER 7

Ethical Considerations for Christians in Sport

"And whatever you do, whether in word or deed, do it all in the name of the Lord Jesus, giving thanks to God the Father through him."

Colossians 3:17 (NIV)

LEARNING OBJECTIVES

After studying this chapter, you should be able to do the following:

- Describe Christian responsibilities that adhere to a Christ-centered ethos as a member of the sporting community
- Discuss tensions that arise between competitive sport and the tenets of the Christian faith
- Explain how the Bible is to be used by believers as the authoritative guide to shape thinking, motivation, speech, and conduct within the world of sport
- Distinguish between legitimate strategy and the dishonest and deceptive practices of normative cheating and gamesmanship
- Identify how a Christian athlete is influenced by sport and how sport is influenced by a Christian athlete
- Develop a Christ-honoring perspective about winning and losing

The score was 6–0, and the coach instructed his players to maintain possession of the ball but no longer shoot so that the score would not become even more lopsided. The setting was a women's soccer match in Costa Rica during a collegiate U.S. team's participation in a short-term soccer-specific sports ministry trip. A Costa Rican observer noticed that the players were no longer seeking to cash in on clear scoring opportunities and asked why. He was informed that the team did not want to run up the score. This concept was new and strange to him—what did it matter if the score was 1–0 or 25–0? The man's inquiry raises these questions: Is running up a score indicative of poor sportsmanship? Is it universally poor sportsmanship, or does it depend on a cultural perspective? Will a score enhance or diminish the priorities of a sports ministry initiative?

This chapter will explore ethical considerations in sport as they relate to Christians within athletic endeavors. Are competition and Christian faith even compatible? What are some of the ethical issues confronting the Christian in sport, and how does one integrate one's faith in a meaningful response?

The Hammer Analogy

Consider a simple hammer, a tool that has been in existence for centuries. In the hands of a carpenter, this tool can be wielded masterfully to construct cabinets, build a table, erect a fence, and handle a host of other beneficial projects. The hammer itself was designed for positive construction. As a part of God's creative genius, His image bearers follow His nature by creatively developing a useful a tool. However, place that same hammer into the hands of a criminal, and it can be misused as an instrument of destruction. The hammer itself is not the problem. The hammer's intended design was to build and construct. The problem arises with the hammer's use. Can the same be said of sport? Does sport have the capacity to be used as an instrument to build the bonds of human relationships? Will sport be used by participants to build qualities of character and personal disciplines? Will sport be an instrument through which God will call men and women to Himself in the service of His divine purposes? Or will sport be misused to glorify self-seeking adulation, disrupt relationships, promote dishonesty, and become the platform for a host of abhorrent behaviors? Used properly, sport can influence the Christian, and the Christian (as God's image bearer) can influence sport. Sport as a tool has the potential for either good or evil purposes.

A New Christ-Centered Ethos

"And you call yourself a Christian?" The sarcastic tone of this retort is frequently uttered when a Christian athlete fails to live by the perceived expectations of conduct ascribed to a follower of Jesus. All too often the criticism of this question is justified. Christian conduct regularly falls short in all walks of life, including the arena of sport. How are **Christian ethics** to be demonstrated in the life of the Christian sportsperson? What behaviors set apart the Christian fan and competitor when compared to spectators and athletes who do not share the same worldview?

Believers experience an ongoing clash between the flesh and the Spirit, between the old life separated from Christ and the new life immersed with His presence. A biblical distinction is drawn between the "fruit of the flesh" and the "fruit of the Spirit" (Galatians 5:19-25). Jesus contended that though He and His followers live in this world, they are not a part of it; this draws a distinction between worldly and heavenly mindedness and affections (John 15:19; 17:14-16). The world is equated with darkness and a spiritual blindness bound by the devastating effects of sin (Ephesians 4:17-19; 2 Corinthians 4:4). Jesus is described as a light who exposes darkness, opens blind eyes, and sets the captives free (John 3:19-21; 8:18; Luke 4:17-19). When born again, the followers of Jesus are filled with His presence, and His light becomes a part of their new nature (Matthew 5:14-16). This new nature is set free to yield itself in obedience to Christ. Followers of Jesus gain a new worldview perspective and are called to live differently from their past (2 Corinthians 5:15-17). Not only are they

Christian ethics—The biblical morals that guide and govern beliefs, values, and subsequent standards of behavior as the believer seeks to know and follow the will of God.

called to live differently, but they are also equipped and empowered to do so by the indwelling presence of the Holy Spirit (John 16:13-15; Acts 1:8). Hatred is replaced with love. Forgiveness replaces retaliation and revenge. A worldly perspective is replaced by a God-mindedness.

Throughout Scripture, believers are repeatedly exhorted to fully live the new life they have embraced in Christ (Galatians 5:25; 1 John 2:3-6; 2 John 2:9). They are to live according to a new Christ-centered ethos. How does the Christian athlete integrate these principles as he or she competes in the sport arena? Is it even possible? Are the demands too contradictory? Kretschmann and Benz assert, "Christian athletes, as a distinguished group among competing athletes, are supposed to be people with specific and distinctive moral guidelines in everyday life that they validly integrate in competitive sports as well" (Kretschmann and Benz 2012b, 5). Michael Shafer challenges Christian athletes and spectators "to gain a richer understanding of how their faith offers formative principles to guide their attitudes and behaviors as well as provide spiritually meaningful reasons for participating in sport" (Shafer 2015, 1). Christian athletes are not to leave their faith in the locker room as they enter the athletic arena. Their faith is an integral part of their spiritual newborn essence, foundational to their identity in Christ, and influences every sphere of their lives, including sport participation.

A Work in Progress

Despite the call and equipping to live a new life, the Christian is a work in progress. As a work in progress, he or she will make mistakes and falter at times. Positionally, he or she is considered brand new and a child of God (2 Corinthians 5:17; John 1:12-14; Romans 8:16). Experientially, a spiritual tension exists between the old and new self (Romans 7:18-8:2). In Paul's letter to the saints at Philippi, he prayed that the work begun in them would be carried on "to completion until the day of Christ Jesus" (Philippians 1:6 NIV). He acknowledged that a new believer is a work in progress. Likewise, he spoke about his own journey not yet being complete. He pressed on toward that which Christ Jesus had in store for him (Philippians 3:12-14). He, too, was a work in progress. Being a work in progress is not an excuse for negligence or wrongdoing, but rather is an explanation for the mistakes made along the way. The Christian athlete is called to a new standard of conduct, a new Christ-centered ethos, but he or she is not yet perfected in this new way of living. He or she will experience the growing pains of transformation, moving away from a life apart from Christ to one in which He is more fully Lord. With the help of the indwelling Holy Spirit equipping, motivating, and admonishing them, Christian athletes learn to adhere to a new perspective about their athletic endeavors. Mistakes and shortcomings will be made along the way—a common innate process of life in the quest toward spiritual maturity.

The Tension Between Competitive Sport and Christian Faith

When considering Christian ethics and sport, a foundational question is one of competition's compatibility with faith. Mentioned in chapter 5, this question is now more fully developed within the specific framework of ethical considerations. How is faith in Jesus Christ and adherence to His word to be applied within the realm of sport? First, it must be acknowledged that a tension exists between the nature of competitive sport and the character expectations of the Christian faith. Some would argue that the very nature of sport is self-focused and contrary to the tenets of the gospel, which is deemed other-focused. Kretschmann and Benz cite Jan Boxill: "The intrinsic nature of competition is immoral because competition is selfish, egoistic, involves treating others as means, as enemies to be defeated, or as obstacles thwarting one's victory or success to be removed by any means possible" (2012b, 6). Nancy Lay believes the nature of competition disqualifies the Christian from participation and concludes that sport and religion are altogether incompatible.

Sport is concerned with competition, with beating someone. Religion, on the other hand, is concerned with loving everybody and with humbleness. Thus, . . . Is it inconsistent with Christian principles to want to win when someone else has to lose? Yes, it is inconsistent. It is not Christian. (Lay 1993, 11, 18)

Hoffman addresses the dissonance between competition and Christianity, asserting that sport feeds into human nature's urge to place oneself at the front of the line with little regard for the interests of others. A commitment to win is simultaneous to making someone else lose. Victory is at the expense of one's opponent (Hoffman 2010). He goes on to recount the dilemma faced by 1980s tennis champion Andrea Jaeger. As a Christian athlete, she struggled with the success she experienced on the court at the expense of the person she had defeated. Hoffman describes Jaeger's turmoil:

> Even before a shoulder injury cast a cloud over her career at the age of 19, she had been pondering the disconnect between her faith and the spirit required to win on the tennis tour. Eventually she realized that her faith could no longer allow her to play her hardest when doing so brought so much disappointment and suffering to those who were victims of her talent. . . . Today Jaeger is an Episcopal nun. "I did my best according to my values and morals," she says. "I did my best according to what I believe to this day that God does approve of: 'Be true to who you are in the person I have molded you to be.'" (Hoffman 2010, 163-164)

Jaeger's departure from tennis can be appreciated because of her personal conviction about the integration of her faith and sport. For her, the nature of competition was difficult to reconcile with her Christian tenets. Yet other devout Christians view sport and competition differently. These differences of opinion highlight a tension existing within the Church community as she seeks to understand the ethics of sport from a theological perspective.

The Compatibility of Competitive Sport and Christian Faith

Robert Ellis constructs a case for play as a part of God's creative order. In his view, sport is an organized subset of play and is likewise considered a part of God's creative design through His image bearers (Genesis 1:27) as they emulate the divine pattern of creativity. He suggests that "play is somehow understood to be part of what it means for human persons to be the imago dei" (Hoven, Parker, and Watson 2019, 39). He continues by citing Hoffman: "All forms of play are expressions of the same characteristic human response to the world, a response so universal—evident in animals as well as humans—that it is difficult not to believe that it is a part of God's design" (Hoven 2019, 39). Ellis takes his argument a step further by adding competition as an essential component of sport: "Sport is always a contest, it always involves trying to 'win'—though sometimes the opponent we are trying to beat is really ourselves, or our best previous performance" (Hoven 2019, 42). Is the step Ellis takes from play to competition legitimate? Ordained minister and NFL head coach Frank Reich believes that competition is ingrained in almost everything. He appeals to "God's Dominion Mandate—to be fruitful and multiply, to rule over and to subdue the earth (Genesis 1:28)" as the "seed that breeds the competitiveness in each one of us" (Reich 2002, 1). Greg Linville suggests that nature provides multiple examples of expressions of competition. Trees compete for sunlight as their branches

Christian ethos: Is competitive sport compatible with Christian faith?

extend skyward, and roots dig deep within the ground to gain sustenance from the soil (Garner 2003, 175). God's image bearers are exhorted to care for creation and further develop its potential as faithful stewards. According to Treat, God intends for His creation to be enjoyed and for play to be further developed as an expression of creativity and as an offering returned to Him with gratitude:

The God who bounds in love and kindness created a world of delights and placed His beloved image bearers in it with an invitation to enjoyment. Creation is not merely a resource to be used for productivity, it is a gift to be received and enjoyed. This is the idea of where "play" comes in, which is implicit in humanity's calling to develop and delight in God's creation. To play is to creatively enjoy something for its own intrinsic good. . . . God is honored and takes joy when His sons and daughters delight in His workmanship. The world is—as it has been said—the theater of God's glory; but it is also the playground of God's goodness. (Treat 2015, 4, 5)

Michael Shafer concurs with Treat's sentiments, acknowledging sport as a God-given gift to be enjoyed and as fundamental for human flourishing.

Sport is a part of God's design for human flourishing. It is a gift to be enjoyed. . . . Leisure, not work, is the basis for culture. To say that play is merely rest from and for work is to devalue the significance of play as a fundamental component of human flourishing. More importantly, the purpose of leisure is not a means of preparing for work but a form of worship. Play is an expression of gratitude to God who gives the gift of sport. . . . We must recover the spirit of play in sport and see athletic activity neither as a trivial form of entertainment nor as a means of some external end but as an expression of who we are as human beings—an expression filled with grace, gratitude, and a spirit of worship. (Shafer 2015, 5,7)

Christian athletes can embrace physical activities as spiritual opportunities, from kneeling in prayer or singing a hymn to swinging a tennis racket or heading a soccer ball. The bodily movements, when presented to God, are themselves offerings of gratitude rendered for His glory (Hoven, Parker, and Watson 2019). The physical action is a visible display of the heart's position—a desire to thank God for the ability and opportunity to play.

Competition is central to the tension that arises between sport and Christian faith. How can Christian principles coexist with the demands inherent in competition? Treat considers the etymology of competition:

The Latin com-petito literally means "to strive together," rendering sport a "mutually acceptable quest for excellence." As iron sharpens iron, competition enhances play. Michael Goheen and Craig Bartholomew rightly argue that it is cooperation, not rivalry, that is at the heart of competition: "In sports, teams or individuals agree cooperatively to oppose one another within the stated goals, rules, and obstacles of the game." (Treat 2015, 6)

Treat's view casts competition in a positive light as a mutually agreed-upon method to relationally engage and improve one another. Most people will agree that competition can lead to abhorrent behaviors. The "win at all costs" mentality can lend itself to an endless list of degradations: cheating, dishonesty, self-centered pride, gambling, substance abuse, assault, and so on. Is competition inherently evil and thus to be avoided by the Christian? As previously mentioned, Lay contends that it is incompatible with the Christian faith. Ellis offers a different position:

The bad is a distortion of the good, and because competition can sometimes have a harmful impact this does not mean it is always necessarily bad—instead, we want to assert that competition is bad only when it becomes a distortion of the good. Competition is, as we have established, an important part of our enjoyment of the games we play. But it is more than mere enjoyment. We can argue that competition makes us and our opponents better players—and that this, in turn, enhances our enjoyment of the games we play. (Hoven, Parker, and Watson 2019, 42-43)

Ellis acknowledges that competition can be misused with evil intent. Since the entrance of sin in the human experience, every aspect of our lives has become broken and in need of the reconciling grace of God. Competition has not escaped the need for this reconciliation:

Sport can be, and often is, a site of sin. There is a sense in which all the world is broken, and sport is no exception. . . . Sport can be a site of sin but also a site of salvation, then. . . . In salvation we speak of God saving us from brokenness and mending our lives, drawing us into God's

Interview With a Professional

Rev. Scott Steltzer

Associate Director at Summer's Best Two Weeks, a Christian sport and recreation camp

BA, Grove City College

MDiv, Pittsburgh Theological Seminary

Rev. Steltzer has served on staff at SB2W since 1999. He has coached, taught, and led campers and staff ages 8 to 22 for 22 summers. He also has coached youth football and baseball in his community for the past 13 years. Rev. Steltzer enjoys developing, implementing, and refining the practical theology of competition that shapes the sport experience at SB2W.

Courtesy of Scott Steltzer.

What is SB2W's ministry objective?

Our ministry objective is to transform sport culture by training holistically Christian athletes who compete Christ-consciously rather than selfishly. At SB2W the glory goes to God as competitors seek to put God first, others second, and themselves third. This "I'm Third" motto is based on Jesus's articulation of the greatest commandment in Mark 12:30-31.

How is competition implemented strategically within SB2W programming?

SB2W intentionally creates an intense competitive experience for campers that mirrors the competitive atmosphere they experience on their sport teams at home. The rivalry between two teams at camp purposefully reinforces within the athlete's heart the drive and desire to win. This strategy is conducive to providing many opportunities for staff to coach the hearts of young athletes in the heat of competition. SB2W teaches campers to integrate their faith in how they compete and to put winning in proper biblical perspective.

Can you provide an example?

Staff are trained to identify the heart issues (anger, frustration, and discouragement, for example) that reveal themselves outwardly as campers earnestly compete. Coaching the heart is when both coaches and referees use moments of transition and postgame debriefing as opportunities to speak truth to the hearts of competitors. These teachable moments help campers not only see and understand the root causes of their feelings and behaviors but address them in a transformative way (Romans 12:2).

How is competition compatible with Christian faith?

The root of the word *compete* means "to strive together." When striving to win is the highest goal, idolatry flourishes. When winning is the only goal, destruction is rampant. Competition is compatible with faith only when Christians place honoring Christ as a higher goal than winning. At SB2W, we put **S**triving for **B**est ahead of striving **2 W**in. Striving for best—meaning God's best, other's best, and our own best interests—in light of God's Word, is our first priority (Philippians 2:3-8). SB2W does not diminish the importance of winning but elevates the primacy of honoring Christ in all areas of life.

Why does SB2W use competition as a tool for discipleship?

Competitive sport is one of the best tools to reveal the heart issues in campers' lives and to address those issues in a timely and transformative manner. The good news of the gospel is relevant to every minute of play. The sport field becomes the laboratory, where what is learned in Bible study is worked out practically in the lives of campers. Lessons learned are then transferred to sport experiences back home.

What key ethical issues arise amid competition, and how does SB2W address them?

Intense competition does not build character but reveals the sins of one's heart. SB2W has identified pride (self-glorification), apathy, idolatry, anger, fear and anxiety, despair, selfishness, and passivity as some of the most prominent root sins of competitors' hearts. In order to coach the heart most effectively, SB2W has developed themed competition talks that precede each sport event to prepare athletes to compete in a worshipful way and to consider as they compete. At the end of the competition period, campers debrief their experience related to the theme of the competition talk that day.

Is there anything else you would like to share about the use of competition within the context of SB2W's ministry?

The vast majority of coaching in sport is directed at improving the team and its players physically and mentally. They prepare their bodies and minds to compete optimally. At SB2W, we have the time and space to focus a greater amount of attention on the players' hearts. We address athletes' motivations, desires, attitudes, perspectives, insecurities, and passions with the truths and promises of Scripture. The results are spiritual fruit in the lives of competitors.

---

presence. In our reaching out in sport, though we may not know it, we are reaching out for this same God who made us in imago dei. (Hoven, Parker, and Watson 2019, 45)

Linville concurs with Ellis that competitive sport needs redemption. He also concludes that biblical narrative casts a positive light on sport, uses it to explain spiritual lessons, and never condemns it (Linville 2014).

Contrasting Andrea Jaeger's discomfort with the despair she caused her defeated competitors is the account Ellis provides of Wimbledon tennis champion Andy Murray:

When a reporter sympathized with Wimbledon tennis champion Andy Murray for playing in the era of Djokovic, Federer, and Nadal, rather than at another time when he might have won more trophies, Murray retorted that while he might have won more trophies in another era, he would not have been such a good player: playing against these great players has made him as good as he is. (Hoven, Parker, and Watson 2019, 43)

Murray recognized the personal benefits of playing against formidable competition. It improved his own performance. The lesson of competition is two-sided—learning how to win and learning how to lose. The exception might be a sport like soccer when the outcome's result can be a tie. A ministry that intentionally uses competition as a means for discipling the Christian athlete is Summer's Best Two Weeks (SB2W). In Interview With a Professional, Rev. Steltzer, the associate director at SB2W, explains the rationale behind the use of competition for discipling

people in the Christian faith. He endorses its use as an opportunity to build constructive qualities within the lives of young athletes.

A Divide Between the Sacred and the Secular

A dualistic approach segregates the separate worlds of the sacred from the secular: the holy and the unholy. Traditionally, Christianity is assigned to the sacred and sport to the secular. Yet the principle of the incarnation disrupts this dualistic perspective. Jesus, the very essence of sacred, takes on human flesh and identifies Himself with secular nature. He introduces the holy within the realm of the unholy. With His presence, the unholy cannot remain the same. Jesus is salvation, an offering of redemption. He redeems the secular and transforms the profane to make it holy. Through His divine grace, forgiveness, and healing, Jesus restores His creation to its original God-honoring purpose. The secular is transformed for the redeemed pleasure and purpose of the sacred. Therefore, sport can be redeemed from its secular domain and reconstructed to serve the sacred.

The Christian athlete no longer views the world of sport as a mere secular endeavor. Sport is infused with sacred intentions, an opportunity to connect with the Creator:

Many believe that God is exclusively concerned about religious activities, forgetting that God is the God of all creation, sacred and secular. All of life is under His dominion and concern. Theologian John Stott said, "Our God is often too small because He is too religious. We imag-

ine that He is chiefly interested in religion—in religious buildings, religious activities, and religious books. Of course He is concerned about these things, but only if they are related to the whole of life. According to the Old Testament prophets and the teaching of Jesus, God is very critical of 'religion,' if by that is meant religious services divorced from real life, loving service, and the moral obedience of the heart." . . . We have to be careful that we do not segregate spiritual life from other areas of life. To think that ministry only happens during a Bible study or on Sunday mornings inhibits us from promoting the integration of Jesus into all our experiences—especially sport. . . . Jesus did not endorse a ten-step program on how to be a disciple, but rather focused on living out one's faith in the experience of life. (McCown and Gin 2003, 114-115, 154-155)

Incarnational living enables the Christian athlete to view sport as an exercise of spiritual life, interpreting athletic talents and passions as God-given abilities to be fully cultivated and presented back to Him as expressions of thanksgiving and worship.

As previously mentioned, competitive sport instills an ever-present tension for the Christian athlete. The desire to live incarnationally butts heads with the spirit of competition as evidenced by Gary Warner's frustration in his book *Competition*:

My faith had no application to my competitiveness. I was the same old person between the baselines. I cursed, I lost control, I was obsessed with winning. I would manipulate and do whatever it took to win. I slid into bases with my spikes high, and if a baserunner did not get down to the double play, I had no qualms about putting the ball between his eyes. From the bench I heaped abuse on opponents and referees. After all, this was competition. This was being an athlete. And no one modeled a Christian difference for me to see. (Warner 1979, 45)

Warner's sentiments are not uncommon. Many Christian athletes question the inconsistency of their faith within sport. Warner's final sentence reads not only as an explanation, but also as a plea: "No one modeled a Christian difference for me to see." It is a sad commentary but so often true. Besides evangelism, sports ministry must address discipleship—assisting athletes to not only come to

Christ, but to actively live like Christ and to make a compelling difference within the athletic arena. As more Christian athletes live the faith they confess, Warner's pleas for role models will be addressed. A representation of Christlikeness within the sport arena is visible as participants yield to the abiding presence of the Holy Spirit, allowing the qualities of His nature to empower, direct, and characterize them. As His presence increases, others will recognize the difference and be encouraged to live and do likewise; at least a viable choice will be evident for them to follow. Recall in chapter 2 how the lineman playing next to Naismith apologized for spouting a foul word in his presence. Something about Naismith led to the apology, a recognition of a different way of living; in this case, a higher standard of conduct was modeled by Naismith and acknowledged by the personal conviction of his teammate.

Sportianity: A Critical Review

As sports ministries were advancing in the 1970s (namely, Fellowship of Christian Athletes [FCA], Athletes in Action [AIA], Pro Outreach, and Sport Chaplaincy Ministries), *Sports Illustrated* writer Frank Deford wrote a three-part series critiquing "Jocks for Jesus" in what he termed **Sportianity**. At that time, he concluded that sport was influencing Christianity more than Christianity was influencing sport (Deford 1976c). Though his critique is often cynical and paints in broad strokes a picture of prominent sports ministries, he raises issues relevant for reflection:

Don Cutler disagrees with the movement's lack of social concern. "If the New Testament says anything, it is that this man poured himself out for you, and now it is your responsibility to pour yourself out for others." . . . In the process of dozens of interviews with people of Sportianity, not one even remotely suggested any direct effort was being considered to improve the morality of athletics . . . no one in the movement—much less any organization—speaks out against cheating in sport, against dirty play; no one attacks the evils of recruiting, racism or any of the many other well-known excesses and abuses. Sportianity seems prepared to accept athletics as is, more devoted to exploiting sport than serving it. (Deford 1976a, 18-20)

Sportianity—A cynical term combining sport and Christianity coined by *Sports Illustrated* writer Frank Deford in the 1970s critiquing several emerging sports ministry organizations.

Despite a critical analysis of emerging sports ministries, Deford did acknowledge a broadening perspective of FCA's focus by quoting then vice president of FCA's finances, Ron Morris, a former collegiate basketball star and ordained Methodist minister:

[With respect to FCA] I see a danger in our being overly evangelistic. It is important for us to understand where we stand. We're not breaking new ground. We're not even reaching the uncommitted kid. The boy we get has almost always been raised in a church, his mom and dad are members. We provide a strengthening process, the identification of a peer group. We get these kids to camp, we get them to play together on a team, and their trust factors go up. Through this athletic camaraderie you have an affirming process, and, unfortunately, in life we don't get affirmed too often, do we? We ought to understand that what the FCA does best is affirm, not evangelize. (Deford 1976b, 3, 4)

Morris recognized that sports ministry is more than evangelism; it should also help shape, encourage, and affirm the Christian athlete through an intentional process of educational discipleship. Too often quality behavioral traits are merely hopeful byproducts of sport participation rather than planned for specifically (Brown 2003).

Pre- and Postgame Prayers

According to Deford, many viewers take issue with public displays of pre- and postgame prayer, suggesting that the players' prayers lack authenticity and meaning. He adds, "Game-day religion has become a sort of security blanket, something on the order of superstition" (Deford 1976c, 14). Without knowing the posture of their heart, it is presumptuous to assume that the players' prayers lacked genuine meaning. Yet Deford's criticism might accurately assess the experience of some—but not all—Christian athletes and sport enthusiasts. Prayer does not have to become a rote, ritualistic, or superstitious exercise. Granted, times of perplexed questioning, doubt, and bewilderment will arise. Even the psalmist exhibits such displays of lament over the apparent futility of labored prayer (Psalm 22 and 80). Routine does not reduce the need for prayer, nor does it encourage its neglect. Christian disciplines are not limited to exciting mountaintop encounters with God but are likewise manifest when He seems to have abandoned His people within the valley of the daily routine.

Ministry Expansion Caution

Many current sports ministries encompass more than athletic evangelism. However, ministry expansion must be approached with caution. Ministries have specific points of focus and cannot effectively engage every human need that arises. They must use their resources appropriately and be faithful to the mission to which they have been uniquely called. If they attempt to address every need and issue, they might overextend themselves and become ineffective to serve their primary objective. They need to honestly evaluate their own limitations and pour themselves fully into the Kingdom role to which they are equipped and called to exercise, regardless of the voices that might critically suggest otherwise (1 Corinthians 12; Romans 12:3-8).

Christian Ethics Through a Biblical Lens: Linville's Three-Step Process

Greg Linville, sports ministry specialist and founder of the Association of Church Sports and Recreation Ministries, provides a traditional three-step biblical interpretation process to help Christian athletes determine their approach to ethical conduct.

1. First is the relevant study of Scripture and the application of appropriate **biblical hermeneutics**. What does Scripture say? How does it read within the context of surrounding verses, chapters, and the Bible as a whole? How was it interpreted and applied by the original readers? Linville states, "Even though the first-century rule may no longer be relevant for those living in the twenty-first century, its basic principle may well still be applicable" (Linville 2014, 140).

2. Step 2 identifies the principle that has been determined through the study of Scripture. What is the specific directive God commands? How does this principle align itself with commands found in other Scripture passages? Do other biblical texts provide additional inference for it even if they do not directly address the topic?

3. Step 3 is the action point used because of the conclusion formulated through steps 1 and 2. This step determines the thought, word, or behavior to be taken or avoided (Linville

---

biblical hermeneutics—The study of the Bible, interpreting God's revealed truth and values so that God's people can hear and understand His will as expressed through His word.

2014). The objective of this three-step process is to develop a biblical-mindedness that will honor God through conformity to His desires. As the Lord's prayer recites, "Your will be done" (Matthew 6:10)—not empty words but a heartfelt conviction to live by.

This process is adapted and built on here. An assumption to this approach is the understanding that the Bible is the revealed word of God and authoritative to address human behavior and ethical concerns. The Apostle Paul's affirmation of the believers at Thessalonica is consistent with this view of Scripture.

And we also thank God continually because, when you received the Word of God, which you heard from us, you accepted it not as a human word, but as it actually is, the Word of God, which is indeed at work in you who believe. (1 Thessalonians 2:13 NIV)

A biblical **worldview** will conflict with society's deeply imbedded secular perspective. A contemporary expression speaks of "my truth," "your truth," "her truth," "his truth." Yet the search remains for "the truth." In a world conflicted about the concept of absolute truth, the compelling words of Jesus resound: "I am the truth" (John 14:6 NIV). God is truth, and when He speaks, His words are true. God's word is not merely His truth; it is *the* truth. It may lack popularity, but God's word and the standards He discloses are not subject to human revision or negotiation. The Creator does not need advice from his creation. The issue at hand is how to accurately understand what God has declared and to live accordingly in obedience. This task is difficult. Seeking *the* voice is befuddled by the onslaught of variant lesser voices competing for attention. Throughout Scripture, God warns about false teachers who twist and misrepresent His word by maligning what He says and flagrantly proclaiming what He does not say (Jeremiah 14:14; 2 Timothy 4:3, 4; 1 John 4:1-6). The prophet Isaiah bemoaned the day when the discernment of good and evil are flipped upside down: "Woe to those who call evil good and good evil, who put darkness for light and light for darkness, who put bitter for sweet and sweet for bitter" (Isaiah 5:20 NIV).

The New Testament speaks about those who will reject the truth in preference for falsehoods:

For the time will come when people will not put up with sound doctrine. Instead, to suit their own desires, they will gather around them a great number of teachers to say what their itching ears want to hear. They will turn their ears away from the truth and turn aside to myths. (2 Timothy 4:3-4 NIV)

They exchanged the truth about God for a lie . . . (Romans 1:25a NIV)

Spiritual inquiry necessitates spiritual discipline. Seeking the counsel of God begins with prayer, asking the Holy Spirit to illuminate the reading of Scripture, or **biblical illumination**. In the New Testament, Jesus frequently spoke in parables. He often concluded a parable with the words, "Whoever has ears to hear, let them hear" (Mark 4:9, 23 NIV). This phrase references the illuminating presence of the Holy Spirit, who teaches and enables His word to be comprehended by the listener (John 14:26). The seeker's yearning is to hear God's voice, to understand His word as He intends it, to envision the world through His eyes, and to apply His instruction according to His will. The prayerful reading of the Bible is deeper than solely an academic pursuit; it is an exercise of dependent faith. Whether it is a biblical scholar or an unschooled group of fishermen (Acts 4:13), all are humbly dependent on God for the revelation of truth. Without the help of His illumination and divine guidance, the Bible will only be printed words on a page and subject to misrepresentation.

Governing Principles for Ethical Behavior in Sport

In addition to Linville's three steps are several principles to govern one's insights regarding Christian ethical behavior in sport. Consensus among Christians is not always reached when discussing ethics and related actions. Opinions can differ, and growth in understanding frequently occurs when healthy discourse is permitted and encouraged. Christian thinkers are to participate in discerning dialogue as the counsel of God is wholeheartedly sought and enacted. Iron sharpens iron better than iron sharpens putty. God blesses and enlightens those who earnestly seek Him (Matthew 6:33; 7:7). A key question to ask is, What

---

worldview—A philosophy or interpretation of life that seeks to explain human origins and meaning. Worldview searches for answers to questions such as "Who am I?," "Why am I?," "How did I get here?," and "Where am I headed?"

biblical illumination—The work of the Spirit of God as He enables His revealed word to be understood. He opens the mind to understand and the heart to respond with conviction.

are the nonnegotiable tenets of the Christian faith? One nonnegotiable is the centrality of Jesus to the Christian faith—His identity as the Son of God who offers redemption through His sacrificial death and subsequent resurrection. A second nonnegotiable is the truth in what He says as revealed in His Word.

Contrasting Viewpoints in a Pluralistic Society

Within a pluralistic society, differences of opinion occur when worldviews emerge from dissimilar foundations. These differences can be quite extreme and often lead to polarization. How does the Christian athlete balance respect for those with opposing viewpoints without compromising his or her deeply held, biblically based convictions? Unfortunately, disagreement is too often equated with nonacceptance. Jesus frequently was criticized for mingling alongside the outcasts and despised members of society (Luke 19:7; John 4; 8:1-11). He embraced the sinners, saying He "came to seek and to save the lost" (Luke 19:10b NIV). He often ate with them, but it is important to note that He did not participate with them in their sinful behaviors. It is also important to note that encounters with Jesus most often concluded with a life-changing decision. The corrupt tax collector Zacchaeus encountered Jesus and was no longer the same person. He returned the stolen funds he had received through ill-gotten gain and would cheat no longer (Luke 19:8-10). Jesus did not condemn the adulterous woman but told her to "go and leave your life of sin" (John 8:11 NIV). Saul no longer persecuted the followers of Jesus but became an outspoken preacher of the name he had once tried to silence (Acts 9:1-19; Galatians 1:23, 24). How does the Christian athlete engage a teammate, a coach, or an opponent who overtly contradicts his or her Christian standards?

> We should see athletic competitions as opportunities to witness to Christian faith. Christian athletes must "live in the world" of contemporary sports but not "of that world." In sports (as in other human cultural endeavors such as the arts, sciences, academia, political life and so on), opportunities abound to witness to the gospel way of life. Christian athletes can be role models of sportsmanship, fair play, discipline, and integrity. (Kerrigan 2008, 26)

It must be understood that standing for Christian principles likely will be viewed as the rejection of a person because acceptance has become equated with the endorsement of one's behaviors and choices. Consequently, Christian athletes will face mockery and ridicule for not embracing conduct that violates their faith-based convictions. How does one lovingly live in the world but not be a participant or celebrant of worldly vices? Is love strong enough to live within the dynamics of this dichotomy?

Respect and Human Interaction

Respect for others is foundational to productive human interactions. Self-control and civility among those expressing differing points of view should always dictate conversations and debate. Contemptuous attitudes and dismissive labeling are indicators of poor reasoning and an attempt to win the argument by shutting down the opinion of others rather than through listening and persuasive rationale. Additionally, "Some have even argued that life requires the moral courage to love our enemies" (Clifford and Feezell 2010, 118).

A Willingness to Listen and Judgmental Attitudes

Closely related to respect is a willingness to listen. Too often people listen to respond rather than to understand. Differences of opinion may be characterized as judgmental. Typically, the accusation of judging is associated with condemnation. This sentiment only depicts one aspect of a judgmental attitude. Judgment has two components: that which is disapproved and that which is approved. When distinguishing between right and wrong, true and false, and good and evil, a determination (judgment) is required. The question is, What is being approved in contrast to what is being disapproved? Discussions about Christian ethical considerations in sport will give rise to differing opinions and judgments. The one who disapproves may be denounced as judgmental. Yet the counterpoint opinion is equally judgmental by the assertion of what one approves. Thus, opinions need to be freely expressed and evaluated based on the merits of their rationale and authority. Dismissive labels and accusations of judgment should not be employed to silence strong differences of opinion. Recall the previous quote from the prophet Isaiah (5:20) when he prophesied about a day when good would be judged and scornfully condemned as evil, and evil would be judged as acceptable and celebrated as good.

Created in the Image of God

Always keep in mind that humanity is created in the image of God—the player, the coach, the opponent, the official, the fan. Despite the fall (Genesis 3), a vestige of God's image continues to distinguish humanity from the other creatures of His creation.

The world we live in is substantially broken. The reality of creation's brokenness affects every part of God's world, and every human endeavor and aspiration, every relationship, and all human structures. . . . The image of God in human persons is not completely destroyed in creation's brokenness. Human persons remain rational, relational, creative, open to God, and playful (Hoven, Parker, and Watson 2019, 41).

Sport participants should not be objectified. Sport is only one component of participants' identities. They are mothers, fathers, daughters, sons, sisters, brothers, wives, husbands, neighbors, employees, citizens—the list could stretch to great lengths. They should not be treated as inanimate chess pieces being maneuvered on the board of life. Each person, though broken by sin, uniquely exhibits the creative handiwork of his or her Creator and should be treated accordingly.

Repudiation is difficult but consider the example of Jesus. He is the perfect living embodiment of love and truth. He welcomes all to come to Him: "Come to me, all you who are weary and burdened, and I will give you rest" (Matthew 11:26 NIV). He welcomes the least and the worst. Some receive His invitation while others choose to reject Him. Ultimately, Jesus' earthly ministry concluded by being falsely accused, spat on, mocked, beaten, scourged, and nailed to a Roman cross. If the most gracious embodiment of perfect love was so treated, should His followers expect to be treated any differently? Jesus foretold:

If the world hates you, keep in mind that it hated me first. If you belonged to the world, it would love you as its own. As it is, you do not belong to the world, but I have chosen you out of the world. That is why the world hates you. Remember the words I spoke to you: "A servant is not greater than his master." If they persecuted me, they will persecute you also." (John 15:18-20 NIV)

The Scriptures are filled with examples of people who had to choose between obedience to God or a pursuit apart from Him. A few examples follow:

- Adam and Eve chose to listen to deceit and the allure of a forbidden fruit over obedience to God. The consequence was bondage to the slavery of sin (Genesis 3).

- Mordecai refused to kneel to Haman because God alone was to be the recipient of such honor (Esther 3).

- At great personal risk, Esther chose faithfulness to God by saving her Jewish people from the evil plot of Haman (Esther 8-9).

- Shadrach, Meshach, and Abednego chose obedience to God and an ensuant fiery furnace rather than worshipping an idolatrous golden image (Daniel 3)

By permission of SB2W

Sport participants are not to be objectified. They are sons, daughters, brothers, sisters, husbands, wives, neighbors—real people created and bearing the image of God.

- Daniel chose obedience to God and a den of hungry lions over praying to King Darius (Daniel 6).

- The apostles chose obedience by continuing to preach about Jesus, despite threats and being commanded by the Sanhedrin to no longer speak of Him. Peter and John's words clearly explain their motivation: "Judge for yourselves whether it is right in God's sight to obey you rather than God. For we are not able to stop speaking about what we have seen and heard" (Acts 4:19 Berean Study Bible).

The Christian athlete can be comforted and encouraged by the example of these biblical narratives. Their lessons are as applicable today as they did when originally penned. Christianity expressed within sport will manifest spiritual conflicts, necessitating difficult choices and decisions. As the Scriptures illustrate, God has strengthened and enabled the saints of the past to persevere, and He is faithful to do the same today. Whether a public figure or an obscure coach or athlete in a small town, God's promise is for each. For the sake of those who will respond by coming to Jesus, whether few or many, the Christian influence within sport is worth the insults and rejections. Consider Tim Tebow's football career (see Sports Ministry in Action), an example of the experience faced by many Christian athletes who perform in the public eye.

Ethical Consideration One: Pagan Associations With the Origins of Sport

In chapter 2 a clear association was made between the origins of sport and ritualistic pagan religion. Ancient temples were strategically constructed near athletic venues. Statues of gods lined the streets. Ritualistic prayer and worship were offered, and pledges of allegiance to pagan gods were customary among athletes and spectators alike. The sky around the arena was often blackened with smoke rising from animal sacrifices. Precontest athlete processions were led by the priests of gods such as Zeus and Nike. Hoffman suggests that the pagan religious ceremonies were "as integral to sport spectacles as 'The Star-Spangled Banner' or the seventh inning stretch to American baseball" (Hoffman 2010, 24). Throughout the centuries, this association has frequently led the Church to withdraw from sport as a tainted activity. Because sport has historic pagan associations, does it preclude the Christian from participation? What about other pagan activities? Pagans historically have prayed, expressed worship through song and dance, and performed ceremonies like those conducted by the Christian Church. Should Christians no longer pray, sing, or worship because pagans have exercised these practices in their religious observances? Can the activities of sinful humanity be restored as proper

SPORTS MINISTRY IN ACTION

Choosing Obedience in the Face of Ridicule and Rejection

Tim Tebow is a highly decorated athlete. He was Florida's Mr. Football as he led Nease High School to the state title during his senior year. He won two NCAA national titles at the University of Florida and was the first-ever sophomore to win the Heisman Trophy. In 2010 he was drafted by the Denver Broncos. Born in 1987 to missionary parents in the Philippines, Tebow developed a strong passion to serve God by serving people (Tim Tebow Foundation 2021).

Tebow's playing career received national attention, not only for his credentials, but because of his Christian identity. He is known for kneeling in prayer, which reporters coined as *Tebowing*, postgame interviews in which He thanked God for his ability to play, and Bible verses written in his eye black. Public sentiment is divided over Tebow, from adoring adulation to insulting mockery. Admirers appreciate his philanthropic endeavors and the convictions of his Christianity. Football analysts note flaws in his playing skills while others ridicule the demonstrative nature of his faith (Bishop 2011). Tebow provides an example of the spiritual divide that exists within American culture. Christian athletes like Tebow will be scrutinized for authenticity, yet no one will reach perfection. Regardless, the life and message of the Christian athlete and sports ministry initiatives will not always be embraced. Ridicule and rejection are to be anticipated.

CASE STUDY

Defeating Sport Idolatry

Idolatry occurs when God's rightful position as Creator and sovereign Lord is supplanted by someone or something else. The Old Testament Scriptures abound with examples of idolatrous behavior (Exodus 32; Numbers 25:1-3; Judges 3:7; 1 Kings 16:31-33; 2 Kings 17:7-17; 2 Chronicles 28:1-4). Though idolatry may be the manifestation of misguided human craftsmen who shape images of metal and carved wood (Isaiah 44:9-20), its origins are connected to a spiritual conflict with demonic associations and persuasions (Psalm 106:36-39; Revelation 9:20-21). Idolatry violates the first two admonitions of the Ten Commandments:

> I am the LORD your God, who brought you out of Egypt, out of the land of slavery. You shall have no other gods before me. You shall not make for yourself an image in the form of anything in heaven above or on the earth beneath or in the waters below. You shall not bow down to them or worship them. (Exodus 20:2-5a NIV)

Despite repeated warnings, when the people of God stray from Him and mingle with people who have rejected their Creator, it influences them to adopt erroneous customs and falsehoods (Psalm 106:35). God disdains idolatry (Ezekiel 20:7) and demands the abandonment of idolatrous alliances (Joshua 24:14). The Scriptures exhort obeying God and fleeing from spiritual infidelity (1 Corinthians 10:14), because those who succumb to temptation's allure have no part in His kingdom (1 Corinthians 6:9-10; Galatians 5:19-21). The New Testament expounds on the heart of idolatry by emphasizing "fleshly" behaviors as idolatrous expressions of evil desires, impurity, lust, and greed (Colossians 3:5).

C.T. Studd abandoned his cricket career because, for him, cricket had become an idol. His identity, passion, and energy were completely tied up with receiving sport-related accolades. His idolatry was not expressed through the worship of images made of wood or gold, but by the position of his divided heart. Cricket had usurped the rightful place of God in his life. A four-part blog by Cede Sports provides applicable insights into the dilemma that likely challenged Studd and confronts the modern Christian athlete with the appeal of sport idolatry:

> When I examine the deeper emotions surrounding my sports, one of the things I find when I go beneath even the deep belief in my heart is a passionate drive to excel or win. If I probe around about that longing, I discover this longing to excel is really a longing for glory—for greatness and the recognition by others of that greatness. This is where it gets both interesting and hard. If I am really honest, even as a Christ follower this longing for glory is not very often about God's glory but instead is very often about my glory. I want what winning and sports' achievements bring from our culture—the respect, the honor, the admiration, the trophies—or, in other words, the glory, my glory. It is hard to acknowledge this because to do so shows the self-centeredness of my heart—the orientation of my longings toward me. (Cede Sports, 2018)

Throughout Scripture, God's remedy for idolatry is heartfelt repentance (2 Chronicles 7:14; Isaiah 55:7; Acts 2:38). God has created humanity for relational fellowship with Himself and with one another. He instructs His followers to listen, to live in obedience to His commands (Deuteronomy 6), and to denounce anything that might deter their faithful following.

Discussion Questions

1. Read Deuteronomy 6. When God's people were preparing to enter the Promised Land, He gave them specific instructions. What were those instructions and warnings that would enable them to live in the land they were about to receive?

2. How can sport become an idol? What characterizes sport idolatry?

3. How does God's instructions, as recorded in Deuteronomy 6, apply to the Christian athlete?

4. What is God's remedy for idolatry, and how can it be applied to the life of a Christian athlete?

expressions before God? Certainly, people themselves are redeemed and transformed through encounters with Jesus. According to the Bible, the image of God has been corrupted within humanity's experience. Everyone now born into this world is in spiritual darkness, separated from God, and under the direction of pagan loyalties (Ephesians 2:1-3). The human condition is dreadfully hellacious (Romans 3:9-18). However, God has not abandoned His creation to the deserved fate of their apostasy. Through His boundless grace and forgiveness, people can be changed, no longer to live for deceptive, self-seeking, destructive passions, but rather set free to live as He intends (Ephesians 2:4-10; 4:22-24). If peoples' lives can be changed, so, too, can their activities. Sport is subject to God's redemptive plan and transforming power.

The story of redemption in scripture is not one merely of rescuing souls from the fallen creation but rescuing embodied souls and renewing all of creation (Colossians 1:15-20; Romans 8:18-25). The final vision of salvation is the enthroned Jesus declaring, "Behold, I am making all things new" (Revelation 21:5). (Treat 2015, 13)

Human activities such as sport can be redeemed because redemption is the nature of the gospel. Sport can be embraced by the Christian community as an authentic gift of God to be enjoyed. It is the responsibility of the redeemed Christian athlete to be a catalyst in the redemption of sport.

Ethical Consideration Two: Sport and the Sabbath

"Remember the Sabbath day by keeping it holy" (Exodus 20:8 NIV). The **Fourth Commandment** was instituted by God to grant rest and refreshment from one's labors. Rest follows the divine pattern exhibited in the Genesis creation account. On the seventh day God rested from all His work (Genesis 2:2-3). "God is not resting because He is exhausted but is desisting from His work of creation" (Elwell 1989, 12). God's rest is one of completion, a delight and satisfaction with what has been made: "God saw all that He had made, and it was very good" (Genesis 1:31 NIV). Sabbath rest is not necessarily a cessation from activity but allows believers to pause and reflect on God as Creator and Initiator of the new, redeemed creation He offers in Christ.

Desecration of the Sabbath

The desecration of the Sabbath has been a criticism of sport throughout the ages. As cited in chapter 2, runners Eric Liddell and Gil Dodds held to strict interpretations of the Fourth Commandment. Both men refused to race on Sundays in adherence to their conviction that obedience to God's command was of greater importance than medals and adulation. Historically, fundamentalist believers have viewed observance of the Sabbath as an indicator of one's Christian faith. In the 1920s evangelist Howard S. Williams expressed this sentiment while commenting on professional football's Sunday games: "There will not be a single Christian [in attendance], probably; however, hundreds of church members will be there" (Putz n.d.). Williams' opinion was indicative of many believers of his era. The most renowned American evangelist, Billy Graham, also originally held an unwavering conviction about the Sabbath:

In 1953, Graham used his newspaper column to answer a question about whether a Christian could play "big-time baseball or football." Graham responded by encouraging Christians to participate in professional sports as long as they "maintained their testimony by consistent Christian living, by contagious Christian enthusiasm, by fair play and good sportsmanship, and keeping the Lord's Day." Over the next few years Graham continued to urge Christians to stand strong when it came to the Sabbath. "The world needs today people with conviction enough with things Christian to refuse to conform to the popular trend," he wrote in 1955. "People with sufficient regard for the highest things to say, 'Not today, thank you,' when asked on the Lord's Day to turn from work to play rather than from work to worship." (Putz n.d.)

Because of their affiliation with Campus Crusade for Christ, football stars Donn Moomaw and Bob Davenport were a part of the team known as the 1954 "UCLA's Eleven from Heaven". Upon graduation, Moomaw and Davenport refused to play professionally because they believed playing on Sunday was a sin and would compromise their Christian witness (Putz n.d.). Graham eventually softened his position about sports and the Sabbath. Though he personally adhered to a strict Sabbath observance, he did not want this discussion to divert him from his primary

Fourth Commandment—One of the Ten Commandments given by God to Moses on Mount Sinai. It reads, "Remember the Sabbath day by keeping it holy" (Exodus 20:8 NIV).

evangelistic mission of proclaiming the life-changing message of the gospel. He encouraged individuals to wrestle with the issue of Sabbath observance, to prayerfully seek God's counsel, and to decide on their response accordingly:

> *"We must not submit to a legalistic Christianity that is encumbered with commands and prohibitions,"* [Graham] *stated in response to a question about opening a business on Sunday. "Our first and greatest commandment is to love God and to love our neighbors as ourselves. Therefore, you must make the final decision in this matter." (Putz n.d.)*

How do Christians participate in sport while honoring the Lord through obedience to the Fourth Commandment? Where is the line drawn between what honors and what desecrates the Lord's admonition about the Sabbath? Two extremes are to be avoided: (1) dismissing the Fourth Commandment as no longer relevant and (2) structuring pharisaic regulations that smother the day with oppressive limitations and guilt-ridden axioms. The words of Jesus shed light on these questions: "The Sabbath was made for man, not man for the Sabbath" (Mark 2:27 NIV).

Sports and Lord's Day Issues

In his book *Christmanship*, Linville provides an insightful chapter titled Sports and Lord's Day Issues. From a biblical perspective, he provides a theological summary of the Sabbath. Using the example of Jesus in Matthew 12, Linville summarizes the Christian's responsibility to the Sabbath Day mandates concerning work. He provides three types of actions that would honor the Lord through Sabbath Day toils.

1. *Acts of necessity:* duties or responsibilities that ensure and protect the general health, life, and safety of people and the created order (Matthew 12:1-4)

2. *Acts of mercy:* duties or responsibilities that have to do with aiding someone in need (Matthew 12:9-14)

3. *Acts of ministry:* Christ clearly taught that ministry was to take place on the Lord's Day. These duties or responsibilities include anything that provides worship, fellowship, Christian teaching, or evangelistic outreach (Matthew 12:5-8) (Linville 2014, 149).

Linville goes on to say that too many followers of Christ have "nothing more than a faith of conve-

nience" and are unwilling to make personal sacrifices or to align themselves more fully with biblical principles. He adds a perceptive question: "Is it the Lord's day or just the Lord's hour?" (Linville 2014, 150, 154).

Sunday and Youth Sports

Youth sports and travel teams frequently schedule games on Sundays, causing families to make the difficult choice between childhood developmental games and church attendance. How are priorities determined? What balance is sought that best honors the Lord? Does the question of honoring the Lord even enter the equation? In an interview with Mary Kassian, cofounder of the True-Woman Movement, writer Tony Reinke provides five suggestions for parents to consider (Reinke 2018).

1. Consider a league with fewer demands. Unfortunately, many high-level programs schedule games and tournaments that include Sundays. However, some leagues do not schedule Sunday events. Is playing at a lower level without a Sunday commitment an option?

2. Weigh the cost—this evaluation is not only financial. What will the cost be in terms of time, travel commitments, and as a lesson in priorities? Will Sundays be involved, and how many? Is one Sunday conflict acceptable? What about five? How about ten? Is there a limit?

3. Embrace the consequences of a missed practice or game. Choosing to attend church and miss a Sunday practice or game may result in a team penalty such as limited playing time or sitting out the next contest. Is the sacrifice worth it?

4. Be creative about church attendance. Is there an early service that would allow both church attendance and team participation during the same day? Two questions arise with this suggestion. One has already been mentioned by Linville when he asked if the Sabbath is the Lord's day or the Lord's hour. The other question is one of focus. Will attention during church be distracted by thoughts of the upcoming game? What about attending church as part of traveling to a game? Can Sabbath rest be observed on an alternative day?

5. Let the decision be a family discussion. It is good for children to observe their parents

wrestling with spiritual concerns, to hear about the struggles of applying biblical principles to real-life circumstances.

These are teachable moments that reveal priorities. Is Christ central to life, or has sport become an idol that supersedes Him?

"Athletics is such a competing god," Mary says soberly. "I think it is so critical that the parents are always checking their own hearts. I needed to check my heart through our process. Where are you drawing your identity? Where are you drawing your sense of meaning? What is in your heart? If this were to end tomorrow, what would be left in terms of your sense of wholeness and well-being, and who you are? Are you drawing that from the Lord? Is hockey a bigger delight for me than God is? I asked my son to wrestle with that question on an ongoing basis too." (Reinke 2018)

Too often, Sabbath discussions emphasize what should not be done on the Lord's Day. Perhaps greater attention can be given to what should be done.

Ethical Consideration Three: Considering Gamesmanship

"I never teach cheating to any of my players, but I admire the guys who get away with it. The object of the game is to win and if you can cheat and win, I give you all the credit in the world," said former Detroit Tigers manager Sparky Anderson (Eitzen 2012, 130).

It is admirable that Sparky Anderson did not actively instruct his players to cheat. Yet his thinking about cheating is problematic—cheating is acceptable if the cheater can get away with it. His message is clear—cheat, but do not get caught. He also expresses a truncated view of a game's objective by elevating winning as the primary focus. What about the *process* to attain the result? Is the final score all that matters? Closely associated with cheating is **normative cheating** and

gamesmanship. An example is fighting in ice hockey. Penalties are assessed for fighting as a rule violation, but fighting is quite normal and typically expected during a game. Fighting in hockey is so prevalent that a satirical joke says, "I went to a boxing match and an ice hockey game broke out." Most teams have a player designated as their "enforcer" who administers ice justice on behalf of the team.

Is **gamesmanship** justifiable for the Christian, stretching the rule boundaries to the very edge without crossing over to a defined violation? The message of normative cheating and gamesmanship is identical—winning has greater importance than playing fairly. Reconsider Anderson's perspective that cheating is fine if it is not discovered. Can the Christian athlete or coach adopt this philosophy as his or her own? Will the Christian athlete ever play in total secret with undisclosed actions and motives? It might be possible to fool teammates, coaches, opponents, officials, and fans, but what about God? His omnipresence (i.e., He is always present) cannot be escaped, and His omniscience (i.e., He is all knowing) captures every thought, word, and deed. Can anyone hide from God?

Like life in general, Christians are too often seeking to straddle the lines between acceptable and unacceptable behaviors. They want the assurance of heaven while living as close to the edge of hell as possible. The allure of worldly pleasures offers false hope and empty contentment. Adam and Eve went to the edge and crossed the line. They succumbed to the enticements of a forbidden fruit, the allure of a worldly desire, by choosing to contradict God's instruction in preference for their own. The consequence of their choice was expulsion from their garden paradise, and a relational wedge subsequently separated them from God (Genesis 3). This compromise of values begs this question: Is mediocrity the behavioral standard for the Christian? The warning of Jesus, as recorded in the Bible's final book, leaves little room for doubt about half-hearted devotion.

I know your deeds, that you are neither cold nor hot. I wish you were either one or the other! So, because you are lukewarm—neither hot nor cold—I am about to spit you out of my mouth. (Revelation 3:15-16 NIV)

---

normative cheating—Might involve breaking a stated rule, but the action has become normalized to the point that it has been accepted as a part of the game.

gamesmanship—An attempt to circumvent the rules of play to gain an unfair advantage over an opponent. Technically, gamesmanship might not involve breaking a rule, but it does infringe on the spirit of the game.

Gamesmanship is a form of deception that attempts to get away with something. It diminishes the intentions of the game by seeking loopholes to exploit. Instead, why not focus attention and energy on mastering the skills and strategies of the game by becoming the very best player you can be? It is better to stand tall at the end of competition knowing that you played with complete integrity and gave your best effort because of dedicated work and honest effort.

Legitimate Game Strategy Versus Gamesmanship

What is the distinction between legitimate game strategy and dishonesty cloaked as gamesmanship? During the final minutes of a close basketball game, strategy might dictate fouling intentionally in the hope that the opponent's free throws will be missed. A soccer player might strategically commit a professional foul to keep a faster opponent from a breakaway opportunity. What about trash talk to get into the head of an opponent? Is faking an injury or feinting a foul acceptable strategy or dishonest deception? Consider the example of NBA star James Harden as presented in a paper by Brian Palmiter, then a PhD candidate at Harvard University:

NBA MVP James Harden is the most polarizing superstar in the NBA. His talent is undeniable, but for many basketball purists his scoring accomplishments carry an asterisk similar to the one attached to Barry Bonds' home run record. Harden, to be sure, has never been accused of cheating like Bonds. The complaint against Harden is that a substantial portion of his success is attributable to his unmatched ability to intentionally draw fouls. What is wrong with this? In sportswriter Rodger Sherman's representative words: "The rightful way to score is by throwing a ball into a basket. Free throws are interruptions in the regular course of play, although we accept them as a reward for players whose moves are so effective that no one can guard them legally. Harden, however, often seeks to get fouled as a primary action, subverting the natural order of things. And of course, there are the flops. Harden's game seems cynical, like he is exploiting a loophole.... Scoring simpliciter, however, is not the object of basketball, nor is winning. The object of competing in such a way as to constitute an excellent game of basketball. Only someone who values winning more than the game itself could fail to recognize this. That, in a sentence, is the difference between a gamesman and a sportsman" (Palmiter 2018, 17).

Is Harden guilty of exploiting the intentions of basketball? He is not violating the rules of the game, or is he? What about soccer players who theatrically fall to the ground, often holding the opposite leg that was supposedly brutally assaulted? Are their actions justified as they seek to fool the official in the hope of gaining an undeserved free kick? At what point does such gamesmanship distract from the intent of fair play?

Does the Christian athlete endorse the actions of gamesmanship or normative cheating? Are these actions simply a part of the game, or must the athlete advocate for higher standards? Can a Christian ice hockey player become the team's enforcer who fights opposing players in the name of team justice? Will a Christian baseball pitcher yield to the manager's directive to throw a retaliatory pitch at the next batter's head? Will a Christian coach teach players techniques that will enable them to foul opponents in such a way as to be undetected by game officials? After all, they can get away with it. Is it the Christian community's responsibility to play sport differently from those who do not follow Jesus? Is Christ honored through the acts of intentional dishonest deception, or gamesmanship?

Winning and Losing

"Winning isn't everything; it's the only thing," is a phrase attributed to legendary Green Bay Packers Coach Vince Lombardi. In reality, these words were a reporter's revised version of what he actually said: "Winning isn't everything, but striving to win is" (Martens 2012, 20-21). Winning is a legitimate objective of competition as long as it is pursued the "right" way. The question is, How is the "right" way determined? A "win at all costs" mentality skews the intention of sport. Winning unfairly cheapens the experience, rendering it a hollow victory. Research indicates that the longer one participates in competitive sport, the reasoning of one's moral standards decreases. The possible explanation for this phenomenon is the "winning at all costs" mentality (Woods 2016; Brown 2003).

Striving for Excellence

Legendary UCLA basketball coach John Wooden couched winning within the framework of striving to do one's best:

> I tried to convince my players that they could never be truly successful or attain peace of mind unless they had the self-satisfaction of knowing they had done their best. Although I wanted them to work to win, I tried to convince them they had always won when they had done their best (Martens 2012, 6).

Like Wooden, Wes Neal emphasizes the importance of striving in an attempt to revise one's understanding about game-day results. The central message of his booklet *Total Release Performance* is a redefinition of terms. He begins with traditional definitions of winning and losing: "Winning is to defeat your opponent and losing is to be defeated by your opponent" (Neal 1975, 3). Using Jesus as an example, Neal commends His perseverance to fulfill His redemptive mission. Despite extreme obstacles, Jesus never gave up. Consequently, Neal proposes new definitions specifically for the Christian athlete and coach to consider:

> Winning is the total release of all that you are toward becoming like Jesus Christ in each situation. Losing is not releasing your entire self toward becoming like Jesus Christ in each situation. (Neal 1975, 8)

Neither Wooden nor Neal would reject the validity of maintaining a scoreboard, but both men emphasize the importance of the preceding effort: "It isn't really the winning in sport that ought to serve as a model for life but the excellence we achieve in doing our best to win" (Clifford and Feezell 2010, 118). The process of winning is essential for the satisfaction of victory: "For some fans, the preoccupation with winners grows tiresome. Veterans prefer to watch a well-played and exciting contest" (Woods 2016, 114).

Winning as a Platform

Dave Hannah, the founder of Athletes in Action (AIA), understood the connection between winning and gaining the attention of an audience—a quality team attracts more attention than a team that plays poorly. He says,

> Athletes are no more important to God than anyone else. Yet the world has given them an incredible platform, not just in the U.S., but in other parts of the world as well, where their platform is sometimes even bigger. This visibility is influential, because when spectators and athletes themselves hear the testimonies of our players and see the way they play, it makes an impression. Kids especially are looking for heroes, people to model their lives after. Our players are good. They are coming in first, and that really does influence the kids. (Quebedeaux 1979, 142-143)

Is the process of winning the race as important as the victory itself?

Coach Wooden emphasized the importance of complete effort as much game strategy.

Former AIA basketball player John Sears put it this way: "We need to win to command respect" (Deford 1976a, 3). This sentiment feeds on the notion that the world loves winners. Yet for the AIA teams it was more than just winning. How their teams won (competed) was equally as important as the final result.

> *The fact that they are good and getting better has attracted media and public attention. But that all-important difference—unselfish team-work—is what really affects sports enthusiasts when they see a game. It is AIA's way of demonstrating the gospel as well as proclaiming it. (Quebedeaux 1979, 146)*

Sports ministry adherents strive for athletic excellence, and to do so in the right way. Teamwork, respect for officials and opponents, integrity, caring disposition, work ethic, and much more are characteristic of their faith—a faith not only of proclamation, but demonstration. Faith is not simply a belief, but a verb in action: "I will show you my faith by my deeds" (James 2:18 NIV).

Failure: A Life Lesson Taught Through Sport

Failure is a consistent life lesson taught in sport. Every swing of the bat does not connect for a home run. Every three-pointer does not crease the back of the net. Every athletic contest does not end in victory. Failure in sport corresponds with failure in life. Every

exam does not receive a perfect score. Every interview does not end with a job offer. Attempting something new might not work. Failure must be appropriately processed and includes the ability to bounce back. In their study of faith, morals, and sports, Kretschmann and Benz identified a healthy response to the short-comings encountered by Christian athletes:

> *Christian athletes usually have moral values, which are based upon the Bible in everyday life, as well as in competitive sports. Moral values such as honesty, respect, integrity, and acceptance are thus most important to them. In competitive sport these values are represented through the value of fair play. Although their moral values in everyday life, as well as in sports, are oriented on Christian values, Christian athletes do not necessarily appear to be saints when competing in sports. As they stated themselves, they are just human beings, meaning that they are not perfect and do not always act according to their personal moral guidelines. But what is more important than the fact that Christian athletes also fail from time to time is the way they cope with their failure. If they violate their moral values, the most important thing for them is to reflect and regret their behavior and learn from it. (Kretschmann and Benz 2012a, 516)*

Their study also indicated that Christian athletes believed "God loves you no matter if you are winning or not." This knowledge enabled them to cope with the emotions of winning and defeat. They believed that "God has a plan" and "everything in life has a purpose, which is given by God" (Kretschmann and Benz 2012a, 517). The Christian athlete offers their failures to God and takes comfort in His promise to mercifully forgive and restore them (1 John 1:9). As Jesus calls for His followers to forgive an offender "seventy-seven times" (the expression implies ongoing forgiveness), He will do no less than the same for the repentant heart (Matthew 18:22).

Fun Versus Winning at All Costs

Fun is the motivation of many sport enthusiasts at all levels of competition. However, just as the "win at all costs" mind-set misses the point, so, too, can the "fun is everything" approach. The caution for the serious-minded is to lighten up, and for those with the fun approach to get serious (Clifford and Feezell 2010).

Winning and losing are tools for personal growth and maturation. Sports ministry carefully uses the instructive characteristics of these concepts to enhance the world of sport by teaching and demonstrating how to be a good winner and a good loser. It is not an either-or scenario; both winning and losing can be used in God's service for the betterment of His Kingdom purposes.

The "Salt" and "Light" of Christian Influence

Sport needs the influential "salt" and "light" of the Christian witness (Matthew 5:13-16). Unfortunately, too many Christian athletes have lost their savor and have dimmed their lights within the athletic arena. The admonition for the Christian athlete is to wake up, trim the lamp of life, and be an equipped godly influencer within the world of sport. Standards within sport are going to be followed. The question is, Whose standards will they be? Will the voice of the Christian be heard? Will his or her faith be demonstrated in a winsome and appealing manner? Will observers respond, "That is how the game is meant to be played!"?

SUMMARY

What is learned in life will be applied to sport, and what is learned in sport will be applied to life. Moral ethical codes determine behaviors within sport. Christians participating in sport are held to high ethical standards, ones guided by biblical precepts and admonitions. They experience the clash of pluralistic worldviews of those who acknowledge the authority of Jesus and those who do not. For Jesus followers, sport is no longer a mere secular activity but has become infused with new sacred intentions. This new perception results in seeing and interpreting the world differently. Bearing the image of God, all people are to be treated with respect even when intense differences of opinion surface. As examined, Christian faith informs sport-related ethical decisions such as the compatibility of faith and sport, how to reconcile the historic pagan associations with sport, whether and how to observe the Sabbath, whether to participate in gamesmanship, and how to view the merits of winning and losing. Sport needs the influential presence of biblical principles, and the Christian community is called, equipped, and empowered to deliver accordingly.

REVIEW AND DISCUSSION QUESTIONS

1. What aspect of sport do you find to be most difficult to reconcile with Christian faith?

2. Does the Fourth Commandment (Sabbath rest) influence any of your decisions related to participation in your sport? How?

3. Is cheating in sport acceptable as long as you do not get caught? Explain. By what authority do you base your opinion?

4. What forms of gamesmanship have you experienced or witnessed? Is gamesmanship an acceptable part of the game?

5. Discuss a life lesson you have learned through a time of failure in sport.

6. AIA founder Dave Hannah believed that winning was important to gain the respect of a secular audience. Do you agree with his assessment?

7. How might Christian athletes, coaches, and fans better influence and serve the world of sport through their ethical conduct?

Faith and finances are important puzzle pieces for successful sports ministries.

CHAPTER 8

Financing Sports Ministry

"Stewardship is the act of organizing your life so that God can spend you."

Lynn A. Miller, author and stewardship theologian for Mennonite Mutual Aid, Elkhart, Indiana

LEARNING OBJECTIVES

After studying this chapter, you should be able to do the following:

- Explain the importance of faith as it relates to finances
- Explain the importance of the basic elements of stewardship
- Identify various principles, methods, and tools of sound financial management as they relate to quality sports ministry initiatives
- Describe the basic elements of securing the necessary financial resources and the approaches you believe are best for securing a ministry's funding sources
- Understand the importance and responsibility of honest and consistent communication with a sports ministry's system of financial support
- Understand the challenges that can result for effective sports ministry when available financial resources do not meet budgeted goals

Picture the following meeting of sports ministry leadership with their advisory board. At their annual retreat they review how God has blessed their work through the programs offered the previous year. Many stories are shared about the ministry's growth and the spiritual impact it has had on participants. A feel-good atmosphere permeates the room. After a lunch break the group discusses the agenda's next item: the financial report. Shortly into the presentation, the leader reveals a financial strategy employed for the first time ever during the previous year. In an effort to initiate special new opportunities for which they had no funding, they opted in faith to increase their credit limit on their personal credit cards with the intent of raising the money afterward. Six months later, with a significant debt load approaching $50,000, their plan was not working well. In fact, they were barely covering the minimum monthly payments on this recently acquired debt. This, combined with a less than attractive interest rate, quickly caused all the earlier feel-good atmosphere in the room to evaporate. After heated debate cooler heads prevailed, and the board and ministry leadership stepped back, prayed, and set about to develop a plan to rectify the situation. It took time, but within 12 months the ministry was back on track financially with guidelines in place to ensure this did not happen again. The good news is that this sports ministry and its leadership team and advisory board worked together and successfully overcame a significant financial dilemma. In doing so, they effectively navigated the circumstances enabling them to continue ministry with young people through sport for the glory of God.

The sad truth is that mismanagement and poor stewardship have been the undoing of more than one sports ministry. Therefore, it is important to learn not only how to raise funds, but to manage them effectively. This chapter will cover the various ways to do just that.

Financial Considerations in Sports Ministry

It is a well-documented fact that many Americans live right up to their means. Additionally, quite a number of people choose to live beyond their means, as evidenced in the opening story. In other words, they spend all—or in some cases, thanks to credit cards and lines of credit, spend more than—they are bringing in monetarily. Considering the key role finances play in sports ministry, such a style of living is not a luxury that can be afforded by those who minister through sport. Consider the **key two-dollar swing**. That is, living a dollar below one's means is good, as opposed to living a dollar beyond one's means which can prove most detrimental.

Though just two dollars separate the first individual from the second, the results over time tend to be dramatically different. The first individual is content with what the Lord has blessed them with, whereas the second falls into the trap of not only wanting much, but always wanting more, leading to frustration and discontentment. The former is freed to minister effectively, while the latter is restricted, forced to deal with and service his or her debt issues. From the outset, be determined to live within your means. Trust the Heavenly Father each step of the way to meet all needs.

Stewardship

A good plan to follow to help achieve this end, even while in college, involves the **10-10-80 rule.** The first 10 percent of earnings should be given as a gift—a tithe—back to the Lord. This is best illustrated in Malachi 3:10: "'Bring in the whole tithe,' says the LORD Almighty, 'and see if I will not throw open the floodgates of heaven and pour out so much blessing that there will not be enough room for it'" (NIV). Prominent evangelist Billy Graham speaks practically, "We have found in our home . . . that God's blessing upon the nine-tenths, when we tithe, helps it to go farther than the ten-tenths without His blessing" (Lotich 2022). Ask any seasoned Christian and they will affirm, "You cannot outgive the Lord; it is just not possible." The financial lesson is that it is wise to always give generously of one's first fruits to the Lord.

---

key two-dollar swing—The concept of living below one's means and financial resources. Living a dollar below one's means is good, as opposed to living a dollar beyond one's means, which can prove most detrimental.

10-10-80 rule—Give 10 percent back as a tithe of thanksgiving to the Lord, invest the next 10 percent for the future as a resource, and then live off of the remaining 80 percent of what the Lord provides.

The next 10 percent in the 10-10-80 rule should be invested for the future to guarantee additional resources. Living financially within and under 80 percent in a disciplined manner will be fiscally beneficial. Though what has been entrusted to you now is perhaps financially modest by most standards (especially as a college student), how you handle these means will determine your behavior when greater resources are provided. In short, practice good **stewardship** from the outset for His glory, His honor, and sharing the good news of the gospel, in this case through sport.

The simple truth in this life is that God owns everything. Psalm 24:1 affirms this: "The earth is the LORD's and everything in it" (NIV). The realization that nothing truly belongs to anyone enables people to view resources as blessings to be invested wisely for higher purposes and for the benefit of others. As stewards, everything (all possessions) are on loan from the Lord, entrusted by Him to be used in serving Him (MacArthur, n.d.).

Faith is essential as it relates to the finances needed to plan and run quality sports ministry initiatives. According to Hebrews 11:1-3, "Now faith is confidence in what we hope for and assurance about what we do not see. This is what the ancients were commended for. By faith we understand that the universe was formed at God's command, so that what is seen was not made out of what was visible" (NIV). Biblical faith is being certain about one's hopes and realities. In essence, a sports ministry begins as an idea, a hope, and a dream. When we walk in humble faith, God gives birth to the idea, refines the hope, and aligns the dream with His sovereign will.

Without faith it is impossible to please God, but with faith His existence is made known, and He rewards those who earnestly seek Him (Hebrews 11:6). Oswald Chambers captures this concept in his devotional titled "The Discipline of Spiritual Tenacity": "There is nothing noble the human mind has ever hoped for or dreamed of that will not be fulfilled. . . . Our part is to be spiritually tenacious and faithful to our calling" (Chambers 1963).

The frailty of human nature makes faithful stewardship difficult, especially when it comes to finances. Today, depreciation and identity theft are common, and stock market is unpredictable. People place too much faith in the financial system, playing risky games with their funds. Money is important because it reveals who we are. Consider the gospel's message: "For where your treasure is, there your heart will be also" (Matthew 6:21 NIV). Those with the most financial success are often not only smart but generous with their money. They not only safeguard it for future uncertainties, but they also give it away strategically. Cheerfully giving is what makes them who they are before God. Contentment is discovered, forgetting themselves and turning their interests toward the Lord's delight in others. Balance is the key. Do not spend money selfishly but be generous as God directs. Do not hoard it away in a system that can fail. Remember Jesus' core mission was love, acceptance, and forgiveness (Luke 19:10). He also spent much time talking about money and a person's treasure principle (Packer 2011). A study of Scripture reveals that money is mentioned over 800 times and that finances are referenced over 2,000 times. Faith in God's provision for His work is fundamental to successful, sustainable sports ministry endeavors (Evans n.d.).

Spiritual ROI (SROI)

We all know the old saying "practice makes perfect"; however, the reality is that practice makes permanent, whether for good or not, depending on how one practices: "Repeat the same mistakes over and over, and you won't get any closer to performing at Carnegie Hall" (Kay 2014). As noted, managing money well, even while in college, will establish a foundation for good fiscal habits. If one does not manage one's personal money well, neither will one manage the financial resources of a sports ministry effectively. Nurturing and doing habits well is a preparation for personal and family life and for sports ministry, resulting in significant **spiritual return on investment** (**SROI**). In the business world, the acronym ROI (return on investment) is often used as a measure of how much financial benefit is derived from a particular monetary investment. Investing in people spiritually is the heart of relationship-based sports. Simultaneously, we are investing in the advancement of God's Kingdom on earth as told in Matthew 6:20: "Store up for yourselves treasures in heaven, where moths and vermin do not destroy, and where thieves do not break in and steal" (NIV). Such investments are the best investments.

---

stewardship—Appropriately managing the resources and means that God provides and for His glory.

spiritual return on investment (SROI)—The practice of investing one's resources and energies in glorifying God and seeing lives changed through the gospel message. It is an investment that pays dividends in this life as well as yielding eternal returns.

The matter of money management is practical and far too often is not given the attention it deserves. Many view it as a less-than-spiritual undertaking. Yet financial considerations and money management ultimately are important for successful sports ministry initiatives. Whether sports ministry is done by an individual, as a program within a local church, or as an independent organization, financial resources will be needed to make the ministry possible.

Financial Management in Sports Ministry

Not enough attention is given to sound financial management. Realizing the vital importance of managing and handling the financial resources of a sports ministry is the first step in doing it well. Clear lessons can be gleaned from the world of business and finance. The goal is to present the basic principles of financial management as they relate to the appropriate fiscal management of sports ministries. As God provides financial resources, it then becomes the job of the sports ministry leader and his or her team to manage these resources wisely to serve people and achieve quality results.

Identifying the various principles, methods, and tools that lead to sound financial management generally fall into two broad areas in sports ministry, just as they do in the world of business. The first area of consideration is how to secure the necessary financial resources to start and run a sports ministry. The second area involves determining how to best deploy and use these financial resources (Fried, DeSchriver, and Mondello 2020). However, a third, very important area of sound financial management in sports ministry is the intersection of accountability and stewardship. Figure 8.1 illustrates the three broad areas concerning financial management functions in sports ministry.

Determining and Securing the Needed Financial Resources

The individual tasked with managing a sports ministry's money has two main roles. First, he or she must forecast and determine how much money the organization will need to meet its ministry goals. Second, the financial manager needs to work with the rest of the ministry team to determine how they will secure these needed financial resources. Just as in the business world, choosing how financial resources will be allocated can have significant short- and long-term ramifications on a sports ministry (Fried, DeSchriver, and Mondello 2020). The individual tasked with managing the financial resources has a key role to play if a ministry is to be successfully launched and sustainable. The following verses illustrate this point:

Suppose one of you wants to build a tower. Won't you first sit down and estimate the cost to see if you have enough money to complete it? For if you lay the foundation and are not able to finish it, everyone who sees it will ridicule you, saying, "This person began to build and wasn't able to finish." (Luke 14:28-30 NIV)

Determining the needed financial resources for sports ministry that honors God requires careful planning, counsel, and the development of a viable budget. In step one, the planning phase, the dream or desire for a sports ministry is conceived. Much thought and prayer must go into this phase. Here, the team refines the idea for ministry that can work. Once conceived and polished, the second step is to seek counsel from others who have done similar sports-related ministries. Wisdom's counsel declares, "Plans fall for lack of counsel, but with many advisers they succeed" (Proverbs 15:22 NIV). The word *advisers* in the verse is plural for a reason. Different advisers and having a multitude of counselors is a

Area 1	Area 2	Area 3
Securing necessary financial resources	Deployment and wise use of financial resources	Accountability and stewardship

FIGURE 8.1   Areas of financial management functions in sports ministry.

valuable approach because a variety of viewpoints will yield better, stronger perspectives on which to build a new sports ministry. The soundest decisions are made when all angles have been considered. Following this procedure allows a ministry to go from an idea to a potential reality (Got Questions, n.d.). It is important to note that not all advice sought will be agreed upon. "As iron sharpens iron, so one person sharpens another" (Proverbs 27:17 NIV). When one element sharpens another, the substance on the sharpening surface must, by necessity, be harder than the material being sharpened, such as two different types of iron alloys. In like manner, one who is stronger and more experienced in faith can help sharpen another so that he or she can become that much stronger in the process (God's Chemistry Set 2011). This concept holds true for the sharpening and refining of a sports ministry idea as well. If the advice received does not support the ministry plan, it would be wise to pause and consider the wisdom offered.

The third and final step is to develop a viable budget, covering the first three to five years of operation and ministry. Carefully affixing a cost to the various elements of the sports ministry and projecting these annual costs over the first three years (at least) enables the team to forge a plan for securing the needed money and resources. Once a viable budget is crafted, it is beneficial to have experienced eyes review it for accuracy, completeness, and fiscal viability. It is also wise before the first donor is secured and the first dollar of support is received, that the ministry enrolls with the ECFA. This practice will lend immediate credibility to the endeavor.

Once the three steps are complete, the ministry team's leadership should determine how much financial resources will be needed and how funds will be secured. The discussion about money must be approached as spiritual one. As Henri Nouwen remarks, "Fundraising is, first and foremost, a form of ministry. It is a way of announcing our vision and inviting other people into our mission" (Nouwen 2010, 16). In this process, the minister or ministry seeks God to provide the need through His people. The sports ministry team shares the vision and mission with potential donors, asking them to prayerfully consider if and how much they should give (Shadrach 2013, 22-24). These financial needs can be met in a variety of ways, and each individual, church, or organization will need to decide which way is best for them as they prayerfully and diligently seek funding.

The required financial resources can be secured in five main ways. The first approach is referred to as the *tentmaking approach*, which has been around a long time in general ministry endeavors. The second approach involves running the sports ministry as a *self-sustaining business*. The third approach is *support raising*. The majority of sports ministry initiatives follow this third approach. The fourth approach, though not as widely incorporated by sports ministries, is the approach of a *fully funded partnership*. The final approach is a *hybrid model*, a combination of two or more of the first four approaches.

The Tentmaking Approach

The **tentmaking approach** refers to one providing for one's own needs through a job, retirement benefits, or other means in order to minister. The term *tentmaking* comes from the example in Acts 18:1-4 of the Apostle Paul, who was himself a tentmaker. Upon his arrival in Corinth, he met a tentmaking couple named Aquila and Priscilla, and he worked alongside them while teaching in the synagogues and ministering to the Jewish people of the city. The advantage of this self-funded approach is not having to rely on funding from other sources in order to minister. The disadvantages to this approach are time restraints due to other job responsibilities, leaving the minister with less time for ministry itself. Fewer people are involved in the ministry's hands-on prayer support.

Self-Sustaining Business Approach

The **self-sustaining business** practice is common within sports ministries because many provide clinics, camps, teams, leagues, international mission trips, and more. People expect to pay something to be involved in various activities; sports ministry organizations might cover their expenditures plus earn additional revenue to defray ministry and staff expenses. Many ministries that operate this way find that they can offer programs of equal or better quality to secular organizations at a lower price, making their programs more attractive. One of the dangers of this method is the tendency of the ministry to benefit those who are capable of paying. If the ministry is called to reach people who are poor or marginalized, it must be intentional about using income-generating funds to help those who otherwise would be unable to participate.

---

tentmaking approach—Raising funds and support involves sports ministers providing for their own needs and the needs of the ministry through their job, retirement benefits, investments, and other means.

self-sustaining business—A viable way of funding ministry by setting up ministry and periphery activities as a business entity that meets the ministry's financial needs as a whole.

A good example of a ministry as a self-sustaining business is the Indiana Basketball Academy led by former NBA Laker Tom Abernethy. The academy is a shining example of a developmental training academy for young people that is also an incarnational ministry providing high-quality biblical instruction, a key mission of the founders, Tom and his wife, Susie (Compton 2014).

Support Raising Approach

Support raising is a traditional way of funding ministry personnel. Those who respond donate to the organization, which in turn pays the minister. Frequently, the minister must have pledges for full support and several months of consistent giving before beginning the ministry. Relying on others to meet a financial need so that one can devote one's full effort to ministry has biblical examples. The Apostle Paul relied on his tentmaking abilities to meet his personal needs while ministering (Acts 18:1-4). Yet in Acts 18:5 we read, "When Silas and Timothy came from Macedonia, Paul devoted himself exclusively to preaching, testifying to the Jews that Jesus was the Messiah." Silas and Timothy likely brought with them

---

SPORTS MINISTRY IN ACTION
Former NBA Player Combines Basketball, Sports Ministry, and Business

Tom Abernethy's career in basketball has spanned decades, and he has built an impressive résumé. A standout at every level, the Carmel, Indiana, resident has been an Indiana All-Star, an NCAA champion, an NBA player, an Indiana Basketball Hall of Famer, and a founder of the Indiana Basketball Academy (1996). Despite these credentials and accolades, his Christian faith, not basketball, is at the center of his life. His latest new youth program, Bigger Vision BBall, was launched in 2017 and is designed for boys and girls ages 5 to 13. This former Indiana University star has created a sports ministry program combining high-quality basketball instruction while developing strong Christian character through biblical teaching. According to Abernathy, "The concept that I have been thinking about for many years is how to provide excellent basketball teaching to kids and a program that will emphasize fundamentals and skills to go hand-in-hand with excellent Bible teaching." (Tom Abernethy pers. interview 2022) Hundreds of youths have gone through the program, and many aspiring basketball players have benefited from this twofold approach.

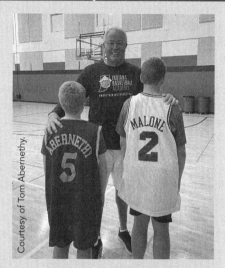

Tom Abernethy joins a couple of young players during a basketball training session.

If there is one word that best describes what we do, we encourage kids. We feel it is important to encourage kids to play and to learn to be the best they can be. With Bigger Vision, it's how to grow your Godly character, how to become more Christ-like. Tough things happen in sports and in basketball. There are so many lessons that can be learned, so as we are teaching these lessons, we are emphasizing the importance of them growing and building their faith. (Morwick 2018)

Regarding the business and financial aspects of this ministry, Tom offers the following: "God has made this whole thing work for us. I wasn't nervous about the project because of my faith in God. Things haven't always gone exactly perfect, but we have had success" (Tom Abernethy pers. interview 2022) Abernethy, who left the commercial real estate world in the early 1990s, acknowledges that he and his wife took a leap of faith to start the academy. It was this faith that helped him achieve success. He concludes, "I always wanted to combine my gifts in basketball with a business setting. It's all about how the kids are treated and taught" (Compton 2014). Possessing a strong faith and trusting God's provision for the founding and sustaining ministry of the Indiana Basketball Academy has been the core of this ministry's success.

---

support raising—This approach establishes a financial goal for individuals and families to meet their annual personal and ministry expenses. This goal is set by the ministry organization. Family, friends, churches, and foundations are approached with the vision and invited to partner with them financially.

a generous gift from the church in Philippi, located in the region of Macedonia (Philippians 4:15-16). Paul did not solicit money from the people to whom he was ministering, which was a common practice in that time. He wanted to avoid the appearance of false motives. Jesus is another example of someone who ministered with the support of others. Prior to his ministry years, Jesus made a living as a carpenter. The Bible does not indicate that he did carpentry during his three-year ministry. In addition to the 12 disciples, a number of women traveled with Jesus, meeting the financial needs of the group from their own resources (Luke 8:1-3). The advantage of this kind of funding is that contributors often have a relationship with the minister. This close relationship builds a partnership of prayer, accountability, and long-term giving.

Support raising can be both challenging and rewarding because interactions with friends, family, and churches are heightened. While it can be easier to talk about money matters with close associates, it also can be more difficult. The wisdom of mentors who have already successfully raised their support will provide experienced and wise counsel. In addition, training in public speaking and how to effectively write support letters are often available through sending agencies (Von Gunten, n.d.). Seeking financial and prayer support expands the scope of ministry partnerships. Supporters are extensions of the mission field. They may not physically be on the ministry location, but their participation is vitally important. Their financial support enables the use of soccer to share the gospel with children in Liberia, or the use of basketball to do the same in Croatia. Their generous support enables lives to be affected for eternal dividends. Praying for the right prayer and financial partners to be on the broader ministry team is essential. As these partnerships unfold, God can be trusted to bless and provide the necessary resources for effective, sustaining ministry (TEAM 2020).

Fully Funded Partnership Approach

Another approach is the **fully funded partnership**. In the church setting the church would incorporate the costs of running sports ministry into its yearly budget. The likelihood of a person with adequate means having a relationship with a minister and sharing a vision for the mission is low, makes this arrangement a rarity outside of the church setting. From the minister's standpoint, it would seem to be a dream come true, but one person or foundation providing funds sometimes results in a feeling of ownership and a desire to direct the minister or ministry rather than simply providing funding for it. Foundations typically require grant proposals, which mandate a level of expertise to produce. Funding is not usually guaranteed for long periods of time, and if the grant is not renewed, the ministry is impeded until a new funding source can be found. The same is true for an individual donor. Should the donor have a reversal in business or his or her interest is drawn in a different direction, the ministry would need to secure new funding.

In the approach of a fully funded partnership, the bulk of the work is done well before the launch of the sports ministry. The vision is created and then shared with individuals or groups who catch the vision and possess the capacity to fund it. The ability to communicate the vision in a clear, compelling, and articulate manner is the key to conveying passion to others. The advantage to this approach is that the sports ministry is freed up to focus on its mission and outreach. This approach has less face-to-face interaction with supporters. It is recommended to have a separate, independent prayer support team with whom to communicate on a regular basis (TEAM 2020).

One example of the fully funded approach is Gospel Patrons, founded by John and Renee Rinehart. At the age of 25, John wanted more than just the American dream of success, wealth, and great possessions. While traveling with his wife in Australia, they met over coffee with an unnamed British businessman, who was a friend of a friend. He shared some profound Christian history with them. The Rineharts recollected him to say, "Behind every great movement of God are generous business leaders who have partnered with those who proclaim the gospel. God raises up people to proclaim the gospel, but he also raises up patrons to support them." In the 1500s, William Tyndale had a patron support him as he translated the Bible into English, a high crime at the time. In the 1700s, a leading preacher of the Great Awakening was supported by Lady Huntingdon. This dynamic is also evidenced in Scripture: Jesus was supported by Mary, Joanna, and Susanna (Luke 8:1-3). The Rineharts found themselves awed by these stories of true partners in the work of the gospel, which led them to wonder what God might do through a new generation of gospel patrons. This in turn led John to take nine months to produce the book *Gospel Patrons*. His premise is simple: God has uniquely gifted each of us to serve His purposes in our

---

fully funded partnership—A minister or organization that is funded by a single large donor or foundation.

Interview With a Professional

Shaun Smithson, State Director, Maryland FCA
Mid-Atlantic Region Talent Advancement Director
BS, Bible, Lancaster Bible College
MA Theology, Liberty University

Courtesy of Shaun Smithson.

Shaun Smithson has spent the past eight years as the team chaplain for DC United of Major League Soccer and five years as the Maryland state director for the Fellowship of Christian Athletes (FCA). As state director, he led a team of 70 staff and hundreds of volunteers as they strive to lead every coach and athlete into a growing relationship with Jesus Christ and His Church. Shaun, his wife, and their four children have lived and served 20 years in Howard County, Maryland, located between Baltimore and Washington, DC, with FCA, Search Ministries, and Grace Community Church, and on several local nonprofit boards.

What was your career path?

My professional career began as a member of the United States Air Force Honor Guard in Washington, DC, and Arlington National Cemetery. After military service I served as a youth pastor at Mount Zion United Methodist Church and then later in the same role at Grace Community Church. My next professional assignment was as the executive assistant to the president of Search Ministries, Larry Moody. At Search Ministries our mission revolved around "conversations about life and faith in the marketplace" through discussion groups that enabled participants to explore Christianity outside of the traditional church setting.

What characteristics must individuals have to be successful in a sports ministry like the FCA?

I would say the characteristics needed to be successful with FCA are high levels of faith and belief in God through Jesus Christ. Beyond this foundation it is important to be a motivated self-starter; possess an entrepreneurial spirit; and be very strong in the areas of integrity, teamwork, service, and excellence.

As you started out with FCA, what resources and training did you find to be valuable in securing your initial financial resources?

FCA provides strong, proven training and resources through the Support Raising Solutions (SRS) organization. SRS runs a program called Fundraising Bootcamp, which gives new staff the tools to share their story. Their book *The God Ask* helped me to better understand the biblical basis for support raising. Finally, I was blessed with an experienced mentor. For me it was the president of Search Ministries under whom I served prior to my present role with FCA.

You teach a course in raising support for the Mid-Atlantic Region for the FCA. Tell us about this program.

The course I teach is a six-week discussion-based cohort. The course is designed to complement the other FCA support-raising strategies and provides a setting where staff working to get funded can encourage and learn from one another while building one another up in the support-raising process. My goal is to build on the foundation of the SRS Bootcamp and in doing so help them get across the finish line to being fully funded and ready to serve.

Is there anything else you would like to share about raising support from your time with the FCA that would provide valuable insights to our readers?

I think one of the most key pieces is the idea of partnership with those who support us. Philippians 4:17 says, "Not that I desire your gifts; what I desire is that more be credited to your account." The focus of Paul's gratitude was not merely for the money itself, but also for the blessings the Philippians would experience as God loves and blesses the cheerful giver. The insight is this: our partners get to answer God's call to be involved with our ministry, and this involvement yields many blessings to all in this special relationship.

What do you consider to be the greatest challenge for raising support for sports ministry work in the next couple of decades?

Presently, most of the challenges in raising support are internal (see Overcoming the Five Challenges to raising support in the next question). I don't see that changing in the next couple of decades. Culture will continue to change and find new ways to portray gospel ministry in a negative light, but God has always provided for His work in the past, and I believe He will continue to be faithful and to provide in the future as well. An example of this is how God has provided through the Covid pandemic. FCA is healthier than ever here in Maryland during this prolonged event. God has raised people up who have generously given in greater numbers for the many young people who need this special ministry through sport. (Shaun Smithson, pers. interview 2022)

Do you know why individuals called to full-time vocational ministry outside the walls of the local church ignore the calling?

You guessed it—many struggle with the idea of raising support. Or at least that is the reason they give verbally. In reality, my reasons were rooted a little deeper. Read on if you think yours might be as well. This is how I arrived at what I refer to as Overcoming the Five Challenges to raising support.

1. *Fear:* The reason for our fear can include all of the other following reasons, but the process begins by admitting that fear might be the main thing keeping us from walking into the ministry that God has called us to. Fear paralyzes us! But we serve a God who has the power to mobilize servants that are willing to present their weakness to Him. This is one reason that the first step to getting fully funded is prayer (Mark 9:14-29).

2. *Pride:* "I love to serve people, but I struggle with asking others to help." Those were the words that a mentor of mine asked me to say back to myself slowly the first time I told him why I didn't like raising support. After I repeated them, he humbly said, "That is pride! I know it because I struggled with it too." Many who are daring enough to accept the call to vocational ministry are also prideful enough to think that God wants them to do it on their own. The enemy's chief lie is, "You will be fine on your own." But anyone who has ever accomplished something significant knows that this is simply not true. God designed us to be a part of a team. Even more precisely, he designed us to be a part of a body with Him as the head: "The eye cannot say to the hand, 'I don't need you'" (1 Corinthians 12:21). Neither should we say to those who have the ability to support our ministry, "I don't need you."

3. *Doubt (in your calling):* A wise man reminded me early in my support-raising process that if God had truly called me to vocational ministry, He also called others to support my ministry. This was meant to provide confidence, but it also raised a question: Are you called to full-time vocational ministry? All are called to serve, and for some, their secular job will be a great tool for their ministry. For others, the outside job keeps them from equipping the saints in the way that they know God wants them to. If you fall in the first category, please don't let anyone pull you away from the profession you are in. If you fall in the second, have confidence to find an encourager who can remind you when your confidence waivers (1 Timothy 1:7). If you are not sure, seek counsel from trusted advisors (Proverbs 15:22).

4. *Laziness or lack of discipline:* While most considering full-time ministry are not inherently lazy, almost all will struggle with the amount of work and discipline it takes to become fully supported. Those called to vocational ministry must be willing to work as hard, and sometimes harder, than their peers in secular jobs. And they often must be willing to accept less pay. This takes motivation, discipline, character, and a love for Jesus that says, "Lord, to whom shall we go? You have the words of eternal life" (John 6:68 NIV). However, even with all of the above, most will have "I quit" days in the process of becoming fully funded. For this reason, you owe it to yourself to find an accountability partner early on who can hold you to the goals you set for yourself (1 Corinthians 9:24-27).

5. *Lack of faith (in God's ability):* In Matthew 6:24-27 Jesus says,

> No one can serve two masters. For you will hate the one and love the other; you
> will be devoted to one and despise the other. You cannot serve God and be

> *enslaved to money. That is why I tell you not to worry about everyday life, whether you have enough food or drink, or enough clothes to wear. Isn't life more than food, and the body more than clothing? Look at the birds. They don't plant or harvest or store food in barns, for your heavenly Father feeds them. And aren't you far more valuable to Him than they are? Can all you worries add a single moment to your life?" (NLT)*

The clear answer is no. Your worries cannot add anything to your life. But God can. Do you trust Him enough to provide for the things you need in life and ministry? If so, prayerfully prepare your budget now, and begin the journey of becoming fully supported. You will not regret it.

---

generation (Acts 13:36). Most of us will not end up being preachers or missionaries, but God is writing a great story, and He has a part for each of us to play (Ephesians 2:10). The mission of *Gospel Patrons* is to inspire and empower a new generation who will build the Church, bless the world, and finish the Great Commission. This book might prove helpful in support raising, especially as it relates to the fully funded category (Gospel Patrons, n.d.).

When it comes to the concept espoused in *Gospel Patrons*, the following two quotes are particularly poignant:

> *With Christ, it is not how much we give, but what we do not give that is the real test."* (Oswald Chambers, 1874-1917, Scottish evangelist)

> *I have held many things in my hands, and I have lost them all; but whatever I have placed in God's hands, that I still possess. (Martin Luther, 1483-1546, German theologian)*

Hybrid Combination Approach

Hybrid models of funding combine parts of some or all of the above methodologies in the quest for funding ministers and ministry. Rarely will any individual or organization use one of the four methods exclusively. As organizations grow, it becomes necessary to employ multiple funding strategies. While individual ministers within the organization might be required to raise their support, the organization might have a development director who pursues foundations and large donors. The organization might also employ fundraising activities like golf tournaments or inter-

national trips, or it might promote sponsorship of specific ministry activities like sponsoring a child, a well to bring fresh drinking water to a specific village, leadership training, or medical or educational materials that ministers can use to meet the needs of those to whom they are ministering.

This list of funding methods is ever-expanding as people and organizations become more creative in attracting funding for ministry. No one-size-fits-all approach can be applied to securing financial resources. The minister seeks God knowing that He is the provider of all that is needed. Then the minister reaches out to the potential supporter asking God to call him or her in like manner.

Having covered these five main ways of securing adequate financial resources—tentmaking, self-sustaining business, support raising, fully funded partnerships, and hybrid models of funding—additional financial considerations, as these relate to creating, running, and sustaining successful sports ministries, will be addressed.

As noted earlier, the third area of consideration that has significant bearing on sports ministry is the mutual combination of accountability and stewardship. In the business world those companies that are most accountable to and transparent with their various constituencies tend to be more successful over time. This fact is equally true in the financial management of gifted resources to sports ministries. Those who support sports ministry initiatives invariably possess a strong desire to know that their gifts are being put to good use. Quality accountability is best achieved by transparency and effective two-way communication between supporters and the sports ministry team. This supportive process is ongoing

---

hybrid models of funding—A combination of some, or in some cases, all of the following methods of securing funding: tentmaking approach, a self-sustaining business, support raising, or a fully funded partnership. This approach is often employed as an effective strategy as rarely will any individual or organization use just one of the four methods exclusively.

and is not only financial, but also includes spiritual components of prayer and various expressions of encouragement. Thus wholesome stewardship is achieved as God-honoring gifts are properly rendered for the intended purposes of the prescribed work.

On Financial Transparency

One of the best ways to achieve financial accountability is through transparency. Mark Twain is reported to have said, "If you tell the truth, you don't have to remember anything." The same is true of **transparency** as it relates to financial accountability. Always tell the truth fully in oral and written communications. All communications and reports need to be in conformity with applicable laws and regulations and in conformity to biblical mandates. Being truthful is the best way to ensure the establishment and maintenance of a strong, trusting relationship between all parties. Technically, most would not necessarily consider transparency to be a financial term or metric, yet as a concept it has become increasingly important in the world of business today. Transparency has always been of key importance in sports ministry initiatives. Transparency and positive two-way communication assist greatly in managing donor expectations and demonstrating that the gifts of one's supporters are appreciated and being put to proper use.

The Mission of ECFA

Sports ministry managers have a neutral third-party ally that helps significantly in this area of accountability with their ministry's supporters. For over four decades, the Evangelical Council for Financial Accountability (ECFA) has served Christ-centered ministries of every kind to enhance trust in relationships with their donors, supporters, and constituencies.

The ECFA has created the "Seven Standards of Responsible Stewardship," which are applied to accredited member organizations. These seven standards demonstrate a ministry's compliance with established standards for financial accountability, transparency, fundraising, and board governance. The Christ-centered ministries accredited by EFCA include but are not limited to churches, denominations, educational institutions, rescue missions, sports ministries, and camps. These many types of tax-exempt 501(c)(3) organizations represent nearly $30 billion in annual revenue. A relationship with the

ECFA is a mark of a ministry's good faith compliance with all ECFA standards.

The ECFA's Seven Standards of Responsible Stewardship represent principles drawn directly from the Bible and are fundamental to demonstrating integrity in stewardship. The goal is to genuinely live the words of the Apostle Paul in 2 Corinthians 8:20-21: "We want to avoid any criticism of the way we administer this liberal gift. For we are taking pains to do what is right, not only in the eyes of the Lord but also in the eyes of man" (NIV). ECFA-accredited ministries are committed to upholding the following Seven Core Standards:

- *Standard 1:* Every organization is committed to a written statement of faith that clearly reflects biblical truth and practices.

- *Standard 2:* Every organization shall be governed by a board of five or more individuals, the majority of whom shall be independent of the ministry.

- *Standard 3:* Every ministry shall prepare fiscally complete and accurate financial statements. These statements shall be reviewed annually by an independent certified accounting firm.

- *Standard 4:* Ministries shall be appropriately managed to ensure that all its operations are responsibly conducted. The ministry will demonstrate conformity with applicable laws and regulations as well as taking into consideration biblical mandates.

- *Standard 5:* Current financial statements shall be provided upon written request as well as providing any other legally required or requested reports and disclosures.

- *Standard 6:* Ministries shall subscribe to and demonstrate compliance with ECFA's Policy for Excellence in Compensation-Setting and Related-Party Transactions.

- *Standard 7:* The guidelines for stewardship of charitable gifts are covered through Sub Sections 7.1-7.5 covering categories such as truthfulness in communications, donor expectations, charitable gift communication, acting in the best interest of financial supporters, and meeting guidelines for appropriate compensation percentage levels for securing charitable gifts (Evangelical Council for Financial Accountability n.d.).

---

transparency—The extent to which supporters and donors have ready access to a sports ministry's leadership team and the ministry's financial information and overall fiscal health (Chen 2021).

Basic Elements of Financial Management in Sports Ministry

In this section we will discuss the importance of taking advantage of tax-exempt status and the key value this legislation provides for sports ministries. Additional attention will be given to the areas of fixed costs versus variable costs, the importance of controlling costs and expenditures, and the importance of learning and implementing best practices. This section closes with a look at what defines success in sports ministry both from a results standpoint as well as a financial standpoint.

Viability of 501(c)(3) Tax-Exempt Status for Sports Ministries

As previously discussed in the section regarding the ECFA, tax-exempt 501(c)(3) Christ-centered ministries, such as sports ministry organizations, churches, denominations, educational institutions, rescue missions, and Christian camps, collectively represent nearly $30 billion in annual revenue (Evangelical Council for Financial Accountability, n.d.). Applying for and securing 501(c)(3) status is important for those who run sports ministry efforts. A 501(c)(3) is a corporation that receives tax-exempt status from the Internal Revenue Service (IRS). In order to secure this status, a corporation must file a Recognition of Exemption form. While services are available to do this for an organization, it is best to apply directly to the IRS and pay the one-time application fee. The following are key elements to know about the 501(c)(3) application process.

What Does 501(c)(3) Status Mean?

The status of 501(c)(3) means that a corporation is exempt from paying federal taxes on revenues and income generated in the organization. It does not exempt the organization from filing tax returns. Filling out IRS Form 990 is required each fiscal year to account for the income received by the organization. The financial data of a 501(c)(3) is subject to public review, whereas a private organization is allowed to maintain its books without such scrutiny from the public. Nonprofit 501(c)(3) organizations must follow the required organizational rules regarding its articles of incorporation and its board of directors. The scrutiny is on how much of the incoming revenues are reinvested toward fulfilling the mission of the organization. The sports ministry can pay salaries, but these salaries must be considered reasonable compensation (Leonard, Haskins, and Bottorff 2021).

What Is Required to Maintain 501(c)(3) Status?

The primary required responsibilities are the annual filings of Form 990 and any subsequent schedules accompanying the form. This form has four parts: The first part reviews the details of the organization's mission and volunteer base. The second part summarizes the ministry's annual revenues. The third part details expenses, and the fourth part summarizes net assets. Aside from filing the annual tax forms, the organization (the ministry) should avoid engaging in activities that could jeopardize its tax-exempt status. The following list, though not exhaustive, addresses some activities that should be avoided:

- Operating in a manner unrelated to the mission of the organization
- Not filing a return for three consecutive fiscal years
- Not operating for the benefit of public interest
- Participating in political campaigns at any level as an organization

Additional restrictions are placed on nonprofits and are covered in the appropriate IRS regulations on its website (Leonard, Haskins, and Bottorff 2021). Some of the pros and cons of becoming a 501(c)(3) nonprofit are shown in table 8.1.

How to Apply for 501(c)(3) Status

Before applying for 501(c)(3) status, a sports ministry must complete all preliminary paperwork required at the state level. The next step involves applying for and securing an Employee Identification Number (EIN) with the IRS by completing Form SS-4. Depending on the form chosen, this process can take between one to two months, for the 1023-EZ form, and up to six months, or longer, for the 1023 form. All required forms and a documentation checklist are available on the IRS website. Once approved, the IRS will send a Determination Letter, which should be kept with the organization's bylaws and tax filings (Leonard, Haskins, and Bottorff 2021).

TABLE 8.1 Advantages and Disadvantages of Tax-Exempt Status

Advantages	Disadvantages
Tax advantage: The tax-exempt status allows the sports ministry to put more money into the fulfillment of the mission and goals.	*Administrative work:* Nonprofits require detailed records that must be kept along with annual filings to the IRS.
Grant eligibility: Many public and private grants will not consider allocating funds to organizations unless they are registered with the IRS as a 501(c)(3).	*Shared control:* Most states require a 501(c)(3) to have several members on the board who are responsible for electing officers who determine the policies of the ministry organization.
Formal structure: Maintaining a formal structure keeps founders and volunteers separate from the organization. This is important because it helps to limit liabilities of the organization away from founders, board of directors, and volunteers.	*Public scrutiny:* Nonprofits are dedicated to the public interest and therefore are subject to having their records and accounts reviewed by the public upon request. This review includes all administrative and staff salaries as well as all expenditures.

Adapted from K. Leonard, J. Haskins, and C. Bottorff, "501(c)(3) Application: How to Obtain Nonprofit Status," Forbes Advisor, last modified September 29, 2022, www.forbes.com/advisor/business/501c3-application-online/..

Fixed Costs Versus Variable Costs in Managing a Sports Ministry

Fixed costs are consistent expenses a sports ministry has, regardless of how many programs or how much ministry the organization is doing. Rent, telephone, Internet, insurance, salaries (e.g., hourly employees running the office), registration, and insurance (if the ministry has vehicles) are examples of fixed costs. The **variable costs** are expenses that change depending on how many programs or how much ministry the organization does. Sports ministry program costs might include facility rental, uniforms and equipment, coaching stipends or volunteer gifts (depending on whether coaches are volunteers or paid), transportation, and food. Fixed costs tend to represent a high percentage of the overall ministry costs. Though financial cuts can be made to the category of fixed costs, such cuts can only be minimal at best before the overall ministry becomes unstable and no longer financially viable. The same is essentially true for variable costs because these represent the expenses of the actual programs provided by sports ministries. Therefore, it is important to carefully plan projected costs and budgets and the needed financial support for each of these categories.

Controlling Costs

Controlling both fixed and variable costs must be an intentional and diligent focus of the ministry's leadership. If the ministry's office space is in a corporate complex, a possible way to lower these costs might be to look for a local church with extra space that might charge a lower rent or even no rent. Variable costs require more diligence because they are numerous and sometimes fast and furious during peak ministry times. It is important to have a budget for sports ministry programs ahead of time and for the program leader to understand the budget and oversight. If program leaders are not financially trained nor aware of program budgets, they could jeopardize the overall budget with last-minute decisions that are less than well thought out and that result in spending money needlessly.

To build a projected budget, a program director determines the total amount of anticipated revenue and expenditures. In figure 8.2, the Cumulative Cash Flow line (line 42) for March and April, trip expenses exceeded income considerably. The shortfall would require either a rapid increase in contribution funding or a delay in payment for airfare. Upon the trip's completion, the use of a budget sheet enables the ministry to compare estimates with actual numbers to determine the accuracy of its $2,615 budget projection.

---

fixed costs—Ongoing expenses such as rent, telephone, insurance, salaries, and so on.

variable costs—Expenses that fluctuate or are periodic such as a one-time cost for a special program or project.

SHORT TERM SPORTS MINISTRY TRIP BUDGET

Account	Income	January	February	March	April	May	June	July	Aug	Sep	Oct	Nov	Dec	Total
40300	Income: Short-Term Trip	2000	2000	4000	10000	10000	14800							42800
40301	Mission % Short-Term Trip	-200	-200	-400	-1000	-1000	-1480	0	0	0	0	0	0	-4280
40318	Prev Yr Inc: Short-Term Trip													0
40395	Misc: Short-Term Trip													0
														0
														0
														0
														0
														0
	Total Income	1800	1800	3600	9000	9000	13320	0	0	0	0	0	0	38520
	Expenses													
60303	1099 staff: Short-Term Trip													0
60306	Utilities: Short-Term Trip													0
60310	Supplies: Short-Term Trip					250								250
60311	Food: Short-Term Trip						3200							3200
60325	Insurance: Short-Term Trip					200								200
60330	Ministry Materials: Short-Term Trip					100								100
60340	Telephone: Short-Term Trip													0
60351	Training Camp: Short-Term Trip													0
60360	Printing: Short-Term Trip	750				100								850
60361	Promotion: Short-Term Trip	150	150	150										450
60362	Recruiting: Short-Term Trip													0
60370	Shipping: Short-Term Trip			325	400	100								825
60378	Game Costs: Short-Term Trip						850							850
60385	Airfare: Short-Term Trip			20300										20300
60386	Lodging: Short-Term Trip						2580							2580
60387	Ground Transport: Short-Term Trip						850							850
60388	Set-Up Trip: Short-Term Trip	1100												1100
60390	Equip/Uniforms: Short-Term Trip				3250	800								4050
60395	Bank Charges: Short-Term Trip													0
60398	Other Expense: Short-Term Trip													0
60399	Misc Exp: Short -Term Trip						300							300
														0
														0
														0
														0
														0
	Total Expenses	2000	150	20775	3650	1250	300	7780	0	0	0	0	0	35905
	Monthly Cash Flow	-200	1650	-17175	5350	7750	13020	-7780	0	0	0	0	0	2615
	Cumulative Cash Flow	-200	1450	-15725	-10375	-2625	10395	2615	2615	2615	2615	2615	2615	

FIGURE 8.2   Sample budget sheet showing a short-term sports ministry trip budget.

Creating an income statement as shown in figure 8.3 is an example of a tool to keep program directors accountable and provides helpful information for planning future program budgets. Depending on the ministry's accounting software, reports can be run that cover the length of the program, as in the example, or for an individual month. These report categories compare the budgeted amount with what was actually spent. The basketball league was budgeted to finish with a deficit (-$380), which the church was projected to absorb. In actuality, the league spent $937 more than its net income. The Year-to-Date (YTD) Variance column shows the difference between the actual cost and the budgeted amount. The uniforms and court rental line items were the largest expenses that caused the league to spend more than it had budgeted.

Best Practices

Considering financial best practices for ministries, the starting place is what the Bible refers to as "stewardship." Finances belong to God, and He entrusts them to His followers and the ministries to which He has called them (see Matthew 25:14-30, the parable of the talents). God's money is to be managed in such a way as to gain profit for the owner. Care should be taken in ministry to use finances wisely to accomplish the vision and mission of the organization.

To gain a further understanding of best practices, it would be wise to take an economics or accounting class as a part of the undergraduate academic experience. The best leaders of sports ministry endeavors are both effective (i.e., achieving the goals of their mission statement in a quality manner) and efficient (i.e., making the best use of their resources) To do this it is important to know how to create and read financial statements, balance sheets, income statements, and annual reports. Remember, effectively managing personal financial resources is a key first step toward being able to do the same as a leader of a sports ministry in the future. Another best practice that can be personally instituted while in college is to avoid the accumulation of significant college personal debt.

Defining Whether a Sports Ministry Is Successful

An organization's vision and mission statements provide the foundation for measuring its success. FCA, for example has a mission statement that reads, "To lead every coach and athlete into a growing relationship with Jesus Christ and His church" (Fellowship of Christian Athletes, n.d.). For people who support the organization financially, it is reasonable for them to want to see evidence of coaches and athletes led to faith in Christ and growing in that faith. The organization has the responsibility to share these stories with its constituency. The Bible talks about fruit primarily in how a person's relationship with God is displayed. "The fruit of the Spirit is love, joy, peace, patience, kindness, goodness, faithfulness, gentleness and self-control" (Galatians 5:22-23 NIV). Bill Bright, founder of Campus Crusade for Christ (now Cru) said, "Success in witnessing is simply sharing Christ in the power of the Holy Spirit and leaving the results to God" (Bright 2007). Besides fulfillment of organizational mission, successful ministry is also measured by a consistent balanced budget, exercising fiscal responsibility, and the use of designated funds as intended.

Understanding Financial Challenges in Sports Ministry

This section will explore practical topics such as how the American economy affects the raising of support for sports ministry work and what happens when financial support erodes or disappears altogether. This section closes with a discussion and example of the importance of sports ministries cooperating with one another versus competing against each other.

Effect of the American Economy on Raising Support

The effect of the American economy on raising support varies from sports ministry to sports ministry, with very little research focused on the topic as it relates to this ministry area. Statistics from *The Annual Report on Philanthropy in America* show that even though the economy took a hit in 2020, charitable giving increased 10 percent from 2018 to 2020. Giving by individuals and foundations increased, though giving from corporations sharply decreased. The largest recipient of charitable giving was religion (the generic term for churches and ministries) (Qgiv 2021). The conventional fear was that if the economy turns for the worse, giving to sports ministry initiatives would erode as well. Whatever the economic situation may hold, in good times and bad, ministries have been able to remain confident and have faith in the God who provides.

XYZ Church
Income Statement Youth Basketball League
For the six months ending March 31
<revenues> = positive variance   <expenses> = negative variance

		Curr Month(s)	Curr Month(s)	YTD	YTD	YTD
		Actual	Budget	Actual	Budget	Variance
	Acct Code					
Revenues						
Donations	30001	250	0	250	0	<250>
Player Fees	30002	12,000	12,600	12,000	12,600	600
Misc Income	30003					
Total Revenues		12,250	12,600	12,250	12,250	350
Expenses						
Coach Wages	81001	4,250	5,000	4,250	5,000	750
Ref Wages	81003	1,800	1,600	1,800	1,600	<200>
Supplies	81005	84	150	84	150	66
Min Mat'l	81007	520	575	520	575	55
Uniforms	81009	2,890	2,250	2,890	2,250	<640>
Equipment	81011	649	600	649	600	<49>
Promotion	81013	287	300	287	300	13
Awards	81015	592	560	592	560	<32>
Photos	81017	265	195	265	195	<70>
Court Rental	81019	1,850	1,400	1,850	1,400	<450>
Misc Exp	81021					
Total Expenses		13,187	12,630	13,187	12,630	<557>
Net Income		-937	-30	-937	-380	

FIGURE 8.3   Sample income sheet.

Effects on a Sports Ministry When Financial Support Erodes or Disappears

As any household knows, when the family brings in less money, decisions need to be made accordingly. The same is true for ministries. In 2016 the International Mission Board of the Southern Baptist Convention retired or let go of 983 missionaries (just over 20 percent of its total) because of a budget shortfall caused, at least in part, by economic downturn (Zylstra 2016).

Ministry programs that generate funding to cover costs would likely continue while programs that are subsidized might be discontinued. For missionaries or ministers who raise support and experience shortfalls in income, they might need to consider taking on a second job, if allowed, which means less time in ministry, or possibly leaving the ministry altogether.

Interdependence and Cooperating Versus Competing: FCA and AIA/Cru

Cooperation versus competition with other sports ministries is important. Ministries that share a commitment to the true gospel should be interdependent and supportive of each other. Perhaps the best example of this in action is seen in the relationship between John Erickson, former president of the FCA, and Bill Bright, the former president of Campus Crusade (and by extension AIA).

CASE STUDY

Sports Ministries: Cooperating Versus Competing

The year was 1972 when John Erickson, who was 45 at the time, became president of the Fellowship of Christian Athletes (FCA). He had just lost his quest to become a U.S. Senator from the state of Wisconsin, but he had won the NBA championship in his role as the vice president and general manager of the Milwaukee Bucks in 1971. At the time, John stated that he would commit to the top leadership post of the FCA for a total of three years. Instead, in God's economy, he would go on to serve as the president of the FCA for 15 years, which would become the longest tenure of any FCA leader (Atcheson 1994).

Erickson succeeded in many ways in his role as leader. He and Durand Holladay, chairman of the trustees, created and implemented the first ever coordinated budget that brought together all the income and expenses of the FCA. Another area John excelled at was building bridges and relationships with other sports ministries. He flew to Hope College in Michigan to meet with Bill Bright, who was the president of Campus Crusade (now known as Cru), to discuss their recently launched athletic ministry, Athletes in Action (AIA). The two leaders spent two hours on their knees in prayer, praying that their differences would be reconciled and that they would not actively or passively compete with each other. They prayed that their relationship would be one of cooperation for advancing God's Kingdom through athletics and sports. From that night forward, they forged a new relationship built on trust. Years later when the FCA was going through a tough time financially, Bill Bright attended one of their banquets and gave John a check for $1,000 in a ringing endorsement of their desire to cooperate and work together. This early spirit of partnership and cooperation resulted in annual meetings between the presidents and leadership of FCA, Campus Crusade, Youth for Christ, Navigators, Young Life, AIA, and Pro Athletes Outreach to pray for their ministries and to share and encourage one another in the Lord's work (Atcheson 1994). Cooperative partnerships can accomplish much more in building God's Kingdom rather than competing with one another. The faith of John Erickson was once again evidenced when at the age of 86 he received the NABC Guardian of the Game Award for Leadership at the NCAA Final Four. Upon accepting the award, he shared how the sport of basketball changed his life but that it was Jesus who gave him life, citing Romans 12:1-2.

Therefore, I urge you, brothers, and sisters, in view of God's mercy, to offer your bodies as a living sacrifice, holy and pleasing to God—this is your true and proper worship. Do not conform to the pattern of this world, but be transformed by the renewing of your mind. Then you will be able to test and approve what God's will is—His good, pleasing and perfect will. (NIV)

Discussion Questions

1. Why are cooperative efforts between sports ministry organizations important?
2. How did Erickson and Bright approach the subject of cooperation versus competition?
3. How was their spirit of cooperation evidenced?

SUMMARY

This chapter introduced the financial considerations of and their importance to creating and running viable, God-honoring sports ministry endeavors. Significant attention was paid to the concepts of stewardship and creating viable platforms for spiritual return on investment (SROI). Attention also was drawn to the various means of securing financial resources for sports ministry. Through basic financial management skills and best practices, sports ministries are better prepared to face the financial challenges and achieve quality and continuity over time.

A study of Scripture reveals that money is mentioned over 800 times and finances are referenced over 2,000 times, so the saying "Follow the money" has credence. In sports ministry, how money for ministry is obtained and wisely deployed speaks volumes about its leaders.

Sports ministry is not for the faint of heart. Possessing a strong faith and believing that God will provide the financial needs of such endeavors is paramount. Once the financial resources are provided, managing and stewarding these resources in a God-honoring manner becomes a key focus. Sometimes it is a fine line between being solvent and insolvent, between being a viable ministry and economic entity or not, as noted earlier in this chapter with the concept of the key two-dollar swing.

In His ministry, Jesus often discussed money in cautionary tones, with the understanding that His disciples were to be faithful stewards. Money is to be viewed for what it is—namely, a resource to assist in the process of making disciples and growing His kingdom through the use of sport.

REVIEW AND DISCUSSION QUESTIONS

1. How important is faith as it relates to the finances needed to plan and run a successful sports ministry?
2. What is the key thing to understand about stewardship before you can be a good steward of God's resources?
3. What is our stewardship role as followers of Jesus Christ?
4. What are the basic elements of securing needed financial resources and which approach do you believe is best one to take in order to secure ministry funding?
5. What approach would you take to ensure that you communicate in an honest and consistent manner with your financial and prayer partners?

Courtesy of Dayton Daily and Athletes in Action.

Maintaining quality facilities represents the responsible stewardship of resources, valuable tools for more important spiritual work at Athletes in Action, Xenia, Ohio.

CHAPTER 9

Sports Ministry Facilities

"Stewardship is the use of God-given resources for the accomplishment of God-given goals."

Ron Blue, author and financial consultant

LEARNING OBJECTIVES

After studying this chapter, you should be able to do the following:

- Explain the importance of planning as it relates to developing a viable, quality sports ministry facility
- Appreciate the value of the option of renting versus the benefits and challenges of repurposing an existing facility for sports ministry initiatives
- Identify when building a new sport facility represents the best option for a ministry effort
- Understand the important steps involved in concept design and development of a new sport facility from architectural drawings, to permits, through the construction phase, and to final completion
- Understand the challenges involved in maintaining a high-quality facility

Almost every top NBA star, including some of the biggest stars of the 1990s and 2000s—Michael Jordan, Larry Bird, Charles Barkley, and Shaquille O'Neal—have spent time training in the Solheim Center on the campus of Moody Bible Institute (Derrick 2020). The Solheim and Moody Bible Institute were the training camp location for the first three United States men's Olympic basketball Dream Teams. They also served most visiting NBA teams in town to play the Chicago Bulls and have hosted over 10 of the NBA's annual predraft camps, the WNBA's tryout camps, and international teams on U.S. tours (Conklin 2002).

The Bible school's relationship with international and professional basketball began shortly after the Solheim Center's official opening in 1991. This relationship began when former Moody athletic director Sheldon Bassett invited his friend John Hammond, assistant coach for the Los Angeles Clippers, to check out the new facilities. Hammond was impressed, stating, "It was just great; state-of-the-art in every aspect. I mentioned something to the NBA about it, and things just sort of evolved from there" (Conklin 2002).

The association between the NBA and Moody Bible Institute had to be one of the most unique and oddest couplings to occur in the world of sport—an amiable relationship of the secular with the sacred that no one would have predicted or imagined. The benefits accrued to the Bible college have been significant. The school's founder, Dwight L. Moody, a successful businessman himself, would no doubt appreciate the monetary and public relations benefits of this unique partnership. Under Bassett, the college has nurtured a relationship with the NBA through mutual respect by training their student workers to 'show that they belonged in the room' or in this case, to 'show that they belonged on the gymnasium floor.' This subtlety is a seemingly small yet important trait when involved in sports ministry within the professional sporting ranks. Bassett instructed the students to treat everyone with respect. They were there to serve, not to ask for autographs, photos, or the like. They were taught to behave professionally and to serve their guests well. The students followed Bassett's instructions, and as a result, the relationship between the NBA and Moody Bible Institute flourished. The outcome was a life-changing experience for many students. An example of one positive result was the desire of many Bible majors to expand on their experience with NBA players and with the association of basketball-related events. The college created a new major, Sports Ministry and Lifetime Fitness, as a practical and tangible means to accomplish their goal (Conklin 2002).

The Solheim Center was designed to serve as the main athletic, recreation, fitness, and sports ministry facility for the Moody Bible Institute. The facility is a multilevel building of over 70,000 square feet with an adjoining 120 × 75-yard (110 × 69 m) soccer field and three adjoining collegiate level tennis courts. The Solheim features three university-regulation basketball and volleyball hardwood courts, a 1/9th-mile running track, four racquetball courts, an auxiliary gym, a weight room, an aerobics room, and classrooms. The total cost of this center approached $7 million and is named in honor of Karsten and Louise Solheim, longtime friends and supporters of the Moody Bible Institute. Karsten was the inventor and developer of Ping golf clubs. He and Louise grew the company into a successful enterprise (Moody Bible Institute, n.d.). The Solheims desired the center to be designed for outreach and sports ministry to the neighboring children around the Moody Bible Institute (Solheim Foundation, pers. interview 1998). The relationship with the NBA has proven to be significant, but the greater impact was the development of the new sports ministry major and the neighborhood outreach program.

Playing on the classic hardwood of a gymnasium floor, experiencing a day on a soccer pitch, or feeling the freshly manicured grass of a baseball diamond evokes special memories. There is no doubt that quality facilities make a difference in the sporting experience. The same holds true for the settings chosen for sports ministry activities. Just as effective sports ministries need quality leadership prepared with well-conceived plans, these same ministries need quality facilities to achieve their desired ends.

This chapter will cover the importance of the planning process for securing, or in some cases developing, high-quality sports ministry facilities. Consideration will be given to the span of available facility options—free, renting, or buying an existing property to repurpose—concluding with the creation of a comprehensive new sporting facility or complex. Particular attention will be given to the cost factor of each of these options, balancing the stated needs of the proposal with available financial resources. In the case of proposing and creating a comprehensive new sporting facility, particular attention will be accorded to the steps involved in concept design and development, from architectural drawings and permits, through the construction phase to final completion and occupancy. The basics of maintaining a high-quality facility that serves its intended purposes also will be addressed.

The Importance of Planning for the Right Sports Ministry Facility

Sporting events are designed to be memorable. The best facilities contribute to achieving these goals by creating an enjoyable sporting ambiance. Sports ministry initiatives are to take the same care to ensure a transforming sport experience. Planning and selecting the right facility is an important undertaking for a leadership team. It all starts with a well-thought-out plan. Failure to plan well can come at a steep cost.

Often sports ministries lack a viable plan of action for their facilities. Instead of being pragmatic and cost effective, they simply build and add facilities when they could rent or avail themselves of free facilities such as city parks (Garner, n.d.). Some people subscribe to the often-misquoted line from the movie *Field of Dreams*: "If you build it, they will come" (Koehler 2020). This becomes an emotional rally cry for a call to build without any regard to whether this is the best strategy. The only time a new facility should be built is when a need is clearly demonstrated, more ministry is enabled, and other options to achieve these ends are not available or feasible. Facilities do not win anyone to Christ. However, sports facilities can become powerful tools for sports ministry leaders who intentionally develop relationships and the sharing of the good news of Jesus Christ (Garner, n.d.). Creating a clear plan of action for facilities should be viewed as a critical first step in the creation of a special sports ministry experience. Will A. Foster captured this idea of a quality, well-thought plan in greater depth: "Quality is never an accident; it is always the result of high intention, sincere effort, intelligent direction and skillful execution; it represents the wise choice of many alternatives" (Tortschnekkel 2009).

Seven Planning Principles

The following seven planning principles, adapted from *Guidebook for Planning Church Recreation Facilities* (Garner and Nicholson 2006), represents advice that will prove helpful in designing a viable sports ministry facility plan.

1. *Count the cost.* New construction is a major undertaking. Two questions should be asked at the outset: Is this what God desires? Is now the right time? Other practical issues must be examined, such as the facility demands and budgets for programming, additional staffing, new equipment, maintenance, utilities, insurance, and so on.

2. *Develop a facility master plan.* Such a plan will help ensure the best stewardship of the facility and how it functions in accordance with the mission and vision of the ministry.

3. *Ensure your ministry really needs the facility.* Does the proposed facility meet the programing needs of the ministry and contribute to the greater goal of sharing the gospel and changing lives? People will respond with financial, emotional, and prayer support if they trust the leadership and recognize the ministry benefits of the proposed new facility.

4. *Learn from others.* Review as many similar situations as possible, solicit and carefully consider their suggestions and advice, and move forward accordingly to refine the plan.

5. *Designate a point person.* Someone needs to be in charge and steer the plan. Ideally, this person has previous experience in this area.

6. *Incorporate these building blocks (figure 9.1).*

7. *Form follows function.* The purpose of the sport facility and its operation determines the design. Securing the services of a professional sport facility consultant could be a wise choice and will most likely result in significant savings. (Garner and Nicholson 2006)

The plans need not be complicated. A clear, concise, and simple approach is better. The plan begins by defining the sports ministry team's vision, mission, goals, and objectives. This starting point establishes

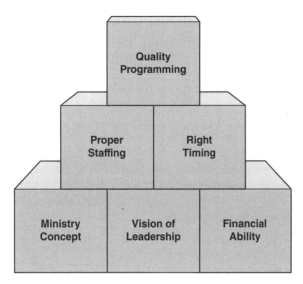

FIGURE 9.1 The building blocks of a successful planning process.
© Human Kinetics, adapted from illustration by Kiel McClung.

a foundation for determining the best type of sport facility needed. This need will arise from the planned sporting activities and events and their targeted ministry populations. Once the plan is established, the next step is conducting a feasibility study, which examines all potential options from renting to the construction of a new facility. This study is critical because of the amount of financial resources that could be at risk.

Conducting a Quality Feasibility Study

The importance of **feasibility studies** cannot be understated. They provide essential data to clarify the vision, concept, and necessary planning for the successful completion of the project. **Clarity of concept** and a careful accounting of the costs are crucial to achieving the goals for the development of a new facility.

Though a sports ministry can research how to conduct feasibility studies and can do it alone, it is wise to seek counsel from those who have successful experience, gleaning knowledge from their valuable insights. Once the study has been completed and

determined to be viable, the creation of a thorough plan of attack is in order.

Every sports ministry facility starts as an idea or dream of a possibility. Before these ideas and dreams can be realized, they need to be tested and refined. Significant resources, both physical and financial, come together in such projects. In many cases, these resources are provided by generous donors who believe in the idea and embrace its vision. This support can affirm the creation and sustainability of a new facility. This refinement of the idea and evaluation of its viability are best done through the creation of a quality feasibility study.

Throughout the United States and around the world, sports ministry and recreation centers are producing high-quality, dynamic sport and recreation programs that include the additional dimension of changing lives through evangelism and discipleship. The Sports Facilities Advisory Group (Sports Facilities Companies 2018) attests to the importance of feasibility studies and provides the following five reasons for their use before leaders commence with a new facility project.

Reason One: Feasibility Studies Demonstrate the Viability of the Vision

In soccer there is an expression popularized by former men's U.S. National Team coach Bob Gansler, "See the field," which encourages players to be aware of their surroundings and assess the possibilities for the best tactical decisions. This visionary concept is analogous to the discussion about conducting a quality feasibility study, which enables leadership to "see the field"—that is, to explore the possibilities. They can determine if they are **rightsizing** the scope of their project's vision.

Reason Two: Feasibility Studies Help Define Goals and Objectives

Ideas and dreams are only as good as their implementation. A feasibility study helps clarify the goals and benchmarks needed for a project's viability. Such a study brings clarity to the costs of constructing a facil-

---

feasibility studies—Reports assessing key factors that dictate project viabilities such as prospective users of the facility; financial costs; and projections for revenue, marketplace, and ministry potential. These studies refine success and the plan's sustainability and help the leadership team set goals for the facility's use.

clarity of concept—The ability to understand the need for a newly developed sport facility or complex, clarify a well-defined plan for the facility's usage, and assess the ministry goals it will meet.

Rightsizing—Careful planning that ensures that the sporting facility will meet current needs as well as anticipated future opportunities, and that it will be viable. Rightsizing also applies to optimal staffing to manage the facility operations and ministry efficiently.

ity as well as the costs of maintaining its operation. This information will assist greatly in determining the anticipated physical and financial resources needed prior to the project's commencement.

Reason Three: Feasibility Studies Help Develop a Viable Plan

As goals are defined, a feasibility study will provide a better understanding of the next steps in the overall development process. The idea is then developed into a program that can be illustrated and justified with a **pro forma financial statement**. Creating a high-quality pro forma will greatly enhance the process of seeking financial support through various sources. An unrealistic positive projection is a potential problem with pro forma statements. They tend to portray a more successful projected outcome than what actually occurs (Bragg 2022). Therefore, especially as Christian leaders of such initiatives, it is important to present as accurate a picture as possible to financial donors and supporters. Max De Pree said it best: "The first responsibility of a leader is to define reality,"—and, in this case, to define reality accurately (De Pree 2004).

Simultaneous to developing this pro forma plan is to produce a viable budget outlining the projected financial results based on certain assumptions and market factors. In addition, an economic impact study demonstrates how the proposed sport facility will provide tangible life benefits to the surrounding community as well as added revenue to the local economy. A well-done economic impact study can result in additional support for the project from local government and businesses.

Reason Four: Feasibility Studies Prescribe an Optimal Plan

Arguably the most significant benefit of a feasibility study is the specific information regarding requirements for sustainability over time. By understanding the development costs, sources of support, financial resources, and potential benefits for the surrounding community, project leadership will gain a better understanding of the business model needed to achieve and sustain success. The various components of a feasibility study will serve as a road map, describing the optimal path for the creation of a high-quality complex.

Reason Five: Feasibility Studies Provide an Identity

When planning a new sport or recreation facility, a feasibility study will provide a better idea of the target audience and the needs of those being served as well as a strong sense of identity in the process (Sports Facilities Companies 2018).

Determining What Type of Sport Facilities Are Available for Effective Ministry

The planning process needs to be realistic and practical. There is nothing wrong with starting modestly. As growth occurs, additional options will surface. Besides ministry needs, additional factors must be considered including facility accessibility, staffing, and budgetary implications. Time and scheduling restraints can also play a role in the decision-making process.

Facilities That Are Free of Charge

Depending on availability, local parks and recreation departments might provide playing fields, outdoor basketball courts, and similar sport facilities free of charge or at a reduced rate. Lower overhead costs for the organization can be passed along to participants, enabling access for participants at all economic levels.

Parks and recreation departments often partner with nonprofits for a wide array of sport and recreational activities. For many such entities, this is a part of their mission statement. This partnership is another example of the importance of securing the designation of a 501(c)(3) nonprofit corporation. The scheduling needs of the ministry and the reliability of the parks and recreation schedule creates a viable approach.

Renting a Sport Facility for Ministry

Sports ministries, like many other youth and adult sport organizations, often rent indoor and outdoor

---

pro forma financial statements—Financial reports that are based on many assumptions and hypothetical conditions that have occurred in the past or might occur in the future. Pro forma statements can be valuable tools to generate investment interest in the sporting facility project under consideration.

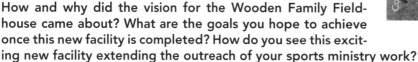

Interview With a Professional

Jonathan Van Horn
Executive Director, Athletes in Action (AIA)
Graduate of Ohio Wesleyan University

What is the mission of Athletes in Action?

Athletes in Action is a caring community passionate about connecting people to Jesus Christ. AIA serves to build spiritual movements everywhere through the platform of sports so that everyone knows someone who truly follows Jesus. Our vision is to see a day when there are Christ followers on every team, in every sport, in every nation.

How and why did the vision for the Wooden Family Fieldhouse came about? What are the goals you hope to achieve once this new facility is completed? How do you see this exciting new facility extending the outreach of your sports ministry work?

We had previously made an attempt at building the fieldhouse in 2006. It was not a good process nor done with the right feasibility process. It was tabled, but the idea was still present. Fast-forward to 2015, and we entered into an agreement with Sports Facilities Advisory to do a feasibility study. They were fantastic. We looked at 24 different models and concluded that AIA should add an indoor component for the reasons of financial sustainability on the campus, the mission of AIA, and its impact on the global network.

What are some of the challenges you have encountered and had to overcome while creating this project? How challenging was the process of securing funding, and how long did this process take?

It has taken seven years to get to the amount needed to break ground. It has been harder and longer but refining. Due to the length of time, we have gone through two different pro formas that have helped us focus better and caused us to incur cost and material increases. We are more fully understanding what it will require to run a facility and making adjustments as we move toward breaking ground for the building phase.

What role has the local community of Xenia, Ohio, played in this project? How will this project positively affect the local community?

Xenia has helped secure some Covid funding for extending the water line as well as leverage some other local resources for infrastructure costs. We are making sure our programming is supported by and will benefit local youth activities. It will create an estimated 500,000 annual turnstile experiences to our campus, thus bringing needed business to the city of Xenia. We have met with local developers around other small businesses that are potentially being built as a result of our project as well.

Do you have any advice for others in sports ministry who are considering building sport facilities?

Use a professional advisory firm like the Sports Facilities Advisory and be thorough in doing your due diligence. Be open-handed, pray, get neutral, and make sure you thoroughly evaluate all facts and circumstances.

sport facilities for their various programs and events. Conversely, sport complexes make their facilities available to sport groups in exchange for rental income or to serve the community (Sadler Sports and Recreation Insurance 2006). Renting sport facilities represents the next level of cost-effective sport ministry. Often, nonprofits are granted a more favorable rental or lease arrangement. Even at market rate, this approach provides additional savings. Advantages include not being responsible for the cost of routine maintenance and, in some cases, utilities.

The selection of a rental option is based on meeting the ministry needs in the most cost-effective manner.

The Benefits and Challenges of Repurposing an Existing Facility for Sports Ministry

The next level of sport facility options involves purchasing existing buildings or fields and **repurposing** them for the ministry's goals and objectives. The

SPORTS MINISTRY IN ACTION

The Fellowship of Christian Athletes (FCA) Demonstrates the Value of the Option of Renting Sports Facilities

The FCA is one of the largest sports ministries in the world. It enjoys a strong base of prayer support and financial giving through its extensive network of ministry partners, sponsors, and donors. Arguably, it has the financial clout necessary to build not only one new sport complex, but perhaps several new such complexes around the country. And yet, the FCA's go-to strategy is to partner with churches and local high schools, colleges, and universities to secure the needed sport facilities.

Employing the strategy of renting facilities for its sport camps enables regional FCA ministries to exercise good stewardship by stretching its financial resources in a cost-effective manner. A new facility can cost anywhere between $10 and $30 million to build, not to mention significant financial resources required to run and maintain it annually. Additionally, when a sports ministry builds and owns a facility, it must work hard to ensure that it is being used on a regular basis to make the investment worthwhile. Conversely, renting a sport facility enables a ministry, as in the case of the FCA regional sports camps, to pay an agreed-upon amount for only the weeks it needs. The cost savings of renting a facility over building and owning one is significant (Fellowship of Christian Athletes n.d.).

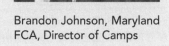

Brandon Johnson, Maryland FCA, Director of Camps

In 2004 Brandon Johnson earned a spot on the FCA Lacrosse High School National Elite Team, and it was here that he placed his faith in Jesus. He went on to play lacrosse for four years at Robert Morris University, graduating in 2009. In 2012 he joined the FCA as an area representative in Carroll County, Maryland. That same year, he and his wife, Ashli, were married. Today Brandon serves as a multi-area director for the FCA in central Maryland, serving Carroll, Frederick, and Howard Counties. One of his chief responsibilities is serving as the director of the camp programs for the Mid-Atlantic region.

FCA Camps are popular for aspiring athletes of all ages and abilities.

repurposing—The process of adapting, changing, or using a facility for a new purpose such as converting a dormant warehouse into a gymnasium or indoor soccer field, or transforming a vacant lot to create sport fields.

opportunities at this level are many and limited only by a leadership team's vision and creativity. Often, these real estate opportunities involve dormant properties. The longer they have been undeveloped, the more attractive the selling price generally is. A creative sports ministry team will see the potential of the property. If the sale price is right and **sweat equity** of the board and support team is sufficient, a renovation plan can proceed.

When Building a New Facility Is the Best Option

When considering building a brand-new facility, the decision should be based on the genuine need for such a sport facility or complex, New builds are typically the most expensive of all the sport facility options. They are complex projects to take from concept to completion. Building a new facility enables the ministry to design with the needs of its community demographics and programming in mind. A **request for proposals (RFP)**, also known as *requests for bids (RFB)*, will be created. (Such proposals can also involve a preliminary step, a request for qualifications (RFQ), which help to ascertain that a construction company meets the minimum requirements for building the facility in question.) Qualified companies respond with detailed proposals. From this, a company is selected. The process is competitive in nature and generally involves sealed bids. It helps the ministry secure the services of a qualified company within the range of their projected costs (Examples. com, n.d.). The best RFPs show what is needed for the project, including all costs, materials, and labor figures. The respondents should demonstrate that they possess the requisite equipment, people power, and access to materials to accomplish the task. They additionally should show that they possess the experience, credentials, and knowledge to solve problems as they arise in the construction process (LetsBuild 2019).

An RFP document should be written in a clear and straightforward manner, and it should be kept as simple as possible while covering the entire scope of the proposed construction. The seven steps shown in figure 9.2 will help the ministry leadership team simplify the RFP process.

FIGURE 9.2   REQUEST FOR PROPOSAL (RFP) DOCUMENT STEPS.

1. *Be clear.* An effective RFP is clear about the scope of the project and the end goals. Clarity of presentation and answers to questions sought will enable a better comparison of the various proposals.

2. *It is all about the details.* Detail the elements of the construction project and the proposed timeline for completion. These aspects need to be clear and uncomplicated so that potential companies will not opt out of the bidding process.

3. *Determine the audience.* What prior construction experience does the company have in building similar structures? Can you visit their previous building sites? Do they have references and endorsements? What best qualifies them for this project?

4. *Decide what you need.* Create a uniform response format to obtain consistent comparable information from the bidding construction entities. Detail what form you want the proposals to be submitted.

5. *Outline the RFP.* Outlining the RFP into sections and subsections further organizes the process and provides response continuity.

6. *Write the RFP.* Based on steps 1 through 5, write in a clear and concise manner.

7. *Edit the RFP.* Be sure that the final proposal is free of typos and grammatical errors. The document should read well; be easily understood; and follow a logical, organized progression. Eliminate redundancy and contradictory requirements (Baker 2017).

Adapted from D. Baker, "7 Steps to Writing an RFP That Gets High-Quality Responses," Super Copy Editors, last modified August 29, 2017, www. supercopyeditors.com.

---

sweat equity—The financial value generated by a ministry and its supporters who freely give of their time and labor to renovate and repurpose the facility. A special bond of unity and ownership is created between team members as they work together.

request for proposals (RFPs)—Documents that solicit the submission of bids by contractors to take on a construction project from start to finish. RFPs are sometimes referred to as RFBs (requests for bids).

CASE STUDY

God Gave a Radical Vision:
The Story of One7 Ministries and Its Facilities

The story of One7 Ministries in Charlotte, North Carolina, is the result of a radical, life-changing vision that God gave to David Garrett. It was a vision brought to life on his return to the United States after a series of international mission trips. He realized he did not have to travel far to live the Great Commission; he could live it in his own country. Shortly thereafter, his church (Higher Ground Baptist Church, Tennessee) commissioned him as an independent missionary in Chicago, where he began to work with refugees from all over the world. His work with the poor, the needy, the suffering, and the broken families of inner-city Chicago brought Matthew 25 to life for him. After four years of ministry, David felt the Lord leading him to serve in Charlotte, North Carolina. This call was to the most culturally diverse, broken, and dangerous area on the east side of Charlotte. Gang activity, crime, and drugs were pervasive. The gospel mission of his ministry was one of peacemaker, reconciler, and advocate for the weak and suffering. His work and vision grew, and in 2006 Garrett was hired by Forest Hill Church to be a pastor for two local inner-city church plants in his target area. This opportunity enabled him to continue discipling youths and to become involved in the lives of these church families.

David Garrett is the Executive Director of One7, an inner-city sports ministry in Charlotte, NC.

In 2008, David felt God calling him to take another step of faith and start his own 501(c)(3) nonprofit. The ministry One7 was founded, drawing its name from a conversation between God and Jeremiah, the Old Testament prophet. Jeremiah found his purpose, vision, and direction while learning how to face his fears and doubts: "Before I formed you in the womb I knew you, before you were born I set you apart; I appointed you as a prophet to the nations" (Jeremiah 1:5 NIV). Garrett built this ministry on this biblical truth. From the start, One7 faced spiritual warfare and persecution. Gangs robbed them, set their facilities on fire, slashed the tires on their ministry van, and even shot at David not once, but twice. Yet through it all, those being ministered to were seeing real life changes. Families were being healed and restored. God was working in a powerful way.

Between 2011 and 2013 God expanded the One7 vision, and the ministry was able to purchase an 18-unit apartment complex complete with meeting areas where they now serve hundreds of youths and their families each week. This unique model is a spiritually fruitful one. God equips One7 Ministries to train and disciple leaders to take the message of Christ with them everywhere they go. Through a partnership with Elevation Church, God provided for an outreach center, which was completed in 2016. This facility is another tool in the effort to reach even more people with the gospel. These are examples of two distinctly different facilities being used to further practical ministry.

Through the years God has richly blessed the One7 family as they seek to fulfill His audacious mission of changing the east side of Charlotte. Their work has become multifaceted through apartment sponsorships, serving meals, tutoring, and giving opportunities at Christmas. One of their special ministries is the One7 Soccer Academy, headed by Nhiet Rocham. Nhiet grew up in this ministry and went on to earn a BS in sport management from Columbia International University. He runs One7's soccer programs and manages the oversight and maintenance of their regulation outdoor soccer pitch, indoor soccer surface, and basketball court. The programs he

> continued

Case Study   > *continued*

oversees are kept affordable by supporters of One7, who keep the community costs down by splitting the expenses for the academy's travel soccer matches. Nhiet sums up his work: "It is hard work, but it is really encouraging when you see the fruit in the lives of our players as they grow. The changed lives from our work is special." Nhiet Rocham is an example of God multiplying the ministry efforts of One7 and the spiritual results that can occur when individuals are faithful to God's call (One7, n.d.).

Discussion Questions

1. What facilities are part of the One7 Ministry?
2. How has the One7 Ministry demonstrated creativity in securing the facilities it uses in its ministry work?
3. Beside sport, how else does One7 minister?

David Garrett (front row left) and Nhiet Rocham (back row second from left) pictured with several of their star One7 soccer players.

Once all the RFPs are received (by a predetermined final submission date), the review process begins in earnest for the sports ministry team and their board of advisors. This part of the process begins with prayer. The next step is a careful review and study of each proposal, narrowing the field to a select few contractors. Some respondents might be too general, and alternatively, some RFPs might be too specific. After deliberation, seeking counsel, and prayer, a decision is ready to be made. The winning bid will meet and answer every task or question proposed, doing so at a reasonable cost with its best values clearly articulated (LetsBuild 2019). The experience and quality of the construction company, balanced with the total proposed costs, should guide the team to a final decision. As experience has shown, one bid proposal will usually rise above the rest.

A Closing Thought on Sport Facility Options

Cost is clearly an important factor in the process, but it is not the only consideration, and sometimes it is not even the most important. The issue of cost is more about stewardship and the wise use of the financial resources supplied by God. However, saving money

and landing in the wrong facility is not the right way to proceed either. A balance must be struck between financial stewardship and obtaining the right facility.

The Process of Creating a New Sport Facility: From Concept to Completion

Building a new facility can be a daunting task for a sports ministry to undertake. The following is an overview of the phases most construction projects go through once a bid proposal has been awarded and contract details are finalized. The goal in this section is to provide a general sense of what goes into creating a new sport facility, from technical drawings to completion of the project.

Construction projects have many moving parts that require thorough planning and continuous oversight. Such projects necessitate well-coordinated orchestration and the efforts of knowledgeable, experienced professionals. Breaking down the construction process into segments or construction phases make the whole process more manageable and yield far better results (Scalisi 2021).

Preconstruction Phase

The first stage is generally referred to as the *preconstruction phase*. Schedules are detailed, and the various entities such as architects, engineers, construction managers, and contractors come to an agreement on their respective roles in the upcoming construction phase. In addition to the actual construction contract, this stage is marked by significant pieces of paperwork, from architectural renderings, site plans, and structural drawings. The structural drawings include electrical, HVAC mechanical, and water and plumbing drawings (Fried 2015). This phase involves such activities as the approval of site plans, surveying, engineering, design, and permits. It provides a road map for the rest of the project to follow. Since the construction project has not broken ground yet, the risks associated with this phase are minimal (Scalisi 2021). This phase is likened to the calm before the storm. Virtually all construction projects encounter challenges and problems along the way. The goal of the preconstruction phase is to anticipate as many of these potential issues as possible and set contingency plans. These plans will help avoid possible negative financial impacts in subsequent phases of the project. A simple tip and good discipline to follow involves making as few changes as possible to the construction plan once the plan and the cost of the project have been agreed upon. Changes in plan, often referred to as *change orders*, can be costly.

Sitework and Foundation Phase

The second stage is the *sitework and foundation phase*. This stage represents the beginning of construction, and starts when the project breaks ground, which involves a formal groundbreaking ceremony. Key project leaders and community officials put foot to a fancy shovel, dig up some dirt, and provide a photo opportunity as they lift their shovels sending ceremonial dirt airborne. Once the ceremony phase is complete, the work of site preparation begins. Site preparation can vary from relatively simple (e.g., leveling a generally level site and removing trees and natural undergrowth) to quite complex (e.g., leveling significantly uneven terrain, demolishing existing buildings, mitigating ground water issues and contaminated land). Driving areas, staging areas, and provision of utility lines are done at this time. Crews then prepare the site by grading the property and excavating for the foundations and footings that will follow. The general contractor, architect, engineer,

and surveyor are important personnel during this phase. Subcontractors enter the process; they pour concrete and set the foundation for the building elements (Scalisi 2021). Inclement weather can become a challenge during this stage and should be considered because it can adversely affect the project timeline and project costs.

Rough Framing

The third stage commences with the *rough framing* as the building starts going vertical. This phase is a big undertaking, because the structural steel framing is attached to the foundation and the building starts to take shape. With the steel in place, crews pour the concrete flooring and the framing subcontractors erect the walls, giving the building its main structure (Scalisi 2021).

Exterior Construction

The next stage involves the remaining *exterior construction*, "drying in" (weather proofing and sealing off) the building from the elements. During this phase, all siding, roofing, and any brick or plasterwork is done, as well as installation of all windows and doors (Scalisi, 2021). The building can now withstand inclement weather, and the majority of the construction work moves inside.

All the elements related to mechanical, electrical, and plumbing (MEP) take center stage once the building envelope is sealed. Mechanical contractors install the HVAC systems and associated ductwork. The electricians install electrical panels and pull wire throughout the entire building. The plumbers ensure that all pipes for water supply and drainage are properly installed. Additional subcontractors install fire suppression and fire alarm systems (Scalisi 2021). Where applicable, in the case of a multifloor structure, subcontractors work on required ADA elements such as elevators and ramps.

Fixtures and Finishes

The final stage of construction includes all *fixtures and finishes*. At this point, the building starts to take its final form, inside and out. This stage is busy, with the number of subcontractors increasing significantly as they finish the flooring, walls, ceilings, and everything in between. Exterior landscaping contractors are also at work during this phase. The greatest risk in this phase involves communication issues over finishes, materials, pricing, and possible changes to the specifications of the project (i.e., change orders). Retaining a quality general contractor to represent the interests of the client is valuable. Make as few changes as possible.

Once all the major stages of construction are completed, it is time to wrap up the project. During this closeout phase, the general contractor thoroughly goes through a punch list of items—usually small items—that need to be squared away. As these are agreed upon and taken care of, final payments can be made. Once a certificate of occupancy is secured, the facility can officially open (Scalisi 2021).

Additional Sport Facility Construction Considerations

While building a new indoor sport facility is a significant undertaking from concept to completion, the building of the outdoor sporting complex can be an equally daunting task for a sports ministry to undertake. The following is an overview that covers key areas to consider in order to achieve the desired results. The goal in this section is to briefly address the choice of playing surfaces, whether natural or artificial, for sports fields; the importance of the appropriate lighting for the facility; providing buildings for severe weather conditions; and, finally, carefully planning the construction of a quality parking lot with a sufficient number of spaces to meet the anticipated program needs.

Sporting Fields

For playing fields, the type of turf chosen—natural or artificial—is an important decision. Well-manicured natural turf is generally preferred by athletes and coaches alike, although artificial turf continues to improve with each passing year. Artificial is not without its own maintenance considerations but is much less challenging to keep up than natural grass. For warm-weather climates, artificial turf can become hot during the summer months, to the point of being dangerous for participants. Unpredictable wet-weather climates favor artificial turf because of the playability and consistency of field conditions. No matter what type of field, irrigation and drainage systems are key

considerations. Snow removal can become problematic on a natural grass field in comparison to a turf surface. Flood plains need to be considered when selecting a field location. This situation can work, but it presents another layer of regulations for the sport facility (Earthnetworks 2019).

Lighting Considerations

With any sporting complex, it is important to have the appropriate lighting, not only for hosting night games and matches, but for safety and security. The best practice and the most cost-effective approach for lighting is LED lighting (light-emitting diode), which significantly reduces the monthly electric bill. LED bulbs last longer and run cooler than other lighting options (Earthnetworks 2019).

Severe Weather Considerations

Another issue to consider is inclement and severe weather conditions and events. The most common and sometimes unpredictable threats are lightning and, depending on the location, tornados. These weather events can result in significant injuries to participants, guests, and staff and in some cases can result in fatalities.

Lightning is the most common and dangerous threat that outdoor complexes experience. When building a facility, consider constructing safe sheltering facilities for field complexes. The installation of a reliable lightning detection system complete with a warning horn or siren is recommended (Earthnetworks 2019).

Parking Considerations

An often overlooked but necessary consideration is parking, which falls under the category of **supporting infrastructure**. The parking area should be safe with well-marked pavement, curbs, appropriate lighting, and proper drainage. If hosting large sporting events, camps, or tournaments, 50 to 100 spaces per field should be allotted, with 100 spaces preferred. Parking lots should be a reasonable and convenient walk to the sporting fields or facility. If running baseball or softball events, a significant system of safety netting

---

supporting infrastructure—All the elements, such as sidewalks, parking, landscaping, and lighting, that enhance the overall experience of the main sporting facility, whether fields, a stadium, or an arena.

should be added. This system includes protection for spectators as well as the vehicles in the parking lot. Signage for liability purposes is also recommended (Earthnetworks 2019). Parking for individuals with disabilities, complete with marked spaces and signage, and appropriate ramp access to sidewalks and all elements of the facility are required by the Americans with Disabilities Act (ADA) legislation.

Maintaining a High-Quality Sport Facility

A key topic in managing sports ministry facilities is the development of a comprehensive maintenance plan. Keeping up a facility helps provide a quality experience for everyone and ensures a clean and safe environment. It facilitates positive public relations and increases the ongoing value of the ministry. Work done as unto the Lord should be done well. A plan of preventative maintenance enables the facility and ministry to last longer. Reactive maintenance, or fixing things as they breakdown, usually ends up costing more in the long run (Mid America Specialty Services, n.d.).

Preventative maintenance involves being proactive in daily and weekly inspections of all elements of the facility. This enables the management team to identify and correct problems before they become greater. Benjamin Franklin's quote still rings true today as it relates to preventative maintenance: "An ounce of prevention is worth a pound of cure." A comprehensive plan in this category needs to be more than just wiping down surfaces, mopping floors, and taking out the trash, and it addresses not only maintaining all the elements of the facility, but also invests in repairing, restoring, and updating elements before any problems arise. The end result is a sport facility that provides (1) greater safety and reduced risk of injury to all involved; (2) better compliance with legal regulations and liability; (3) greater levels of ambiance and a sharp, clean appearance; and (4) a greater return on investment by creating better experiences and lower operating costs (Mid America Specialty Services, n.d.). Incorporate this approach consistently over time, and the program will gain a reputation of being a high-quality sport facility. The words of Aristotle are fitting: "Quality is not act. It is a habit."

SUMMARY

Sport facilities and complexes are best viewed as tools, which, when placed in the hands of a skillful sports minister, can result not only in a special sporting experience, but more importantly, in changed lives touched by the gospel of Jesus Christ. It is tempting to put too much emphasis on the facility and its upkeep and not enough on the reason the facility exists in the first place. Upkeep and preventive maintenance of facilities are indeed important. Such activity represents responsible stewardship of resources and is clearly the right thing to do. Keep the mission of sharing the gospel at the forefront while maintaining facilities that reflect well on the ministry: "But everything should be done in a fitting and orderly way" (1 Corinthians 14:40 NIV).

Another key topic covered in this chapter involved carefully and prayerfully considering what sport setting and facility options are available to leaders of sports ministries. If the budget is lean, free or low-cost facilities are viable options worthy of consideration. The next level of renting provides many cost-effective opportunities. If the financial resources and support are available, purchasing an existing property and repurposing it for sports ministry has been shown to work. In the same category, building new sports facilities for ministry, if truly justifiable, is a great way to create all that is needed from the outset. Devising a viable plan, providing quality, and continuity within the sports ministry initiatives are essential. The facilities are a valuable tool for the more important spiritual work of seeing lives changed to God's glory through sports. According to Andrew Murray, "The world asks, 'What does a man own?' Christ asks, 'How does he use it?'" (Murray n.d.).

REVIEW AND DISCUSSION QUESTIONS

1. How did the Moody Bible Institute student workers show that they belonged in the room, or in their case show that they belonged on the gymnasium floor with NBA players who were their guests in the Solheim Center?

2. Why is planning and selecting the right facility and setting for ministry through sport so important?

3. Is the oft misquoted line from the movie Field of Dreams, "If you build it, they will come," a true statement in sports ministry facility initiatives?

4. Do sport facilities win anyone to Christ? If not, what is the point?

5. John Garner outlines seven planning principles. Which one struck you as being particularly important, and why?

6. Why are feasibility studies so important?

7. If you were to choose an option for a sport facility, would you rent, own and repurpose, or build new? Explain your choice.

eer/iStock/Getty Images

Faithfully knowing and following legal obligations are essential spiritual disciplines in the practice of sports ministry.

CHAPTER 10

Legal Considerations

"But everything should be done in a fitting and orderly way."

1 Corinthians 14:40 (NIV)

LEARNING OBJECTIVES

After studying this chapter, you should be able to do the following:

- Understand the basic elements of the United States legal system and legal terminology
- Identify the key legal issues facing sports ministries and their facilities
- Grasp the importance of quality facility management and how a proactive risk management program better ensures safety for participants in your ministry
- Understand the importance of accountability as both a positive and preventative action
- Identify the importance of securing sound legal counsel and legal support as needed

Imagine a university coach of a nationally ranked men's soccer team who is presently in the midst of a three-game losing streak midway through the season. He is already in quite the foul mood on the afternoon of this story. He and his team are trying to figure things out and right the ship at practice. The team seems a bit lethargic and unmotivated as they are practicing set pieces and restarts. As a result, the mood of the coach turns from foul to angry. The coach calls his team together, and with fire in his eyes, he proceeds to change the direction of the practice session. He simply states, "If you are not going to train with heart and energy, you are going to run until you find some heart and energy." He points out three landmarks near the pitch—a set of pine trees, a telephone pole, and the scoreboard. He informs all 24 players that they are to run as hard as they can around these three markers and back to him. The first 12 back are done. The next 12 do it again, at which point the first six to finish are done. The last six will run again, and so forth.

The coach lines them up and gives the signal, and they take off like a bunch of wild horses. The pack is jostling for position as they clear the set of pines. Half of the team clears the second landmark, the telephone pole, when three of the players tangle and clatter to the ground. As the coach watches he shakes his head, when all of a sudden, there are multiple desperate calls and gestures that something is wrong. He and the assistant coach jog to the scene. Noticing the increasing panic of the players, their jog becomes a full sprint. Upon arrival, one of the players is on the ground with a significant, profusely bleeding gash in his calf. The coach takes a player's practice jersey and applies pressure to the wound. One player is sent to retrieve the athletic trainer, and a second goes to the fieldhouse to call for an ambulance. The trainer arrives and starts administering a more professional level of care. Shortly thereafter, the ambulance arrives, and the player is secured onto a medical gurney, put into the ambulance, and taken to the emergency room. After the injured player's departure, the coach talks with the remaining players to figure out what happened. It seems the telephone pole had a long anchor wire staked to the ground with a large metal spike. The spike had protruding metal burrs that were uneven and very sharp. The injured player caught his calf on one of the burrs on the anchor spike while turning the corner, resulting in the injury. The player eventually fully recovered. Fortunately for the coaches and the university, no lawsuit ensued.

This cautionary tale offers many lessons. In this case, even before the season began, the coaching staff should have inspected the soccer field and its surroundings. Had the coaches inspected their three-landmark course, they would have had the situation corrected. The greater lesson for the coaches is the importance of well-thought-out plans. Throughout this chapter, planning and proactive management that mitigates risk, as they relate compliance to legal considerations, will be significant themes. Additionally, the need for knowledge of the law and its impact on the sports ministers, their programs, and their facilities will be covered. The objective is to enable sports ministers to organize quality programing in well-maintained facilities with the assurance of safety.

organization, community, society, or nation. Laws are dynamic and can change over time. This accumulation of rules and regulations is designed to govern our behavior and actions and to bring a sense of order to business relationships, contracts, personal rights, and individual responsibilities (Pedersen 2019). Some of the most important issues facing those who run and manage sports ministries and their facilities are tort and contract-related issues. These represent legal issues that will be encountered by leaders and managers on a regular basis. Other legal matters such as constitutional law and property law, though encountered far less frequently, are still important matters to understand (Fried and Thibault 2015).

A Basic Description of the U.S. Legal System and Legal Terminology

The law can be defined as a system of regulations designed to govern the conduct of the people of an

A Brief Description of the United States Legal System

The federal system of government in the United States is established by the U.S. Constitution. The constitution provides specific powers to the federal government through the legislative branch (i.e., Congress). All power not delegated to the federal government remains the legal domain of the states through their state legislatures. Each of the 50 U.S. states has its own state constitution, structure of government, legal codes, and judicial system. The U.S. Constitution establishes the judicial branch of the federal government and specifies the authority of the Supreme Court and federal courts. Federal courts have exclusive jurisdiction over certain types of cases, such as those involving federal laws. In certain other areas, federal courts share jurisdiction with state courts. State courts have exclusive jurisdiction over the majority of cases. The executive branch (i.e., U.S. president, state governors, and administrative agencies) makes up the final branch of government established by the U.S. Constitution (Federal Judicial Center 2016).

Sources of Law

Four major sources of law exist in the United States:

1. *Constitutional law:* the U.S. Constitution and the constitutions of each of the individual states
2. *Statutory laws:* federal laws enacted by Congress as well as laws at the state level that are enacted by the respective state legislatures
3. *Administrative law:* rules and regulations enacted by federal and state government agencies
4. *Common law:* represents federal and state court decisions (Pedersen and Thibault 2019).

Constitutional Law

Constitutional law interprets and deals with the actual implementation of the U.S. Constitution, and it addresses some of the fundamental relationships within our society. This includes relationships between each of the states, the states with the federal government, the interaction of the three branches (executive, legislative, judicial) of the federal government, and the rights of individual citizens in relation to both federal and state government. The area of judicial review is a key process and subject within constitutional law. Judicial review enables the Supreme Court to take an active role in ensuring that the executive and legislative branches of government abide by the U.S. Constitution (Cornell Law School 2019). A basic understanding of constitutional law, its legislation, and its procedures are helpful to sports ministries in knowing how to protect and defend their legal rights under the law should the need arise. Most constitutional law is directly related to the

protection, interpretation, and practical application of the Bill of Rights, the common name for the first ten amendments of the Constitution. These rights provide a wide range of legal protections for United States citizens and the enterprises they undertake. Many constitutional laws have been developed over the years as a result of various Supreme Court rulings. The end goal of all of these rulings is ideally to clarify and fairly apply citizen rights in various situations. Constitutional law is often referred to as the supreme law of the United States. Individual states and their respective municipalities have their own varied laws, but these local laws must always uphold all the policies and procedures of constitutional law (Indeed Editorial Team 2022).

One amendment to the U.S. Constitution, the First Amendment, and the concept of the Establishment Clause can have a key impact on sports ministry programs. The First Amendment reads as follows: "Congress shall make no law respecting an establishment of religion or prohibiting the free exercise thereof; or abridging the freedom of speech, or of the press; or the right of the people peaceably to assemble, and to petition the Government for a redress of grievances" (Congress.gov, n.d.). The importance of this amendment is noted in the two provisions it establishes concerning religion. The first provision is known as the Establishment Clause, which prohibits the government from establishing a religion. It is noteworthy to point out that the precise definition of "establishment" is unclear, though many opinions abound. Historically, it referred to the government being prohibited from creating state-sponsored churches or religion. The second provision, referred to as the Free Exercise Clause, ensures that all citizens have the protected right to practice their religion as they please so long as the practice does not run afoul of public morals or compelling government interests (United States Courts, n.d.). Virtually all jurists would agree that the Establishment Clause does protect religious activity from a number of governmental encroachments such interfering with a religious organization's selection of leadership and staff, as well as scriptural and doctrinal standards adhered to and followed. In fact, this clause exempts or accommodates religious entities and institutions such as sports ministries from hundreds of federal, state, and local laws whereby compliance on the ministry's part would conflict with their religious beliefs and conduct (Hamilton and McConnell, n.d.). Sports ministries have significant protection under the Establishment Clause to run biblically sound, God-honoring organizations. The Free Exercise Clause ensures that they can carry out their ministry work in the manner they determine to be best.

Statutory Laws

Statutory laws vary from regulatory or administrative laws, which are passed by executive agencies, and from common law, which are created as a result of prior court decisions. Statutory laws are generally strictly interpreted and applied (HG.org Legal Resources, n.d.). Statutory concerns at the local, state, and federal levels cover such items as tax laws, Occupational Safety and Health Administration (OSHA), health code regulations affecting concession operations, and similar legislation (Fried 2015).

Sports ministries need to file appropriate legal documentation and tax forms annually to maintain their 501(c)(3) status as a nonprofit organization. Their facilities and ministry settings need to be properly maintained and safely conducted per OSHA regulations. The workplace needs to be a positive, nontoxic environment that is free from negative behavior such as sexual misconduct or harassment. Additionally, some states now require criminal background checks for coaches, staff, and volunteers involved in youth sports. Even if not required, sports ministries should consider being proactive and voluntarily do the same. Other examples will be covered elsewhere in the chapter.

Administrative Law

Administrative law governs the creation and operation of federal and state administrative agencies. These agencies are granted significant delegated power by Congress and state legislatures to not only enforce existing laws, but also to create new rules concerning relationships between such agencies, other government bodies, and the public at large. Generally, the mission of such agencies is to protect public interests and to ensure the public good is not denied. It is important for sports ministries to understand administrative agencies to ensure compliance with their various regulations and requirements (Cornell Law School 2017).

Common Law

Common law represents the body of laws derived from judicial decisions as opposed to being derived from existing statutes. Such laws in the United States were originally fashioned on English common law. In time the American legal system matured to the point where common laws were formed through direct precedent cases or by analogy to comparable areas of previously decided law. Most common law is found at the state level, though a limited body of federal common law does exist (Cornell Law School 2020). Judges and courts establish common law through judgments and written opinions that are legally binding for future court decisions in the same jurisdiction. Common law is best viewed as precedent decisions used to fill the gaps not covered by civil law statutes. Common law changes over time (Legal Knowledge Base 2022). The common law system places significant weight on the judicial decisions rendered in prior similar cases. This is done to help ensure similar results in similar cases. It is important to note that the courts are bound by such decisions of the higher courts by a legal principle known as **stare decisis**. The only time this would not occur is when the court determines a given case to be fundamentally different from prior cases heard by the court system. When this occurs, the final ruling is likely to create a new precedent for future cases and rulings on the subject (Legal Dictionary 2015). Becoming well versed in common law is important for sports ministry leaders so they can prevent detrimental legal actions as have previously affected similar ministries.

State Legal Systems

State legislatures create and enact laws for governance in legal matters not covered at the federal level. As previously noted, state laws and statutes must uphold and be consistent with federal laws. The key is to realize that state statutes might be more restrictive than similar federal laws. However, state laws can never be less restrictive than federal laws. Two specific categories of law, torts and contracts, are legal matters always handled at the state level, on a state-by-state basis (Pedersen and Thibault 2019). For sports ministries, these two categories are very important to understand.

Tort Law

The primary goal of **tort law** is to provide relief and compensation for damages incurred by civil wrongs, rather than criminal offenses, and in the process, deter others from committing the same harms. Torts generally fall into three categories: intentional, negligent, and strict liability. Intentional torts are those wrongs for which the defendant knew, or should have known,

---

statutory law—Written laws that are passed and enacted by legislative bodies.

stare decisis—A legal doctrine whereby a decision previously reached by a court of law is then used as the final decision rendering authority in all future legal cases that are based on similar circumstances or facts. Pronounced ster-ē-di-'sī-səs.

tort law—Civil wrongs (as opposed to criminal offenses) for which legal remedies exist for harm caused.

Interview With a Professional

Pat Stewart

Past President and CEO of Missionary Athletes International (MAI), 2002-2018

Prior to his time with MAI, Pat Stewart spent 20 years in various business management positions. While working in the health insurance field, he was asked by friends within MAI to consider joining their board of directors, which he did in 1998.

What was your journey to becoming a board member and then as MAI's president and CEO?

Having traveled to Mexico with my collegiate soccer team, I was familiar with the concept of sports ministry and gladly accepted the board position. It provided me an understanding of how MAI was using soccer to minister both domestically and internationally. The Lord drew my heart toward the ministry when I participated in one of the international short-term outreach trips. I was happy that I could use my business experience to help in the organizational leadership at the board level. When the mission began looking for a president and CEO, I was asked to interview and subsequently hired.

Can you speak to the importance of legal attention as a sports ministry organization leader?

I believe that the leader of an organization has a personal as well as a professional responsibility for compliance to all applicable laws. Failure to be aware of legal obligations can lead to reputational damage, financial penalties, or even criminal charges. There is definitely a price to comply, but the price paid in time, effort, and resources is generally much lower than the price of noncompliance.

Did you have legal resources available to you when you stepped into the leadership role?

Fortunately, the ministry had a local attorney familiar with the ministry and provided pro bono service. Having someone to call with general legal questions is a huge help when not an attorney yourself! There were times, however, when we needed to consult with specialized attorneys in areas like immigration, employment law, and even religious liberty. Even if you, as the leader, are an attorney, there will be times or situations that will require expertise that you do not have. As a Christian organization, we desire to do the best job possible, not just to avoid trouble with the government, but because we are called to a high standard. As the Scriptures implore us, "Whatever you do, work at it with all your heart, as working for the Lord, not for human masters" (Colossians 3:23 NIV).

Another great resource for the ministry has been the ECFA and their seven standards. As we strive to be an authentic and transparent ministry, the standards direct us to best practices. They guide us and have helped us establish a statement of faith as well as mission and vision statements. These statements are important keys for the development of the organization's culture and directing the goals and objectives of day-to-day ministry. Articulating our values enables us to communicate our ministry more effectively to new staff.

Have legal concerns changed over your time with MAI? What might the future look like?

The legal environment is dynamic; it will always be changing. With changes in laws, government, and culture, the organization must be ready to adapt. One area of change is the level of scrutiny that has come with the success of our teams on the field. Social media, combined with our teams playing in secular leagues, sometimes places our values in conflict with those of the leagues. Unfortunately, in the U.S. culture, people today are looking for, and even trying to create, controversy around the exercise of religious freedom outside of the Church. They have difficulty understanding how we operate as a religious organization within a secular environment. Since we are not a church, there are people who would like to restrict the exemptions we have as a religious organization (such as hiring people who share our religious values) or impose on us the values of the league, which may be in conflict with our own religious beliefs.

> continued

While people are quick to cite the separation of church and state, governments (local, state, and federal) seem to be increasingly eager to regulate or restrict religious practices. For example, athletic facilities owned by municipalities or local governments can adopt anti-discrimination language in their contracts, which could potentially be used to deny sports ministry organizations access to public facilities. This emphasizes the importance of having relationships with attorneys or legal groups that know and can defend religious freedom issues.

Risk management and liability issues are also noteworthy. Anyone working with children should be vetted with a background check. The ministry should have requisite levels of liability insurance, workers' compensation coverage, and an emergency plan of action for all programs, and should provide adequate staff training.

What advice about legal issues would you give to future sports ministry professionals?

Because sports ministry does not always look like a religious organization, it is important that Scripture permeates your organizational structure. Scripture is to be evident in your mission and vision statements, policy and procedure manuals, and all other materials so that those questioning your status as a religious organization will clearly see that you are. More important, this clarity will help drive your ministry's culture and be a reminder for everyone of the reason we facilitate sport—to create an environment where the gospel of Jesus Christ can be communicated. Sport is a big part of what we do, but it does not supersede ministry. By being authentic in your practice of ministry and diligent in the small things, and by paying attention to legal realities and trends, you are setting yourself up for effective and fruitful ministry. (Pat Stewart, pers. interview, 2022)

what the results of his or her actions or inactions would be. Some examples of this type of tort are crimes such as assault, battery, wrongful death, fraud, and trespassing, any of which can form the basis of a lawsuit for damages by the injured party. Tort crimes can be the basis for legal action and lawsuits. Sports ministries need to expect the unexpected and be prepared for such potential actions against their ministry if a grievance occurs under their supervision. They also need to carefully, and prayerfully, consider their response when the opportunity to file a lawsuit might be justified. Though a ministry could file a lawsuit, would it glorify God to do so?

A person has a responsibility and duty to behave in a reasonable manner when interacting with others. When an individual fails to do so and causes harm to others, they can be legally deemed to have acted with **negligence**. Strict liability wrongs do not depend on the exercise of care by the defendant but are established when a particular action causes damage (USLegal, n.d.).

Elements Necessary for Any Negligence Claim

Claims of negligence can occur with sports facilities and their operators. Four elements are necessary for

a negligence claim, and all four elements need to be present for the claim to be considered valid.

1. *Duty:* Some duties of facility managers include the provision of a safe facility—a facility that is regularly inspected with needed repairs made in a timely fashion. It is also the duty of management to provide fully trained and attentive staff, capable of executing supervisory responsibilities.

2. *Breach of duty:* Facility managers and staff are required and expected to act in a responsible manner and exercise reasonable judgment with the goal of preventing dangerous situations for potential harm.

3. *Proximate cause:* Even if evidence of a breach of duty exists, that breach might not be the direct cause of harm or injury to someone. Proximate cause implies that an injury or a harm caused was the direct result of someone's breach of duty.

4. *Injury or damages:* Any negligence claim will require someone to have been injured physically, emotionally, or both.

If any of the four elements are missing, the claim is deemed invalid (Fried 2015). Other defenses can be

---

negligence—A legal term that refers to the failure of one party to use reasonable care, resulting in injury and damage to another party.

taken against negligence claims such as comparative or contributory negligence, assumption of risk, and immunity. The effectiveness of these defenses varies from state to state. The manager of a facility must familiarize him- or herself with the laws that apply to the programs and facilities and must manage the entity within these regulations. Something to keep in mind is the familiar saying of boxer Jack Dempsey: "The best defense is a good offense" (Goodreads, n.d.). As leaders and managers of sports ministries and facilities, it is key to be proactive by diligently maintaining and caring for the facilities and safety of all guests.

Contract Law

Contract law preserves and encourages the rights of two or more parties to enter into agreements (Moorman, Reynolds, and Siegrist 2019). **Contracts** are used on a regular basis in sports ministry operations when they buy and sell goods, provide services and programs, provide employment agreements, and purchase various forms of insurance. A good contract has specific, clear terms to avoid disagreements and misunderstandings as each party seeks to fulfill its obligations.

A valid contract has four essential parts:

1. *Offer:* One party makes an offer and states the terms it is proposing.
2. *Acceptance:* This involves accepting or agreeing to another party's offer, which then makes the contract complete. In the case of acceptance, the party that accepts and agrees to the terms of the original offer informs the offering party accordingly.
3. *Consideration:* A valid contract requires that each party provide something in the process. Contracts are best understood as a two-way street, with each party giving something up or ordering to get something they want.
4. *Mutual intent to enter into an agreement:* For a contract to be valid, both parties must show that they intend to be bound by the agreed-upon terms (Legal Career Path, n.d.).

An additional element of contract law that applies to sports ministries is the element of **capacity**. Some people cannot enter into a contract and be legally bound by its terms because of their age, mental status, or mental state. For example, individuals under the age of 18 cannot be bound to a contract because of the assumption that they would not understand what they are agreeing to, regardless of the appearance of their maturity. This is particularly applicable to sports ministry programs when a facility asks or requires minors to sign a waiver form. In such cases, the parents or guardians of these children also should be required to sign a waiver (Fried 2015). Partnering with a quality law firm can prove most helpful when drafting contracts.

Additional Legal Considerations for Sports Ministries

Sports ministries need to be alerted to several additional legal areas and address these in the various initiatives they undertake. Essentially, a sports ministry is comparable to a business, and it needs to ensure compliance with the following legal considerations.

Employment Law

A host of federal, state, and local laws govern and affect the American workplace. Hence, leaders of sports ministries need to possess a working understanding of how these laws affect the work they do. In the case of large sports ministries such as the Fellowship of Christian Athletes (FCA) and Athletes in Action (AIA), they have human resource professionals who guide practical compliance. For smaller sports ministries it is important to have access to professional legal support to achieve these results. Given the complexity of employment laws, understanding them and properly implementing them can be a daunting challenge.

Nonprofit religious organizations such as sports ministries are granted some exceptions and exemptions to legal standards that apply to other corporate entities, yet they still must follow some legal standards. Employment law can become a balancing act of preventing state interference with ministry governance while protecting and respecting the rights of ministry staff under the law. An example of a direct application to sports ministry is the religious

---

contract—An agreement between two parties to do (or not do) a particular act as it relates to an exchange of goods, services, properties, or money.

capacity—The ability to enter into a contract.

exception as it relates to hiring practices. Prior to 1972 this religious exception applied to positions and activities that were considered strictly religious in nature. Congress expanded the exception in 1972 to include all of a religious organization's activities. In the case of a sports ministry, leadership can require that all staff and coaches be professing Christians who agree with the mission and doctrinal position of the ministry (Baptist Standard 2010).

Leaders of sports ministries have a number of resources available to them. On the federal level the United States Department of Labor provides resources on its website focused on positive compliance assistance (Office of Disability Employment Policy, n.d.). A valuable church ministry resource is www.churchlawtoday.com, run by Richard Hammar, an attorney and certified public accountant based in Springfield, Missouri. The publication *Keeping Your Church Out of Court*, provided by the Texas Baptist Christian Life Commission, is also widely used. This publication provides forms a ministry can use to answer legal questions, create job applications, and formulate personnel policies. It is a source of advice for conducting affairs under federal and state laws that provide legal protections and insulations (Baptist Standard 2010).

Labor Law

A number of federal laws directly apply to churches and faith-based ministries such as sports ministries. It is important to adopt clear policies and guidelines to ensure the ministry complies with all applicable legal requirements. The following is a list of the federal employment laws that apply to religious organizations (Church Law 2020):

- Title VII of the Civil Rights Act of 1964
- Occupational Safety and Health Administration Act of 1970 (OSHA)
- Americans With Disabilities Act (ADA)
- Family and Medical Leave Act of 1993 (FMLA)
- Age Discrimination in Employment Act (ADEA)
- Patient Protection and Affordable Care Act (ACA)
- Fair Labor Standards Act (FLSA)

Key Legal Issues Facing Sport Ministries

The pursuit of litigious action is prevalent in today's society. It has become the preferred recourse for individuals to resolve their grievances. Whether the legal claim is substantive and has potential merit or is frivolous and legally baseless, it is a current reality. As a result, risk management in the context of minimizing exposure to legal liability has become an inescapable part of the job for administrators of sports ministries and their facilities. In view of this reality, it is important that the leaders of these ministry initiatives possess a working knowledge and understanding of the legal issues related to their programs (Green 2015).

Lawsuits are a concern for all organizations. It is recommended that the ministry maintain a strong relationship with qualified legal counsel who readily identify with the mission of the organization. Such a law firm will prove valuable not only in the startup phase, but for years to come. The ministry's legal partner should be able to process all legal paperwork such as application for 501(c)(3) nonprofit status, development of a strong risk management plan, creation of waiver forms, assistance with securing adequate liability insurance, and other related legal matters (Fried 2015).

Lack of Understanding and Knowledge of Legal Elements and Responsibilities

A deficient understanding of fundamental legal principles can become a stumbling block for administrators. In many cases, they do not recognize the need for substantial legal knowledge or expertise, or they have not had the opportunity to be trained in the subject. Addressing this shortcoming and gaining the knowledge and necessary expertise is essential to running effective programs and proper facility management. Once armed with this knowledge, the manager can craft best practices and risk management strategies to better serve his or her constituencies and avoid liability issues. A well-informed and responsive leader is a

Interview With a Professional

Jeremy Evans

Chief Entrepreneur Officer, Chief Entrepreneur Officer, Founder, and Managing Attorney at California Sports Lawyer

BA, political science, UCLA

JD, Thomas Jefferson School of Law

Master of laws in entertainment (LLM), media and sports law, Pepperdine University

MBA, entertainment, media, and sports management, Pepperdine University.

Courtesy of Jeremy Evans.

Jeremy M. Evans is the chief entrepreneur officer (CEO), founder, and managing attorney at California Sports Lawyer, representing entertainment, media, and sports clientele in contractual, intellectual property, and dealmaking matters. Evans is an award-winning attorney and industry leader based in Los Angeles. Beginning in 2021, Jeremy has served as president of the California Lawyers Association, the largest statewide bar association in the United States. He hosts and executive produces a weekly podcast, number one in its category, *Bleav in Sports Law*, and writes a weekly column. He also teaches sports law and industry courses for graduate sport management programs at California State University, Long Beach and at American Military University. He serves on the Board of Advisors for the Rose Bowl Legacy Foundation.

His clients range from Fortune 500 companies to entrepreneurs, athletes, entertainers, models, directors, television showrunners and film producers, studios, writers, individuals, and businesses in contractual, intellectual property, formation, production, distribution, negotiation, and dealmaking matters. Prior to opening California Sports Lawyer, Evans worked as a graduate law clerk at the Superior Court of California, advising judicial officers in civil and criminal law and motion matters. Prior to law school, he worked as the associate director for corporate finance at Quinn Emanuel Urquhart & Sullivan, LLP. He has also worked as a legislative aide and field representative in the California State Legislature and continues to work on local and national campaigns. He founded two international entertainment, media, and sports law negotiation competitions to give back and help train the next generation: the National Sports Law Negotiation Competition at his law school alma mater and the California Sports Lawyer Negotiation Competition at the iconic Rose Bowl Stadium.

What was your career path?

Growing up, I had a passion for the law and politics. Initially, after watching many *Law & Order* episodes, I wanted to become a district attorney after working for a couple state legislators and a large law firm in California. During law school, my experiences working for two civil litigation law firms and the public defender, while competing in the Tulane International Baseball Arbitration Competition in New Orleans and serving in several different volunteer roles (president of the Student Bar Association), I was reintroduced to my passion for entertainment, media, and sports law. I grew up playing baseball near Hollywood, so I loved the industry and creative work being done. Once I finished my graduate clerkship at the Superior Court, I opened my own law practice after meeting with many different attorneys to gain wisdom and insight. I trademarked California Sports Lawyer and built a brand through three principles: geography, branding, and community. It is important to position yourself professionally in such a way that you are where the action is happening, creating content and distributing it on social media, joining organizations, and taking on leadership roles where you can have a direct impact in your community and success.

> continued

With your significant background in sports law, what advice would you give to individuals who are running, or seeking to create, 501(c)(3) sports ministries from a legal standpoint?

Charitable organizations are a major part of all talent, whether in sports or entertainment. Agents and their lawyers often advise that starting a charity is great to impact your community and give back, but also to help with financial management. Charitable organizations are one of the areas where athletes can direct money and resources to a cause of their liking.

What websites, online tools, and resources would you recommend to those who work in sports ministry?

I think that the Fellowship of Christian Athletes is a great organization. I would recommend joining a church community. Consider participating in or leading a Bible study. I also think it is a good idea to read and listen to podcasts and books on faith, business, and so on.

What do you see as the future challenges in the legal world especially as it relates to sports and sports ministry?

Values. Find what matters to you, and fight for it.

Do you have any additional thoughts or advice you would like to share?

Your family and friends are everything. Be in constant prayer. Keep the faith, and be encouraged by challenges, which help grow your faith in Christ (Jeremy Evans, pers. interview, 2022).

---

critical asset for the management of sports programs and facilities (Fried 2015). From sports program designs to program execution, from facility design to ongoing facility maintenance, numerous legal requirements and responsibilities are involved. These need to be understood and consistently practiced to protect the ministry initiatives from negative legal issues.

Americans With Disabilities Act (ADA) Requirements for Sport Programs and Facilities

The legal issues that arise with the proper (or improper) interpretation and application of the Americans With Disabilities Act (ADA) as they relate to youth sport activities and facilities need to be addressed. Individuals with disabilities are required by law to be able to enjoy full and equal access to the goods, services, facilities, privileges, advantages, and accommodations offered by the sport facility. This applies to all sport facilities, whether they are private, nonprofit, or public (Fried 2015). Addressing the needs of persons with disabilities begins by considering the challenges faced by individuals who seek access to the facilities and the programs offered (Green 2016). Under ADA law, a place of public accommodation must create greater access and remove physical and architectural barriers when such removal is readily achievable. When removal

is not reasonably feasible, the facility is required to provide alternative means of accessibility. All new facility construction is required to be fully accessible and usable, with very few exceptions allowed (Fried 2015). Noncompliance with ADA regulations can result in significant penalties and fines. However, this should not be the motivation for compliance. As a sports ministry, providing accessibility to such individuals should be viewed not as an inconvenience, but as another opportunity to minster and serve through sport. It will require additional planning, investment, and support elements. In the end, it represents the right thing to do.

Practical and inexpensive ADA solutions can be implemented. Consider the following suggestions forwarded by Gil Fried, JD. Facility managers should perform a complete facility and program review to discover what ADA deficiencies and problems exist. Training should take place focused on creating program-wide attitude changes related to serving individuals with disabilities. The following six steps are recommended:

1. Designate one staff member to be the ADA liaison and expert for programs and the facility. Provide this individual with the requisite training to fulfill this role. Choose an individual to lead who will own the spirit of these legal requirements.

2. Conduct a comprehensive ADA facility audit. A detailed report should be created outlining the work and remediation that still needs to

be done, as well as developing a plan for doing the work and meeting ADA needs.

3. Evaluate all program policies, procedures, and facility practices and how they affect individuals with disabilities. Any deficient elements should be noted, a plan formulated, and corrections made.

4. Acquire and maintain auxiliary aids that support elements of accessibility.

5. Evaluate ADA accessibility plans to determine if they are working in practical ways for those they are designed to serve.

6. Confer with the ministry's accountant to determine whether investments in ADA remediation qualify for any tax breaks (Fried 2015).

Comprehensive Online Resource for the Americans with Disabilities Act (Corada) is an ADA-related resource that provides thorough insights ensuring the program and facilities meet and fulfill ADA legal requirements. Corada's mission is to make a great accessible experience routine. Through its platform and solutions, over 2,000 businesses and organizations have learned how to identify and improve their accessibility efforts. Corada's platform provides users with the ability to search articles covering best practices as well as over 400 federal, state, and legal case study documents through its accessibility search engine. Corada also provides an extensive list of certified products that are compliant with accessibility codes and standards. This listing provides businesses with a wide variety of product solutions for ADA legal requirements (Corada, n.d.). Making great accessible sporting experiences the norm rather than the exception is important to individuals with disabilities and their families. As leaders of sports ministry programs this is an achievable goal.

The Importance of a Proactive Risk Management Program

Spiritually, we are called to do four things:

1. Love God before ourselves (Matthew 22:36-38)

2. Love and serve others (Matthew 22:39-40)

3. Share the hope found in the gospel of Jesus Christ (1 Peter 3:15)

4. Make disciples (Matthew 28:19-20)

These four items lead to a fruitful Christian life and producing a sports ministry that makes a difference in the lives of those served (Cachila 2016).

In addition to these spiritual principles, four tasks are important for developing programs:

1. Work hard at preventing problems.

2. Appropriately solve problems when they occur.

3. Create special experiences.

4. Make these experiences as memorable as possible.

Special and memorable sporting experiences are powerful tools used to love and serve others, share the gospel, and make disciples. As noted earlier, legal liability cannot be eliminated entirely because some accidents and occurrences are unforeseeable. However, leaders skilled in the first two elements of preventing and appropriately solving problems can significantly minimize their facility's legal exposure and liabilities. This in turn will protect the financial bottom line and reputation (Sports Field Management 2018).

Legally, the prevention of problems and the way in which they are solved are critical to the success of the sports ministry. If the ministry is taking over an existing facility, an audit should be done of all elements that will be used in the programming. Items that need attention, repair, or replacement should be taken care of before the programs begin. If a new facility is being built, the leadership team should work closely with the general contractor to construct a safe and easily maintained facility. It cannot be overstated how important it is to give careful forethought to legal regulations and how these will affect the design and supporting elements of the facility. Steps should be taken to ensure that the facility is fully accessible and meets the spirit and the law of the ADA.

Once the sports ministry is operational, several areas should be prioritized to keep the users' experiences positive. Highlighting the areas of safety, quality maintenance, training of staff, waivers, and liability insurance all play a part in creating an ongoing **proactive risk management program**. Though legal liabilities cannot be eliminated entirely, employing

---

Proactive risk management program—A program designed to identify risks before they occur and to supply actions taken to mitigate such risks. The objective is to provide a special sporting environment that is enjoyable, safe, and well maintained.

this proactive approach can dramatically lower the overall legal risks.

Safety

Operating a safe sport facility is critical to limiting liability. Individuals at the facility can only win a lawsuit if it can be demonstrated that they suffered harm or property damage. Without demonstrating such harm, injury, and loss, their lawsuit will be without merit. Even in cases when an unforeseeable accident or injury occurs, facilities that can demonstrate taking all reasonable efforts to ensure visitor and guest safety will be exposed to far less liability. On the other hand, groups generally will be held liable for injuries and harm caused by situations that they knew—or should have known—were dangerous. The phrase "should have known" tends to be interpreted in a broad manner. If something is known to be a potential hazard, the correction is required to be made promptly. If unaware of the dangerous element, the court could still find the facility responsible because the problem should have been known (Sports Field Management 2018). Regular inspections of the facility and all its elements is a critical strategy. The importance of valuing an ongoing, high-quality maintenance program, with installments made daily, weekly, monthly, and annually depending on the various needs of the facility, cannot be emphasized enough.

Storm-Related Considerations

The inherent danger of lightning should not be taken casually. Lightning strikes the United States about 25 million times per year. It has been said that all injuries and deaths from lightning strikes have one common element: a majority of those struck were outdoors and in generally unsafe places like an open field, construction loading and unloading zones, in a tent or pavilion, or under a tree. Lightning is random and unpredictable, and it does not discriminate. Another commonality with these unfortunate events is that survivors usually say that they did not think that the lightning was that dangerous or that close. On average, two to four dozen people die per year from lightning strikes in the United States alone. Similar outcomes are avoided each year by individuals willfully choosing to play it safe and get indoors. They heed the phrase from the NOAA National Weather Service, "When the thunder roars, go indoors!" (Cwik 2016).

Lightning has been known to strike on the most beautiful of days. It is often brought on by the buildup of the day's heat, an oncoming thunderstorm, or the remnants of a storm that fell apart or appears to have fallen apart (hence why some survivors say they did not think it was that dangerous or that close. A sobering fact is that lightning has been known to strike up to 10 miles from the heart of a thunderstorm (Cam 2019).

Usually, the only predictor of lightning is the sound of thunder. If you hear thunder or see lightning, everyone should take shelter immediately, preferably in a fully enclosed brick-and-mortar building. Exercising due caution without delay will go a long way toward managing the situation correctly, meeting the expectations of all involved, and legally mitigating for unsafe weather conditions. Safety and evacuation plans are predetermined and practiced in advance so that everyone is prepared for potential weather-related concerns. Leadership has the responsibility to formulate the plan and apprise all staff of its execution. In the case of a soccer camp, if no brick-and-mortar buildings are in close proximity, consider an alternative site for the camp. It is ideal if the sport facility is equipped with a reliable lightning detection system complete with a warning horn or siren. In certain parts of the country, this warning system will prove valuable in the event of extreme weather such as a tornado.

If competing in an away sporting contest and no safe shelters spaces are available, at minimum, ensure team bus or vans are located nearby and available as a viable safety option. This solution might be less than ideal but is the next best option. Many believe that vehicles are safe from lightning due to their rubber tires, but this is a myth that has been proven false. Lightning bolts are so powerful that they will travel through tires and melt them in the process. The team van or bus is safe because of the metal cage surrounding the occupants inside the vehicle. It might seem counterintuitive because metal is such a good conductor of electricity, but the metal cage of the vehicle actually directs the lightning charge around those inside and safely into the ground (Russo 2020).

Temperature-Related Considerations

Extreme heat indexes are high-risk occasions. Sports ministry programming needs to follow precautions to avoid dehydration and other potential heat-related health risks. Three types of heat illnesses are common:

1. *Heat cramps:* These cramps can be quite painful and are the result of involuntary contractions of the exercising muscles. The cause is usually attributed to a lack of hydration and the substantial loss of fluid through excessive

sweating. Those suffering from heat cramps should be removed from the heat source and given water to drink. They should rest and, at the most, do some passive stretching of the affected muscle groups. Though this is the least serious form of the heat illnesses—and recovery usually occurs quickly—heat cramps should be treated properly. If left untreated, heat cramps could progress to heat exhaustion.

2. *Heat exhaustion:* This is a dangerous condition brought on by rigorous activity taking place in a hot environment. It can result in the participants' body temperature elevating up to 102 degrees Fahrenheit (39° Celsius), usually associated with significant sweating. Other signs and symptoms include cool, moist, pale, ashen, or flushed skin; headaches, nausea, dizziness, a rapid pulse, and general overall weakness. This serious condition requires immediate treatment by getting the individual to a cool, shaded area; elevating his or her lower limbs; providing hydration; and providing cooling ice packs and cool wet towels. It is wise to seek qualified medical advice or emergency medical services. If left unchecked or poorly treated, heat exhaustion can escalate into heat stroke.

3. *Heat stroke:* This is a true medical emergency and represents a life-threatening condition. Internal body temperature can rise to 104 degrees (40° Celsius); the skin might appear red, hot, and dry; yet the victim might still be sweating profusely. Symptoms are similar to those of heat exhaustion but at a higher, more profound level. Those suffering from heat stroke can appear very confused and exhibit an altered state of consciousness. Seizures and a loss of consciousness can occur. Actions should include rapid cooling protocols and calling emergency medical personnel to the scene immediatcly (Spengler 2006).

Numerous proactive measures can be implemented to prevent heat-related illnesses in sporting activities on hot days. First, include proper training and instruction for dealing with heat. Second, provide ample opportunities for fluid replacement before, during, and after the sport activity. Third, encourage participants to wear light-colored, loose-fitting clothing. Fourth, train staff to monitor and recognize the signs of potential heat-related illnesses. Also, provide certified athletic trainers on site if possible (Stop Sports Injuries 2019). Be sure the sport facilities provide ample areas to get out of the sun and into the shade. In addition to providing water coolers for ample hydration, include sponging options of cool, wet towels and ice packs. If available, a water sprinkler system is helpful. The most effective means of treating heat-related illnesses is preventing them from occurring in the first place.

The opposite extreme of heat-related concerns are precautions related to oppressively cold temperatures and windchills, such as hypothermia and frostbite. Even something as common as sunburn and the availability of sunscreen needs to be considered, especially when working with children and youths. Some regions have weather-related air-quality concerns that could hamper participants with respiratory conditions. Regardless, weather is a factor in the planning and execution of sports ministry programing.

Emergency Preparedness

Awareness of the potential dangers and preventative action plans is the responsibility of those who lead and run outdoor sports ministries. First, ministries are committed to doing what is right. Second, appropriate child supervision and safety practices is an expectation. Third, **legal liability** issues could result if due consideration and preparation is not provided in the event of inclement weather and lightning potential.

When overlooked, emergency preparedness can cause significant legal repercussions such as demonstrating that the management of a sports ministry event was negligent, either intentionally or unintentionally. Even when steps are taken to create a safe environment for sporting activity, accidents and injuries will occur. What happens before, during, and after an emergency event can determine the eventual outcome. Dealing with emergency situations requires the creation of an advanced plan of action ensuring resolution should the need arise (Gershom and Peer 2008).

The best way to ensure appropriate emergency preparedness is to develop a quality emergency action plan (EAP). While such plans are not mandated by law, best practices clearly point to their need in sports ministry, protecting the safety of athletes, coaches, support staff, and spectators in the case of a medical emergency. The following outline details 10 elements of a comprehensive EAP (DeLench 2015).

---

legal liability—The risk answerable in law that an organization undertakes for injuries and property damage occurring at a facility. Such liability cannot be eliminated entirely because some accidents and occurrences are unforeseeable.

- Provide on-site recognition of, evaluation of, and immediate first aid for the occurrence of injury or illness (e.g., heat stroke, sporting injuries such as neck and spine injuries, concussions).

- Develop a plan for the availability of individuals designated to provide emergency medical care (e.g., advanced first aid and CPR certified) and to oversee contacting emergency services (e.g., ambulance service and 911).

- Detail and review various medical emergency circumstances and how the team will respond with either on-site care or transportation to an emergency room or physician.

- Ensure that every staff member has a cell phone with emergency care access numbers, as well as information on the hospital or urgent care facility to be used. Ensure cell phone service is available at the site.

- Ensure those responsible for calling emergency medical services (EMS) are well-versed in placing an EMS call and have accurate directions to the location.

- Secure and maintain accurate lists of all participants' emergency contact information for parents or guardians so they can be reached in case of injury or medical emergency.

- Secure and maintain an accurate list of medical concerns and conditions for each participant (e.g., asthma and allergies).

- Provide a signed medical release and treatment authorization form for each participant.

- Assign staff to monitor injured participants during medical emergencies.

- Provide the appropriate medical emergency equipment and ensure it is in appropriate working condition (e.g., rescue inhalers and EpiPens). Provide training in the proper usage of any such items.

Injuries and medical emergencies can happen at any time at a sports ministry event. Proper training of staff and a quality EAP can make all the difference in the outcome. Although the preparation and creation of such plans can be labor intensive, they can result in minimizing the risk and saving someone's life. Free EAP templates are available from organizations such as the National Alliance for Youth Sports (Better Coaching 2022).

When creating such EAPs, consider investing in required training in first aid, CPR, and water safety instruction for leadership and staff. Such training experiences will provide staff with the confidence to remain calm and controlled when administering assistance and aid.

Facility Maintenance

Outdoor sports fields and indoor courts are to be maintained so they are playable and safe. Basketball courts need to be level, in good repair, and provide sufficient traction. However, outdoor sport fields can be tolerated with minimal unlevel surfaces, divots, uneven grass, or worn-out artificial turf surfaces. Poor field and facility conditions can result in injuries to participants and increase the risk for potential legal action. Such factors also extend to the areas immediately adjacent to indoor and outdoor game surfaces such as curbs, walls, and fences. Any space or area used for active sport needs to be evaluated for safety. Consideration for spectator areas with concerns related to slippery surfaces, appropriate seating, safe walkways, lighting, disability access, parking lots, and so on are also integral safety protocols. Consider every element of the facility and then ask, "What could possibly go wrong here?" The leader or facility manager is expected to maintain a safe facility and anticipate potential risks and dangers. The work of problem prevention and solving in sport facility management needs to be a part of the daily routine.

Training Staff and Workers

Good employees are the lifeblood of quality facilities that are organized, well maintained, and safe. Leadership should train staff to understand the high priority of safety operations. Clearly articulated policies should be established for all workers follow. A culture of "see something, say something (or do something)" needs to be cultivated so that it becomes second nature. Every team member needs to be vigilant about proper maintenance and reporting any area considered to be a safety concern. Routine inspections are to be conducted to ensure everything is in working order and proper supervision is taking place (Sports Field Management 2018).

Waiver Forms

Any sporting activity or event comes with inherent risks. A **waiver form** involves an individual surrendering a known right (figure 10.1). A signed waiver can protect the sports ministry against liability from

---

waiver form—Acknowledges the inherent risks associated with participation in sport and the individual's responsibility to assume these risks, waiving any claims against an organization for injuries or damages sustained.

FIGURE 10.1   SAMPLE WAIVER FORM

Consent for Voluntary Athletic Participation

ASSUMPTION OF RISK AND RELEASE WAIVER

I am aware that playing or practicing in any sport can be a dangerous activity involving MANY RISKS OF INJURY. I understand that the dangers and risks of playing or practicing in any sport include, but are not limited to, death; serious neck and spinal injuries that may result in complete or partial paralysis or brain damage; serious injury to virtually all bones, joints, ligaments, muscles, tendons, and other aspects of the musculoskeletal system; and serious injury or impairment to other aspects of my own body, general health, or well-being.

Because of the dangers of participating in any sport, I recognize the importance of following the coach's instructions regarding playing techniques, training rules of the sport, other team rules, and to obey such instructions. All participants, voluntary or otherwise, have the responsibility to help reduce the chance of injury. Therefore, all volunteers, including but not limited to coaches, assistants, athletes, nonparticipant observers, and so on who voluntarily participate in an athletic program or activity for *[insert organization]* must obey all safety rules and regulations, report all physical problems to the coach and athletic trainer or medical staff, follow a proper conditioning program, and inspect personal protective equipment daily. Proper execution of skill techniques must be followed for every sport, especially in contact sports.

As a volunteer, including but not limited to coaching, an assistant, athlete, nonparticipant observers, and so on who is voluntarily participating in athletic programs and activities in the *[insert organization]* program and by signing below, I voluntarily agree to assume and/or incur all risks of loss, impairment, damage, or injury of whatever kind, including death, that may be sustained or suffered or associated by my participation in any athletic program or event whether or not the result is in whole or in part from acts or omissions, negligence, or other unintentional fault of the events or activities of *[insert organization]*.

In addition, I (including my heirs, assigns, and personal representatives) agree to release, hold harmless, and indemnify *[insert organization]*, the physicians, and other practitioners of the healing arts treating me from and against any and all liability, claims, demands of any kind and nature, actions, causes of action, lawsuits, expenses, or losses (including attorneys' fees) of any kind and nature whatsoever arising by, or in connection with or on account of property damage or personal injury (including death) arising out of or attributable to the individual's travel to and from or participation in any event(s) or activities in relation to *[insert organization]*.

This Assumption of Risk and Release Waiver applies to *[insert organization]* and all of its trustees, officers, directors, managers, servants, agents, staff, volunteers, employees, advisors, and representatives and remains in effect until such time as it is no longer valid.

I have read and fully understand the voluntary athletic participation information above, and I acknowledge that I agree to the contents and provisions in this document.

Participant's name: _____ Date: _____
(Please print)

Participant's signature: _____   _____

Participant's address: _____

Participant's social security number: _____Date of birth:_____

Signature of parent or guardian (required if participant is under 18 years old and single):

_____

Emergency contact information in the event of an emergency:

Name and relationship: _____ Phone: _____

Name and relationship: _____ Phone: _____

Adapted by permission from Huntington University Athletic Department Consent Form.

CASE STUDY

Soccer Goals: 40 Deaths and 59 Injuries in 38 Years

On a weekend in May 2017 in Tennessee, a two-year-old was killed by a soccer goal, which, when it was blown over by strong 30- to 40-mile-per-hour winds, landed on top of her. At the time this news was reported, it was unknown whether measures had been taken to properly secure the soccer goal. In a press release, the complex in question assured the public that the staff would conduct a thorough review of safety guidelines on and off the field. This terrible accident once again highlights the dangers of sport equipment that is not properly and safely secured. High winds are not the only risk factor

Securely anchored soccer goals are a standard preventative safety measure.

when it comes to soccer goals. The players themselves can end up being the source of the danger as noted by a mother of 13 children, all of whom have regular access to the soccer fields near their home: "One of the things we watch out for is making sure the little ones don't play inside the net or try to climb the goals. Kids will hang on the goals like monkey bars" (Cameron 2017).

A similar event took place in Ohio in 1998 and resulted in the court case *Zivich v. Menor Soccer Club*. This case was significant because the Ohio Supreme Court ruled that waivers signed by parents on behalf of minor children were enforceable in the state of Ohio. From 1979 through May of 2017, 40 deaths and 59 serious injuries have resulted from fallings soccer goal posts. As sad as these statistics are, the even more disheartening statistic is that the frequency of such deaths and injuries has not decreased (Cotton 2017). The knowledge, expertise, and equipment are all available to end these tragic events.

Professionals who run soccer complexes possess enough expertise and experience to bring an end to these senseless injuries and deaths. Everyone on staff needs to take ownership of the problem and be vigilant to ensure that soccer goals are properly anchored. Providing a safe environment for patrons of the facility is required. The best way to prevent lawsuits is to prevent accidents, injuries, and deaths (Cotton 2017).

Discussion Questions:

1. Is it possible to defend a facility, staff, and leadership who do not provide a safe sporting environment? Discuss why.

2. Why would someone who runs a soccer complex think that their soccer goals would not fall over, resulting in injury?

3. Why is it so important to institute a proactive risk management program at a sporting facility?

4. What is the best way to prevent lawsuits?

injuries and damage, even in cases where the injury was caused by the ministry's staff or facility due to negligence. However, the waiver must be well written, otherwise it could fail when challenged in court (Cotton 2017). No matter how many precautions are taken, injuries occur. As a result, it is essential that sports ministries require participants to sign waivers, which will limit, though not entirely eliminate, lawsuits. If participants are minors (under age 18), a parental signature is required. Insurance companies usually require waivers.

Exceptions to the Rule

Injuries that occur from competitive play are a risk generally assigned to the athletes. Athletes assume these risks by simply choosing to play sport, also known as *assumption of risk* in legal terms. This holds true as long as no negligence is demonstrated on the part of a facility due to poor or unsafe playing conditions on a field or court.

Liability Insurance

A sport facility can follow all legal and safety standards and still have unexpected incidences and injuries. Receive counsel from an expert in this category, then secure the recommended amount of liability coverage (Sports Field Management 2018). The support staff needs to be a positive extension of a well-informed and engaged leader. As a sports ministry team commits their work to the Lord and faithfully and proactively practices their operational strategies, should legal matters arise, they will prove to be more manageable.

The Importance of Accountability

A key learning point for the practitioner of sports ministry is the idea of **accountability**. Every plan con-

ceived, every decision made, and every action taken can have legal ramifications. Think of accountability as the positive precursor to successfully navigating the sea of legal requirements that exist in the United States and around the world. Accountability builds trust both within a sports ministry team and with those they serve. Positive accountability is essential to healthy relationships and interactions. It implies that all parties take responsibility for the decisions made as well as the results of those decisions. Some leaders prefer to operate with little or no accountability, but they clearly do so at their own peril, risking damage to the ministry programs. Accountability is not negative and to be avoided, but rather positive and to be embraced and practiced.

People are not naturally prone to taking on accountability. In our sinful, unrepentant state, we are full of pride and arrogance, and we possess a significant inclination toward independence (i.e., answering to no one). The follower of Jesus Christ walks a different path through an accountability to God. Romans 14:12 affirms this accountability: "So then, each of us will give an account of ourselves to God" (NIV). In an apparent irony, surveys have shown that those claiming no faith or religious or spiritual belief indicate a fear of death because of a concern that they will be punished in the afterlife for what they did, or did not do, while on earth (Morrow 2019). Not only does faith in Christ serve as a reminder of the importance of accountability before God, it also encourages accountability to one another. James 5:16 admonishes us to "confess [our] sins to each other and pray for each other so that [we] may be healed. The prayer of a righteous person is powerful and effective" (NIV). Accountability strengthens one another. This is illustrated in Proverbs 27:17: "As iron sharpens iron, so one person sharpens another" (NIV). Accountability is a spiritually positive discipline. When practiced it will prepare a leadership team to meet and exceed the legal requirements of their sports ministry initiatives.

---

accountability—Being responsible for the decisions made, the actions taken, and their outcomes.

SUMMARY

Legal considerations are a reality. First Peter 2:13 says, "Submit yourselves for the Lord's sake to every human authority" and four verses later tells us to "show proper respect for everyone" (NIV). Submitting to the spirit and the letter of the law honors God and shows respect for those God has placed in positions of authority. Once submitted, the response is to "work at it with [our] whole heart, as working for the Lord" (Colossians 3:23 NIV). Those who lead sports ministries should gain an understanding of legal matters and how they relate to the ministry being undertaken. Sport ministers should act in good faith to fulfill the spirit and letter of the law as they provide exceptional sporting experiences in high-quality and safe facilities.

When it comes to legal considerations and sports ministry initiatives, the wisdom of Benjamin Franklin still rings true today: "If you fail to plan, you are planning to fail!" Understand the legal obligations, have a proactive plan to meet these responsibilities, be faithful to follow the plan, and be true to the important work of fulfilling the mission God has given the sports ministry.

REVIEW AND DISCUSSION QUESTIONS

1. For leaders, why is it important to possess a strong knowledge and understanding of the legal responsibilities associated with the sports ministry programs they run and the facilities they operate?

2. Why is an emergency preparedness plan important from a legal standpoint?

3. What is the key to addressing the special needs of persons with disabilities?

4. What is the best way to prevent lawsuits and legal actions against a sporting facility?

5. What is a waiver form, and why is it important?

6. Why is the concept of accountability important in the leadership of sport programs and in the running of sport facilities?

PART III
DEVELOPING A VIABLE SPORTS MINISTRY

Sport is a universal language that connects the nations. A young boy with a soccer ball sits on the pitch at the Hope Center in Calarasi, Romania.

CHAPTER 11

International Sport Mission Trips

"Love . . . Serve . . . Give (in Jesus' Name) . . . And when we grow tired and weary in each of these expressions—Love some more . . . Serve some more . . . Give some more."

The Pursuit, a publication of the National Christian College Athletic Association

LEARNING OBJECTIVES

After studying this chapter, you should be able to do the following:
- Explain the importance of a people-oriented approach to short-term international sports ministry initiatives
- Discuss partnerships as they relate to sport mission trips
- Explain the concept and value of church-based sports ministry
- Identify key administrative and organizational planning components required for an effective international short-term sport mission trip
- Assess the potential benefits for team members who participate in short-term international sports ministry
- Recognize precautions needed to be taken with international short-term sport mission trips
- Understand components of pretrip team preparations and posttrip debriefing strategies

Eleven collegiate student-athletes traveled to Ethiopia in partnership with Sports Friends, the sports ministry branch of Serving in Mission (SIM). Through sport and recreational activities, the team's primary objective was to assist a ministry with street kids from the capitol city of Addis Ababa. Thirty-six young boys, ages 10 to 14, were bused to SIM's Lake Langano retreat location. During the group's preretreat training, Berhanu Kebede, the national director of Sports Friends Ethiopia, explained that the Addis boys were very poor and at the end of the weeklong retreat likely would want to express their thanks but would have nothing tangible to give as a token of their gratitude—except for their tears. Sure enough, the boys were extremely poor. The majority of them arrived with only the tattered clothes on their backs, and the few who brought a change of clothes carried them in soiled plastic grocery bags. At the closing service, tears flowed freely from everyone as mutually shared expressions of appreciation and love. Lives had been touched by sharing a brief moment of life together.

Midway through the week, the boys were asked what their favorite part of the retreat was. As anticipated, they mentioned the bounty of food and the endless games of soccer. Yet the most overwhelming and unexpected response was their bed. Their beds were two-inch-thick (5 cm) pieces of foam cushion, cut three feet (1 m) wide and six feet (2 m) long, were covered with a single sheet, and laid side by side on a concrete floor. These boys were accustomed to sleeping without bedding, and if they were so fortunate to sleep on an old thin mattress, it was laid on a packed dirt floor and shared with others. In hindsight, in one's developed country, how often is God thanked for the provision of a cozy pillow-top mattress resting on a box spring comfortably raised above a carpeted floor?

Lessons learned from short-term sport mission trips often have nothing to do with sport. Sport is simply the venue from which life lessons emerge. This chapter will provide insights and practical guidelines for the planning and execution of an international short-term sports ministry trip.

Benefits of Short-Term Sport Missions

"It is one thing to read a textbook about ministry and customs in a distant land and another to actually see the faces, know the names, walk alongside, and briefly share life with people from a different culture." This expression has been voiced numerous times as student-athletes travel on international **short-term sport missions**. These trips can benefit the traveler and the native person alike as they encourage one another in shared Kingdom work. Meaningful relationships are established, and perspectives are expanded as individuals engage the world together. Within a mission context, the practice of **perspectivism** does not imply compromising the values of biblical principles but is an attempt to gain deeper cultural understanding. God has created a diverse world filled with remark-

able customs and traditions. His revelation of Himself supersedes any one particular people group. Despite being plagued by the distortions of sin, a glimmer of God's image persists within each culture. As cultures interact, the revelation of God is more fully disclosed. Culturally diverse Christian communities worship, pray, and exercise spiritual disciplines differently. These differences can be appreciated and can enlarge one's understanding of God and His global Church (Elmer 2006). Short-termers often experience three key benefits from their travels:

1. An increased sensitivity for the needs and work of full-time cross-cultural missionaries (which increases advocacy for mission support within one's home church)
2. The possibility of entertaining a calling from God to pursue a full-time mission vocation
3. Creatively applying lessons learned on the mission field to expand ministries within the Church and community back home

The local church is a key partner in short-term mission projects. A primary objective of short-term ministry teams is to help build connections between the local church and the unchurched people reached

short-term sport mission—An abbreviated trip lasting as brief as a week or extending to a few months. Typically, participants catch a vision for sport-related service while assisting an ongoing cross-cultural ministry.

perspectivism—An attempt within a mission context to gain deeper understanding, see through the eyes of others, and gain their insight by learning to think like them.

SPORTS MINISTRY IN ACTION

The Lasting Effects of Short-Term Sports Ministry Trips

Team members of a short-term sports ministry mission trip frequently experience an expansion of their own mission perspective and a continuation of active ministry participation. An example of ongoing ministry involvement following an initial sports ministry trip is Sunshine (Leonard) Beshears. Beshears was a collegiate All-American soccer player who graduated with a degree in art from Houghton University, New York.

Beshears was introduced to global missions through her home church, a Christian and Missionary Alliance church that emphasized support for long-term international missions. She had little knowledge of or exposure to short-term trips or sports ministry.

Her first experience with an international sports ministry trip was during year one at Houghton in the spring of 1998. The women's soccer team partnered with Missionary Athletes International (MAI) and traveled to Australia. The team played 16 matches in 10 days against clubs, the national indoor team, and at the University of Sydney. They also ran soccer clinics and provided school assembly programs where the gospel was presented through skits, songs, and personal testimonies. This trip was pivotal in Beshears' understanding of faith, the influence she had as a believer in Jesus Christ, and how God desired for people of all nations to know Him. It showed her how God's gifts, talents, and abilities (including sport) can be used in a way to bring Him glory while planting seeds of hope and love. She experienced what she refers to as "a lightbulb of truth," a connection between faith and her passion for sport as a common-ground relational platform through which to demonstrate the love of Christ.

Subsequent to that first sports ministry trip, Beshears participated in several additional short-term trips. For example, in 2001, Houghton Women's Soccer partnered again with MAI, and she traveled to Ethiopia. Upon graduation, she joined the Charlotte Lady Eagles full time, a women's soccer ministry of MAI. Through this association, she had the opportunity to participate in short-term trips to Ethiopia, Brazil, Germany, Thailand, Singapore, and Laos between 2003 and 2008. All of these trips used sport as a platform to build relationships, show the love of Jesus, and bring the truth of the gospel to others.

As recent as 2022, Beshears has continued her short-term mission endeavors as a member of her global mission's team at Vintage Church in Randleman, North Carolina, serving with Global Partners in the Czech Republic. The trip's objective was to live and love like Jesus through service at Euro Camp, a sport-driven, English-language learning camp (Sunshine Beshears, pers. interview 2022).

International short-term sports ministry trips have lasting effects, influencing lives well beyond the 2- to 3-week mission itself. It increases mission awareness and the effective use of sport as a ministry tool.

during the mission project. This connection enables new converts or interested parties to be served and discipled. The ministry of Sports Friends, the sports ministry branch of SIM, is founded on the principle of **church-based sports ministry**. Cofounder of Sports Friends, Brian Davidson, elaborates on this concept in Interview With a Professional.

The Importance of Partnerships

Partnerships are essential for international short-term projects. Frequently, a touring group is connected to the in-country host through a sending agency. For example, a college athletic team is the touring group, and they travel with a sports ministry organization that serves as the sending agency (e.g., Surge International and Sports Friends), who connects them to the host. The host ministry is the in-country church or mission organization that the touring group will serve alongside. Partnerships are expanded through the addition of prayer teams committed to praying for the short-term project and its participants. Financial supporters are included in the partnership. Their contributions are investments yielding eternal dividends, enabling team members to cover ministry and accommodation expenses. The most common partnerships are the home churches represented among the ministry team members themselves.

church-based sports ministry—An intentional use of the platform of sport for making disciples, who in turn make disciples who are likewise connected to a local church or a church-planting strategy.

Interview With a Professional

Brian and Chris Davidson

Current Hockey Team Chaplain and Sports Ministry Director at Liberty University

BS, Bible, Houghton University

MA, Christian ministry with an emphasis on discipleship, Liberty University

More than 37 years of sports ministry experience

Former Adjunct Professor of Sports Ministry at Liberty University

Cofounder, with wife Chris Davidson, of the Charlotte Eagles Soccer Club 1991

Cofounder, with the Davidson and Johnston families, of Sports Friends International 2001

Former Sport Chaplain with Orleans Firebirds and Wareham of the Cape Cod Baseball League

Four-time Hall of Fame inductee: Gates-Chili High School; Houghton University (as individual soccer player from 1978 to 1982 and as part of the 1979 soccer team); United Soccer Leagues

What is church-based sports ministry (CBSM)?

It is an intentional use of the platform of sport for making disciples, who in turn make disciples who are likewise connected to a local church or a church-planting strategy. Being convinced that no one should live and die without hearing God's good news, one uses one's passion and talents in sport for the cause of Christ in a gathering of like-minded sporting people as a discipleship initiative connected to a body of believers.

Why is church-based sports ministry important?

Prioritizing and emphasizing the connection of sports ministry initiatives to a local church or church-planting strategy is imperative because God Himself established the Church as the primary location for disciple making. The church is our meeting together place—*episynagogen*, or the formal gathering of God's people for worship—where we spur each other on to good works (Hebrews 10:24, 25). The body of Christ (1 Corinthians 12), which is built up and mature, attains the whole measure of the fullness of Christ, devoted to teaching, fellowship, the breaking of bread, and prayer, equipped for works of service (Ephesians 4:11-13; Acts 2:42).

How is church-based sports ministry implemented?

By top-down and bottom-up approaches—in other words, the sharing of the vision to church leaders and church planters (the top) and the teaching and training of the Christ-following men and woman, boys and girls, to enter the local sport community with an intentional and strategic approach to using sport for disciple making. The encouragement I personally have for implementation of a CBSM is for Christ-followers to go into the local sport community to make new friends, build relationships, meet needs, and share the gospel message with those who do not have a personal relationship with Jesus Christ. Also, to find those who believe in God but have not been living to please God with their lives or are no longer connected to a local body of believers. Engagement in sport with a missional mindset and through a relational ministry strategy is essential to the CBSM strategy.

Can you provide an example of this?

In a cross-cultural setting, I would encourage the Sport Friends Strategy, which I had the privilege to cofound in 2002. Here is the implementation strategy used then and now: we equip churches and church planters to use sport to make disciples of Jesus Christ among young people, their families, and their communities in four key ways:

   1. *Share a vision* for local churches and church planters to use sport as a ministry tool. We believe sport is a powerful tool for crossing barriers, building relationships, proclaiming the gospel, discipling believers, and planting churches.

2. Train Christian leaders to start up sports ministry teams in their local church or as part of a new church-planting effort. We train church and mission leaders in how to develop fruitful sports ministries that will make disciples of Jesus Christ in a variety of contexts.

3. Equip coaches for sustainable ministry through ongoing support, encouragement, and trainings. We mentor, disciple, and significantly invest in these coaches' lives and ministries, helping them to live, lead, minister, and coach for the glory of God.

4. Develop leadership capacity of sports ministry coordinators, who will provide vision, guidance, and management of the local sports ministry movement and develop coaches at the local church level.

In 2021 there are 294,000 youth connected to ongoing, sustainable, nationally led, church-connected sports ministry initiatives around the world. To learn more or listen to and watch God stories from this ministry, go to www.Sports-friends.org.

Is there anything else you would like to share about church-based sports ministry?

In the United States I would encourage outward thinking whereby Christ followers go into the local sport community to play, coach, officiate or serve in a sport management staff role. For example, with regards to local youth sport, I would encourage Christian families to connect with other families who are either far from Christ or not connected with a local body of Christ followers in the youth sport community. As a family, begin by praying for the families that are on your team. Then ask the Spirit of God to help you discern the needs of one or more of those families. One example might be a single mom who needs help with providing equipment for her child or a ride to and from practice or a game. Also, ask God to help your family make personal connections with others on the team. Perhaps you can host a team gathering, organize a tailgating party, or coordinate going to a camp, clinic, or college game together. Perhaps invite one family for dinner at your home or to a restaurant. There are a myriad of possibilities and ways to care for as well as connect with team members and families. As you do, make the priority of your heart to have these families experience the aroma of Christ from you, experience God's love through your family's love for others, come to church with your family, hear your personal God story, and listen to the gospel message. A group of like-minded families engaged in the youth sport community—regardless of age, gender, sport, or level of play—in every church can meet for prayer time, learn how to share their faith, share experiences, and learn how to become disciple makers.

Types of International Short-Term Sports Ministry Trips

Most often, the type of sports ministry initiative is determined by the gifts and abilities represented within the team and the ministry needs of the host church or mission. Is the group a team of athletes representing a variety of sports, or is it a sport-specific team? Do individual members have special gifts and abilities (e.g., gifted singers, musicians, dramatists, artists, speakers)? Beside sport, can the team as a whole or in subgroups be trained in effective music, drama, dance, or some other ministry capacity? Common types of short-term sports ministry trips include the following:

1. *Work project:* This might involve an athletic team embarking on a construction, painting, renovation, or clean-up project. Manual labor is the emphasis of this type of service.

2. *Sport camp or clinics:* These events enable athletes to use their sport talents directly as an instructional means to engage campers within a sport-specific setting.

3. *Match or game ministry:* Teams with compatible skill levels of the touring team play exhibition contests. An evangelistic message or a faith journey typically is shared with spectators and opposing team members. This sharing might occur during a predetermined intermission time or at the game's conclusion. Team-to-team sharing can occur during a postgame meal together. Besides formal organized match ministry, many occasions might arise for informal match play, including small-sided games.

4. *Large-scale sporting events:* Events such as Euro Cup, World Cup, and Olympic Games are sites where sports ministry teams can piggyback on the gathering of large crowds.

5. *Small-scale sporting events:* These can include events such as athletic-themed school assemblies, vacation Bible schools, church youth group gatherings, orphanages, and refugee camps. Abbreviated athletic contests, demonstrations, relay races, and classroom question-and-answer visitations are among the services provided.

6. *Evangelism-specific ministry:* This might involve sport demonstrations, rallies, or street ministry accompanied by evangelistic messages and appeals.

7. *Combination ministries:* This involves elements from any or all of the other types mentioned and is the most commonly used method.

Depending on the gifts and abilities represented among team members, any of the seven ministry types might be interspersed with music, drama, or other types of constructive ministry expressions. Well-performed, message-enriched mime dramatizations can be quite effective, particularly when language is a barrier.

Short-Term Sports Ministry Precautions

Humble service is the benchmark disposition for short-term sport missions. Teams venture forth to serve an existing host ministry. The intention of short-termers is not to fix or instruct the work of the host ministry.

Rather, they themselves are to have teachable spirits, learning from their in-country counterparts as they mutually serve and strive together. Questions replace answers, dialogue supplants lecture, discovery substitutes correction so that respect and nurtured trust characterize their partnership. Human nature leans toward **egocentrism**, measuring new experiences by one's own personally established standards. This disposition evaluates everything as inferior and in need of modification. Traveling teams need to be aware of this tendency and not succumb to its demeaning allure. Closely related is **ethnocentrism**. Loyalty and delight in one's own culture are admirable traits, but they should not interfere with an appreciation for another culture's differences. The emphasis of egocentrism is that "my way" surpasses "your way," while ethnocentrism assumes "our ways" trump "your ways" (Elmer 2006). Understanding one's own attitude is essential within cross-cultural training so that safeguards can be put up to assure enhanced partnership and relatable communication.

The Importance of Service and Relationship Building

Career missionary Richard Reichart emphasizes the importance of service and relationship building in short-term mission projects. His insights are consistent with this key priority within sports ministry:

Besides formal match ministry, sports ministry teams should always be prepared for the emergence of informal sport contests and impromptu small-sided games.

---

egocentrism—A form of self-centeredness; a belief that one's own perspective is superior and the best way to proceed in thought and action.

ethnocentrism—Viewing one's own cultural standards as the measure to evaluate the customs of another culture.

It is hard for missions work teams to realize that they have come primarily not to do projects but to meet people. Despite the obvious agenda of building a latrine, or painting a seminary on a two-week timeline, it is essential to never let what you are doing get in the way of the people around. It may be much more important to leave a wall undone or a board uncut in order to be sensitive to the people around you. North American project-minded people are often considered impersonal or impatient because of their production mentality. Action-oriented, energy-efficient, goal-driven people find it hardest to fit in to a short-term working visit and often leave frustrated and unfulfilled. (Reichart 2001, 73)

He illustrates this concept through the example of a short-termer he refers to as Ted. Ted exhibited numerous imperfections as a team member—at times too loud and not the most skilled. Yet Ted did something exceptionally well—he kept his attention focused on people:

Ted had come to see and to serve. He did not pound nails nearly as well as his fellow team members. He did not play any instruments and he certainly could not sing. About all Ted did was make friends with the kids. He loved them, and they loved him. When I go back to the town where his team worked, they do not ask about Rory, who could sling concrete with the best of the men, nor do they ask for Alice, who was bilingual and gave a stirring farewell charge. They do not even ask for Andrea, who could play her flute like an angel. When I go back to the town they are always asking for Ted, who took time to play with the people. (Reichart 2001, 73)

Sport is a tool, a relational bridge between groups of people. It is not to supplant its purpose by becoming the focal point. People, not sport, are the focal point of sports ministry.

Administrative Responsibilities

Planning an international sports ministry trip takes time and includes numerous details. It is not unusual to allow nine months or more of lead time when preparing for an international trip. The following sections include important administrative duties associated with a short-term international sport mission tour.

Travel Documents

An up-to-date *passport* is a primary required travel document. A new passport will cost in excess of $125 and closer to $200 if expedition is needed. Many countries require three to six months' validity remaining on a passport before allowing entrance or issuing a travel visa. A *visa* is often required and is placed within a passport, granting the holder official entrance and specifying the length of stay in a country.

Effective sports ministry is people oriented, sharing a moment of life together.

CASE STUDY

Are Short-Term Sport Missions Worthwhile?

Debate is ongoing about the validity of short-term sport missions. Critics claim that such ventures are too often occasions for glorified spiritual tourism, enabling participants to visit exotic countries and encounter people from different cultures. They contend that these trips are more about the experiences of the visitors rather than the people and ministries they came to serve. They assert that the essential ministry foundation of meaningful relationships develop over time, and the brief duration of a 10-day tour does not allow for these to adequately flourish. Money is also mentioned. Rather than raising funds for a trip, send contributions to existing ministry workers, churches, and sports ministry organizations within a developing country.

Advocates for short-term sport missions do not deny the benefits of participant experience. In fact, they believe this component to be a worthwhile objective, allowing team members to gain first-hand knowledge about cultures different from their own. As their understanding broadens, it can increase their respect and concern for populations living in another country. Often university student-athletes confess learning more during a 10-day trip than they did sitting in a classroom for an entire 15-week semester. The objective of a short-term trip is not an either-or proposition between the visitor or the visited; it is to benefit both. These endeavors can also prove to be a testing ground, potentially affirming a call to full-time vocational service. Likewise, the tour can lead others to a completely different calling, again the trip proving to be the catalyst to hearing God's voice. The question about money is a worthwhile discussion. It begs the question, Should expenditures in other programs also be reevaluated for merit? For example, is money being wasted on weekend retreats, a week at summer camp, youth outings to an amusement park? Should a $25 one-year-guaranteed ball be purchased rather than a $60 three-year-guaranteed one? In God's economy, what is too little or too much?

Discussion Questions

1. Are short-term sport mission tours worthwhile?

2. Is it better to finance short-term sport mission trips or allocate that money differently?

3. How might pretrip training and posttrip follow-up help with the service of participants?

A visa can cost between $150 and $200. Information about the cost of securing a passport and visa can be found on the website for the U.S. Department of State Bureau of Consular Affairs. The website also provides worldwide State Department travel advisories. *Vaccinations* are frequently recommended or mandated, and documented proof is required for entry by some countries. Required vaccinations vary from country to country. The most common types of vaccinations include hepatitis A, hepatitis B, typhoid, cholera, yellow fever, rabies, meningitis, diphtheria, polio, tetanus, anthrax, and Covid. Vaccinations can be expensive. Some health plans cover travel vaccination costs, but some do not. Information about health-related implications for travel can be obtained at the websites for the U.S. Centers for Disease Control and Prevention and the World Health Organization.

Budget Planning

When estimating anticipated group international travel costs, aim high. It is better to raise more funds than needed than to experience a shortfall. The following line items need to be considered in the estimate:

- *Travel expenses:* This is typically the most expensive line item and includes airfare, ground transportation to and from the airport within the country of departure and return, and ground transportation within the host country. Also account for any additional airline baggage fees.

- *Travel documents:* These include passports, visas, and vaccination records. Photocopy passports and store in a safe location in case information is needed in the event of a lost passport.

- *Entry and exit fees:* Some countries levy an entry or exit fee at the airport upon arrival or departure.
- *Vaccinations:* Consider any required or recommended vaccinations. The group leader should maintain a spreadsheet with the vaccination records of all participants and their blood type. Note any additional medical needs represented within the group (e.g., diabetes, asthma, dietary restrictions).
- *Housing:* Securing housing within the host country. Will host churches or families be used? Will hotel or hostel accommodations be necessary? What about any housing needs during travel to or from the host ministry location?
- *Meals:* Take into consideration all in-country meals and meals during travel.
- *Translators:* If traveling to a country that speaks a different language, translators will be needed.
- *Ministry-related expenses:* The purchase of Bibles, pamphlets for distribution, facility rental fees and the cost of game officials, and postgame meal gatherings with the opposing team and officials are typically expenses incurred by the sports ministry team.
- *Gifts:* Game ministry often includes a gift exchange between teams. Key members of the host ministry are acknowledged and thanked with gifts as a token of appreciation.
- *Traveler's insurance:* Most trips require the purchase of group travel insurance. Collegiate student trips frequently require the purchase of an International Student Identity Card.
- *Team gear:* Will the group need to purchase game-day uniforms, T-shirts, warm-ups, and so on? Identical team travel bags are convenient to locate at airport baggage claims. Years ago, traveling teams would wear identical clothing during travel to assist in accounting for everyone at congested airports. Since 9/11 this practice is no longer recommended because identifiable clothing makes groups stand out as potential targets. It is now recommended to draw as little attention as possible to a traveling group.

- *Medical and athletic training supplies:* This includes first aid necessities such as bandages, gauze, topical antibiotics, athletic tape, and wraps.
- *Miscellaneous:* It is wise to include a line item for unanticipated expenses.

International Travel Packing

Always check with the airline regarding the number of allowable checked and carry-on bags and the size and weight limits? Additional costs might be incurred if these limits are exceeded. Depending on the ministry location, laundry access might not be available, so items might need to be handwashed in sinks and hung up to dry. It is quite common to wear items multiple times between washings. When packing, take into consideration the subliminal message that is sent by the choices being made. Extravagant adornment can thwart one's approachability. As Linda Drury points out, "This is a time to lay aside some of your personal preferences and offer this trip to the Lord. This trip is about God's work and not about your personal sense of style. More of Jesus, less of me" (Drury 2005, 21).

Traveling as a sports ministry team involves two sets of packing considerations. The first is team travel needs: stocked medical kit, team equipment (e.g., balls, scrimmage vests, ball bags, cones), ministry supplies (e.g., brochures, pamphlets, Bibles). The second is individual travel needs. See figure 11.1 of actual packing lists used by a collegiate women's soccer team on a soccer-specific sports ministry trip to Ethiopia.

Trip Itinerary and Emergency Contacts

A daily itinerary is constructed with projected times for activities. Task-oriented cultures tend to be more sensitive to time, whereas relationally oriented cultures are not so driven by the clock. Flexibility and adjustments are common and need to be expected (Elmer 2006). It is not a new concept to recognize that people from different cultures interpret time differently. Sarah Lanier distinguishes between hot- and cold-climate cultures. Countries of the southern hemisphere are considered hot climate (i.e., Africa, South America, Pacific Islands), whereas northern hemisphere countries are cold climate (i.e., Scandinavia, Canada, Russia). Theories abound about why climate seems to create behavioral and attitudinal differences about the global observance of time.

FIGURE 11.1   SAMPLE INTERNATIONAL TRAVEL PACKING LISTS

Packing List for Ethiopia for Team Equipment

- ❏ 24 Deflated soccer balls and 2 ball bags
- ❏ Rack of 48 practice cones
- ❏ 36 scrimmage vests (3 sets of 12 in blue, red, and yellow)
- ❏ 3 hand-held air pumps for ball inflation along with extra needles
- ❏ Fully stocked athletic-specific medical kit (prewrap, athletic tape, ankle wraps, bandages, dressings, athletic scissors, topical antibiotics, ibuprofen, plastic ice bags)
- ❏ 24 give-away uniform kits (jerseys, shorts, socks)
- ❏ 60 give-away team T-shirts
- ❏ give-away collected used soccer shoes
- ❏ missionary-requested items: peanut butter, granola bars, oatmeal, unlined paper, crayons, markers, sunscreen, insect repellent, baby Tylenol
- ❏ host gifts (T-shirts, caps, mugs, blankets)
- ❏ game-day gifts (team banners, fliers)
- ❏ ministry supplies (Bibles, pamphlets)
- ❏ team travel bags
- ❏ large plastic bags (to cover team bag and medical kit during games in case of rain)
- ❏ (If needed to reduce the total number of bags, and if space is available—some of the above items will be placed in individual team member travel bags.)

Packing List for Ethiopia for Individual

One checked bag (large bag with wheels) and one carry-on (backpack). Bags will be lugged throughout airports, so keep this in mind when packing. Ethiopians are quite modest—consider this when packing attire.

- ❏ Bible and devotionals
- ❏ Notebook
- ❏ Pen or pencil
- ❏ Shorts
- ❏ T-shirts (no spaghetti strap tops)
- ❏ Pants
- ❏ Skirts
- ❏ Sneakers and soccer shoes
- ❏ 2 uniform kits (jersey, shorts, socks, shin guards)
- ❏ Team warm-up jacket and pant
- ❏ Toiletries (soap, shampoo, toothpaste, toothbrush, deodorant, lip balm)
- ❏ Bath towel and face cloth
- ❏ Swimsuit
- ❏ Laundry or plastic bags (to store wet or dirty clothes)
- ❏ Hand sanitizer
- ❏ Sunscreen, lotion, insect repellent
- ❏ Granola bars and other personal snacks
- ❏ Toilet paper (2 rolls)
- ❏ Money

- ❏ Passport and copy of passport
- ❏ Immunization record (yellow book)
- ❏ Backpack or small bag (sling bag)
- ❏ Towelettes or baby wipes
- ❏ Flashlight
- ❏ Medications (ibuprofen, malaria medications, Imodium)
- ❏ Glasses and contacts if needed
- ❏ Socks and undergarments
- ❏ Clothes for church (skirt and polo for women, khakis and polo for men)
- ❏ Sweatshirt or fleece jacket (it can be cool in the morning)
- ❏ Cap or hat
- ❏ Camera and film
- ❏ Travel alarm clock
- ❏ Outlet converter

- It is best to find someone with whom to split shampoo, soap, conditioner, toothpaste, and so on to make bags lighter.
- For anything that needs charging—cannot just be plugged into the wall—a converter is needed.
- A passport copy should be kept with you and one left at home.
- Keep a contact info sheet inside your luggage (in case the exterior contact info tag is removed).
- Restrictions on carry-ons: liquids cannot exceed 3 ounces and must be placed in a clear sandwich-size baggie. (Otherwise, place in your checked bag.)

Lanier believes that the world was once more hot climate and relationally based. She speculates that the emergence of the industrial revolution introduced a new time-sensitive structure (Lanier 2000). Regardless of the origins of these differences, knowing that cultures view time differently will aid in the development and execution of a trip itinerary. For example, a cold-climate soccer sports ministry team scheduled a match for 6:00 p.m. with a team in a hot-climate country. When scheduled, the assumption was for the game to kick off at 6:00 p.m.. However, their fellow competitors interpreted the schedule to mean the time when players were to begin gathering at the field. Consequently, after relational pleasantries and pregame warm-ups, the kickoff took place at 7:00 p.m. Depending on the location and culture, sports ministry teams might wish to build buffer times within their daily itineraries.

Itineraries should be left with key contact people back in the mission team's home country. They will need to know the group's location and how they can be reached in case of an emergency. Similarly, the mission team needs to be able to contact people on the home front. Include multiple alternative contacts in case one cannot be reached. It is a good practice for the ministry team to check in regularly with their home contacts to keep everyone appraised and to update the prayer support partnership.

For international travel, plan to arrive at the airport a minimum of three hours prior to departure. Processing a large group can be prolonged, and the group should allow adequate time for the unexpected. As previously mentioned, prior to 9/11, many groups wore matching identifiable attire so they could easily find one another in crowded airports. For safety concerns this practice is now discouraged so that the group can maintain a low profile. Groups can sometimes become loud because dialogue volumes increase to be heard above the crowd. Consequently, leadership needs to continually encourage a quiet presence, reminding the team to avoid any sudden outbursts of laughter or conversation.

Pretrip Team Training and Posttrip Debriefing

Pretrip training acquaints the team with a foundation for anticipated cross-cultural ministry. Regardless of the amount and type of preparation, nothing can be substituted for the experience itself. There will always be hindsight details that could have better equipped a team for service. Nevertheless, pretrip training creates a ministry vision and begins the bonding process essential for the team to work together harmoniously.

Since sports ministry is a spiritual mission, the practice of spiritual disciplines is indispensable. Prayer should guide the team from start to finish, seeking God's intervention for wisdom and discernment throughout the process. Not only should the team actively pray, but each member should seek prayer partners to join with them. Team members should encourage one another to maintain their own spiritual fervor, consistently imploring the Lord for guidance through the reading of His word, worship, and prayer. After all, a dry well does not serve the needs of a thirsty community.

An important foundation is to assess how the particular project aligns itself with a biblically based theology for the use of sport within a ministry setting. In essence, the group is asking itself, why do this and how does it fit within the scope of the overall gospel mandate? Closely related are the partnering ministries, especially the mission and specific goals of the host in-country ministry. Team members need to adopt and further elucidate a clear vision for how their efforts will fit with the ministry plans and objectives of the partnering host.

Fundraising

An international sports ministry trip can be expensive. Expenses can be divided into two components: (1) team expenses (e.g., ministry materials, gifts, team gear, equipment) and (2) individual expenses (e.g., airfare, meals, housing). Fundraising is a part of pretrip training as members work together, pray for sufficient funds, and build team dynamics in the process of implementing creative fundraising projects such as car washes, bake sales, donation work projects, dinners, auctions, and so on. Group fundraising efforts can be used to offset team expenses or to supplement the support of participant accounts. Individual fundraising represents the bulk of needed funds. One of the most widely used methods for individual funding is an appeal through a financial support letter (figure 11.2). Typically, a training session focuses on the content of a well-worded letter and allows time for team members to compose their own letters. Early in the funding process, an initial monetary deposit from team members signifies an individual's commitment to the trip, and a funding schedule is developed so that targeted goals are met in a timely fashion. It is a good practice to have all fundraising completed a month prior to departure. Since support raising takes time, it is wise to schedule this instruction in an early training session.

Some arguments have been made that the expenses of a short-term sports ministry project are not worth the investment—that the thousands of dollars would be better spent on a full-time sports missionary rather than on a two-week venture. This rationale may have merit. As a part of their pretrip training, it is worthwhile for team members to wrestle with this question so that a theologically informed rationale can affirm their support-raising efforts. Reichert addresses the

Postmatch interaction of teams at a clubhouse in Vienna, Austria.

argument with the story of the woman who poured expensive perfume on Jesus' head (Matthew 26:6-13). His disciples protested, claiming that the perfume could have been sold at a great price and the money given to the poor. Certainly, an offering to the poor would be a worthy cause. Yet Jesus commends the woman and declares that she has done a beautiful thing, preparing His body for burial. Reichart compares this complaint about the woman's perfume with the sentiment of a wasted investment in short-term missions:

> The real bottom line of any investment in this very extravagant enterprise of world evangelization, no matter how limited, is not what it will cost you, but what it has already cost Him. The financial feasibility of the missionary enterprise can only be accurately measured in terms of the worth of the One we serve, not in terms of the apparent 'wastes' involved. . . . You can be sure that what you invest in Christ's Kingdom by way of time and money will never be lost. It will not be "wasted." The "waste" will always be worth it because the goal of getting the Gospel to every creature is worthy of everything we have to give. (Reichert 2001, 43)

Differences of opinion may exist about short-term missions and their funding. The question is not so much about the money, but rather the discernment of God's calling. The response to God's call is faithful obedience. And when God calls, He provides the means for the call to be accomplished.

Cultural Overview

An overview of the culture and language spoken in the host country is essential. What characterizes the people? What sports are popular, and who participates and watches? What is the political climate? What about the spiritual climate? How does the Church view sport? And what is their perspective about using sport as a ministry tool? Should the sports ministry team be made aware of traditions and customs? What clothing is considered acceptable or unacceptable? Does the team need to take any precautions regarding their conduct? If possible and available, during a team training session, invite a person native to the country to speak to the group and answer questions related to cultural nuances. They might also provide simple language tutelage.

Ministry Preparations

The team also needs to learn about the ministry aspects of their trip. What ministry strategies will the team employ? Will the gospel be presented through faith journeys, object lessons, and devotional messages? Will the team use drama, mimes, music, dance, or other expressions? Will individual team members be responsible to fulfill specific roles? How will sport be used? Will team members hold clinics or instructional camps? Do team members know how to lead and organize these instructions? Will there be match ministry? If so, players need to be equipped for fitness through pretrip sport-specific training sessions. Regardless, all anticipated physical and spiritual programmatic strategies should be well prepared and sufficiently practiced. When possible, allow participants to organize and lead ministry components. For example, gifted musicians can select and lead songs, gifted dramatists can organize skits, and so on. Everyone should prepare and practice gospel communication skills.

Miscellaneous Details

Practical team logistics should be reviewed (e.g., paperwork and proper documentation such as passports, visas, insurance, and vaccination records). What conduct and behavioral expectations are encouraged? What about punctuality, the upkeep of room accommodations, water courtesy, servant attitudes, grateful hearts, and a smiling disposition that replaces the temptation to complain and grumble? A checklist should be developed for both team and individual packing needs. Trip itinerary and travel details should be reviewed. Maintaining spiritual fervor is encouraged. Some groups elect to follow a common study guide or devotional so that members share a unified approach as a personal discipline.

Posttrip Debriefing

An individual pretrip analysis can be made to discern anticipated trip expectations, and these anticipated expectations can be evaluated upon return from the trip to compare expectations to reality. During the trip, daily journal entries are encouraged so that participants reflect on their experience. What are they observing? What place does sport have in the culture? Who participates, and who spectates? Are

FIGURE 11.2

FINANCIAL SUPPORT LETTER

Financial support raising is required for the majority of short-term sports ministry mission projects. Funding is typically provided through churches, family members, and friends. One widely used method to share about a ministry project is a financial support letter. The letter should be concise while providing essential details for the reader. Key components to include in the letter are:

1. The partnering organizations (in the sample letter the partnership includes Surge International, a college sports ministry class, the Hope Center in Romania, and Surge International in Salzburg, Austria)
2. A brief introduction of the partnering ministry
3. A brief explanation of the specific ministry details
4. The location and date of the trip
5. The total amount of funds to be raised and how the funds will be used
6. Instructions about contributing to the project
7. Personal contact information
8. A concise personal update about oneself and what this trip means to the participant

Sample Support Letter

Dear _____,

I am excited to inform you that our university sports ministry class (comprised of members of the women's soccer team) is partnering with Surge International for one of their unique short-term soccer-specific ministry projects.

Surge International, a 501(c)(3) nonprofit organization, is using the world's most popular sport, soccer, to share the Christian message of hope around the world. Players and staff of Surge International have ministered in over 40 countries of the world through large-scale evangelistic festivals, homeless outreach, prison ministry, student ministry, refugee outreach, outreach to drug addicts, soccer relief work, church planting, youth soccer tournaments and clinics, school assemblies, soccer match ministry, and leading small-group Bible studies. Currently Surge is sharing Christ in Austria, Bolivia, Burundi, Kosovo, Mexico, Mongolia, Peru, Ukraine, Romania, and the United States.

The project I have been accepted for is The Global Player Initiative – Amateur, set in Romania and Austria. I will be part of a soccer ministry submersion. Our short-term mission trip will expose me to European missions and Surge's ongoing work in Romania and Austria. In Romania we will work alongside the Hope Center, located in the midst of an impoverished region outside of Bucharest. Our primary focus in Austria will be working alongside churches in Salzburg that have invested in the lives of a large refugee population. Soccer will be prominently used as a ministry tool throughout our trip. We will be preparing for this trip during the spring semester at Houghton and traveling on site in Romania and Austria from May 13 to 24, 2018.

[Personalize your letter with a brief update about you (e.g., your university, what year you're in, your major). Keep it concise.]

In order to participate in this program, I have to raise $2,400, which is tax deductible. These funds cover all expenses (airfare, ground transportation, housing, meals, ministry supplies, etc.). I would appreciate your prayerful consideration of helping to support our work. Our goal is to have all funds raised one month prior to our departure (around April 15). To learn more about Surge International, please go to www.surgesoccer.org.

Bringing Hope through Soccer, make checks payable to: Surge International

Mail checks to my attention at: _____
_____*Name*

PO Box #: _____
Your PO Box

_____   _____   _____
City   *State*   *Zip Code_*

Contact me if you have any questions:

_____   _____
Email Address   Phone Number

Sincerely, _____
Name

Prior to mailing, the support letter should be reviewed by the supervisor of the trip to ensure that all pertinent information is accurately provided. Most trips include dates for reaching progressive fundraising goals. The mailing of support letters should coincide with the group's fundraising dates so that adequate time is provided to reach the goal. Short-term fundraising enables the participant to experience a glimpse of what full-time missionaries do as a way of life. Raising missional financial support is a humbling process and an exercise of prayer-filled faith. When individuals make contributions, a follow-up note of thanks should be sent, preferably within two weeks of receiving the gift. Contributors should also be included as recipients of posttrip summary reports.

Reprinted from Surge International/Houghton University (2018).

sport-related **gender ideologies** prevalent? Do men and women view and experience sport differently? What methods of sports ministry were effective, and which ones were ineffective? What improvements to pretrip training are recommended? Team leadership might wish to provide probing observation questions in advance so that each team member has a guideline to follow and reflect on. Through daily written and scheduled group reflections, team members process posttrip debriefing concerns throughout the trip. Daily mini-debriefing sessions are enriching and helpful so that processing one's experience is not delayed and crammed into the end of the trip when fatigue skews perspectives. Cultural comparisons between one's own and the host country are quite normal. Team members must be reminded that their exposure to a new culture is quite limited due to the brevity of their trip. Personal assessments, both good and bad, might be distorted because of the trip's limitations.

Helpful Travel Tips

Lessons are learned with frequent travel experience. Several reoccurring items are helpful to know for advance planning and preparation so that the group is not caught off guard.

Water and Food Safety

Water and food safety are essential during international travel. Untreated water can be full of potential harmful contaminants. Only consume bottled, boiled, or purified filtered water. If tap water is not filtered, avoid rinsing toothbrushes with it. Be careful when showering to not swallow unfiltered water. Avoid ice in a beverage if the ice has originated from an unfiltered source. The same can be true of uncooked vegetables that have been unsafely rinsed. Local

gender ideology—How a culture defines masculinity and femininity and what is deemed to be manly or womanly.

residents' immune systems have built up tolerance with their water sources, but members of the ministry team are vulnerable. Despite safety precautions, water consumption is important to maintain healthy levels of hydration during regular game ministry competitions and activities. Initial signs of dehydration include thirst, loss of appetite, dry skin, fatigue, lightheadedness, dizziness, chills, and headache. As dehydration worsens, these symptoms intensify and can become dangerous—even life threatening—as total body fluid decreases. One easy method to detect body hydration is to observe the color of one's urine. Cloudy, darker brownish-yellow urine signifies an increased level of dehydration. When dehydration occurs, the loss of electrolytes can be replenished through the consumption of sodium and potassium salts found in most sport drinks.

Water courtesy might need to be practiced. Many underdeveloped countries do not have excessive quantities of water. Consequently, lengthy showers should be avoided. Conservation efforts might dictate a quick rinse, lathering with soap while the water is off, and concluding with a final rinse. The availability of hot water might also be an issue—another reason to limit the length of one's shower. A closely related water issue is the use of toilets. Some countries do not flush toilet paper. Instead a can or basket is placed next to the toilet for the disposal of toilet paper and feminine products. Outhouses with a simple covered hole in the ground or discreetly finding a place in nature might also be one's only option. Toilet paper might or might not be supplied in public facilities.

Wash hands thoroughly with soap and water before eating. Many sinks and showers will run unfiltered water. It is safe to use it for bathing and washing hands, but as much as possible avoid water in the vicinity of the mouth and from digesting it. Depending on the circumstances (availability of safe food sources), avoid uncooked food apart from fruit and vegetables that can be peeled or shelled. Food should be thoroughly cooked and kept hot. Avoid raw fish and meats that are still red or with juices that are pink. Food from street vendors might not be safe. Keep in mind this food safety motto: "When in doubt, avoid."

Sunburn

Sunburn can derail the effectiveness of a sports ministry athlete. Liberal use of sunscreen is recommended. Also maintain a proper attitude concerning the in-country mission. Is basking in the sun to return home with a deep tan the team's objective, or is drawing attention to the Son the priority?

Malaria Precautions

Malaria precautions are necessary if traveling within a region prone to **malaria**. Half of the world's population is at risk from this disease, and it accounts for roughly one million annual deaths worldwide. Children under the age of five are particularly vulnerable, and it is estimated that every two minutes a child dies from it. A majority of malaria deaths occur in Sub-Saharan Africa (World Health Organization 2022). Proper malaria preventative measures are quite effective, but none have a 100 percent rate of efficacy. Common medications include Malarone, Doxycycline, and mefloquine, and strict adherence to a physician's medicinal directives is critical. A couple side effects that might be experienced with the use of malaria medications include a greater susceptibility to sunburn and vivid nightmares. Some medications require continued use for several weeks after departure from a malaria-stricken region. Travelers who ignore this instruction have been known to contract the illness weeks following their return home.

Electrical Power

Some countries have a limited electrical power grid or are serviced through gas generators during specific daily hours. Consequently, power outages and electric unavailability are to be anticipated with a flexible plan of action.

Travel Is a Ministry Opportunity

Ministry is not limited to formalized, intentional works of service, but is an ongoing way of life during a short-term trip. Courtesy exhibited during a flight; a kind word to an attendant, bus driver, and housekeeper; and a genuine engaging smile can go a long way to brighten a day and set the tone for service. Jesus demonstrated the ability to notice the least among the clamoring attention seekers—the humble generosity of a poor widow (Mark 12:41-44), the heartfelt plea of a disfigured man with leprosy (Mark 1:40-45), the ostracized adulterous Samaritan woman (John 4:1-42), and the accepting innocence of young children (John 19:13-15). Following the

---

water courtesy—An intentional consideration of the water resource needs of others ahead of one's own comforts.

malaria—A potentially life-threatening flu-like illness contracted through the bite of an anopheles mosquito.

example of Jesus, travel transitions enable team members to exercise their sight awareness, noticing the least in their midst. It is also an opportunity to practice secret prayer—praying for a passerby, for the community, local churches, team members, and the formal team ministry occasions. Depending on the circumstances, downtime transitions can foster team-bonding opportunities to catch up with one another and to help process experiences.

The Ministry of Rest

Rest is a gift and spiritual discipline that enables team members to recuperate and reenergize. Due to the compressed schedule of a short-term mission project, days can be packed with activities. Even though the team might have served multiple groups, each new group will be experiencing the team for the first time, and they need to be given the best refreshed attention possible.

SUMMARY

Anecdotally, international short-term sport missions have been blessed by God as evidenced by the vast number of people whose lives have been influenced positively by this form of ministry. Recipients of this work have heard the good news of the gospel, and participants have seen the hand of God as He has worked His pleasure in their midst. Sport, or any other ministry methodology, is never to supersede the Message Himself. The method is subject to change, but the Message is eternal as is the One who transforms lives. The logistical details entailed in the preparation and execution of a sports ministry tour can be tedious, but the ensuing results overwhelmingly render the efforts so worthwhile. Prayer commences the procedural planning and trip preparations. Prayer sustains the trip during its execution. And prayer concludes the trip, offering the results into the hands of God.

This chapter has addressed the importance of partnerships and relevance of connecting sport mission trips to the local church as a church-based enterprise. We have discussed a variety of types of trips most commonly used in a sport context. Administrative responsibilities, pretrip training, and posttrip debriefing have been reviewed. A key component of short-term ministry is the spiritual fervor and gracious servant attitudes of the participants—keeping the focus on people and how to best build meaningful relational connections with them.

REVIEW AND DISCUSSION QUESTIONS

1. Discuss the significance of a church-based sports ministry.
2. Identify some precautions to be taken when traveling to serve a host ministry.
3. For participants, what are some of the benefits of serving in a short-term sport mission?
4. Discuss the importance of water while serving on a short-term project.
5. Consider the amount of money needed to fund a short-term project. Is it worth it, or could the money be better spent elsewhere?
6. If you could travel anywhere in the world on a short-term sport mission trip, where would you go and why, and what sport would you use?
7. Have you personally participated in an international sport mission trip? If so, what pretrip preparation would you like to have had to better equip you for your experience? If you have not been on such a trip, is something preventing you?

Courtesy of Grace and Truth Sports Park.

Local church sports ministry is for all ages, from the very young to senior saints and everyone in between.

CHAPTER 12

Sports Ministry in the Local Church

"The local church cannot ignore the potential of sport and recreation ministry as a bridge into the community. . . . Jesus did not take up a synagogue stance and wait for needy people to join him there. He spent his earthly life out of the normal religious environment of his day."

Bryan Mason, UK Coordinator for Church Sports and Recreation Ministry (CSRM) and Author

LEARNING OBJECTIVES

After studying this chapter, you should be able to do the following:

- Understand the importance of connecting sports ministry objectives to the overall mission of the local church
- Discuss the typical church-based sports ministry settings
- Identify and evaluate church sports ministry funding options
- Explain the distinctions and similarities of sports ministry represented in churches of various sizes
- Discuss the types of local church sport and recreational ministry programs
- Explain how local church sports ministry broadens leadership development, roles, and opportunities through nontraditional realms of giftedness and talents

Hundreds of balloons were filled with an assortment of muck—watered-down chocolate and pistachio puddings, shaving cream, and multicolored liquid gelatins—inflated, and readied for quasicompetitive contests. Competitions included Batter Splatter, (a pitched balloon batted by a teammate), Balloon Volleyball Catch, (balloons tossed over a net and caught by team members inside their extra-large bib overalls), Splat Seat (team members racing to chairs and popping balloons by sitting on them) and Jump Pop (popping elevated balloons with a pointed headband). Relays included Flour Prune Face (a tray of flour embedded with prunes, which contestants secured in their mouths without the use of their hands), Grab Bag Whistle (competitors raced to bags of wrapped food items such as peanut butter crackers, sardines, and boiled eggs, unwrapped an item, ate it, then whistled), Bobbing for Prunes (teams raced to large pans filled with soupy chocolate pudding and plunged face-first to bite into a prune with their teeth), and Egg Eye (a team member atop a 12-foot [4 m] A-frame ladder cracked an egg and tried to land the yoke on the partner's nose lying beneath them). This annual contest was a church-sponsored recreational activity known as the Yuk Relays. Its motto: "Dress for a mess."

Members of the youth group were encouraged to invite friends to participate in the relays. A seventh-grade boy by the name of Chris responded to an invitation and attended the inaugural event. At the time, Chris was unchurched and from a fatherless home. He enthusiastically competed in each activity, but with every gross encounter with muck he loudly squawked a four-letter expletive. Chris soon learned that profanities were unacceptable in the youth group, and the penalty levied was ten push-ups per occurrence. Chris performed several hundred repetitions that day. Frequently, when penalized, he exploded with additional expletives, which served only to double, triple, or quadruple his number. Needless to say, at the conclusion of the relays, due to his record number of push-ups, the youth leaders surmised that Chris likely would never make a return visit to the group. Yet he did. In fact, Chris became a regular active attendee. Not only did he attend the youth meetings but also the teen Sunday school class and the morning worship service. He was embraced with gracious love as exemplified in the lives of imperfect yet caring church leaders. In time, Chris took to heart the repeatedly communicated and demonstrated message of the gospel, received Jesus as Lord and Savior, and publicly acknowledged his decision by being baptized. Years passed, and as an adult, Chris served the congregation as chair of the missions committee and played drums for the worship team. In his 30s, he penned the following words at the conclusion of a Christmas greeting to the youth leaders who had supervised the group and the annual Yuk Relays: "As I gaze back into the past occasionally, I just want to thank you both for what you've done for me. Who knows if I ever would have found Christ. So, thanks again." What began as a simple invitation to attend a fun-focused series of competitive relay races proved to establish an initial relationship that grew to foster meaning and trust. The Yuk Relays were not sport specific, but they were sportlike and certainly competitive. This account provides a glimpse into the potential effectiveness of sport and recreational ministry in the life of a church. However, a distinction needs to be made between the use of freestanding sport and recreational activities and an intentional programmatic church sports ministry.

This chapter will discuss components of sustained, intentional local church sport and recreation ministries. Church and community demographic assessments, ministry objectives, and programming will be examined. Examples of church sports ministry operations based on church size will be discussed, and the benefits and shortcomings of each will be considered.

Assessing Ministry Mission and Objectives

How will a local church sports ministry complement the overall mission and objectives of the congregation? Do church leaders embrace a vision for sports ministry, and will they encourage its implementation

Prune Face, which involves bobbing for prunes face first in a pan of liquid chocolate pudding, is a race in the annual church youth group Yuk Relays.

for their members and community? Will the focus of the sports ministry be **in-reach**, **outreach**, or a combination of the two? Establishing friendships and authentic trust are characteristic of outreach efforts. Members plant seeds of faith as they model Christianity to their neighbors. As appropriate occasions arise, church members share specifically about the application of their Christian faith to their daily lives, inviting their nonchurched acquaintances to consider experiencing faith applications for themselves.

The Yuk Relays fit in the category of a recreational activity with a broader, intentional purpose. It combines both in-reach and outreach components and use **recreation event invitation**. Such events include a ministry strategy and are incorporated into the broader ministry plan.

Are all age groups targeted, or will the focus be narrowed to specified ministries for children, youths, young adults, adults, or older adults? Will programming be developed for persons with cognitive or physical disabilities? Will sports ministry initiatives stand alone or be integrated into existing programs such as church Sunday school classes, vacation Bible school, youth group, missions, Bible study and discipleship classes, and worship services? Answers to questions such as these will be determined by the specified ministry objectives.

Assessing Church and Community Demographics

What are the needs represented within the church and surrounding community? What resources does the church have to conduct sports ministry strategies? What strengths and weaknesses exist? Will programs be coordinated through paid staff personnel, volunteers, or a combination of both? What sport passions, gifts, and abilities are represented within the congregation and local community? What key community contacts can the church use as resources? Does the church have adequate facilities to host and support sports ministry projects, or will it be necessary to acquire the use of community recreational sites? Can area churches partner together? What about the availability of partnerships with sports ministry organizations (SMO)?

The location of a church might dictate the best types and forms of sports ministry. For example, a church located in a cold-climate, mountainous region might consider winter sport activities such as skiing, skating, ice hockey, sledding, hiking, whereas a church located in a warm-weather, beach environment might consider swimming, surfing, jogging, or beach volleyball. Each church assesses its own specific

---

in-reach—Programming geared to benefit existing church members and active participants, promoting discipleship and fellowship opportunities that build and strengthen cohesive bonds of relationship with one another.

outreach—Equipping church members to engage the local and regional communities, building relational connections as a gospel witness.

recreation event invitation—A fun-focused activity designed to welcome invitees to a nonthreatening, relationship-building form of recreation.

demographics to determine what makes the most sense and what its unique niche is. Does the church build on the foundation of existing sport passions, or does it have the resources within its own community of faith to introduce something new? For example, Indiana is a state known for basketball. Does an Indiana church build on this already popular regional passion? What if the church has an interest in and resources for street hockey? Does the church launch a form of sports ministry with this less-familiar offering as a more unique activity?

Four Typical Church-Based Sports Ministry Locations

Churches typically depend on four sites for sports ministry locations: on site, in the community, a jaunt event, and short-term missions. Larger churches frequently are best suited to provide their own on-site sport and recreational facilities. They might have their own gymnasium, fitness or weight room, ball fields, and outdoor courts. They might have the capacity

SPORTS MINISTRY IN ACTION

Sports Ministry Practitioners Take the Lead at Zeal Church

Philip and Kaylin Tuttle are lead pastors at Zeal Church in Manchester, New Hampshire. The Tuttles were both stellar collegiate athletes. Upon graduation, Philip played three seasons with Major League Soccer (MLS) after being drafted by the San Jose Earthquakes in 2011. Philip became a follower of Jesus around the time he embarked on his professional soccer career, which led him to perform the duties of a team chaplain. Having received a ministry invitation, Philip eventually left the MLS to become a full-time missionary to the state of New Hampshire through service with the Fellowship of Christian Athletes (FCA). Kaylin came to Christ while in high school, and her newfound faith led to impassionate conversations with teammates about Jesus. A collegiate All-American soccer player, Kaylin became formally introduced to sports ministry in college, and during a short-term trip to Ethiopia, God opened her heart to a love for the nations. In His timing, the Lord brought together Philip and Kaylin, marriage ensued, and a prototypical version of a modern-era Aquila and Priscilla partnership in ministry commenced (Acts 18-19). They have held numerous positions throughout their 10 years of ministry, but one constant has remained: sharing the gospel through the platform of sport. They are sports ministry practitioners.

A large refugee population, predominantly from the African nations of Democratic Republic of Congo, Rwanda, Tanzania, and Zambia, has settled in Manchester. The Tuttles have provided pastoral leadership for their church, encouraging the congregation to embrace and welcome these new families into their community. Despite cultural and language differences, the introduction of a soccer ball ultimately has helped to create a bond of friendship around sport. The church has organized soccer camps as well as spring and summer training sessions. These efforts have been well received by the refugee families because many of the youth have neither the money to pay for quality training nor the opportunity to receive instruction from Christian coaches. Church members who might have felt uncomfortable teaching or leading a Bible study have come alive coaching and playing with the kids, having discovered a valuable ministry investment that best suits them. Other members provide meals, distribute donated clothing, and run educational tutoring programs.

Though productive, the refugee sports ministry has also encountered difficulties. Language barriers are an ongoing struggle, and transportation has proven to be problematic. Many of the families lack vehicles and need the location of ministry activities to be within walking distance. Finally, most of the youths have only experienced informal play; consequently, structured training sessions are frequently hampered by distractions, which necessitates instruction about appropriate behaviors.

A primary church goal is to help rewrite the future of Manchester by breaking the cycles of abuse, poverty, addictions, and other destructive paths. The congregation affirms the power of Jesus to transform lives as He heals brokenness and infuses His people to become hands of hope in the face of despair. Prayer is at the core of their endeavors, believing God to be the source of fruitful ministry, changed lives, and restorative love. Zeal Church serves as an example of a congregation that recognizes community needs and how the powerful tool of sport can be implemented when humbly surrendered to the hands of God (Kaylin Tuttle, pers. interview 2022).

to organize their own leagues or to serve as a host for community leagues and sporting events. Pathway Community Church in Fort Wayne, Indiana, had sports ministry in mind as a part of their construction and renovation plans:

> When we expanded our building in 2018, our heart was to embrace more people from our growing community. With that attitude, we began to open our grounds for various sporting events—both for the Pathway family and for community groups. In addition to hosting the Carroll High School rugby teams and various local soccer and flag football teams, we've created opportunities for PCC adults and youth to enjoy athletics together. Our hope, as we open our physical space, is that we will create room for deeper connections and opportunities for people to encounter Jesus Christ. (Pathway Community Church, n.d.)

On Site

SMOs frequently partner with churches and use their on-site facilities to conduct sport-specific programming such as camps and clinics. An example is On Goal, a soccer SMO established by Tom Fite when he partnered with Pleasant Hill Baptist Church to run a soccer camp in Milford, Ohio, in 1985. The ministry has since grown to now include eight full-time staff. Their mission statement begins: "On Goal partners with churches around the United States and in Brazil and the UK to combine soccer excellence with the life-changing message of Jesus Christ through quality soccer programs" (On Goal, n.d.). Another SMO that frequently uses church facilities is the Fellowship of Christian Athletes (FCA), often for the purpose of conducting their Huddle groups. Their partnership with a local church is particularly resourceful when the church is located within close proximity of a high school. An advantage of on-site church sports ministry is the ability to foster the church's positive welcoming environment and its involvement within the community. Its accessibility helps diminish the perception that the church is only interested in other-worldly concerns. It creates stronger impressions that the church is made of real people, which helps to break down perceived barriers of approachability.

Community

Churches without adequate on-site facilities to host sports ministry programming can explore the use of community recreational facilities such as local school fields, track, and gymnasiums; public parks; fitness centers; bowling alleys; swimming pools; jogging and biking trails; trampoline and dodgeball parks; skating rinks; miniature golf courses; and shuffleboard courts. Partnerships with area churches that have their own facilities can also be considered. Does a local SMO have athletic facilities? For example, Athletes in Action (AIA) has excellent facilities at their Xenia, Ohio, location. Their 250-acre campus features outdoor synthetic turf fields (two soccer fields, two softball fields, a baseball field, and a football and soccer field), an indoor sports performance

A neighborhood soccer training session, a ministry of Zeal Church in Manchester, New Hampshire.

center, and a high-low ropes challenge course for team building (Athletes in Action, n.d.).

An example is the Grace and Truth Sports Park (G&T) in the suburbs of Rochester, New York. G&T, a ministry of First Bible Baptist Church, maintains beautiful outdoor athletic fields for soccer, flag football, lacrosse, baseball, and softball. They also manage sites for sand volleyball, cornhole, spike ball, croquet, archery, and basketball. According to G&T's director, Tom Street, the Sports Park has two foundational purposes:

The main goal of the Sports Park is to provide a space for our athletic programs to impact the community by creating new and better followers of Christ. Grace and Truth Athletics provides multiple sport and recreational activities for members of our community to register. We hope to provide a quality athletic experience for children and adults through our many programs. It is our hope that at the end of each program, every participant is a better player of their sport, while also taking time to show them more about the Lord.

The second purpose of the park is to provide quality fields for community leagues and organizations to use. Our intention is that our Sports Park environment would stand out as an exceptional and positive experience, in the hope that people will ask what makes us unique. It would be our pleasure to explain the reason behind why a church would own a Sports Park open for the community to visit and use. (Grace and Truth Sports, n.d.)

Public use of church facilities necessitates well-managed and maintained operations. First, whatever is done is to be offered as "unto the Lord," and such offerings are to be the first-fruits (the very best) of resources, talents, and effort (Colossians 3:23; Proverbs 3:9). Second, the service rendered on behalf of one's neighbor demands quality for the best possible reception. A shabby job is not impressive, indicates a lack of concern or respect, and ultimately will be interpreted accordingly.

Another aspect of community is the growing number of churches entering teams within community-based leagues. Individual members also elect to play on community teams rather than on a church-sponsored team. In either circumstance, an advantage of joining community-based leagues and playing on their teams is the opportunity for church members to expand their sphere of influence by reaching out beyond their inner circle and the four walls of their building. Churches disciple members through training classes to help participants know how to conduct themselves and to be an effective witness within community sport settings. Are they being witnesses by exhibiting the character qualities of the **fruit of the Spirit** in the midst of competitive

Courtesy of Grace and Truth Sports Park

Grace and Truth Sports Park, a ministry of First Bible Baptist Church near Rochester, New York, serves the area with well-groomed fields for a variety of sport and recreation activities.

---

fruit of the spirit—Representative godly characteristics as described in Galatians 5:22-23—namely, love, joy, peace, patience, kindness, goodness, faithfulness, gentleness, and self-control. Followers of Jesus are exhorted to embrace and incarnate these qualities.

sport? Followers of Jesus are exhorted to embrace and incarnate these qualities. It is one thing to demonstrate godliness in a church setting, but it is another to demonstrate it on a ball field or basketball court. The athletic arena is a testing ground that reveals the authenticity of one's faith. It is also a pruning ground, enabling the believer to be refined as he or she learns to become increasingly Christlike in daily living. Both the churched and unchurched person can benefit from shared community sport involvement. The churched athlete's character is refined, while the unchurched player recognizes that something is different about his or her churched teammate. Perhaps the Spirit of God will speak to his or her heart, wooing him or her to further explore a faith commitment of their own.

In addition to witnessing through godly character qualities, church sportspersons are trained to communicate their faith effectively and on how to lead someone to Christ. Timing sensitivities are important. It is important to be aware of two extremes: being too timid and not speaking up when the opportunity is afforded, and being too impatient, aggressively imposing one's faith by steamrolling the listener without regard to his or her readiness. Prayerful sensitivity to the Holy Spirit's guidance will indicate when and how to communicate the gospel. Chapter 6 has addressed components of effective gospel communication, and one of the most effective means cited is the ability to explain one's own faith journey concisely. Personal story is powerful and relatable, but one's story cannot be in word only. As mentioned in previous chapters, consistent incarnational gospel living is mandated and serves to confirm the credibility of spoken words.

Jaunt Event

Another setting for sports ministry is a **jaunt event**. Excursion activities are broad in nature and include soft activities such as camping, canoeing, hiking, and sledding as well as hard activities such as mountain biking, whitewater rafting, downhill skiing, and hang gliding (Pedersen and Thibault 2019). Jaunt events also can include sport spectator activities such as group travel to a professional or collegiate game and visiting a sport hall of fame, exhibit, or museum.

Short-Term Missions

The fourth church-based sports ministry location is short-term missions. Churches frequently engage in missions related to poverty, education, disaster relief, medical practices, and construction projects. Why not consider sports ministry either as a standalone mission or in cooperation with one of the other endeavors? A church might have sufficient numbers and interest to field their own team for match ministry, conducting sport camps and clinics, and so on. If more people and resources are needed, an opportunity exists to expand partnerships with other churches to be better equipped with the necessary skills, personnel, and leadership staffing required to fulfill a successful sports ministry initiative. Churches might elect to travel internationally (addressed in chapter 11) or remain in country, focusing on a variety of population groups such as immigrants, Native Americans, or urban dwellers, or assisting the ongoing work of a SMO.

Hosting Events

Churches of all sizes regularly host sport-related events, speakers, and programming. These events build fellowship among regular attendees and provide opportunities to invite guests who might not feel comfortable attending a traditional worship service but will attend a sport-themed program. Watch parties, guest speakers, and athletic films are popular options.

Watch Parties

A popular sport-related church program is hosting gatherings around major sporting events such as the Super Bowl, World Cup, World Series, Final Four, and Stanley Cup. The ministry objectives should determine what events to highlight and how to proceed. During the planning process, viewing guidelines, policies, and legality need to be confirmed. Organizations such as Christian Copyright Solutions and Church Law and Tax Group can be consulted. A membership fee likely is required to access their materials and to receive their counsel. Many churches are already members of such organizations as a part of their authorization use for sheet music and audio recordings. Using the Super Bowl as an example, Brotherhood Mutual provides NFL copyright guidelines, which include the following:

1. Games being shown can only use the normal church service AV equipment. No rental equipment can be leased to augment viewing.

---

jaunt event—An excursion sport or recreational activity that takes place away from one's usual geographic location.

2. An admission fee cannot be charged, but an offering can be collected to help cover expenses incurred by the church.

3. Promotional materials should avoid the use of NFL, Super Bowl, or participating team logos (Brotherhood Mutual, n.d.).

Whatever the sporting events, copyright protocols need to be thoroughly examined and upheld.

Will the event be solely in-reach, or will it also include an outreach component? Will pre-, mid-, or postgame programming be developed (e.g., welcome, introductions, announcements, a keynote speaker)? Will a meal or snacks be included? Will the church's large screen projection and sound amplification be needed? How will seating be arranged to maximize enjoyment, viewing, and meaningful interaction?

Athletic Guest Speakers

As mentioned in chapter 3, the YMCA introduced Athletic Sundays whereby a prominent Christian athlete was invited to deliver a message or speak about his or her faith commitment. The notoriety of an athlete often draws people who otherwise would not attend a religious service. With the popularity and influence of athletics within the social dynamic of a congregation, would church leadership devote a Sunday service or a portion of the service to hear the perspective of a respected Christian athlete? What about speakers for Sunday school classes, youth meetings, vacation Bible school, banquets, and fellowship events? Professional athlete guest speakers might be too expensive for many church budgets; other options for consideration include local Christian high school, community, and collegiate coaches and athletes.

Christian-Themed Sport Movies

The quality of Christian-based motion pictures has improved over the years. Film provides a powerful medium for the depiction of faith within real-life circumstances. It enables audiences to relate to the message content and ask cogent questions about everyday living. These films can serve as a source of encouragement and become a compelling appeal for the conviction of change in one's perspective, motivation, and behavior. Stories portrayed in film provide inspirational examples of determination, perseverance, spiritual fortitude, self-sacrifice, and evidence of God's interventions in the lives of His people. Besides motion picture entertainment value, audiences can be guided through postfilm discussions, or leadership might let the film's message speak for itself. Based on ministry objectives, churches elect to host special film nights or include movies as a part of existing programs. Table 12.1 provides a list for consideration, along with a brief film synopsis.

Other noteworthy films to consider include *A Mile in His Shoes* (2011, baseball), *Catching Faith* (2015, football), *Full Count* (2019, baseball), *Glory Road* (2006, basketball), *Home Run* (2013, baseball), *Invictus* (2009, rugby), *McFarland* (2015, cross country), *One Hit From Home* (2012, baseball), *Queen of Katwe* (2016, chess), *Seven Days in Utopia* (2011, golf), and *42* (2013, baseball). Similar to hosting watch-party events, the planning committee needs to explore viewing protocol legalities.

Funding Church Sports Ministry

Besides capable staffing, every church program requires adequate funding to cover expenditures. Will sports ministry have a line item in the annual church budget? Will it need to develop funding through donations and registration fees? What if the targeted ministry recipients are a part of a low-income or an impoverished community? Will a scholarship assistance program be available?

Budgeted Line Item

When a church adds a line item to its budget, this suggests that the item is a priority and deserves full congregational support. This line should be itemized into sections including staff, resources, materials, and programming, and then is broken down into further sections. For instance, staff are itemized like any other ministry position (i.e., salary, benefits, housing, travel reimbursement, continuing education). Programming can be itemized to include specific events, especially if they occur regularly (e.g., movie nights, league expenses, guest speakers). In the case of churches with their own sport facilities, itemized lists include utilities, custodial, and maintenance.

Contributions

Special events or activities might need contributors to assist with expenses. For example, a short-term sports ministry trip might require funding that indi-

TABLE 12.1   Sports Movies With Subject and Description

Movie title	Subject	Description
American Underdog (2021)	Football	Depicts the roller coaster football career of Kurt Warner and the faith on which he and his wife ultimately relied.
Chariots of Fire (1981)	Olympic track	The story of two British runners competing in the 1924 Paris Summer Olympics: Harold Abrahams, a Jewish sprinter who faced public prejudice and antisemitism, and Eric Liddell, the son of missionaries who ran for the glory of God. The film was nominated for seven Academy Awards and won four, including Best Picture.
Facing the Giants (2006)	Football	A fictional account of a Christian football coach and his influence on his team both on and off the field.
Greater (2016)	Football	Brandon Burlsworth, a devout Christian who is considered by many to be the best college walk-on to ever play the game. His faith and work ethic landed him a spot on the University of Arkansas football team, where he became an All-American. Eleven days after being drafted by the Indianapolis Colts, Burlsworth encountered tragedy that stunned everyone and begs the persistent question, Why?
Overcomer (2019)	Basketball and cross country	The fictional story of a high school basketball coach whose faith is tested by economic hardships and the loss of jobs. He becomes the new cross-country coach at a neighboring high school (Leeman 2021).
Soul Surfer (2011)	Surfing	Through her strong faith in Jesus, 13-year-old Bethany Hamilton learns how to adjust to life after losing her arm to a shark attack. Eventually, she finds her way back to the surf and embarks on a new life chapter.
The Mighty Macs (2011)	Basketball	The incredible story of Coach Cathy Rush and the Immaculata College women's basketball team. Only two years removed from college herself, Coach Rush took a rag-tag team to national prominence. (Naismith Memorial Basketball Hall of Fame, n.d.).
Unbroken (2014) Unbroken: Path to Redemption (2018)	Olympic track	Shot down during World War II, Olympian Louis Zamperini's 47-day survival adrift in the Pacific Ocean, only to be captured and tortured in a Japanese prison camp, leads to lessons about perseverance, God's grace, and forgiveness.
When the Game Stands Tall (2014)	Football	The journey of Bob Ladouceur, football coach at De La Salle High School. With no previous coaching experience, Ladouceur took over a team that never had a winning season and transformed them into a powerhouse. At one point the team set a national high school football record with 151 consecutive victories. During his 34-year coaching career, Ladouceur had 20 undefeated seasons and at his retirement had amassed a career record of 399–25–3 (Associated Press 2013).
Woodlawn (2015)	Football	Based on the 1973 Birmingham, Alabama, Woodlawn High School football team, this story tells how spiritual revival helped the team and community confront racial tensions.

vidual participants cannot afford on their own. As mentioned in chapter 11, support-raising appeals can be made to friends, family, and members of the congregation. A partnership develops between active participants and those who financially and prayerfully back them. Another example is the expenses needed to host a specific guest speaker whose costs are greater than the budget line. Contributions could be sought to pay for the overage.

Registration Fees

Some programming is paid for by the participant themselves. For instance, leagues and the use of fitness facilities might require registration or membership fees. Jaunt events might incur a cost that participants pay. These costs should be kept as minimal as possible so that participation can be maximized.

Scholarships

Encouraging participation is essential for sports ministry programs. Whenever possible, participation should not become prohibitive because of the costs. For church and community members who cannot afford the costs, scholarship assistance programming is developed. Scholarships might become a budget line item, or they could be connected to appeals for contributions. Later in the chapter, Camp JYC will be highlighted. Annually, they raise funds and receive contributions so that as many community children can be campers at their overnight facility.

Church Sports Ministry Resources

Churches have access to valuable resources for sports ministry implementation and oversight through networking and equipping sports ministries. These organizations provide accessible online materials, and several provide in-person consultation. Exploring their websites enables churches to see what is available and most useful for their communities and congregations.

- *The Association of Church Sports and Recreation Ministries (CSRM):* CSRM provides numerous resources and training opportunities for the local church, including books, podcasts, certificate training, and an extensive video library. Many of their resources are linked with Overwhelming Victory, a branch of CSRM. (CSRM, n.d.)

- *Additional equipping SMOs:* Additional equipping SMOs are Cede Sports and Unchartered Waters (UW). Like CSRM, they are dedicated to equipping churches for sports ministry. AIA and the FCA also have numerous resources that benefit local churches including devotional and topical studies and athletic testimonials. Their websites offer an abundance of print, audio, and video materials.

Equipping Responsibilities for the Sport Minded

There is no question that the mission of the local church includes the responsibility to equip its members with the instruction and resources to live godly lives. Classes are regularly held to study the Bible and to relate its teaching to an array of subjects: parenting, family living, women of God, men of God, spiritual disciplines (prayer, worship, giving, biblical interpretation, evangelism), world missions, spiritual warfare, spiritual counterfeits, spiritual gifts, the second coming of Christ, and social responsibilities (poverty, racism, sexuality, abortion, human trafficking, environmental stewardship), to name a few. Messages are delivered from the pulpit, Sunday school classes instruct, and special seminars are held tackling these topics and more. These subjects are important and worthy of being addressed. Yet does the sporting community have a place to address its needs both within and outside the church? Instructional guidance can be provided about how to be a Christian athlete, coach, and spectator, including topics such as the application of positive character traits and the struggles commonly associated with sport (e.g., pride, self-sacrifice, perseverance, teamwork, discipline, sportsmanship, motivation) and how to handle victory and defeat, success and failure. Church leadership can think creatively about addressing the broader scope of needs represented within their communities and include ministry for the sport minded.

---

church polity—The governing principles used to guide congregational structure, operations, and authority. It maintains the spiritual eligibility of office holders, the office expectations, and the length of service.

Four square match at Camp JYC, a sport and recreation camping ministry of the First Baptist Church of Franklinville, New York.

Developing Church Sports Ministry Leadership

Church polity has its roots in the Bible and guidelines from texts such as 1 Timothy 3:1-13 and Titus 1:6-9 are typical references used by churches to define candidate qualifications. Just as requirements for leadership roles and training are needed for church board members and Sunday school teachers, likewise coaches, league coordinators, and others involved in sports ministry have equipping and spiritual competency needs. The church will delineate the leadership qualities sought and might include attributes such as the following:

- Consistent Christian testimony that models a passion for the Lord
- Shows the fruit of the Spirit in his or her life
- Strong relational skills and desire for interaction with people
- Practices faithful spiritual disciplines (prayer, Bible study, church attendance)
- Has a heart for servant-leadership, respects others, and is respected
- Enjoys sport and recognizes it as a powerful tool for ministry

Like any other church leadership role, a church seeks devout Christian leaders to fill sports ministry supervisory roles. However, on occasion a congregation might elect to incorporate a gifted, high-character non-Christian in a coaching or administrative role as a way to minister to that person specifically. If this practice is adopted, such individuals should be partnered with a strong Christian mentor so as not to neglect the essential Christ presence.

Examples of Local Church Sports Ministries

Church size is not determined by the expanse of facilities but instead is measured by the average weekend attendance. Church attendance patterns can fluctuate seasonally. For example, a cold-climate church with an extensive population of older persons might encounter a reduction during the winter months as snowbirds migrate south for warmer destinations. Other congregations experience summertime attendance lulls as families exit for vacations. Local population cycles also influence numbers. Expanding neighborhoods tend to support church growth, whereas churches in high-transition locales experience frequent attendance shifts. Opinions differ when it comes to classifying churches by size. For the current discussion, the following figures will be applied:

church size—Measured by the average weekend attendance.

Interview With a Professional

John Garner

BS, Recreation, Mississippi College

MRE (Master of Religious Education), Southwestern Baptist Theological Seminary, Fort Worth, Texas

Connections Pastor, Clear View Baptist Church, Franklin, Tennessee TN

Adjunct Professor, Oklahoma Baptist and Belmont Universities

John Garner has 20 years' experience as a recreation and sports minister in the local church. He has served 18 years with LifeWay Christian Resources as a consultant, editor, and manager for sports ministry, and has served the local church as senior pastor and in various other ministry positions along the way. John is the author and editor of *Recreation and Sports Ministry Impacting Postmodern Culture* and has authored more than 70 articles in various professional, educational, and religious publications. He is a conference leader and speaker specializing in recreation and sports facility design, programming, and management.

What attributes do you consider most essential for a local church to possess in order to have a vibrant sports ministry?

A church must have three things to be successful using sports ministry: (1) The *vision* and support of the pastor and church leadership. (2) *Intentionality* is when each league, class, and activity has as its reason for existence: the sharing of the gospel with prebelievers and the discipleship of believers. The ultimate goal is to make multiplying disciples of all who are involved in recreation and sports ministry. (3) A *called and trained minister* will have a passion for using nontraditional means for sharing the gospel and discipleship. This leader will be more likely to keep a ministry on track in sharing the gospel and discipling believers.

What are some of the common hurdles facing local church sports ministry?

The most common hurdle is helping the average church member see how leisure activities, which include sport, can be used as a valid gospel tool. This needs to come in the form of pulpit support and a public celebration when someone comes to know Christ as a result of being involved in sport and recreation ministry. Testimonies from participants, stories in the church newsletter, on a blog, on a Facebook page, on Instagram, and so on will help people understand why recreation and sports ministry is used. If church members see results, they might understand and see the use of their own leisure pursuits as an opportunity to reach people using informal, nonthreatening activities that they personally enjoy.

Another hurdle is thinking you can't do recreation and sports ministry without a facility. Churches should start without a facility, holding events at facilities found in their community (e.g., schools, partnering with businesses, and the local parks and recreation departments). Once this ministry is successfully established without a facility, the need to expand the ministry through the use of a church facility will become evident. The church can then be confident that a recreation and sport facility will enable them to grow the ministry to new heights as they reach and disciple people.

Do you distinguish between recreational activities and sports ministry?

My philosophy is that both recreation and sports take place during leisure time. Therefore, leisure services (recreation) provided by the church encompass both recreation and sports for all ages, from preschool to senior adults. Anything people do in their leisure can be a tool for ministry, be it sports, a ceramics class, yoga and aerobics classes, sport camps, fishing, wellness clinics, fitness, games, motorcycle clubs, day camps, and so on. So including recreation activities and sport under the umbrella of recreation seems a good fit. Perhaps a better term would be *leisure services ministry*. Today, however, many churches use the term *sports ministry*. To the average church member, the term *sports ministry* carries the connotation that this ministry is exclusively about sports, thus leaving out preschoolers and senior adults, who don't traditionally participate in sport. If that is what the church needs and desires, then the term *sports ministry* is perfectly fine. Some churches are including recreation activities as a part of their sports ministry, which works also. If that is the case, time and effort must be spent educating the church that all ages and activities (such as cited earlier) are included under the title *sports ministry*.

What recommendations do you have for students preparing to serve in local church sports ministry?

(1) Be sure you are called by God and have a heart for ministry. As a church staff member, a sports minister will often be called on to "perform other duties as assigned." Because of budget constraints, it is not likely that a sports minister will work only as a sports minister. In most churches, the sports minister will have two areas of ministry to cover such as students and sports, family and sports ministry, or others. The church will view the sports minister as a minister first who uses sport as his or her ministry tool. (2) Be a mature, practicing, committed, multiplying believer. (3) Be a team player. Good staff relationships with other ministry staff are vital. The goal of sports ministry is to win and disciple believers so that they can be involved in all of church life. In essence, sports ministry prepares and funnels people to church membership, the church's groups ministry, worship ministry, children's ministry, discipleship ministry, and so on. The day that the church staff recognizes that the sports ministry sends them new people is the day the sports ministry and minister gain new cheerleaders. No one on church staff works in a vacuum. (4) The undergrad should endeavor to grow in people, organizational, and administrative skills. The student must learn to juggle schedules, work with maintenance personnel, work with a leadership team, read and create spreadsheets, understand budgeting processes, organize league schedules, understand promotion and publicity concepts, and so on. If a facility is involved, the undergrad should be aware of risk management issues, learn how to recruit and work with volunteers, and learn business concepts because running a ministry or facility is like running a small business. This often can be done by taking an introduction to business class.

What do you foresee as the future of sports ministry in the local church?

America and the world are sports obsessed. In America, we have more leisure time than ever before in our history. People work to support their leisure pursuits. This affects business and culture. Leisure is not used in pursuing sports only. Young adults are more diverse in their leisure activities, with social events, fitness, and wellness as high priorities. Every parent wants his or her children to learn sports; families desire instructional leagues for their children and family-oriented social events. The aging of America has more older adults concerned about health and wellness. All of this bodes well for the local church. In the future, the church will have more opportunities than ever to use leisure event tools (anything people do in their leisure time) to capture the imagination of people to influence them for Christ. As a new generation of leaders are called and trained, they will find churches looking for culturally relevant ways to reach people with the message of Christ. I see a bright future for sports ministry. Young pastors, who are part of this leisure-oriented culture, expect the aforementioned desires for their families. Many will see ministry opportunities here. They will seek out called and trained sport and recreation ministers. (John Garner, pers. interview 2022)

- *Small church* equals an average weekend attendance of 200 or fewer (represents the majority of U.S. churches).
- *Medium church* equals an average weekend attendance of 201 to 400.
- *Large church* equals an average weekend attendance of 401 to 2,000.
- *Megachurch* equals an average weekend attendance that exceeds 2,000.

This section will consider examples from the two ends of the church size spectrum: a sports ministry from a small church and one from a megachurch. Ministry principles can be deciphered from each and applied to any size church.

Sports Ministry in a Small Church

Sports ministry within a small church is typically dependent on the vision of a solo pastor or an enthusiastic member of the congregation. Either the pastor will take on oversight responsibilities alone or will enlist the assistance of volunteers from within the church. Most often small churches do not have their own sport or recreational facilities but are dependent on the procurement of community alternatives. An exception to this assumption is the First Baptist Church (FBC), a small church located in the western New York village of Franklinville. This congregation provides a model for what God can accomplish through visionary enactment, and the principles exhibited can serve the purpose of sports ministry replication regardless of church size.

Understanding the value of outdoor sport and recreation, FBC began a camping ministry in 1951 by obtaining the use of a nearby public park. Several years later, in 1958, the congregation voted to accept a gift of 160 acres of land on the outskirts of the village. Their missional vision expanded, and facilities (known as Camp JYC) were progressively constructed, predominantly through the labor of their own members. Today, the church operates an insulated year-round lodge equipped with a full kitchen, a walk-in cooler and freezer, an office, an infirmary, and a large hall accommodating a maximum of 360 people. A modern bathhouse, multiple camper sites, and eight cabins with a total of 101 beds provide residential options. Because of the camp's strong sport and recreation emphasis, facilities have been added to include a full-size outdoor basketball court; an inground pool; a four-square court; an outdoor volleyball court; a gaga ball pit; a graded multipurpose sports field; hiking trails; a disc golf course; a playground; horseshoe pits; an archery range; and a stocked fishing pond furnished with canoes, kayaks, paddleboards, and paddleboats. Future plans include the addition of a .22 rifle marksmanship range, a pickleball court, and a zipline (Camp JYC, n.d.).

Members of the church serve in camp leadership to coordinate all facets of their own summer residential camp weeks geared toward children and teens. Adult members serve as cooks, maintenance crew members, teachers, sport and recreation coaches, and camp nurses. In recent years, an increased number of campers have come from unchurched backgrounds. Consequently, JYC has adjusted curriculum content and ministry emphasis, described as "Intro to Jesus 101," to address this need more specifically. When not operating their own sport and recreation programs, the camp is available for scheduling by other churches and organizations. The camp is funded through camper registrations, donations, fundraisers, rentals, grants, and as a line item in the annual church budget. A unique source of additional funding has been generated through safe, environmental timber harvesting from the camp's wooded terrain. This congregation demonstrates key lessons to be learned about a small church's application of sport and recreational ministry implementation:

1. An accurate assessment of their regional demographics (including an awareness of the types of sport and recreational activities that best complement local interests)
2. Creative use of their own resources, giftedness, and abilities
3. The ability to grow internally and disciple generational leadership
4. A willingness to review, evaluate, and adapt curriculum and ministry to best meet the needs of the constituents they serve
5. A sense of ownership experienced by working together—a bond of cooperative, shared ministry that includes the vast majority of the congregation and represents all ages
6. Making the most of congregational resources and a willingness to give of themselves—an investment of time, abilities and skills, and finances
7. The importance of building a visionary connection between the sport and recreational ministry and the overall mission of the church
8. A strong trust in, consistent prayer to, and dependence on God to do what appears to be impossible

Through the faithful stewardship of a generous gift of land, FBC Franklinville's Camp JYC is an exemplary example of what a small congregation with a big vision from a bigger God can accomplish (Martin Hatch, pers. interview 2021).

Sports Ministry in Medium and Large Churches

As churches grow in size, vocational staffing is added, most commonly assistant and associate pastors, youth ministers, and worship directors. These new positions provide an increased specialized ministry focus. Sports ministry responsibilities might become a part of a yoked role such as assistant pastor and minister of recreation, minister of youth and sports ministry, and pastor of young adults and sports ministry. These churches might provide some of their own sport and recreational facilities such as a gymnasium, ball field, or playground. With a few exceptions, specifically designated sports ministry positions are more frequently found in larger churches. Previously highlighted in this chapter is Grace and Truth Sports Park, a ministry of First Bible Baptist Church, near Rochester, New York. FBC is an example of a church that fits this category.

Sports Ministry in a Megachurch

American megachurches continue to grow in number and attendance. The Hartford Institute for Religion Research publishes a study of megachurches every five years. According to their most recent study (2020), approximately 1,750 megachurches exist in the United States. These churches are predominantly evangelical and characterized by an increasing presence of multiracial attendees. The study indicates that 47 percent of these churches have opened a satellite or branch location, and 48 percent have helped plant a new congregation. The average weekly attendance is 4,092, while the average sanctuary seating capacity has consistently remained 1,200 for several years. Consequently, the number of weekly services has grown. Annual budgets hover around $5.3 million, with 96 percent of church income coming from participant contributions. The percentage of budget breakdown is consistent with the percentages also found in small and mid- to large-size churches: 50 percent for staffing salaries and benefits, 20 percent for facility and operations, 15 percent for programming and materials, 11 percent for missions and benevolence, and 4 percent designated as other. With greater overall resources, if desired, megachurches have the capability to staff and resource sports ministry programming. The megachurch survey indicated that 12 percent of these largest congregations place a strong emphasis on sports groups, 38 percent had some sport emphasis, and 50 percent had no emphasis (Bird and Thumma 2020).

An example of a megachurch sports ministry is found at the Mount Pleasant Christian Church in Greenwood, Indiana. This church features a Community Life Center with full-time staffing that includes a director, a wellness coordinator, and two sports coordinators. Facilities include two hardwood gymnasiums; an elevated track; a mirrored fitness room; and a weight and cardio room equipped with free weights, nautilus, and cardio machines. Their programming and facilities sponsor wellness activities such as cardio and strength training, aerobics, indoor cycling, Zumba, power Pilates, kettlebells, pickleball, senior toning, REFIT dance, total body strength and conditioning, and nutrition classes. Adult league sports are organized in basketball, volleyball, golf, and softball. Children and youth league opportunities include baseball, basketball, soccer, volleyball, and summer sport camps. Annual memberships are reasonably priced for families, individuals, seniors, students, and drop-ins (Mount Pleasant Christian Church Community Life Center, n.d.).

Expanded resourcing (staffing, facilities, funding, programs) is an advantage of larger churches. With greater numbers they have more points of connection throughout the local community. Professional staff provide undivided attention to further develop sport and recreational programming. A potential shortcoming is the struggle to maintain a common vision and gospel emphasis across multiple channels of communication.

A Precaution

When incorporating recreation and sport within the life of the church, *ministry* must be the foundational focus. The activity itself cannot usurp the purpose. If recreation and sport activity become the pinnacle of attention, the church will be guilty of reneging its gospel responsibility and will simply function as another community rec program. The ongoing oversight of church leadership is essential to provide adequate vision casting, training, oversight, and guidance as they invest in those under their supervision to maintain a healthy and proper ministry balance. Prayerful assessment and review are necessary, just like any other ministry evaluation of the church.

SUMMARY

Sportspersons represent another realm of giftedness within the constituency of the congregation. Their leadership can be developed, and their talents employed to engage an unreached sector of the community. In-reach programming enriches the fellowship of active participants, while outreach builds a connecting bridge to neighbors. It is not an either-or proposition; both are indispensable components of church sports ministry. Churches of all sizes are capable of using the powerful tool of sport. Each church should assess the needs and interests of its congregants and examine the demographics of its surrounding community to determine what best fits its overall mission. Once the vision is cast, plans can be implemented, and the results evaluated for improvement.

REVIEW AND DISCUSSION QUESTIONS

1. What has been your experience with recreation and sport in a local church environment?
2. Why is it important for sports ministries to align their objectives with the overall objectives of the church?
3. Discuss advantages and disadvantages of church size when it comes to sports ministry.
4. Explain the importance of prayer as it relates to local church sports ministry.
5. Discuss qualities essential for a local church sports ministry leader.
6. What community demographics should be considered when considering a sports ministry?

Sports ministry organizations use all types of sport and recreational activities to build compelling relationships.

CHAPTER 13

Sports Ministry Organizations

[Reflecting on the use of snowboarding for Christ] "On the other side of the globe God was planting His vision. This was not one dude's idea. This was a divinely inspired thing. Later down the road we would meet each other, and whoa! You have the same idea. . . . We're doing it and he's doing it over there—how crazy is this! That's been the heaviest impact on me . . . to watch God unfold the vision all over the world."

Josh Stock, SFC USA Founder and International Director

LEARNING OBJECTIVES

After studying this chapter, you should be able to do the following:

- Discuss the relationship and tensions between church and parachurch ministries
- Understand biblical principles about ministry specializations
- Identify the types of sports ministry organizations (SMOs), their history, and their ministry focus
- Compare objectives and methodologies employed by SMOs
- Explain key characteristics, expectations, and core values of effective SMOs
- Recognize the emphasis placed on relationships employed by SMOs to meet spiritual and physical needs
- Determine which SMO would be most appropriate for one's own setting

In September 2016 Disney Studios released the movie *The Queen of Katwe*. Based on the book by the same title, author Tim Crothers tells the incredible story of child chess prodigy Phiona Mutesi. Living in the Katwe slum of Kampala, Uganda, Phiona had little hope, yet her life was forever changed when she was introduced to the game of chess by an indigenous sports missionary, Robert Katende. Defying the odds, Phiona became an engrossed student of the game and entertained the dream of one day achieving the status of grandmaster. She competed locally, regionally, and eventually became Uganda's national chess champion. She went on to compete internationally and represents an amazing rags-to-riches story of perseverance and accomplishment. Katende, and Kampala's Agape church, was not only instrumental in Phiona's chess accolades, but it also discipled her in the Christian faith. What initially began with one chess board, one coach, and a handful of impoverished children has grown to become a thriving chess academy that operates with this motto: "Transforming Lives Through Chess One Move at a Time" (Sports Outreach, n.d.).

Mutesi's story has a direct sports ministry connection. Years prior to her birth, Russ Carr, a collegiate soccer coach from Santa Barbara, California, experienced a personal awakening while touring Central America with a U.S. State Department–sponsored soccer team. He was burdened by the disturbing scenes of extreme poverty. His mind would not allow him to be freed from the images of devastating human need. Something had to be done. Carr eventually left the collegiate coaching ranks, devoted himself to full-time sports ministry and became the founder of Sports Outreach International (SOI), a ministry committed to evangelism and discipleship through sport while also addressing the needs of poverty.

In 1988 Carr traveled to Uganda to present the idea of a football (soccer) crusade to church leaders. The proposal was initially met with overwhelming laughter. Soccer was considered evil because of its association with bribery, witchcraft, corruption, and prostitution. If a soccer player came to Christ, the player would renounce soccer and no longer play. They also did not think Ugandans would take an American soccer team seriously because worldwide, the quality of American soccer was not highly regarded. After much prayer, the church leaders consented and decided to try something that seemed spiritually and culturally unacceptable at the time.

In preparation, three significant events transpired. First, the Ugandans instituted a 24-hour prayer chain. The prayer chairman, a man with only one lung, said, "I can't play football, but I can pray." Second, upon his return to the United States, Carr contacted Missionary Athletes International (MAI) and formed a team largely of players from their Southern California Seahorse squad. Third, a popular Ugandan goalkeeper, David Dronyi, came out of retirement to play in net for the Seahorses. His addition drew national attention and bolstered the crusade's credibility among Ugandans.

The crusade was highly successful. Nationally televised games were played before as many as 25,000 spectators. The Seahorse team astounded onlookers as they competed at the highest level, even beating Uganda's second-best team. "We were such a novelty," reflected Carr. "Americans playing soccer was such a strange thing to them. They honestly didn't believe we could kick a ball and walk at the same time" (Russ Carr, pers. interview 2022).

Responding to gospel presentations, approximately 5,000 Ugandans came forward after the soccer matches to make decisions to follow Christ, and only eternity knows how many additional decisions were made by fans watching the televised broadcasts. The impact of the crusade convinced church leaders that sport could be used as an effective ministry tool. Prayerfully, Carr determined that SOI Uganda would be best served by training indigenous missionaries and only use traveling U.S. teams to provide periodic support, assistance, and encouragement.

Our sports ministry models and principles have proven countless times to be cross-cultural and effective. They have been developed and fine-tuned throughout the years. Soccer and chess are our primary activities, but have also included basketball, volleyball, softball, baseball, and just about any activity that gets kids running around! It all leads to relationships and opportunities to connect off the field with the gospel message and life applications. We partner with churches in the places we minister to connect people to a local body of believers. (Sports Outreach, n.d.; Carr, pers. interview 2022)

Phiona Mutesi represents a living example of the fruit of sports ministry efforts. She was yet to be born when a prayerfully planned and successfully accomplished soccer crusade led to the founding of SOI Uganda. Communities have since been, and continue to be, reached through the service of this organization. As the New Testament reveals on multiple occasions, Jesus blessed a few fish and loaves of bread to feed thousands of people (Luke 9:10-17; Matthew 15:29-39). Analogically, when placed in the hands of Jesus, small experiences and ideas can be multiplied and reshaped to fulfill His kingdom purposes. While in Central America, God burdened Russ Carr with a penetrating glimpse of poverty. That glimpse eventually multiplied into a vision for sports ministry as Carr presented the few fish and loaves of his life to Jesus.

This chapter will explore aspects of sports ministry organizations (SMOs). The relationship and tension between the Church and SMOs will be discussed. Biblical principles guide the development of best practices for an SMO. Although previous chapters have specifically identified several SMOs (i.e., YMCA, FCA, AIA), additional ministries will be highlighted here.

SMO as Parachurch

Numerous Christian services have sprung up that offer specialized ministries such as mission agencies, relief and development organizations, educational institutions, campus evangelism and discipleship ministries, teaching and resource providers, and SMOs. These specialized groups have come to be known as **parachurch ministries**. The prefix *para* means "beside" or "alongside." Some parachurch ministries have originated in local churches and have denominational connections. But largely, many parachurch ministries structurally operate independently from a specific church association. This lack of church origin and affiliation has led some **Christian apologists** to criticize the legitimacy of what they refer to as "so-called parachurch ministries." Parachurch proponents argue that this lack of church affiliation is a strength because it allows these organizations to cross over individual church or denominational boundaries and provide a plurality of service to the Church as a whole (Lausanne Movement 1983). An exhaustive dialogue about the

role and validity of parachurch ministry is neither possible nor the purpose of this chapter, but a cursory discussion will follow.

A Question of Origins and Authoritative Operation

Parachurch ministries are not themselves a church, nor should they be considered a replacement or substitution for a church. Critics contend that the New Testament does not provide examples of specialized ministries apart from those originating from within the church herself. Christian apologist John Stott affirms the necessity of specialist ministries while maintaining that the crux of the debate centers around the question of whose responsibility and authority it is to initiate and operate them:

> *All are agreed that specialist functions require specialist organizations (e.g., for Bible translation, student evangelism and cross-cultural missions); but who should initiate and operate them? That is the issue. The argument in favor of parachurch organizations is largely historical, namely that under God they have made a much greater contribution to world evangelization than has the Church. This is indisputable. The contrary argument begins with scripture rather than history, asserts that only the Church can claim to be a divine creation, and concludes that ideally the Church should itself undertake necessary specialist tasks. It is not easy to reconcile these appeals to history and scripture, to reality and to the ideal. But since evangelicals desire in all things to be guided by the Bible, we should be able to grade specialist activities thus: independence of the Church is bad, co-operation with the Church is better, service as an arm of the Church is best. (Stott, qtd. in Lausanne Movement 1983)*

The Church's Primacy of Ministry

In Acts 6 a dispute arose about the oversight of the daily distribution of food among widows. The apostles determined a course of action based on the primacy of their work:

---

parachurch ministries—Christian organizations that come alongside the Church universal to enhance ministries that local churches might not be equipped to perform alone.

Christian apologist—A scholarly theologian who seeks to defend the Christian faith through accurate biblical interpretation and application of the Scriptures.

So the Twelve gathered all the disciples together and said, "It would not be right for us to neglect the ministry of the Word of God in order to wait on tables. Brothers and sisters, choose seven men from among you who are known to be full of the Spirit and wisdom. We will turn this responsibility over to them and will give our attention to prayer and the ministry of the Word. (Acts 6:2-4 NIV)

From this passage, prayer and the ministry of God's word were two essential duties of church leadership. Service to the widows was important, but that work was delegated so that the apostles' chief responsibilities would not be diminished "in order to wait on tables." This form of specialized ministry has its role in the life of the Church. Jon Saunders observes,

A Christian publisher is a type of parachurch ministry. Books are a tremendous resource that bolsters the ministry of the church. . . . Yet a local church cannot—and probably should not—spend time picking out paper quality, finding mass-producing machines, researching binding techniques, and advertising books. They need help. This is where a parachurch ministry can step in. Publishers serve the greater mission of the Church by doing things the Church is unable to. They assist; they do not replace. (Saunders 2015)

Saunders' observation is quite rational—delegatory specialization is needed as a part of pragmatic church function. Likewise, Exodus attests to the same when Jethro visited Moses and observed him serving as judge for the people. Jethro determined that the workload was too great for one person alone and recommended that Moses appoint capable officials to share this responsibility. He listened to the counsel and appointed judges, thus dividing the responsibilities to make them more manageable (Exodus 18). Affirming Stott's assertion, the need for specialized ministries within the Church is valid so that the primary task of prayer and attention to God's word are unhindered—the debate remains procedural, namely, concerning origins and operational authority.

Ministry Model Usurps a Corporate Model

The organizational structure and function of the Church exhibits corporate-like characteristics, yet these qualities do not usurp the ministry model for church polity and operations. The same is true for SMOs. *Ministry* is the emphasis. J. Mack Stiles writes,

Modern corporate culture values efficiency, risk management, clean organizational structures, and a strong financial ledger. Corporate culture and structure are routinely imported into parachurch ministry leadership. As a result, many parachurch organizations then also place a high value on what raises the most money, minimizes risk, or produces the most efficient management structure.

But these are not the values that bring spiritual revival, passion for the gospel, or people who are willing to lay down their lives for Jesus. Are there things to learn from modern corporate culture? Sure. Should they be our highest values in ministry? Never. Consequently, parachurch ministries need an understanding of management and money that runs counter to worldly culture.

There needs to be a constant, radical call for the management of parachurch ministries to be like what they call their staff and members to be like. A political, corporate leadership erodes a biblical mindset. When that happens in the leadership of a parachurch organization the death of the real ministry is not far behind.

Healthy parachurch ministries need to issue constant, radical, internal calls for the organization to be driven by the gospel rather than by management principles, finances, and fundraising. That way, the ministry looks like a ministry from top to bottom. (Stiles 2011)

Faithful adherence to ministry is essential. Borrowing a repeated expression popularized by sports minister Brian Davidson, "It is sports MINISTRY, not SPORTS ministry."

Affirmation and Accountability

The Church has been established for the fellowship of believers and for their governance. As ministries function, they do so within structured accountability. A concern that arises with parachurch ministries, including SMOs, is one of accountability. These ministries should not merely be accountable to themselves but should be affirmed and accountable to the Church at large as represented through an affiliated association of churches or a single local church answerable to a larger governing church body. Checks and balances are necessary to maintain sound biblical theology and proper stewardship of financial, personnel, and ministerial resources. The Lausanne Movement exists in part to connect and unite church leaders around healthy dialogue about important church-related issues including the role of parachurch organizations.

The place and role of so-called para-church organizations have been ongoing subjects of discussion and, sometimes, sources of tension and contention in church circles. That debate has frequently had the effect of polarizing participants into distinct camps and impeding evangelization endeavors.

Some Christians seriously question the validity of all groups other than traditional congregations. Others have no problem in accepting their own denominational groups (such as seminaries, mission-sending agencies, or the denominational structure itself) but reject, or at most concede secondary status to non-denominational organizations.

At the opposite end of the spectrum are those who advocate acceptance of para-church agencies not merely as biblical, but as equally "church," in the congregational sense.

Most, however, would probably adopt a position somewhere between these two extremes. They would recognize those special non-congregational Christian ministries (or parachurch groups) as necessary tools in the Kingdom of God, while clearly differentiating between them and churchly congregations of believers. (Lausanne Movement 1983)

Ideally, SMOs should emerge and operate as a function of the Church. Yet how is "church" to be defined? Is it merely adherence to a gathering in accordance to formalized, structured, institutional bylaws? What about Christian neighbors congregating in a private home for prayer—is that a gathering of the Church? What about Christian friends praying and worshipping God around a campfire? Is it a gathering of the Church when a Christian athletic team joins together to hear a devotional word?

When God stirs the heart of an individual or a small group with a common inspiration, is it no less His work being manifest in the midst of His people? Does He only speak through the auspices of designated church leaders? What about someone like Amos, a simple shepherd of Tekoa who tended sycamore fig trees yet who was appointed by God to be His prophet (Amos 1:1; 7:14-15)? Is perceived "structure" inhibiting the exercise of the work of God's Spirit among His people? Recall the perplexity of Jesus' disciples as recorded in Mark 9. A man, who was not one of the inner circle, was driving out demons in Jesus' name. "'Do not stop him,' Jesus said. 'For no one who does a miracle in my name can in the next moment say anything bad about me, for whoever is not against us is for us'" (Mark 9:39-40 NIV).

The disciples were bound by a preconceived concept that ministry had to fall within a particularly defined parameter. Yet Jesus—who often did not follow the supposed rules, as evidenced by His response—viewed the situation differently. A note of caution is due here—by challenging the notion of the limitations that structural boundaries often enforce, in no way does it imply that anything goes, as individuals and groups claim, to hear a word from God. Wise biblical discernment is required to distinguish between the leading of the Holy Spirit and the promptings of fleshly yearnings. The Church is the agency to test and affirm the counsel of God's direction. The debate over the relationship between church and parachurch ministries can be a healthy dialogue as long as adherence to biblical guidelines are sought and followed.

Exemplary Characteristics for a SMO

Parachurch SMOs abound. God uses them to multiply and build His kingdom. What are some of the essential characteristics of a thriving SMO? Here is a representative working list of eight qualities that should be sought and actualized:

1. The ministry's focus is on the lordship and saving grace of Jesus (Hebrews 12:2-3).

2. The Bible is affirmed as God's word and serves as the ministry's counsel and directive (Acts 17:11; 1 Thessalonians 2:13; 2 Timothy 3:16).

3. The Church affirms the ministry (Acts 6:6; 13:3).

4. The gospel admonition of evangelism and discipleship is central to the mission (Matthew 28:18-20; Acts 1:8).

5. The core spiritual disciplines are diligently practiced (1 Thessalonians 5:16-18; Colossians 3:16).

6. Active participation and accountability in a local church is expected of all ministry staff and participants (Hebrews 10:22-25).

7. They are good stewards of time and resources, and are fiscally responsible (Matthew 25:14-30).

8. The fruit of the ministry is good and praiseworthy (Matthew 7:15-23; John 15:8).

Interview With a Professional

David Walton
President, Push The Rock
BA, The Kings College (1976)
MBA, Lehigh University (1981)

David Walton began his association with Push The Rock in 1998 as the chairman of the board of directors and now leads the entire organization as president. He supervises strategy and vision and shepherds the leadership team. David also spends time speaking on behalf of Push The Rock, sharing its vision and fundraising.

David spent 39 years in various departments at PPL Corporation, implementing an automated metering system and improving customer service, and served a term as vice president of business solutions and operations.

David played basketball in high school and college. He once held his high school's single-season and single-game assists record. After graduating he spent time coaching youth basketball and soccer. He coached his U12 soccer team to a state championship.

David grew up in the love and care of a Christian family and came to Christ at a young age. However, faith was never his own until multiple basketball injuries made him realize that it was only Jesus who could satisfy the longing in his heart.

What is Push The Rock's ministry objective?

Our ministry objective is to use sport to bring people to Christ. Our repetitive contact philosophy helps us develop trust with participants so that we can share the hope of the gospel with them. Our programs, which include camps, after-school programs, homeschool physical education programs, sport clubs, clinics, mission trips, and chapels, all include a gospel or devotion component.

What is behind the name of the organization?

The name Push The Rock has a dual meaning. We started as a basketball ministry, and the phrase "push the rock" is a slang term to push the ball up the court. The Lord is the rock in whom we put our trust. We are pushing and sharing the rock of Jesus. Our verse is "Trust in the Lord forever, for the Lord, the Lord is the rock eternal" (Isaiah 26:4).

Why are sports ministries like Push The Rock necessary?

Sport is a great way to connect with people and open doors for the gospel. People who do not go to church will often come to a sports outreach. Organizations like PTR partner with churches, schools, and other organizations to open doors for them. From an economic standpoint, it is not practical for every organization to have a sports outreach.

What connection exists between PTR and the local church?

A significant number of our programs are in partnership with a local church. This partnership is particularly important for our summer camps and mission trips. Our goal is to connect participants to a local church after our event is over.

What is most rewarding to you about the ministry of PTR?

We have the incredible opportunity to connect many people to the life-changing message of the gospel. Many of our participants never go to church and might never hear about Jesus and what He has done for us. They love sports, and we get to share through the universal language of sport. On a personal level, I get to combine my passion for sport with my passion for Jesus.

What recommendation do you give to students who are considering sports ministry as a vocation?

If you love Jesus and love sport, it is an incredible way to combine your passions. If you are undecided, I would recommend you pursue an internship with a sports ministry to confirm the fit.

How is competition implemented strategically within PTR programming?

All of our programs, including competitive teams, include a spiritual component. Our primary goal is to get our participants to play for Christ on the field of sport. We ask each one to consider making a commitment to the Lord, to play for Christ, their primary objective above winning. (David Walton, pers. interview 2022)

By the power of God, humble specialized service that seeks to honor Him and equips the Church is desired. Church and parachurch ministries are partners who strive together for the sake of the gospel. The work of SMOs begins with prayer and is sustained through prayer, and the fruit of transformed lives is an answer to prayer. Ministry is His work done in His way.

SMO Examples

Over the past 50 years SMOs have blossomed, with an extensive variety of sport and recreational types. Sport and recreational opportunities exist for all four seasons of the year. They span the scope of creative ingenuity—using competitive sports (e.g., soccer, basketball, volleyball), snow sports (e.g., skiing, snowboarding, tubing), recreational activities (e.g., hiking, biking, fishing), adventure sports (e.g., white water rafting, rock climbing, kayaking), providing ministry resources (e.g., curricula, devotional studies, video testimonies), and more. Broadly, SMOs can be placed in three categories: domestic, international, and multinational. These categories are loosely interpreted as ministry expansion and withdrawal continually ebb and flow.

Domestic Sports Ministries

Two Christian sport and recreational camps that fit the character of a **domestic sports ministry (DSM)** are Summer's Best Two Weeks and Youth Dynamics.

Summer's Best Two Weeks

Summer's Best Two Weeks (SB2W) originated in 1966 as a local church residential and day camp ministry of Elmwood Presbyterian Church in Syracuse, New York. Led by Jim Welch, the day camp operated at the church while the resident camp was held at the presbytery-owned Vandercamp. Following Jim's relocation to Pittsburgh in 1969, the day camp was hosted by the Fox Chapel Presbyterian Church, and the residential camps were held at the Pittsburgh

Presbytery's Camp Fairfield. The ministry incorporated in 1973 as a nonprofit entity, Christian Camps of Pittsburgh, Inc. The SB2W name originated in the mid-1970s when a magazine, *Presbyterian Life*, printed an article titled "Summer's Best Two Weeks." A camper had summarized his camp experience by declaring it was the "best two weeks of the summer."

In 1981 the 140-acre Lake Gloria site was purchased and developed, and it has operated at capacity ever since. A second camp, located on the shores of Lake Quemahoning, just nine miles from Lake Gloria, opened for campers in the summer of 2003 to accommodate a growing wait list, which had grown so long in the late 1990s that new campers had to wait two or three years to get a spot in camp. Since the very early days, SB2W was committed to reaching inner-city youths by providing opportunities to experience camp. In 2012 SB2W spearheaded efforts for SB2W Citikidz to begin facilitating camp for over 500 campers and inner-city leaders at Laurel Mountain Christian Camp in Rector, Pennsylvania. Citikidz is a separate nonprofit entity, but SB2W is a strong advocate for their ministry.

Athletic competitions in a wide range of sports are a key component of the SB2W ministry. Campers are divided into teams (Galatians and Romans) and compete daily, compiling points to determine eventual camp champions. Through competition, SB2W staff guide campers to learn life lessons. Five principles guide the emphasis on competitive athletics:

1. We believe all of life, every moment, is an opportunity to worship God. The athletic field, therefore, is a place of worship.
2. We believe competition is a microcosm of life. It imitates the emotions of life, involves intensely interpersonal interaction, and reflects culture.
3. We believe the intensity of competition heightens temptation towards sinful thoughts and actions.
4. We believe sport and competition can be used as a means to coach the heart of an athlete, growing them in holiness and godliness.

domestic sports ministries (DSMs)—Ministries that are headquartered and minister within the country of their location.

Life lessons through competitive sport is an intentional component of the SB2W ministry.

5. We are concerned primarily at camp with the identity, purpose, character, and spiritual growth of the athlete during competition. (Summer's Best Two Weeks, n.d.)

SB2W believes that camp should be fun, and they provide ample opportunities for campers to laugh and have a wholesome good time. Yet camp is also meant to challenge campers to return home to live and nurture the lessons learned. To this end, SB2W has developed the 8 Mile Marks to encourage campers as they transition back into their communities. Here is a list of the eight with an abbreviated summary of each:

1. *Get active in a local church:* Do not simply attend; become an actively involved participant.

2. *Study God's word with others:* The SB2W Bible study encounters Jesus through a five-year progression: (a) studying His miracles; (b) studying what the Old Testament says about Jesus; (c) studying what Jesus says about Himself; (d) studying what others said about Jesus; and (e) by examining His parables, studying what Jesus taught.

3. *Serve:* Self-absorption can be combatted by serving others. Serve at home, church, school, and in the community.

4. *Speak and listen to God:* Pray and read Scripture to build a personal relationship with God.

5. *Obey God's Word:* Do not merely be a hearer of God's word; do what it says. Biblical facts and insights are good to know, but they are also intended for life application.

6. *Read about God:* Not only read the Bible, but also read Christian literature such as Oswald Chambers' *My Utmost for His Highest* and Francis Chan's *Crazy Love.*

7. *Flee temptation and seek wisdom:* "Our culture has encouraged adolescent immaturity and immorality instead of adult maturity and responsibility." Seek godly mentors who can help with decision-making and can maintain a watchful eye of accountability.

8. *Compete as a Christian athlete:* Worship God and give Him the glory through athletic endeavors. (Summer's Best Two Weeks, n.d.)

Many camp experiences quickly fade when campers leave the mountaintop to return to life as normal. SB2W's 8 Mile Marks attempts to help campers build on the lessons learned.

Besides campers, the SB2W staff intentionally pour into the lives of the part-time collegiate summer staff. The majority of the college staff are students-athletes, and the camp's principles not only meet camper needs, but also addresses the staff's needs. Academic internship credit is readily available for interested students.

Youth Dynamics

Paul Evans was a 21-year-old life insurance salesman when he called a pastor to request an appointment to discuss a life insurance policy. The pastor promised 20 minutes of his time if the salesman would allow him 10 minutes to share about *his* life insurance plan. Paul agreed, the appointment kept, and his life would never be the same. The conversation with the pastor led to Paul's conversion. His faith was passionate,

Youth Dynamics is a relational ministry challenging youths to a lifelong adventure with Christ and His Church.

and he began to speak about Jesus with students from his former high school. This humble beginning was the start of an enduring teen ministry that eventually became Youth Dynamics.

Youth Dynamics is a relational adventure youth ministry serving throughout Washington, Idaho, and Oregon. Reaching any and all youths 11 to 24 years old, Youth Dynamics offers weekly middle and high school programs, young adult internships, community development programs, rural outreach, leadership opportunities, professionally guided adventure experiences, and Stonewater—Youth Dynamics' amazing 158-acre adventure and retreat facility located in Leavenworth, Washington.

Youth Dynamics' mission is "to invite and challenge youth to a lifelong adventure with Christ and His Church" (Youth Dynamics, n.d.). Committed to reaching youths since 1970, their ministry focuses on using outdoor adventure to promote relationships, individual growth, leadership skills, individual character growth, and community engagement. All adventure activities are professionally guided and follow the highest standards within the industry. These programs include the following:

- Whitewater rafting and kayaking
- Mountaineering and rock climbing
- Hiking and backpacking
- Team building and challenge course
- Custom adventure combo
- Horsemanship

- Retreats and events
- Leadership development
- Winter adventures
- Training and certifications

Youth Dynamics believes that wilderness experiences are powerful to connect youths to God and His creation. They maintain a strong local church emphasis:

Youth Dynamics seeks to work "alongside" the local church and seeks to support and enhance the local church's ministries, not become a church. Youth Dynamics relies on partnerships with churches of multiple denominations to live out our vision and mission. (Youth Dynamics, n.d.)

Additional examples of DSMs include Alpine Ministries, Infinity Sports, and In His Grip Golf.

International Sports Ministries

The category of **international sports ministries (ISMs)** frequently shifts between international and multinational sports ministries because affiliated or branch offices often are established in multiple countries while predominantly being headquartered in one. Push The Rock is an example of this practice. Though headquartered in the United States, their rate of expansion into global fields could readily characterize them as a MSM, even though many

---

international sports ministries (ISMs)—Ministries that are headquartered and minister within one country but also send touring groups to minister in other nations.

of their prime ministries remain stateside. Baseball Chapel is another ministry that could be classified as a MSM. Headquartered in Florida, they are popular with Major and Minor League Baseball in the United States, but they are also strongly associated with leagues in other nations.

Push The Rock

Push The Rock (PTR) originated as a weeklong basketball camp in southeast Pennsylvania. It has since grown into a global SMO. When asked about the best applicant qualities sought for PTR workers, the response emphasized the following:

- Loving the Lord
- Recognizing and endorsing the value of sport as a witnessing tool
- Having a servant-heart for people
- Exhibiting an entrepreneurial and pioneer spirit—being team oriented, creative, and hardworking (Go. Serve. Love. 2019)

PTR describes themselves as "a global leader in sports ministry, impacting the world for Jesus Christ . . . one life at a time." They maintain five essential core values, which are briefly described here:

1. Firm in Our Faith
   - Biblical doctrine, values, and standards are not compromised.
   - Have an inward attitude of Christ-centeredness and an outward display of Christlikeness
   - Christ's gospel is central to each program.
   - Constant prayer is a priority.
2. Kingdom Minded
   - The spiritual growth of all staff, volunteers, and participants are encouraged.
   - Intentionally acknowledge God and His glory in everything.
   - Pursue heavenly treasures rather than earthly ones.
   - Advance partnerships that equip others in Kingdom work.
3. Individual Focus
   - Recognize the individual story of each participant.
   - Know that one-on-one interactions can be moments of truth that can yield a positive impact.
   - Commit to prayer and follow up with every relationship.

- Understand that every interaction is part of a repetitive contact philosophy.
4. Family Oriented
   - Staff and volunteers are embraced and cared for as family.
   - Speak the truth in love through transparency and vulnerability.
   - Be accountable to one another.
   - Share an "all-in" perspective.
5. Innovative
   - Offer an ever-growing diversity of sports.
   - Pursue relationships with diverse cultures, the marginalized, and with those most in need of the gospel.
   - Listen and give due analysis to ideas.
   - Encourage initiative and an entrepreneurial spirit while respecting internal structures.

The PTR values are demonstrated through an array of sports ministries that include a *homeschool program*, a biblically based physical education class that helps families meet academic requirements while challenging students to grow physically and spiritually. Closely related is an *after-school program* in cooperation with a number of Pennsylvania public schools, providing an hour of instruction on the basics of different sports and a 10- to 15-minute chapel message. Southeast Pennsylvania and New Jersey summer *day camps* are organized in partnership with area churches and are offered for boys and girls ranging in age from 4 to 16 years. Most camps are multisport, but an occasional specialized camp is available (e.g., basketball). A *volleyball club* was established in 2005 and provides faith-based teams for middle and high school volleyball players. A *prison ministry* features an adult PTR basketball team that plays inmate teams where mentoring relationships are built and the gospel can be shared. *International trips* include traveling sport teams and individuals ministering through match ministry, camps, clinics, and other related activities. *International internships* are readily available in locations such as Brazil, Costa Rica, Guatemala, and Spain, where PTR has full-time staff. PTR also organizes golf clinics and has recently entered the world of disc golf. In 2021 PTR launched *outreach to refugees* in Clarkston, Georgia, the most culturally diverse mile in the United States. Partnering with a local church, PTR runs four to six weeks of sport camps in the summer for refugees in the community. An *esports* division called Slingshot conducts events at Pennsylvania churches where participants learn their craft from experts and compete in tournaments. Devotional

In partnership with local churches, summer sport camps are one of a variety of ministries offered by Push The Rock.

messages are held at each event (Push The Rock, n.d.).

PTR lives up to their core value of being innovative. Growing initially from a one-week basketball camp, they continually seek to multiply the reach of their sports ministry capabilities and have become a global leader in the field.

Baseball Chapel

As early as 1956, Clyde King provided chapel services for the minor league teams he managed and later for his teams in the majors. During the 1960s, road trip chapel services were initiated by players from the Chicago Cubs and Minnesota Twins. In 1973 Watson Spoelstra, a Detroit sportswriter, approached Commissioner Bowie Kuhn with a proposal to establish an organized chapel program for every major league team (Baseball Chapel, n.d.).

> *While I normally tried to reach conclusions in a thoughtful way, occasionally I followed hunches. I did so in 1973 when Waddy Spoelstra of the Detroit News, a recovering alcoholic, called and asked if I would fund a program of Baseball Chapel services for each major league club, a born-again Christian talking to a Catholic commissioner. Spoelstra, broadcasters Ernie Harwell and Red Barber, plus players like Jim Kaat, Al Worthington, Randy Hundley, Don Kessinger, Don Sutton, and Bobby Richardson had already been conducting such services on a sporadic basis. Spoelstra wanted to organize it for everyone. My answer was yes, and today, there are weekly chapel services across the major and minor leagues. (Kuhn 1997, 298)*

Baseball Chapel, headquartered in Largo, Florida, is a nondenominational evangelical Christian ministry network of over 600 people providing Sunday chapel services, midweek Bible studies, counseling, and discipleship. Besides U.S. Major and Minor League Baseball, the ministry has expanded internationally to include leagues in Mexico, Puerto Rico, Venezuela, Dominican Republic, Nicaragua, and Japan.

Baseball Chapel's four primary ministry focus groups follow:

1. Sunday chapel services for players and coaches for both home and away teams, which typically attract 4,000 attendees each week

2. Intentional ministry to umpires

3. Ministry to players' wives and girlfriends

4. Ministry to nonplayer ballpark personnel (e.g., ushers, security, front office, grounds, concessions) (Baseball Chapel, n.d.)

Due to the high number of Latino players, services are often provided in Spanish. Demands on players' schedules can become a challenge. Consequently, the average length of a chapel service is 20 minutes, and the midweek Bible study is typically 45 minutes. Chaplains attempt to maintain a high profile so that players, coaches, and other personnel become familiar with them and understand they are approachable and available as needs arise (Herd 2006). Baseball Chapel representatives are committed to a Christian worldview approach to life but will seek to minister to all baseball constituents regardless of one's religious beliefs: "Our desire is to encourage baseball people through the message of Jesus Christ, so that

Climbing for Christ—delivering the gospel in the mountains of the world, where other missionaries cannot or will not go

they would understand the importance of following Him" (Baseball Chapel, n.d.).

Additional ISM examples include Ignite International, Surge International, and Uncommon Sports Group.

Multinational Sports Ministries

As organizations expand due to fruitful ministry opportunities, increased interest and the adequate availability of resources and staffing, **multinational sports ministries (MSMs)** develop. Global expansion enables indigenous people to assume greater levels of participation and administrative leadership.

Climbing for Christ

Gary Fallesen had been a spectating sportswriter for nearly 20 years, covering high school, college, and professional sports from the sidelines. Then in 1996, he assumed the role of outdoors writer for *Democrat and Chronicle* the daily newspaper in Rochester, New York. Consequently, he became an active participant in many of the outdoor life stories he covered. His first attempt at climbing was an encounter with Mount Rainier in Washington. In 1998, while training to scale Mount Kilimanjaro, Africa's rooftop, the Lord spoke to his heart with the idea to start a Christian climbing organization. Eventually, God broke through Gary's hesitancy, and Climbing for Christ (C4C) was birthed.

C4C's calling is to take the gospel to unreached peoples living in the world's highest and most remote regions. Its primary purpose is "to go and deliver the gospel in the mountains of the world, where other missionaries cannot or will not go." Recognizing the vast amount of time mountain guides spend with mountaineers, C4C has developed a ministry discipling these guides, porters, and their families, teaching them how to evangelize and disciple others. In 2022, 28 Kilimanjaro guides and porters will have completed their second year of advanced Disciples Making Disciples (DMD) training and will launch into year three, "Discovering the Bible," further equipping them for God's work.

C4C serves to reach Muslims, Hindus, Buddhists, animists (a belief that every natural thing, such as animals, plants, rocks, rivers, and weather bears a soul), and atheists living in the mountains of Majority World nations, most of which are found in the 10/40 Window. It is considered the world's leading unevangelized location, home to people also known as the Unreached Unengaged People Groups. C4C provides indigenous missionary support in nine countries, trains disciples to make disciples, plants churches, distributes Bibles, frees brick factory slaves, delivers medical help, cares for widows and orphans, builds houses of worship, and supports education in mountain villages.

Some of the world's best climbing options are also located in some of the most dangerous places. Ted Callahan said,

multinational sports ministries (MSMs)—Ministries that minister and have affiliated offices in multiple countries.

SFC at Copper Mountain in Colorado, "taking the message to the mountain."

Some of the world's best climbing venues are also sited in some of the world's most dangerous locales. By dangerous, I mean only rife with tangential (and largely unavoidable) concerns such as abysmal sanitation, exotic bacteria, and dodgy, ill-maintained vehicles, but also imbued with objective hazards—crime, terrorism, kidnapping, and war—of a political nature (Callahan quoted in Climbing for Christ n.d.).

Fallesen adds, "Areas hazardous to climbers may be even more threatening to those who are climbing for Christ. But we have better protection. We have the name of Jesus—from whom the wicked enemy flees (James 4:6-7)" (Climbing for Christ n.d.).

C4C has regional chapters throughout the United States and worldwide in Australia, Canada, Indonesia, Tanzania (Kilimanjaro), and the Philippines. Besides these countries, climbing expeditions (labeled Evangelic Expeditions by C4C) have been conducted in Haiti, Malawi, Morocco, Nepal, Nigeria, Peru, and Turkey. As of January 2022, and under God's direction, C4C has completed 112 missions, built 15 churches, and had 2,694 members representing 70 countries (Climbing for Christ, n.d.).

Snowboarders and Skiers for Christ (SFC)

Combining a love for Jesus with a love for snow sports, Snowboarders and Skiers for Christ (SFC) embraces these two passions as the bedrock of their ministry. Rather than being individual Christians living among the snowboarding community, like-minded snowboarders decided to organize and join together. SFC is an MSM that was born in 1995 in New Zealand among a group of international shredders who felt called "to take the message to the mountain." *Shredding* is an expression familiar within ski culture and refers to the camaraderie of the slopes as riders carve through powdered snow, experience the adrenaline rush of speeding down a mountainside, and enjoy conquering all that nature can muster up (Hauge 2019). SFC founders recognized the dark side that plagued so much of the fun-loving, laid-back snow sport community—destructive substance abuse, escalating addiction rates, mental health issues, and an alarming rate of suicide. More than anything, they wanted the shred community to experience the healing grace and love of Jesus for themselves.

Initially, SFC had little organizational structure, quite characteristic of the free-spirited nature of the snowboarding community. Founders wrestled with their shared vision about integrating the gospel with their snow sport passions. Simultaneously and unbeknownst to them, pockets of Christians within the snowboarding community were emerging globally with the same concept for a ministry. Word soon traveled about this shared vision among the various unorganized Christian shredders, and they believed it was a testament to the moving of God's Spirit among His followers. Eventually, SFC drafted a mission statement along with vision and core values statements and a statement of faith. Multiple national chapters emerged and currently exist in 19 countries, along with 85 local expressions.

SFC serves as a values-based organization as opposed to a programs-based one. Each group looks different because they organize themselves to meet the unique needs of their own communities. They do share common core values known as the BRIDGE, which stands for the following:

Believing that faith is grounded in biblical truth.

Relationships are intentionally built, connecting Christian riders to their global network.

Identity of the laid-back, recreation-focused culture is appreciated, but that identity is facing a crisis. SFC is found in an eternal identity with Jesus.

Doing, or selflessly demonstrating a love for Jesus by placing others before self and serving one another.

Gospel, the good news, is what is essential and most important.

Engaging, intentionally meeting people where they are, both physically and spiritually.

SFC has developed an online discipleship curriculum called The Being and Doing course. Their website provides devotional studies, podcasts, a monthly newsletter, announcements about upcoming events, and a video resource library with over 100 selections (Snowboarders and Skiers for Christ, n.d.).

Sports Friends

At first glance, they may have appeared reminiscent of the odd couple. Brian Davidson was a pioneering sports minister with over 20 years of experience, and Tripp Johnson was a successful investment banking executive. Yet they shared compatible competencies that fostered an ideal partnership. During his travels to more than 30 nations, Davidson appreciated the well-meaning intentions of sports ministry efforts, but many were short-lived because they failed to properly resource local churches for sustainability. God gave the two men a vision to develop viable church-based sports ministries in Africa, Asia, and the Americas to reach youth, their families, and their communities. They approached the global mission organization SIM about a possible partnership, and the proposal was readily endorsed. Trusting God's guidance, Johnson left the corporate world to become a full-time sports minister, and in 2002 both men relocated their families to Ethiopia to launch Sports Friends

(SF). Since its founding, SF has served thousands of churches and church planters around the world. Besides Ethiopia, SF has ministered in the African nations of Nigeria, Kenya, Malawi, Zambia, Ghana, Senegal, Niger, and Tanzania; in the Americas in the United States, Ecuador, and Peru; in the Southeast Asian nation of Thailand; and in the United Kingdom (Sports Friends, n.d.).

SF is a ministry of **SIM**, which believes that "no one should live and die without hearing God's good news, and believing to be called of God, they make disciples of the Lord Jesus Christ in communities where He is least known" (SIM website).

SF's four-part strategy seeks to equip churches and church planters to use sport as a means to make followers of Jesus:

1. *Share a vision* for local churches and church planters to use sports as a ministry tool. We believe sports are a powerful tool for crossing barriers, building relationships, proclaiming the gospel, discipling believers, and planting churches.

2. *Train Christian leaders* to start up sports ministry teams in their local church or as part of a new church-planting effort. We train church and mission leaders in how to develop fruitful sports ministries that will make disciples of Jesus Christ in a variety of contexts.

3. *Equip coaches* for sustainable ministry through ongoing support, encouragement, and trainings. We mentor, disciple, and significantly invest in these coaches' lives and ministries, helping them to live, lead, minister, and coach for the glory of God.

4. *Develop leadership capacity* of sports ministry coordinators, who will provide vision, guidance, and management of the local sports ministry movement and develop coaches at the local church level. (Sports Friends, n.d.)

SF has developed leadership training that equips indigenous sports ministers to plant churches within their homelands. Among their online resources, SF provides encouraging videos about their work and inspiring testimonies from people whose lives have been touched.

Additional examples of MSMs include Ambassadors in Sport and Christian Surfers International.

SIM—An international mission with a church-focused vision. Originating in the 1890s as the Sudan Interior Mission, the organization has expanded worldwide and is now simply known as SIM.

Equipping SMOs

As mentioned in chapter 12, the primary purpose of some SMOs is to equip local churches and Christian athletes with resources to encourage spiritual growth through sport endeavors (CSRM, Activ8Sports, Cede Sport, Unchartered Waters). Two additional noteworthy equipping ministries include ReadySetGO and Christians in Sport.

ReadySetGO

ReadySetGO's motto is "making disciples for Christ in all nations in the world of sport and play." ReadySetGO is an equipping ministry, preparing Christ followers to use sport as a ministry tool in and through the Church. They provide an expansive online library of free sports ministry resources.

Their name is derived from a race analogy. *Ready* is the gathering at the starting blocks. Within the world of sports ministry, it corresponds to the gathering of people to catch the vision about the use of sport as a disciple-making tool. *Set* is firmly positioning oneself in preparation to burst out of the starting block. This image denotes the spiritual preparation of equipping followers with the ability to make disciples. *Go* is the pulsating action as the race commences, and it represents the strategy, methods, and actions taken to make disciples.

Runners do not run a race once, but repeatedly compete. Every race follows the same pattern—a time to get ready, set, and go. The same pattern is emulated in disciple making: "Let us run with perseverance the race marked out for us, fixing our eyes on Jesus, the pioneer and perfecter of faith" (Hebrews 12:1b-2a). Jesus is the focus, the model starter and finisher of the great race.

ReadySetGO is a ministry of multiplication, equipping disciples to make disciples, who make disciples (ReadySetGO, n.d.).

Christians in Sport

During the mid-1970s, several British sportspersons began to pray for and discuss the dream of a fellowship network that would unite and encourage Christian sportspersons. They envisioned Christian athletes worshipping and witnessing in teams and clubhouses across the country. Former Oxford University bowler and Anglican clergyman Andrew Wingfield-Digby sensed people's growing excitement about "a marriage of sport and faith. Everyone wanted to raise the profile of Christian presence in sport" (Christians in Sport n.d.). According to BBC tennis commentator Gerald Williams, "We had a feeling that God could do something through Christians in sport if they made themselves available to Him" (Christians in Sport n.d.).

On June 19, 1976, 80 Christian sportspersons gathered for a dinner at the Park Lane Hotel in London. Brian Adams, a British race-walking team member competing in the Montreal Olympics, recalled the meeting: "It was great to be sent off to the Olympics with the mindset that what I'm doing in sport is for God. . . . Your identity is in Christ, and sport is an expression of that identity."

A second dinner was held a year later, followed by a third in 1978, attended by 400 guests. The level of interest in a Christian sports network was flourishing, and the dream came to fruition in 1980 with the establishment of Christians in Sport (CIS). Four years later, Reverend Wingfield-Digby took a step of faith, leaving his clergy position to become the director of CIS.

Prayer sustained and continues to be the organization's bedrock. Since the early visionary days, prayer meetings, and dinners, CIS now supports 10,000 Christians in the world of competitive and elite sports. Over 1,000 leaders have been trained in sports evangelism and discipleship. CIS ministers through sport camps, conferences, prayer summits, and university work, and their network has expanded to 150 countries worldwide. Their website includes practical print and video resources (e.g., testimonies and teachings) to encourage and instruct Christian athletes in a variety of sporting venues (Christians in Sport, n.d.).

SPORTS MINISTRY IN ACTION

The Chicago Eagles Summer Academy

The Chicago Eagles was established in 1997 as one of the soccer-specific ministry branches of Missionary Athletes International (MAI). Since MAI's founding, thousands of children have attended MAI camps. A primary focus of this Midwest ministry has been the training of collegiate and high school student-athletes, equipping them through a variety of programs to be sports ministers.

The Summer Academy is an intensive two-month experience that challenges a player's faith while also training to raise the level of their game. Men's and women's teams compete in the Illinois U23 league and have on-field soccer training sessions four days a week. They receive curricular instruction about the integration of faith and sport. Players serve as role models

Wacky Wednesdays are a fun staff dress-up day at the Eagles' summer soccer camps.

coaching youth camps and sharing about their faith in Jesus. The summer culminates with a two-week international short-term soccer mission trip, working with church partners abroad. In recent years, Brazil has been the trip's destination. Match ministry, instructional clinics, and serving local churches have become their most widely used ministry approaches. An objective of the Academy is to return players to their colleges and universities better equipped physically and spiritually (Chicago Eagles, n.d.).

Melissa Graham is a current collegiate head women's soccer coach and former Academy player. She describes her experience:

> Serving with the Chicago Eagles Summer Academy was a transformational experience. I never would have imagined that a summer playing soccer, coaching camps, and partnering with local churches in Brazil and Chicago would change my life forever. God used those summers to open my eyes to see the life that was waiting for me in Him, to show me what it looks like to daily walk in step with His Spirit, and to fuel my passion for sports ministry. Not only was my life changed, but I was able to experience the Lord move in the lives of my campers, teammates, coaches, and host families. It was a powerful experience to see how God could use the game of soccer to bring the gospel message to so many. (Melissa Graham, pers. interview 2022)

SUMMARY

SMOs serve the mission of the Church through expanded specialized ministry capabilities. They use the popular cultural phenomena of sport to evangelize, disciple, and address the God-designed need of each human heart. Their methodologies might differ by type and substance of activity, but they share the common thread of seeking life transformations through the integration of the gospel with diverse sport and recreational pursuits. Ministering domestically and internationally, SMOs reach the sporting community through sport-minded Christian staff and participants.

REVIEW AND DISCUSSION QUESTIONS

1. What are some advantages of specialized SMOs?

2. Discuss qualities of a healthy SMO.

3. According to some Christian apologists, what is one of the major concerns about para-church ministries? What do you think about this concern?

4. Upon review of the SMOs discussed in this chapter, what are common ministry themes that thread their way through most of them?

5. What unique ministries stood out to you among the SMOs studied?

6. Of the SMOs discussed in this chapter, which ones would you most likely gravitate toward to work for and why?

7. Would you like to see a certain sport or recreational activity developed as a sports ministry? By their nature, should any sport or recreational activities be avoided for consideration?

The greatest cultural barrier to cross is an eternal one—a transfer from death to life.

CHAPTER 14

Cultural and Leadership Considerations

"Sports is a unique all-terrain vehicle that knows no bounds. It is international in scope, intercultural in appeal, and there are no cultural or social hang-ups. It moves swiftly through all the differences—race, religion, age, and gender. Sports is a great common denominator, opening doors to all levels of society. Teamed with ministry, the potential is incredible, the impact is staggering."

Russ Carr, founder of Sports Outreach Institute and Global School of Sports Ministry

LEARNING OBJECTIVES

After studying this chapter, you should be able to do the following:

- Understand the importance of knowing social and cultural norms within a sports ministry setting
- Explain the lesson of servanthood Jesus taught His disciples when He washed their feet and how His instruction relates to sports ministry practices
- Recognize the limitations of adherence to cultural norms through the encounter of Jesus with the Samaritan woman
- Assess the nonnegotiables that are never to be compromised when entering the context of another culture
- Explain why healthy team dynamics are important to a sports ministry organization
- Define friendship evangelism and why it is beneficial

As part of pretrip cultural training, a collegiate women's soccer team met in the home of career missionaries. They were discussing simple Amharic phrases such as "How are you?" "Thank you," and similar courtesies. None of the players had been to Africa previously nor did any of them speak Amharic. They listened and repeated phrases of the new language. Eventually, a player asked how to say, "Where is the bathroom?" The phrase was pronounced and practiced by everyone. The subject of bathrooms prompted the missionaries to speak further about the topic.

Toilet paper was an essential item included in each individual's packing list. Most public facilities (e.g., restaurants, service stations, markets) would have some form of toilet facilities, but toilet paper would not be provided. When traveling "down country," unlike along American highways, rest areas are unavailable. If a stop had to be made, travelers would go behind an ant hill. Ant hills varied in size, but many reached heights in excess of 8 feet (2 m)—plenty of height and width to accommodate privacy.

The missionaries told the team not to take themselves too seriously, to laugh at themselves, and to enjoy each occasion to learn from the experiences of a different culture. They shared a humorous account of one of their down-country trips. Their route would be a three-hour minivan excursion south of the capitol. On this occasion, none of the family members remembered to pack toilet paper. An hour into the trip, the woman realized that her lunch was not sitting well with her, and an immediate stop at the nearest ant hill was warranted. She hastily exited the van and several minutes later reappeared with a sheepish grin, commenting that she no longer had any birr, Ethiopia's paper currency. (At the time of their story, 1,000 birr equated to just under 20 U.S. dollars). The trip briefly resumed when the son likewise needed to make his own emergency stop. He was wearing socks when he exited the van. Upon his return from behind the ant hill, the socks were gone. The imagined visual of the story was humorous, but their message was clear—always have access to toilet paper!

Ironically, a week later, a couple team members would experience their own ant hill story. Traveling the same down-country route as described by the missionaries, an ant hill pit stop became necessary. On this occasion, there was an added dimension; the player with urgent need had toilet paper, but she was recovering from pretrip knee surgery and could not bend to squat. A teammate offered to help, and both quickly scampered out of view behind a large ant hill. They later described the episode. With her warm-up pants dropped to her ankles, the player leaned herself forward while keeping her knee straight. Her teammate facing her, held both hands to provide balance. Their positioning was quite the sight for a busload of Ethiopians who suddenly appeared, traveling off the main road on the two players' side of the ant hill. One can only imagine the impression and bus conversations about the unusual scene they had witnessed of these two white girls!

Toilet paper, ant hills, and buses creating their own roadways are small samplings of the nuances of cross-cultural experiences. Wise leadership and sensitive cultural understanding are needed for effective sports ministry. Christ calls His followers to follow the example of His leadership by engaging the culture of the day. This chapter will explore cultural distinctives and the qualities of servant leadership that thrive when ministering in diverse settings and populations.

Cultural and Cross-Cultural Considerations

Culture is broadly defined. People share a common humanity, but the expressions of this humanity can differ greatly. Learning about culture means learning about people and their customs, values, and way of life. Sports ministry regularly engages in **cross-cultural** experience and communication.

---

culture—A way of life developed over time as people interact in community with each other. It is a social world characterized by everyday codes of conduct, dress, ritual, language, arts, symbols, beliefs, customs, and values.

cross-cultural—A relational comparison between cultures, an examination of their similarities and differences.

Learning about culture means learning about people and their customs, values, and way of life.

Jesus as a Cross-Cultural Type

Jesus' incarnation provides an example of a cross-cultural type. This example is not the typical relationship between two human cultures but is the unique encounter of heaven entering earth. Jesus intentionally leaves the undefiled culture of His domain to physically enter the corrupted cultural realm of this world. His incarnation also lays aside His divine nature, and he becomes a man, identifying with the frailties of human flesh. His example is likened to the differences experienced as one enters an unfamiliar culture. The following passage provides a description of Jesus' incarnation, a profound type of cultural exchange.

> *Who, being in very nature God, did not consider equality with God something to be used to his own advantage; rather, he made himself nothing by taking the very nature of a servant, being made in human likeness. And being found in appearance as a man, he humbled himself by becoming obedient to death— even death on a cross! (Philippians 2:6-8 NIV)*

The incarnation is God's choice to become a servant, a quality of His own divine nature. Throughout His earthly ministry, Jesus exhibits servanthood. He notices the lowly, speaks to the outcasts, and dines with sinners. He blesses children, forgives the adulterer, and heals the marginalized leper. His chosen 12 include commoners—fishermen and one holding the despised occupation of tax collector. If Jesus manifests the virtue of servanthood, then His followers will do likewise.

Elmer's Robe Metaphor

Cross-cultural specialist Duane Elmer proposes two metaphors that represent Jesus and one that corresponds with His followers: a robe and a towel. Referring to Jesus, the robe is His priestly divine nature as Lord. He is the "King of kings and Lord of lords" (1 Timothy 6:15; Revelation 19:16 NIV). He alone can fulfill this role. He alone bears the authoritative name for which every knee will bow and every tongue will confess the truth concerning His messianic identity (Philippians 2:10-11). Jesus is the singular answer to the question raised by the angelic orator of John's revelation:

> *Then I saw in the right hand of him who sat on the throne a scroll with writing on both sides and sealed with seven seals. And I saw a mighty angel proclaiming in a loud voice, "Who is worthy to break the seals and open the scroll?" But no one in heaven or on earth or under the earth could open the scroll or even look inside it. I wept and wept because no one was found who was worthy to open the scroll or look inside. Then one of the elders said to me, "Do not weep! See, the lion of the tribe of Judah, the Root of David, has triumphed. He is able to open the scroll and its seven seals." (Revelation 5:1-5 NIV)*

Elmer's Towel Metaphor

Jesus is also represented in the towel. His servant nature culminates at the washing of His disciples' feet (John 13:1-17). Foot washing was a common cultural practice, a menial task reserved for slaves. The dusty paths and dirt roads of the warm climate were conducive to sweaty, grimy feet. Upon entering a home, the host would typically have the feet of his guests washed. Some rabbis taught that the practice was so demeaning that it was beneath a Jew to do it—even for a Jewish slave (Cosper 2014).

The disciples had been posturing about their own potential for elevated positions. They disputed among themselves who would be the greatest (Luke 9:46; 22:24). James and John approached Jesus with a request that one be seated on His right and the other on His left when He came into His glory (Mark 10:37). When the other 10 disciples heard about this request, they became indignant. They, too, coveted a seat of honor and feared they would be left out if the request made by these two sons of Zebedee was granted. The disciples failed to recognize the example and teaching of Jesus. Their perspective was tainted by the concept of earthly rule, yet Jesus was advocating servanthood, displaying priority for others rather than oneself (Lane 1974).

> [Jesus said,] "Whoever wants to become great among you must be your servant, and whoever wants to be first must be slave of all. For even the Son of Man did not come to be served, but to serve, and to give his life as a ransom for many." (Mark 10:43-45 NIV)

Jesus exemplified servanthood from the moment of His transition from heaven to earth, born in a lowly manger as the earthly son of a carpenter. He would die stretched on a wooden cross, nails impaling his hands and feet, the familiar materials of His childhood trade. He represents the epitome of a man of the towel. He came not to be served, but to serve—to completely give of Himself as the sacrificial lamb of redemption (Elmer 2006). As Jesus wrapped a towel around his waist and stooped down to wash the feet of His disciples, He assumed the role of the least. He was visually reiterating the lesson of servanthood the 12 were to emulate. When Jesus finished washing the disciples' feet, He clarified the lesson for them:

> When he had finished washing their feet, he put on his clothes and returned to his place. "Do you understand what I have done for you?" he asked them. "You call me 'Teacher' and 'Lord,' and rightly so, for that is what I am. Now that I, your Lord and teacher, have washed your feet, you also should wash one another's feet. I have set you an example that you should do as I have done for you. Very truly I tell you, no servant is greater than his master, nor is a messenger greater than the one who sent him.

> Now that you know these things, you will be blessed if you do them." (John 13:12-17 NIV)

It was not beneath Jesus to wear the towel, and His followers were to do the same.

Throughout His earthly ministry, Jesus was preparing the inner circle of disciples for future leadership roles as apostles of the Church. Their leadership style was not to follow the example of the religious rulers of their day. The Pharisees pompously offered public prayers to be noticed (Matthew 6:5; Luke 18:9-14). They chose the seats of honor at banquets and the high places of the synagogues (Luke 14:7-11; 11:43). The leadership of Jesus and His followers was enacted in the role of humble servants.

> A dispute also arose among them as to which of them was considered to be greatest. Jesus said to them, "The kings of the Gentiles lord it over them; and those who exercise authority over them call themselves Benefactors. But you are not to be like that. Instead, the greatest among you should be like the youngest, and the one who rules like the one who serves. For who is greater, the one who is at the table or the one who serves? Is it not the one who is at the table? But I am among you as one who serves." (Luke 22:24-27 NIV)

Like Jesus, His followers were to lead by humbly, wearing the towel.

Wearing the towel does not come instinctively. The natural inclination is to seek recognition and to take the best seat, the top job, the place of honor, the easy path. It is unnatural to serve someone else while dismissing serving oneself. Consequently, the natural must be transformed. Wearing the towel becomes the new natural, a changed essence. In Christ, a person is re-created (2 Corinthians 5:17), and the exhortation of Scripture is to actually live the faith one believes (Galatians 5:25; James 2:17-18). A new perspective is born—viewing people and life circumstances through the eyes of Jesus. The objective is to become increasingly more like Him. The character of a servant heart is paramount as sports ministers encounter various cultures.

Cultural Perspective Awareness

One's own cultural bias interprets the differences seen in others. Upbringing and personal experience shapes understanding whether accurate or not. A desire to serve in another culture is frequently hindered by these presumptions. Intentions might be

Upbringing and personal experience shape understanding about culture.

well-meaning, but a disguised attitude of superiority can undermine the efforts. Elmer identifies several cloaked attitudes of superiority that surface in the midst of serving in a cross-cultural setting:

- *I need to correct their error (meaning I have superior knowledge, a corner on truth).*
- *My education has equipped me to know what is best for you (so let me do most of the talking while you do most of the listening and changing).*
- *I am here to help you (so do as I say).*
- *I can be your spiritual mentor (so I am your role model).*
- *Let me disciple you, equip you, train you (often perceived as "let me make you into a clone of myself"). (Elmer 2006, 17)*

Paul Hiebert, a leading missiological anthropologist, adds a similar list—signs indicating rejection:

- Cutting people off when they are talking
- Laughing at their remarks
- Forgetting their names
- Questioning their facts
- Belittling their comments
- Not trusting them with money or tasks

He knew of a missionary who refused to let the "natives" hold their tickets for fear that they would lose them. "By doing so, he expressed distrust as loudly as if he had said it in words" (Hiebert 1986, 84). Elmer contends that living in a North American culture breeds an attitude of being the most powerful, best educated, technologically advanced, and world leader. Truth can be found in this statement, but it also wields a "better-than-you" mentality. Being aware of one's own predisposed dispositions will help the discerning process as the distinctives of other cultures are examined.

Building Understanding Promotes Friendship Evangelism

Understanding the people to be served is essential in cross-cultural ministry. Getting to know people is an expression of care. It is an investment of time and energy. It sends the message that a person is valued and time spent with them is worthwhile. Years ago, two sports ministry families relocated to a new country and practiced friendship evangelism. They lived in proximity with the people they came to serve. Their entire first year was spent developing relationships by getting to know others. Family members were met, occupations discussed, conversations enjoyed, likes and dislikes discovered—they ate together, played together, spent time together. The gospel was not formally presented, though it was being demonstrated by the care shown. Through mutual interest, a trusting relationship was unfolding, not one of pretense but of genuine heart-to-heart connection. The ministry couples waited for God's timing before they embarked on sharing the gospel. Even then, the sharing was measured to keep pace with the readiness of their friends. In **friendship evangelism** friendship is not sought for the purpose of manipulation. Devoted friends share their deepest concerns and interests. Speaking to anyone about Jesus is an important opportunity, but speaking to a friend increases the fervor of conversation because of the associated personal attachment. Friendship evangelism is not a duty but is motivated by the genuine love for a friend—someone known and for whom there is great care. Too often, ministry is task oriented and agenda driven rather than focused on people. Hiebert emphasizes the importance of caring relationships, ones that genuinely take an interest in the people being served.

> Relationships in mission service must take priority over the task, particularly at the beginning. Trust in the message depends first upon trust in the messenger. Trust building begins with an interest in and acceptance of those among whom we serve. . . . True interest expresses itself in many ways. It is seen in our desire to learn about the people, their lives, and their culture. It is reflected symbolically in our willingness to wear their type of clothes, try their food, and visit their homes. It is demonstrated in hospitality, when we invite the people into our homes and let their children play with ours. . . . No task is more important in the first years of ministry in a new culture than the building of trusting relationships with the people. Without these, the people will not listen to the gospel, nor will we ever be accepted into their lives and communities. (Hiebert 1986, 83,85)

People need to be understood as people, a shared humanity with families, feelings, and dreams. "They" needs to be transformed to an inclusive "we," created in the image of God with an eternal destiny. Building relationships of trust fosters friendship evangelism.

Gospel Contextualization

Communicating the gospel requires spoken and written language. Language is a fundamental component of culture. **Gospel contextualization** is when the biblical message extends to all people groups and is not altered but is communicated differently based on cultural variations.

> Culture runs deep. It is like an iceberg with much more under the surface than above. Understanding this truth is important for two reasons. First, Christians need to actively learn the culture of others. We can seek to understand how people think, what they feel and how they see the world. This is especially true for local churches in North America that now find themselves living next to Muslims, Buddhists, Hindus, and scores of other groups. Our neighbors are increasingly different than us, and it is our gospel responsibility to understand them so we can clearly communicate the good news of Christ to them.
>
> Secondly, culture runs deep in us, too. Our culture subtly influences our foundational beliefs about life, family, faith, and society. Often, we are unaware of how much this affects the way we communicate with others—including how we communicate the gospel. (Cook 2019)

Word definitions might need to be explained. The use of illustrations and analogies will need to be applied with cultural sensitivities in mind. The message is shaped to best fit the cultural understanding of the listeners. Pray for discerning wisdom. Career missionaries and sports ministers Kevin and Cindy Austin accentuate this need to adapt the message to best fit the intended audience:

> Be careful to not lose sight of the ultimate goal. Do not be trapped into thinking my way is the "right way." Always be prepared to share, to listen, and encourage. Trust God and the experts around you. Be a learner. Finally, pray. Pray when you feel like it, and when you don't, pray until you do. (Austin, pers. interview 2022)

Humor and Cultural Faux Pas

The interactions between persons with differing cultural heritages inevitably become wrought with mistakes. As people learn from one another, misinterpretations will arise; they can sometimes be quite humorous. Elmer cites an incident in Kenya while visiting with a Maasai elder:

> As the Maasai elder approached us, our youngest son, Marc, did as he had been told: "Step forward and bow your head. The elder will put

---

friendship evangelism—A relationally oriented form of presenting the gospel. It builds authentic friendships of care and trust, while patiently waiting on God's timing to address spiritual concerns.

gospel contextualization—The adaption of the biblical message for a particular culture.

Kevin and Cindy Austin, career missionaries and sports ministers serving with Wesleyan Global Partners in the Czech Republic: "Pray when you feel like it, and when you don't, pray until you do."

his hand on your head and offer a greeting." It was the way for Maasai children, and we would honor their ways. The Maasai elder proceeded to spit on his head three times. Confusion flooded our minds trying to understand what had just happened. Then Marc stepped back to the side of his mother and said, "Mom, that man spit on me. He spit on me." His mother answered, "Yes, we must wait and see what it means," and the elder stepped forward to greet us in a more traditional, Western way. Later we asked a friend who knew the Maasai how we should interpret the spitting on our son. He laughed and said, "It was a blessing. They do it all the time." Marc didn't feel blessed, and we were skeptical. But with further information we began to understand. The Maasai believe that when it rains on their arid land, God is spitting—God is blessing them. (Elmer 2016, 126-127)

Jesus used spittle as He healed the man with blindness at Bethsaida (Mark 8:22-26).

Learning about new cultures can be stressful, and we might fear the possibility of offending neighbors. Yet they are learning as well, and may share the same anxieties. Awkward encounters with cultural norms and attempts to navigate language barriers can lead to embarrassing situations that can prove to be humorous in hindsight. Here are two such examples.

An American team was in the Middle East sitting in the lobby of a hotel when a woman abruptly leapt from her seat with a horrified expression. She dashed out of the room only to return moments later with the disturbed-looking hotel manager. He asked the team to please not cross their legs when seated because the bottom of their shoes pointed at the woman and her friend. He explained that this posture was an extreme offense in their culture.

On the same trip, the team's leader was first to arrive and take a seat in the church. His action was greeted with much laughter from his hosts, who informed him he was sitting on the women's side of the church.

During a competitive end-to-end soccer match in Austria, the sports ministry team scored a dramatic goal. The team's coach jumped to his feet and excitedly yelled in German what he thought was "We scored! We scored!" only to have the missionary quietly ask him why he was yelling "Shut the gate! Shut the gate!"

Understanding cultural meanings broadens one's perspective, whether it is an ant hill, foot washing, spitting, customs, or language snafus. Mistakes will be made. Do not agonize over them. Lighten up, smile, and learn to laugh. Laughter can be a healing balm in the midst of clumsy awkwardness.

Humor is a great medicine for an excessive sense of self-importance, as it is a sign of inner security and self-esteem. We need to laugh with the people at our mistakes—we make many of them learning a new culture, and they are often very funny. Remember, people are not laughing at us, but at our strange ways and our cultural faux pas. Learning to laugh with them helps us overcome the fear of failure that so often keeps us from trying something new. We learn new cultures best when we try and fail, laugh, try again, and learn from our mistakes. (Hiebert 1986, 86)

Migrants and Refugees as Neighbors

As **migrants**, **refugees**, and **asylum seekers** relocate worldwide, they bring their cultural identities with them.

The vast majority of refugees are hosted by neighboring developing countries. According to the Global Trends Report, in 2020 82.4 million people were forcibly displaced worldwide; 42 percent of those people were children under age 18. The United Nations High Commissioner for Refugees (UNHCR) estimated one million children were born as refugees between 2018 and 2020. In Europe the largest groups seeking asylum came from Syria, Iraq, and Afghanistan. There are also significant numbers from Libya and Somalia. Children seeking asylum represented 18 percent of refugees, and a third of that percentage were unaccompanied minors, a particularly vulnerable group (United Nations Refugee Agency, n.d.).

The Refugee Crisis in Austria

Global crises elicit a ministry response. God's people are called to pray and be equipped for action. Austria borders Germany and faced such a crisis. The crisis peaked between 2014 and 2016 when thousands of refugees were pouring through their country en route to Germany. Many of the refugees were fleeing war and upheaval in their homelands, predominantly from Syria, Afghanistan, and Iraq. The number of refugees grew so large that Germany eventually closed its border, stranding many refugees in Austria. Rewinding for a moment to 2007, two university soccer playing graduates, Nate Brewer (Pt Loma Nazarene University, CA) and Grant Knight (Cedarville University, OH), pioneered a new soccer ministry program, The Global Player Initiative (GPI). Landing in Vienna, they joined Austrian soccer teams and used the platform of soccer to reach not only the soccer community but their surrounding neighborhoods. Bible studies were started at nine different coffee shops in the city, ministry to the homeless and drug addicted took place, and outreach expanded to children of Turkish immigrants who gathered in the parks to socialize and play soccer. Over time the program moved from Vienna to Salzburg with approximately twenty male and female soccer player participants. As refugees began flooding into Austria the outreach shifted attention to these new arrivals. Brewer recounts the scene he witnessed at a major train station in Vienna:

I had read in the newspapers about the refugee wave coming but wasn't prepared at all for the reality of what I saw. At Westbahnhof, every train ending there unloaded a huge amount of refugees. The place was packed with bodies, like a mosh pit at a concert, or a mass of people trying to get in a soccer stadium at the same time. People were yelling in different Middle Eastern languages, presumably Farsi and Arabic, and Austrian officials were trying to direct traffic, but it was impossible. It was chaos. There was nowhere for the people to go, so they just set up camp right there in or around the train station. Men, women, and children, exhausted from the journey, but simultaneously relieved to have arrived in western Europe. (Brewer, pers. interview 2022)

Ministry to the Stranger

Salzburg, Austria, is close to the border of Germany. It is a picturesque region with rugged mountains, lavish cathedrals, and historic castles. It was the setting for the Academy Award–winning movie *The Sound of Music.* As a border city, Salzburg was inundated with stranded refugees. How would they survive? Where would they find housing and food accommodations? They must not be made to feel like outcasts. Leaders from local churches and mission organizations gathered to discuss and pray about these concerns. The refugees needed care. Those gathered knew the Scriptures were filled with mandates imploring God's

---

migrants—People moving from one country to another, primarily to improve their lives through employment opportunities or educational pursuits or to reunite with family members.

refugees—People who are forcibly displaced, fleeing their countries for reasons such as war, persecution, sexual violence, and forced labor. Environmental reasons could also cause one to flee one's country (e.g., drought and famine).

asylum seekers—People in the process of seeking political refuge and protection from the homeland.

people to minister to the needs of the stranger by feeding, clothing, and showing hospitality (Deuteronomy 10:19; Psalm 146:9; Romans 12:13). Jesus declared that acts of kindness shown "to the least" was equated with ministry to Him (Matthew 25:35, 40). Even angels have been the benefactors of such hospitality: "Do not forget to show hospitality to strangers, for by so doing some people have shown hospitality to angels without knowing it" (Hebrews 13:2 NIV). Action on behalf of the refugees had begun.

The Vision of a Soccer Ball

Ministry among the refugees still lacked a point of connection. They were from African and Middle Eastern countries. The people of Salzburg were European. The typical cultural differences loomed large. What could unify and bring this conglomerate of people together? A small church gathering commenced with a 24-hour prayer and fasting vigil, seeking wisdom from God. Upon the conclusion of prayer, a woman said, "It seems strange, but throughout the entire time of prayer, the vision of a soccer ball kept coming to my mind." This woman did not have a soccer background or interest in the sport. A discussion ensued. Soccer made complete sense. All the represented nations played soccer. Despite language and other cultural barriers, soccer unified them and would become the point of mutual connection (Danny Patton, pers. interview 2018).

A Soccer Ministry and the Tournament of Nations

Through the combined efforts of church partners and sports ministries in Austria, Germany, the United States, and Egypt, an organic soccer ministry was formed in Salzburg. Local Austrian soccer participants and clubs joined the cause. Refugee soccer leagues were formed, tournaments conducted, and soccer camps developed for Austrian and refugee children alike. A men's collegiate team from the United States helped kick off future events with a big game that featured a large group of refugees.

A U.S. collegiate women's soccer sports ministry team came to play in Salzburg, and they opened up by playing a match with an Afghan men's team. A couple days later, the women played in the Tournament of Nations, with teams representing each refugee country. Rather than playing as a separate team, the women were split into groups of three and placed on each of the men's teams. It might have violated cultural norms to have Christian women playing alongside Muslim men, but the tournament ran smoothly, and everyone enjoyed the play and interaction. When the day concluded, the women's team joined together to sing a couple worship songs for the men's teams. Translators let the men know the lyrics of each song. The women were only there as part of a short-term mission opportunity, but their participation helped the ongoing ministry of the

A unique exchange of cultures: a soccer match between a collegiate women's team and an Afghan men's team.

Interview With a Professional

Jill Ireland

BSc (Hons), physical education and sports science, Loughborough University

Postgraduate certificate in secondary education, physical education and geography, Loughborough University

BA (Hons), biblical and intercultural studies, All Nations Christian College

Deputy Global Leader and Southeast Asia Regional Coordinator at Sports Friends, a ministry of Serving in Mission (SIM)

Courtesy of Jill Ireland.

After coming to faith through the witness of a university field hockey teammate, Jill's conversion has shaped her calling as she has served in sports ministry ever since, wanting to help others come to know and grow in Jesus within the context of sport. For nine years Jill served with Christians in Sport, based in the United Kingdom, in a variety of roles in student, camp, elite athlete, training, and international ministry, while also playing National Premier League hockey. Sensing a call to cross-cultural ministry, Jill joined SIM's Sports Friends, which trains and equips leaders in local churches to make disciples through sport. Jill has been serving with Sports Friends for 15 years, 9 of which were based in Thailand, leading Sports Friends teams and ministry in Southeast Asia.

What leadership attributes do you consider most essential for a sports minister?

A key attribute essential for any leader is humility—a willingness to learn, to serve, to engage in sports ministry in a way that best serves the needs, context, and situation of the people with whom you are working—not your own needs, preferences, or comfort. We are to imitate Christ's example as highlighted in Philippians 2, taking the nature of a servant.

What are common hurdles faced in cross-cultural sports ministry?

The challenge of entering into, living, and working in a culture that is not your own raises many hurdles: understanding the local language, culture, and values; gaining trust and developing authentic genuine relationships as an "outsider"; building credibility in the arena of sport; working in multicultural teams; listening and learning about the religious context in which you are working and how to live a life that commends Jesus Christ and how to speak sensitively and winsomely about Him.

For you personally, what have been some of the adjustments you have had to make living and ministering in another culture?

So many—months and years of language learning (it's never completed!); learning to adjust to local foods, culture, climate, sports; the challenge of building relationships in a language and culture different from my own; adapting my leadership and management to meet the needs of the context. Living far away long term from family, friends, home church, and community can bring its challenges, though developing new friendships cross-culturally is incredibly life giving and diverse.

How is the gospel presented in your current ministry setting?

Sports Friends seeks to train, equip, and support leaders in the local context to make disciples through sport in their communities. How the Apostle Paul ministered among the Thessalonians is a great example of this (1 Thessalonians 2:8). Paul loved the Thessalonians so much that he was delighted to share not only the gospel of God, but his life as well. We are thrilled to see many Christian coaches around the world modeling this, sharing their lives and love for sport with young people and sharing the gospel as they have opportunity.

Besides evangelism and discipleship, what other needs are being addressed through your ministry?

As a training and equipping ministry, we not only seek to train Christian coaches in churches and church planters to make disciples through sport, but we also want to build capacity for sports ministry within national church denominations and church-planting networks. We do this by training leaders and sports ministry coordinators within national denominations. Sports Friends' primary focus is disciple making, though during the Covid pandemic we responded by supporting our church partners and coaches, and communities in which they work, with food aid and practical needs.

What affects you the most in your ministry?

Lives changed by the gospel! The power and potential for sport to provide an arena for developing genuine, authentic, ongoing relationships through which the gospel can be shared respectfully as lives are shared, as sport is enjoyed, as relationships are developed, as truth is explained, and love is given.

What recommendations do you have for students as they prepare for service in a cross-cultural sports ministry setting?

Be faithful in doing sports ministry and sport outreach in your home context first—this provides the training ground for great learning, building experience, gaining confidence, and developing knowledge, as well as an opportunity to test your calling, attitudes, and skills. Develop a learner attitude; embrace change, spontaneity, and flexibility; and have a healthy sense of humor—an ability to laugh at yourself. These are all essential in cross-cultural settings. (Jill Ireland, pers. interview 2022)

---

churches and career missionaries. The free exchange and availability of information is closing some of the cultural gaps that were so rigid years ago. Sometimes introducing new experiences can broaden cultural understanding if done in a loving and respectful way.

The soccer ministry among the refugees continues to flourish along with other ministries of housing, dinners, winter coat drives, education, job training, and so on. As love is tangibly expressed, members of the refugee community are asking questions about this Jesus they see in the lives of their Austrian friends.

Jesus Adapts to Cultural Norms

Adaptation to religious and social cultural norms are evident in the early life of Jesus. Eight days following his birth, in accord with the law of Moses, Jesus was circumcised. When the time of purification was accomplished, typically at least 40 days after birth, Jesus was presented for dedication at the temple. According to the customs of the law, Joseph and Mary sacrificed a pair of doves or young pigeons. This type of sacrifice was indicative of a poor family who could not afford to sacrifice a lamb (Geldenhuys 1979, 118). Every year, His family traveled to Jerusalem to celebrate the feast of the Passover. On one occasion,

at age 12, Jesus prolonged His visit in Jerusalem to sit with the Jewish teachers. They were amazed by His understanding (Luke 2:47).

As Jesus embarked upon His ministry, He, along with His disciples, were invited as guests to a wedding in Cana. When the wine ran out, Jesus' mother mentioned it to Him. He had six large jars filled with water. Jesus then instructed the servants to draw some to take to the master of the banquet. Upon tasting, the master declared that the customary practice was to serve the best wine first and the cheaper wine after everyone had had too much to drink. Yet they had saved the best for last (John 2:1-12). Perhaps Jesus broke the custom by producing the best wine, but the point is that Jesus attended a wedding, a special social custom of His day.

Jesus attended the feast of tabernacles (John 7) and regularly celebrated the Passover (John 2:13; 6:4; 11:55). He regularly visited and taught in the synagogue (Luke 4:16). When He healed a man with leprosy, He instructed the man to present himself to the priest and offer the sacrifice in keeping with the commands of Moses (Mark 2:40-44). Jesus dined with people (Luke 19:5) and used ordinary customs and daily life traditions as subjects of His parables (Matthew 13:1-9; 18:21-35; 22:1-14; Luke 15:11-32). Jesus declared that He had not come to abolish the law or the prophets, but to fulfill it. He

Surge International/David Irby.

Postmatch worship song at the Tournament of Nations.

commended those who practiced and taught the law (Matthew 5:17-19). He told the crowds to obey the teachers of the law and the Pharisees who sat in the seat of Moses but to not follow their example, for they were guilty of not practicing what they preached (Matthew 23:1-3). Though He participated in the cultural and religious persuasions of His day, He did not observe all of them. He warned about Pharisees and teachers who negated the Word of God in preference for their own man-made traditions (Mark 7:9-13).

Samaritans: Jesus Bucks Cultural Norms

Jesus did not always abide by the cultural norms of His day. An example is His association with **Samaritans**. *Samaritan* was a degrading label assigned to Jesus by the Pharisees when He told them they did not belong to God: "Aren't we right in saying that you are a Samaritan and demon-possessed" (John 8:48 NIV)? Their insult insinuated that Jesus was heretical (Samaritan) and evil (demon possessed). The Pharisees had no qualms about connecting "Samaritan" with "demonic possession" in the same context.

The Good Samaritan

Jesus contradicted the cultural norm when He used a Samaritan traveler as a role model of compassion in His parable commonly known as the "good Samaritan." Unlike the Jewish priest and Levite who passed by a beaten robbery victim lying along the Jericho roadside, the Samaritan man rendered empathetic aid

(Luke 10:25-37). Jesus asked the Jewish law expert which of the three men proved to be a neighbor to the injured man. The expert replied, "The one who had mercy on him" (verse 37 NIV). It is noteworthy that the Jewish expert's response made no mention of the man being a Samaritan, an intentional omission to avoid his lips from such a pronouncement because of his disdain for these people. To him, how could a Samaritan possibly be viewed in a positive light? Yet Jesus lauded the Samaritan's actions and instructed the expert to "go and do likewise" (verse 37 NIV). To champion a Samaritan as the parable's role model was an outlandish breech of Jewish cultural norms.

Jesus and the Samaritan Woman

Jesus' encounter with the Samaritan woman at Jacob's well in Sychar (John 4:1-43) is another episode of a break with cultural expectations. Pharisees intensely disliked the Samaritans and avoided travel through their region as much as possible. If travel were necessary from Jerusalem to Galilee, they would take a longer route to bypass their territory (Morris 1971; Tasker 1960). Jesus did not avoid Samaria. Some commentators suggest that He chose this route because He was in a hurry and passage through Samaria was shorter Yet, Jesus prolonged His visit there by two days (verse 43). Jesus' willingness to enter Samaria and minister to its people foreshadowed the later proclamation of the gospel in the same region by His followers as recorded in Acts 8. They understood and followed Jesus' example to proclaim salvation to all people and in every location.

Samaritans—A people group inhabiting Samaria who held longstanding mutual hostilities with the Jews.

The story of this interview (with the Samaritan woman) and of its sequel makes it clear that, since the advent of the Christ, the people of God is to consist of all, whatever their race, their religious background or their moral standing may be, who acknowledge Jesus as the Savior of the world, who have received from Him the life-giving Spirit, and who worship God in spirit and in truth. (Tasker 1960, 75).

Jesus Dismissed Protocols of Defilement   An examination of Jesus' encounter with the woman at the well reveals several significant breaks with the cultural sentiments of the day. Jesus spoke to the woman, requesting a drink of water. The woman was well aware of the inappropriate nature of His request: "'You are a Jew, and I am a Samaritan woman. How can you ask me for a drink?' (For Jews do not associate with Samaritans)" (John 4:9 NIV). It would not be uncommon for a man to receive water from a woman since women typically were the ones to draw water, but she was a Samaritan. Jews were extremely cautious about personal defilement. According to the Mishnah, a collection of the oral traditions of Jewish law, "the daughters of Samaritans are [deemed unclean as] menstruants from their cradle . . . i.e., they are all regarded as ceremonially unclean" (Morris 1971, 258-259). Jews would not even use the eating and drinking utensils of Samaritans. Yet Jesus disregarded the prospect of defilement. He chose instead to enter into dialogue with this woman and even to drink from a Samaritan cup.

The Significance of Living Water   Jesus directed the conversation to "living water," a spiritual application. Jesus' first miracle was turning water into wine during a wedding feast in Cana (John 2). He later declared that those who were thirsty should come to Him and drink. By believing in Him, "rivers of living water will flow from within them" (John 7:37-38 NIV). New wine and living water were symbolic of the indwelling Holy Spirit who would come to take residence within the lives of Jesus' followers. As Jesus spoke about this living water, the Samaritan woman only understood the physical component of His words. She desired this water so that her tongue would no longer be parched and her visits to the well would become unnecessary. Yet Jesus was speaking about something deeper than physical water.

The Additional Stain of Sexual Immorality   Jesus told the woman to go and call her husband to join them. The woman replied that she had no husband. Jesus commended her honesty and noted that she had been the wife of five husbands, and the man she was currently with was now her sixth. Jesus was not only talking with a Samaritan woman, but He was also engaged in conversation with one who was stained by sexual immorality. How did Jesus know this woman's personal information? She suspected that He must be a prophet and turned the discussion away from herself to a question about cultural religious observances.

Jesus Challenged Religious Norms   The Jews and Samaritans were bitterly divided over the proper place of worship; the Jews contended that the site of worship was Jerusalem while the Samaritans preferred their own temple built on Mount Gerizim (Morris 1971). Again, Jesus disrupted cultural norms, siding with neither the Jews nor the Samaritans.

"Woman," Jesus replied, "believe me, a time is coming when you will worship the Father neither on this mountain nor in Jerusalem. You Samaritans worship what you do not know; we worship what we do know, for salvation is from the Jews. Yet a time is coming and has now come when the true worshipers will worship the Father in the Spirit and in truth, for they are the kind of worshipers the Father seeks. God is spirit, and his worshipers must worship in the Spirit and in truth." (John 4:21-24 NIV)

The woman conceded that when the Messiah came, He would explain all things. Jesus revealed His identity to her with the words, "I, the one speaking to you—I am he" (verse 26 NIV). The disciples, who had gone to town for food, returned to the scene at the well. They were astonished to see Jesus talking with a woman, yet they said nothing. They understood that Jesus did not always adhere to the rabbinic protocols of the day.

No rabbi would have carried on a conversation with a woman. One of their sayings ran: "A man should not be alone with a woman in an inn, not even with his sister or his daughter, on account of what men may think. A man shall not talk with a woman in the street, not even with his own wife, and especially not with another woman, on account of what men may say." (Morris 1971, 274)

The Samaritan Ripple Effect   The Samaritan woman was convinced that Jesus was indeed the Messiah. With great haste and enthusiasm (her water jar was left at the well), she returned to the town and told the people about her encounter with Jesus. The townspeople came to Jesus and urged Him to stay and speak with them. He remained for two days, and many believed Him to be the Savior of the world. Jesus had not only spoken privately with an adulterous Samaritan woman, He was also entertained by an entire town of Samaritans. He associated with a despised remnant. A providential meeting with a lone woman concluded with the ripple effect of an entire town hearing and believing Jesus.

The Principle of Jesus' Example

Once, Jesus was questioned by the Pharisees about His disciples acting unlawfully by breaking the cultural customs of religious law. His disciples had been picking heads of grain on the Sabbath.

> *[Jesus] answered, "Have you never read what David did when he and his companions were hungry and in need? In the days of Abiathar the high priest, he entered the house of God and ate the consecrated bread, which is lawful only for priests to eat. And he also gave some to his companions." Then he said to them, "The Sabbath was made for man, not man for the Sabbath. So the Son of Man is Lord even of the Sabbath." (Mark 2:25-28 NIV)*

Jesus pointed out that the cultural dictates of the Pharisees and their interpretation of the law were overly stringent. The human system of Sabbath observance was restrictive and denied its true divine purpose, as evidenced by Jesus' words proclaiming His Lordship over it. It would not be too great of a stretch to alter the discussion from the Sabbath to cultural norms. Culture has been made for people, not people made for culture, and just like the Sabbath, Jesus is Lord of everything, even of culture.

Jesus' earthly ministry provides evidence of respect for social and religious cultural norms, yet He was not bound captive to them. His encounter with the Samaritan woman reveals that He cared more about her as a person than He cared about obedience to culturally imposed prohibitions. In no way did He feel defiled by being associated with her. Cultural sensitivities are extremely important and need to be appreciated and observed as much as possible, but Jesus' principle is that conformity to culture is not the key. People are more important than adherence to their social norms and customs.

Sports Ministry Application

Respectful appreciation for cultural distinctives is an essential quality for cross-cultural ministry. Demonstrating genuine care by intentionally taking an interest in people and getting to know them will help to build meaningful and trusting relationships. Jesus focused on the needs of people first. He met them within the context of their daily lives: a man born blind seeking sight (John 9) and a woman healed from years of hemorrhaging (Luke 8:42-48), and despite objections, children gathered around Him to be blessed (Matthew 19:13-15). Like Jesus, sports ministers operate within the cultural dynamics of their daily settings. The needs of people come first. Honoring cultural distinctives are important, but humble love might require occasional divergence from cultural barriers. After all, the greatest barrier to cross is an eternal one—a change from death to life, from darkness to light, from lost to found.

Women as an Example of Cultural Norm

The account of Jesus and the woman at the well sheds light on the Lord's endorsement of women. Jesus did not shy away from confronting the Samaritan

Sports ministers serve as role models, especially for young, impressionable observers.

woman's deepest spiritual needs because of a cultural stipulation that a rabbi was not to privately speak with a woman. What about a women's soccer team playing matches in a culture where women do not play? Is it right for them to introduce something that is countercultural? Will their presence inspire young girls and women to play the game? What about a woman in a public setting speaking to a mixed-gendered crowd in a cultural context where men and women are separated when receiving instruction? Sometimes cultural norms need to be lovingly challenged and a new approach needs to be modeled. With advancements in travel and technology, the world has become less isolated and the ability to learn from one another has increased. The world is becoming a melting pot of new ideas with greater acceptance afforded. Sport has been a venue for this exchange of understanding. Worldwide events such as the Olympic Games and World Cup not only highlight sport but also open a window for people to view customs, lifestyles, and values. As women's sport grows worldwide, it challenges preconceptions and ideologies.

A collegiate women's soccer team traveled to a conservative region of Ethiopia. The women wore clothing to fit the cultural norm—long skirts revealing as little of their legs as possible. They were visiting church plants. In this context, the churches had been founded through soccer-specific ministries. When it was discovered that the visiting women were members of a soccer team, an informal match with the men and boys ensued outside the church building. The team played competitively despite remaining in their long skirts. Their male counterparts were surprised by their ability, and one man exclaimed afterward, "They play like men!" At that time, only a few Ethiopian women played soccer; most of them considered it a man's sport. When cultures intermingle, evaluations and adjustments are made as people learn from one another. Gender ideology and the role of women are areas that sports ministry addresses. Women tend to make exceptional sports ministers because of their strong relational skills.

Discernment Implications

When and where to challenge cultural practices is a matter of prayerful discernment. What components of culture are simply accepted? Are there nonnegotiables that are never to be compromised when entering a cross-cultural environment? If so, what are they? When conflicting values surface, are they to be addressed, and if so, how? Are right and wrong the same for each culture? Has Jesus introduced truth that encompasses every culture group? What about church polity, the mode of baptism, the order of a worship service, and so on? Can a sports ministry team offer an **altar call**? What about addressing cultural social norms like the abuse of women, the neglect of people with physical and cognitive disabilities, or the mistreatment of animals? Ministry teams will encounter numerous cultural aberrations. The example of Jesus' encounter with the Samaritan woman suggests that cultural norms do not supersede the needs of people. Yet sports ministry teams cannot randomly claim authority over every disagreeable cultural nuance. Answers to these types of questions require attentive consultation of the Scriptures and sincere, prayerful discernment.

Defining Nonnegotiables

Hypothetical questions give rise to concrete and specific affirmations. For example, throughout this textbook, the Word of God as revealed in the Scriptures is emphatically endorsed. When the Bible speaks, the words are true and authoritative. Just as the Bereans examined the Scriptures daily to confirm the truth of the Apostle Paul's words (Acts 17:11), so too the Bible is the measure for truth in our modern era. The Bible as the revealed Word of God is nonnegotiable. Likewise, when Jesus proclaims Himself as the only way to the Father (John 14:6) and His disciples affirm their belief in Him as the Savior (Acts 4:12, Philippians 2:9-11, I John 5:11-12), the deity and messianic mission of Jesus are non-negotiables. Thus, the written word (the Scriptures) and the Living Word (the word made flesh, Jesus, John 1:14) are foundational nonnegotiables regardless of the cultural setting.

Support for One Another

How ministry teams treat one another speaks volumes to observers about the authenticity of their faith. People want to know if what the faith team members profess is real. A children's chorus sings, "They will know we are Christians by our love."

---

altar call—A public occasion inviting respondents to receive Jesus as Lord and Savior.

People are more important than their social and cultural norms.

This represents not only an outward love for those being served, but also the inward love of the team members themselves. How well does the group get along? Do they enjoy each other and ministering together? Group dynamics is important for effective programmatic ministry but more importantly, for the winsomeness of their presence. Does the spiritual aura of the team attract curious observers? Does the group show they have a certain, different quality about them that is good? Team leadership is responsible for fostering a healthy team dynamic.

Leader-Led Teamwork

A coaching analogy contends a team that plays well together can beat a disunified team with more talent. The bonded chemistry of an athletic team can be formidable. A similar principle can be applied to a sports ministry team or organization. Healthy ministry team dynamics is a foundational objective. What qualities of a team leader help build dedicated team chemistry?

The Aroma of Christ

The most important aspect of leadership is to exemplify the presence of Christ. When an issue of neglect relating to the distribution of food confronted the early church, the apostles gathered together all the disciples and asked them to choose seven men from among themselves to supervise this responsibility. They gave two qualifications for the candidates—they must be "known to be full of the Spirit and wisdom" (Acts 6:3 NIV). To be full of the spirit is to be like Jesus. The life of a sports ministry leader is to diffuse the aroma of Jesus. When the character and life of this person is in view, Jesus is also seen. When they speak, Jesus is heard. A quality about this leader points people to Jesus. This type of leader will demonstrate in his or her own life what he or she expects to see in the lives of the team members.

Humble Servant

The Scriptures and the life of Jesus emphasize the importance of servanthood. The writers of the New Testament often begin their books by identifying themselves as "servants." To be a servant is to bear a humble posture. It is an other-centered approach to leadership. A pompous, self-focused leader enters a crowded room with a demeanor of "Here I am. Look at me. I have arrived." A servant leader enters the same room with, "There you are. How are you? It is good to see you!"

SPORTS MINISTRY IN ACTION

Sports Friends Kenya: Remembering the Forgotten

Ten-year-old Mary is home alone and locked in the house. Her father abandoned the family a long time ago, her mother is at work, while her grandmother is out. Mary has cerebral palsy and cannot speak.

Jane sits on the dirt floor outside. There is no sign of her parents, though her older sister is around. At nineteen years old, Jane has never ventured beyond the front entrance of the family's compound. She has Down syndrome.

Grace calls out to her family as they go about their business. She is a lively seventeen-year-old, who physically is the same size as a five-year-old. She cannot walk, though she can shuffle along the ground. Grace has cerebral palsy. (Coleman, n.d.)

In this region of Kenya, children with disabilities are considered cursed or bewitched. It is believed that their suffering is a result of sin, a punishment for their own sins, or the sins of their fathers. The parents of children with disabilities are ashamed and guilt ridden. The families are the "least" among the community and have overwhelming needs, yet rather than being helped, they are isolated and abandoned.

Sports Friends seeks to minister to the whole person, physically and spiritually. Motivated by the love of Jesus, they look straight into the eyes and hearts of these children with disabilities. Partnering with local churches, they embrace these families with a caring message of hope. Through a camp experience, the children and parents participate in physical activities, games, arts, crafts, singing, and dance. Comfortable housing and meals are provided in a beautiful setting of floral gardens. Joseph, a Sports Friends Kenya coach says, "We are reaching out to the hidden and forgotten in our community, who are at our doorstep."

Parents (typically only the mothers, since most fathers have deserted their families) face tremendous struggles. Like any mother, they want their children to be accepted, loved, and appreciated. Instead they are ignored, looked down upon, and scorned. The camp experience benefits the mothers as much as it does their children. While coaches tend to the needs of the children, parents participate in a trauma-healing program. The truth of God's word speaks against the lies of ignorance and prejudice imposed on these families. They are each made in God's image, regardless of appearance and ability. They are a blessing, not a curse, and are abundantly loved.

Parents share their burdens with one another, realizing they are not alone. The healing of wounded hearts begins. On the final night, a symbolic foot washing ceremony is celebrated as each Sports Friends coach washes the feet of the child and parent they have mentored. The marginalized families are honored and humbly served (Coleman, n.d.).

Like so many SMOs, Sports Friends Kenya uses sport and recreation activities, but their ministry addresses human needs extending well beyond the sporting venue. In this situation, they did not abide by the cultural norm to despise and shun the kids who are disabled and their families. Sports Friends Kenya chose to be countercultural; they chose to love, embrace, and welcome the "least" in their midst. They chose to serve like Jesus and respond according to His word.

"I was hungry, and you gave me something to eat, I was thirsty, and you gave me something to drink, I was a stranger and you invited me in, I needed clothes and you clothed me, I was sick and you looked after me, I was in prison, and you came to visit me." Then the righteous will answer him, "Lord, when did we see you hungry and feed you, or thirsty and give you something to drink? When did we see you a stranger and invite you in, or needing clothes and clothe you? When did we see you sick or in prison and go to visit you?" The King will reply, "Truly I tell you, whatever you did for one of the least of these brothers and sisters of mine, you did for me." (Matthew 25:35-40 NIV)

Dependent

Sports ministry leaders are utterly dependent on God. They might have education, experience, and skills, but nothing surpasses the sufficiency that is found in Christ alone. Figuratively, they understand that in themselves, they are but a clay pot: "We have this treasure in jars of clay to show that this all-surpassing power is from God and not from us" (2 Corinthians 4:7 NIV). The words of Jesus are known, understood, and applied: "I am the vine; you are the branches. If you remain in me and I in you, you will bear much fruit; apart from me you can do nothing" (John 15:5 NIV). This dependency is exercised through a life of prayer. Prayer is ceaseless, petitioning God for guidance, and seeking His counsel.

Teachable

Team-building sports ministers listen. They understand the relational community nature of the group. They value and seek the opinions of others. Group members appreciate being involved in the decision-making process. It gives them a sense of belonging; they feel valued. These leaders' own experiences are important, but they have never "arrived." There is always more to learn. They continue to grow in God's word. Passages read multiple times are alive with fresh insights. They crave and have an enduring teachable spirit.

Imperfect

Leaders serve an infallible God, a quality He alone possesses. Imperfection is the leader's trait, not intentional, but a reality. They have experienced failure and have learned to deal with it. Forgiveness has been received and bestowed to others. They are willing to take risks, step out in faith, and trust God. They know the strength of the spirit but also the weakness of the flesh. God is faithful, and they trust His word: "If we confess our sins, he is faithful and just and will forgive us our sins and purify us from all unrighteousness" (1 John 1:9 NIV). The group is secure because leaders acknowledge their own shortcomings and with such knowledge understand the frailties of others: "Be kind and compassionate to one another, forgiving each other, just as in Christ God forgave you" (Ephesians 4:32 NIV). Those who embrace the grace of forgiveness know how to graciously forgive.

SUMMARY

Exploring cultural differences is rewarding as the expanse of God's creative genius unfolds. His creation is marvelous in its diversity. Sports ministries are cross-cultural whether local, abroad, or both. Through His incarnation, Jesus provides an example of a cross-cultural type. He left the domain of heaven to fully enter the human experience. He attended weddings, observed religious festivals, dined with an array of people, and engaged in the typical social and cultural norms. Yet the needs of people were more important than the adherence to their customs.

Jesus taught His disciples the importance of servanthood. He washed their feet to demonstrate how they, too, were to serve others. He rightly broke multiple cultural barriers when He encountered the Samaritan woman at Jacob's well. His example provides principles for sports ministries to follow. Consulting Scripture and prayerful discernment are needed when leaders are confronted with opposing cultural values. Healthy team dynamics enable effective ministry and serve as a witness for curious observers. Team leaders are responsible for equipping and encouraging the group's chemistry. Qualities of such leaders include diffusing the aroma of Christ, serving humbly, exhibiting utter dependence on God, maintaining a teachable spirit, and acknowledging one's own shortcomings.

REVIEW AND DISCUSSION QUESTIONS

1. Why is familiarity with social and cultural norms beneficial in sports ministry?
2. What are the benefits of friendship evangelism?
3. What instructional purpose was served when Jesus washed the feet of His disciples?
4. How is the instruction that Jesus gave His disciples about servanthood applicable to sports ministry?

5. What do sports ministers learn about culture in the episode of Jesus and the Samaritan woman?

6. Are there nonnegotiables that are never to be compromised when entering a cross-cultural environment? If so, what are they?

7. How should sports ministers respond when values of another culture drastically conflict with the values of the ministry?

8. Identify a person in your life you consider to be a leader. What are the qualities he or she exhibits?

WORKS CITED

Chapter 1

Bada, Ferdinand. 2018. "The Most Watched Sporting Events in the World." World Atlas. July 3, 2018. www.worldatlas.com/articles/the-most-watched-sporting-events-in-the-world.html.

Busbee, Jay. 2013. "Nelson Mandela: 'Sport Has the Power to Change the World'." *Yahoo! Sports*. December 5, 2013. https://sports.yahoo.com/blogs/the-turnstile/nelson-mandela-sport-power-change-world-215933270.html.

Chukwuemeka, Edeh Samuel. March 26, 2022. "Most Popular Sports in the World 2022: Top 10 Most Watched." www.Bscholarly.com/most-popular-sports-in-the-world.

Connor, Steve. 2003. *Sports Outreach: Principles and Practice for Successful Sports Ministry*. Ross-shire, Scotland: Christian Focus Publications.

Das, Sourav. 2022. "Top 10 Most Popular Sports in the World." Sports Browser. May 17, 2022. www.sportsbrowser.net/most-popular-sports.

Dee, Liz. 2014. "The 1969 'Soccer Wars' Between Honduras and El Salvador." Association of Diplomatic Studies and Training. June 18, 2014. https://adst.org/2014/06/the-1969-soccer-war.

Dempsey, Steve. 2022. "Most Watched Sporting Events of All Time." *Stadium Talk*. August 4, 2022. www.stadiumtalk.com/s/most-popular-sporting-events-world-8fc518d95d104c16.

Fox, Judy. 2019. "Exclusive Interview: Nicaragua Olympic Committee." Video. 08:12. Accessed April 5, 2021. www.youtube.com/watch?v=NWkOF9Sc9fE

Fox Sports. 2016. "World Series Game 7 Averages Over 40 Million Viewers." *Fox Sports Press Pass*. November 3, 2016. www.foxsports.com/presspass/latest-news/2016/11/03/world-series-game-7-averages-over-40-million-viewers.

Guiberteau, Olivier. 2020. "Didier Drogba: How Ivory Coast Striker Helped to Halt Civil War in His Home Nation." BBC Sport. March 3, 2020. www.bbc.com/sport/football/52072592.

Henson, Steve. 2012. "What Makes a Nightmare Sports Parent . . . and What Makes a Great One?" *The Post Game*. February 15, 2012. www.thepostgame.com/blog/more-family-fun/201202/what-makes-nightmare-sports-parent.

Howden, David. 2014. "Football-Mad President Plays on While Burundi Fears the Return of Civil War." *The Guardian*. April 5, 2014. www.theguardian.com/world/2014/apr/06/football-mad-president-burundi.

Ignite International. 2021a. "Founder", igniteinternational.org/about#founder.

Ignite International. 2021b. "Our Core Values", www.igniteinternational.org/about#history.

Ignite International. 2021c. "Our History", www.igniteinternational.org/about#history.

Jeremiah, David. 2020. *Forward: Discovering God's Presence and Purpose in Your Tomorrow*. Nashville: Thomas Nelson.

Jones, Jeffrey. 2015. "As Industry Grows, Percentage of U.S. Sports Fans Steady." Gallup. June 17, 2015. https://news.gallup.com/poll/183689/industry-grows-percentage-sports-fans-steady.aspx.

Mason, Bryan. 2003. *Into the Stadium*. Milton Keynes, UK: Authentic Lifestyle.

McCown, Lowrie, and Valerie Gin. 2003. *Focus on Sport in Ministry*. Marietta, GA: 360 Sports.

My Best Ball. 2022. "Cristiano Ronaldo and Messi Have More Social Media Followers than Manchester United and PSG", February 3. https://mybestball.com/cristiano-ronaldo-and-messi-have-more-social-media-followers-than-manchester-united-and-psg/.

90 Min. 2020. "30 Biggest Social Media Accounts", January 29. https://www.90min.com/posts/6546643-30-biggest-social-media-accounts-in-sport.

Pedersen, Paul, and Lucie Thibault, eds. 2019. *Contemporary Sport Management*. 6th ed. Champaign, IL: Human Kinetics.

Reuters Life. 2010. "Sport Combats Conflict, Change Lives: Tony Blair." Reuters Life. January 15, 2010. www.reuters.com/article/us-tonyblair-idUSTRE65E60X20100615.

Swanson, Beth. 2017. "Youth Sports Participation by the Numbers." *Active Kids*. June 29, 2017. www.activekids.com/football/articles/youth-sports-participation-by-the-numbers.

Chapter 2

Baseball Almanac. 2021. "Billy Sunday Stats." Baseball Almanac. January 11, 2021. www.baseball-almanac.com/players/player.php?p=sundabi01.

Baseball Reference. n.d. "Billy Sunday." Baseball Reference. Accessed February 7, 2021. www.baseball-reference.com/players/s/sundabi01.shtml.

Bowman, Zac. 2013. "Massive Overhaul". Accessed August 20, 2022. Massiveoverhaul.blogspot.com/2013/02/paul-anderson.html.

Brown, Elijah. (1914) 1986. *The Real Billy Sunday: The Life and Work of Rev. William Ashley Sunday, D.D.* Chattanooga: Global Publishers.

Catton, Pia. 2010. "Records Fall at Sotheby's Auctions." *Wall Street Journal*, December 11, 2010. www.wsj.com/articles/SB10001424052748704457604576011812643642104.

Coakley, Jay. 2009. *Sports in Society: Issues and Controversies*, 10th ed. New York: McGraw Hill.

Ellis, William. 1936. *Billy Sunday: The Man and the Message*. Philadelphia: John C. Winston.

Evans, Christopher, and William Herzog II, eds. 2002. *The Faith of Fifty Million: Baseball, Religion and American Culture*. Louisville, KY: Westminster John Knox Press.

Garner, John, ed. 2003. *Recreation and Sports Ministry: Impacting Postmodern Culture*, First Edition. Nashville: Broadman & Holman.

Grubb, Norman. 2010. *C.T. Studd: Cricketer & Pioneer (1933)*. Fort Washington, PA: CLC Publications.

Hall, Jennifer. 2019. *Amos Alonzo Stagg: College Football's Man in Motion*. Charleston, SC: The History Press.

Henry, Ed. 2017. *42 Faith: The Rest of the Jackie Robinson Story*. Nashville: Thomas Nelson.

Hoffman, Shirl. 2010. *Good Game: Christianity and the Culture of Sports*. Waco, TX: Baylor University Press.

Jones, Bob, Jr. 1985. *Cornbread and Caviar*. Greenville, SC: Bob Jones University Press.

Keddie, John. 2007. *Running the Race: Eric Liddell—Olympic Champion and Missionary*. Webster, NY: Evangelical Press

Knickerbocker, Wendy. n.d. "Billy Sunday." Society for American Baseball Research. Accessed February 17, 2021. www.sabr.org/bioproj/person/billy-Sunday.

Ladd, Tony, and James Mathisen. 1999. *Muscular Christianity: Evangelical Protestants and the Development of American Sport*. Grand Rapids, MI: Baker Books.

Larson, Mel. 1945. *Gil Dodds: The Flying Parson*. Chicago: Evangelical Beacon.

Lester, Robin. 1995. *Stagg's University: The Rise, Decline, and Fall of Big-Time Football at Chicago*. Chicago: University of Illinois Press.

Linville, Greg. 2014. *Christmanship: A Theology of Competition and Sport*. Canton, OH: Oliver House.

Marshalltown Community Television. 2019. "Billy Sunday Baseball Evangelist." Video, 59:47. April 19, 2019. www.youtube.com/watch?v=visboF6MI-g.

Maryland Department of Juvenile Services. n.d. "Charles H. Hickey, Jr. School." Maryland State Archives. Accessed July 28, 2021. https://djs.maryland.gov/Pages/facilities/Charles-H-Hickey-Jr-School.aspx.

Martin, Robert. 2002. *Hero of the Heartland: Billy Sunday and the Transformation of American Society, 1862-1935*. Bloomington: Indiana University Press.

Mass Moments. n.d. "February 9, 1895: Holyoke Man Invents Volleyball." Mass Moments. Accessed March 3, 2021. www.massmoments.org/moment-details/holyoke-man-invents-volleyball.html.

McCasland, David. 2001. *Eric Liddell: Pure Gold*. Grand Rapids, MI: Discovery House Press.

McCasland, David and Patricia Russell. 2008. "Eric Liddell: Champion of Conviction." Video, 1:40:20. www.youtube.com/watch?v=poE9trD-3CQ

McCown, Lowrie, and Valerie Gin. 2003. *Focus on Sport in Ministry*. Marietta, GA: 360 Sports.

Mitrovich, George. 2005. "The Life and Faith of Jackie Robinson." *Good News*, May/June 2005. Accessed March 3, 2021. www.goodnewsmag.org/2011/03/the-life-and-faith-of-jackie-robinson.

Naismith, James. 1996. *Basketball: Its Origins and Development*. Lincoln: University of Nebraska Press.

New York Times. 1977. "Gil Dodds, Former Mile Record-Holder, Dead at 58." *New York Times*, February 5, 1977. www.nytimes.com/1977/02/05/archives/gil-dodds-former-mile-recordholder-dead-at-58.html.

Paul Anderson Youth Home. 1988. "The Uplifting Story of Paul Anderson." *Saturday Evening Post*. Accessed July 28, 2021. www.payh.org.

Rains, Rob, and Hellen Carpenter. 2009. *James Naismith: The Man Who Invented Basketball*. Philadelphia: Temple University Press.

Rampersad, Arnold. 1998. *Jackie Robinson: A Biography*. New York: Random House.

Ramsey, Russell. 1987. *God's Joyful Runner: The Family-Authorized Biography of Eric Liddell*. South Plainfield, NJ: Bridge Publishing.

Robinson, Jackie. 1995. *I Never Had It Made: Jackie Robinson, An Autobiography*. New York: Putnam.

Robinson, Jackie, and Michael Long. 2013. *Beyond Home Plate: Jackie Robinson on Life After Baseball*. Syracuse, NY: Syracuse University Press.

Rodeheaver, Homer. 1936. *20 Years With Billy Sunday*. Winona Lake, IN: Rodeheaver Hall- Mack.

Stagg, Amos, as told to Wesley Winans Stout. 1927. *Touchdown!* New York: Longmans, Green and Company.

Stark, Douglas, ed. 2021. *The James Naismith Reader: Basketball in His Own Words*. Lincoln: University of Nebraska Press.

Sunday, William. (1932-1933) 2005. *The Sawdust Trail: Billy Sunday in His Own Words*. Reprint of the original, published serially in *Ladies Home Journal*. Iowa City: University of Iowa Press, 2005.

Thomas, Lee. 1961. *The Billy Sunday Story: The Life and Times of William Ashley Sunday, D.D.* Grand Rapids, MI: Zondervan.

Triplett, Harlon. 1975. "Weightlifting Demonstration Ministry." July 16. Presentation at Maryland School for Boys, Baltimore, MD.

Watson, Nick, Stuart Weir, and Stephen Friend. 2005. "The Development of Muscular Christianity in Victorian Britain and Beyond." *Journal of Religion & Society* 7. https://dspace2.creighton.edu/xmlui/handle/10504/64420.

Woods, Ronald. 2016. *Social Issues in Sport*, 3rd ed. Champaign, IL: Human Kinetics.

Chapter 3

AIA. n.d.a. "54 Years and We're Just Getting Started." Accessed March 24, 2021. www.athletesinaction.org/about/history-and-finances.

AIA. n.d.b. "About AIA: AIA Commentary Pro Cycling Chaplains." Accessed February 24, 2021. www.aiacycling.com/what-we-do.

AIA. n.d.c. "Sports Complex, Fields and Facilities." Accessed August 25, 2022. www.athletesinaction.org/sports-complex/facilities/.

Atcheson, Wayne. 1994. *Impact for Christ: How FCA Has Influenced the Sports World*. Kearney, NE: Cross Training Publications.

Athletes in Action vs. Soviet Union Basketball. 1978. Official game program, Anaheim Convention Center, Anaheim, CA.

Cede Sports. n.d. "About." Accessed March 22, 2021. http://cedesports.org.

Cridlin, Jay. 2021. "YMCA Taps Tampa Executive for Next President and CEO." *Tampa Bay Times*, August 9, 2021. https://tampabay.com/news/business/2021/08/09/ymca-taps-tampa-executive-for-next-president-and-ceo.

Cru. n.d. "About Us." Cru. Accessed March 24, 2021. www.cru.org/us/en/about/what-we-do/milestones.3.html.

Curtis, Bryan. 2018. "NFL Scoops From Heaven." The Ringer. March 23, 2018. www.theringer.com/nfl/2018/3/23/17156312/nfl-offseason-scoops-sports-spectrum-matt-forte-adam-schefter.

Faith on the Field. n.d. "About Faith on the Field." Faith on the Field. Accessed March 1, 2021. https://faithonthe-fieldshow.com/about-faith-on-the-field.

FCA. n.d. "Fellowship of Christian Athletes Timeline." Fellowship of Christian Athletes. Accessed March 24, 2021. www.timeline.fca.org.

Hoffman, Shirl. 2010. *Good Game: Christianity and the Culture of Sports*. Waco, TX: Baylor University Press.

Inspired Motivation. n.d. "L.J. Cardinal Suenens Quote on Dreaming." Inspired Motivation. Accessed August 27, 2021. https://inspired-motivation.com/dream-big-pay-the-price-come-true-quote.

Inspiring Quotes. n.d. "Jim Elliot Quotes & Sayings." Inspiring Quotes. Accessed March 17, 2021. www.inspiring quotes.us/author/5319-jim-elliot.

KFA. 2017. "FCA: A Review of the Sports Ministry." KLOVE. April 6, 2017. www.fanawards.com/FCA-review-sports-ministry.

Ladd, Tony, and James Mathisen. 1999. *Muscular Christianity: Evangelical Protestants and the Development of American Sport*. Grand Rapids, MI: Baker Books.

Missionary Athletes International. n.d. "About Us." Missionary Athletes International. Accessed February 24, 2021. www.maisoccer.com/mai-history.

Murchison, Joe. 2008. *Caution to the Wind: Faith Lessons From the Life of Don McClanen*. Kearney, NE: Cross Training Publications.

NCCAA. n.d.a. "About Us." National Christian College Athletic Association. Accessed February 25, 2021. https://thenccaa.org/tournaments/?id=567.

NCCAA. n.d.b. "2021 Annual Convention Speaker: Tom Roy." National Christian College Athletic Association. Accessed June 8, 2022. www.thenccaa.org/sports/2019/4/25Tom_Roy.aspx.

PAO. n.d. "About." Pro Athletes Outreach. Accessed March 22, 2021. www.pao.org/about.

PR Newswire. 2020. "YMCA of the USA President and CEO Kevin Washington to Retire After 43 Years of Service." PR Newswire. Accessed December 3, 2020. www.prnewswire.com/news-releases/ymca-of-the-usa-president-and-ceo-kevin-washington-to-retire-after-43-years-of-srevice-301186198.html.

Pure History. 2012. "History of the YMCA." Pure History. January 4, 2012. https://purehistory.org/history-of-the-ymca-2.

Quebedeaux, Richard. 1979. *I Found It! The Story of Bill Bright and Campus Crusade*. San Francisco: Harper & Row.

Robinson, Jackie. 1995. *I Never Had It Made: Jackie Robinson, An Autobiography*. New York: Putnam.

Robinson, Jackie, and Michael Long. 2013. *Beyond Home Plate: Jackie Robinson on Life After Baseball*. Syracuse, NY: Syracuse University Press.

Shepherd Coach Network. n.d. "About SCN." Shepherd Coach Network. Accessed June 8, 2022. www.shepherd-coachnet.com/about-scn.

SI Staff. 1956. "Hero Worship Harnessed: Stars Turn to Evangelism and Score Hit With Admirers at Rally in Denver." *Sports Illustrated*, February 6, 1956. https://vault.si.com/vault/1956/02/06/hero-worship-harnessed.

Spoelstra, Watson. 1979. "Pro Athletes Outreach: A Training Huddle for Purposeful Pros." *Christianity Today*. March 2, 1979. www.christianitytoday.com/ct/1979/march-2/pro-athletes-outreach-training-huddle-for-purposeful-pros.html.

Weeks, Linton. 2015. "How the YMCA Helped Shape America." NPR. June 2, 2015. www.npr.org/sections/npr-history-dept/2015/06/02/410532977/how-the-ymca-helped-shape-america.

YMCA of Greater Charlotte. n.d. "Welcome to the Harris YMCA." YMCA of Greater Charlotte. Accessed August 6, 2021. www.ymcacharlotte.org/branches/harris.

YMCA Richmond. 2016. "America's Haven: The YMCA at 150." Video, 54:33. August 30, 2016. www.youtube.com/watch?v=sQLPnq_DHo8.

Chapter 4

Batterson, Mark. 2013. *All In: You Are One Decision Away From a Totally Different Life.* Grand Rapids, MI: Zondervan.

Bremner, Steve. 2013. "Are Short-Term Missions a Waste of Money?" Steven Bremner. October 2, 2013. www.stevebremner.com/2013/10/are-short-term-missions-a-waste-of-money.

Bureau of Labor Statistics. 2019. *Number of Jobs, Labor Market Experience, and Earnings Growth: Results From a National Longitudinal Survey.* Washington, DC: U.S. Department of Labor.

Charities Aid Foundation. 2016. "Gross Domestic Philanthropy: An International Analysis of GDP, Tax, and Giving." Charities Aid Foundation. www.cafonline.org/docs/default-source/about-us-policy-and-campaigns/gross-domestic-philanthropy-feb-2016.pdf.

Cru. n.d. "Carl and Noreen Dambman." Cru. Accessed March 26, 2021. https://give.cru.org/0007991.

Duval, Bethany. 2017. *The Art of Cross-Cultural Evangelism.* TEAM. July 25, 2017. https://team.org/blog/the-art-of-cross-cultural-evangelism.

Friesen, R.G. 2004. "The Long-Term Impact of Short-Term Missions on the Beliefs, Attitudes, and Behaviors of Young Adults." PhD diss., University of South Africa.

Greenfield, Craig. 2015. *"Stop Calling It a Short-Term Missions Trip. Here's What You Should Call It Instead."* Craig Greenfield. March 4, 2015. www.craiggreenfield.com/blog/2015/3/4/stop-calling-it-short-term-missions.

Hauerwas, Stanley, and Willimon, William Henry. 2014. *Resident Aliens.* Nashville: Abingdon Press.

Kendall, R.T. 2003. *The Anointing: Yesterday, Today, Tomorrow.* Lake Mary, FL: Charisma House.

Ladd, Tony, and James Mathisen. 1999. *Muscular Christianity: Evangelical Protestants and the Development of American Sport.* Grand Rapids, MI: Baker Books.

Loizides, Lex. 2008. "Factors That Assisted The Spread Of The Gospel." Church History Review. September 19, 2008. https://lexloiz.wordpress.com/2008/09/19/factors-that-assisted-the-spread-of-the-gospel-throughout-the-roman-empire.

NP Source. 2018. "Charitable Giving Statistics." Nonprofits Source. Accessed March 14, 2021. https://nonprofitssource.com/online-giving-statistics.

One Challenge. 2015. "Remembering Bud Schaeffer (Sports Ambassadors)." One Challenge. August 31, 2015. www.onechallenge.org/2015/08/31/remembering-bud-schaeffer-sports-ambassadors.

One Challenge. n.d. "History: How OC Began." One Challenge. Accessed March 25, 2021. www.onechallenge.org/history-how-oc-began.

Pew Research Center. 2018. "Origins and Destinations of the World's Migrants, 1990-2017." Pew Research Center. February 28, 2021. www.pewresearch.org/global/interactives/global-migrant-stocks-map/.

Pew Research Center. 2019. "Pew Research Center Religion and Public Life." Pew Research Center. October 17, 2019. www.pewforum.org/2019/10/17/in-u-s-decline-of-christianity-continues-at-rapid-pace.

Priest, Robert J., Dischinger, Terry, Rasmussen, Steve, and Brown, C.M. 2006. "Researching the Short-Term Mission Movement." *Missiology: An International Review* 34 (4): 431-450.

Probasco, LiErin. 2013. "Giving Time, Not Money: Long-Term Impacts of Short-Term Mission Trips." *Missiology: An International Review* 41 (2): 202-224.

Quatro, S. 2009. *Intentional Outreach: A Guide to Simple Church Sports Ministry.* Maitland, FL: Xulon Press.

Sneed, Stephen. 2019. "Hope for Samson." *Life and Change Experienced Thru Sports* (blog). September 18, 2019. www.laces.org/blog/samson.

Sports Friends. n.d. "Our Strategy." Sports Friends. Accessed March 30, 2021. https://sports-friends.org/strategy.

Srinivas, Arjun. 2018. "The First Ever International Cricket Match." Sportskeeda. December 30, 2018. www.sportskeeda.com/cricket/the-first-ever-international-cricket-match.

Steffan, Melissa. 2013. "The Surprising Countries Most Missionaries Are Sent From and Go To" Christianity Today. July 25, 2013. www.christianitytoday.com/news/2013/july/missionaries-countries-sent-received-csgc-gordon-conwell.html.

Vardhman, R. 2020. "20 Eye-Opening Statistics About The State of Career Changes in 2020." GoRemotely. March 21, 2020. https://goremotely.net/blog/career-change-statistics.

Within Reach Global. n.d.a. "Our Vision." Within Reach Global. Accessed March 28, 2021. https://withinreachglobal.org/about-us/#.

Within Reach Global. n.d.b. "The 10/40 Window." Within Reach Global. Accessed March 28, 2021. http://withinreachglobal.org/1040-window.

World Bank. n.d. "GDP (Current US$)." World Bank. Accessed March 12, 2021. https://data.worldbank.org/indicator/NY.GDP.MKTP.CD?most_recent_value_desc=true.

Chapter 5

Axisa, Mike. 2020. "Houston Astros Cheating Scandal: 10 Things We Learned From MLB's Nine-Page Investigative Report." CBS MLB. January 15, 2020. www.cbssports.com/mlb/news/houston-astros-cheating-scandal-10-things-we-learned-from-mlbs-nine-page-investigative-report.

Barna, G. 2011. "Research on How God Transforms Lives Reveals a 10-Stop Journey." www.barna.com/research/research-on-how-god-transforms-lives-reveals-a-10-stop-journey/.

Calvin, John. n.d. "Of Christian Liberty." Calvin's Institutes. Accessed July 27, 2022. http://ccel.org/calvin/institutes.v.xx.html.

Ellis, Robert. 2014. *The Games People Play: Theology, Religion, and Sport.* Eugene, OR: Wipf & Stock.

Erdozain, D. 2011. *Grace and Play: Christianity and the Meaning of Sport Lectures 1-5*. Vancouver: s.n.

Gill, J. 2020. "Homily for the Feast of the Presentation—Feb 2, 2020." *The Cross Stands while the World Turns* (blog). January 31, 2020. https://thecrossstands.blogspot.com/2020/01.

Grimm, Tommy. 2012. "When I Run, I Feel God's Pleasure." The Connection. August 10, 2012. https://sites.duke.edu/theconnection/2012/08/10/exercising-for-joy.

Harvey, Lincoln. 2014. *A Brief Theology of Sport*. London: SCM Press.

Hoffman, Shirl. 2010. *Good Game: Christianity and the Culture of Sports*. Waco, TX: Baylor University Press.

Hudson, Hugh, dir. *Chariots of Fire*. 1981. Los Angeles: 20th Century Fox.

Huizinga, Johan. 2014. *Homo Ludens: A Study of the Play-Element in Culture*. Mansfield Center, CT: Martino Publishers.

International Mixed Martial Arts Federation. n.d. "What Is MMA?" International Mixed Martial Arts Federation. Accessed July 27, 2022. https://immaf.org/about/what-is-mma.

International Olympic Committee. n.d. "Beyond the Games." International Olympic Committee. Accessed July 27, 2022. https://olympics.com/ioc/beyond-the-games.

Lewis, C.S. 1955. *Surprised by Joy: The Shape of My Early Life*. Orlando, FL: Harcourt.

Major League Baseball. n.d. "Houston Astros Mission, Vision and Values/Diversity." Major League Baseball. Accessed July 27, 2022. www.mlb.com/astros/team/jobs/mission.

Morrison, D. 2021. "25 Motivational Quotes From Vince Lombardi." Leaders. https://leaders.com/articles/sports-leadership/25-motivational-quotes-from-vince-lombardi.

National Collegiate Athletic Association. n.d. "Mission and Priorities." National Collegiate Athletic Association. Accessed July 27, 2022. www.ncaa.org/mission-and-priorities.

Pfitzner, V. 1967. *Paul and the Agon Motif*. Leiden, Netherlands: Brill.

SRS. 2020. "SRS International." Accessed February 2022. https://www.srs-international.org/srs-international.

Weir, Stuart. n.d. "Paul and Sport." Verité Sport. Accessed July 27, 2022. https://veritesport.org/?page=sd_faithandsport_paulandsport.

Willard, Dallas. n.d. "Spiritual Formation: What It Is, and How It Is Done." Dallas Willard. Accessed July 27, 2022. https://dwillard.org/articles/spiritual-formation-what-it-is-and-how-it-is-done.

Willard, Dallas. 1988. *The Spirit of the Disciplines: Understanding How God Changes Lives*. New York: HarperCollins.

Willard, Dallas. 2006. *The Great Omission: Reclaiming Jesus's Essential Teachings on Discipleship*. San Francisco: HarperOne.

Chapter 6

Connor, Steve. 2003. *Sports Outreach: Principles and Practice for Successful Sports Ministry*. Ross-shire, Scotland: Christian Focus Publications.

Chapter 7

Bishop, Greg. 2011. "In Tebow Debate, a Clash of Faith and Football." *New York Times*, November 7, 2011. www.nytimes.com/2011/11/08/sports/football/in-tebow-debate-a-clash-of-faith-and-football.html.

Brown, Bruce. 2003. *Teaching Character Through Sport: Developing a Positive Coaching Legacy*. Monterey, CA: Coaches Choice.

Cede Sports. 2018. "How Do You Know When Sports Are An Idol? Parts 1-4." June 27-July 6, . Cede Sports. www.cedesports.org/how-do-you-know-when-sports-are-an-idol-part-4-2.

Clifford, Craig, and Randolph Feezell. 2010. *Sport and Character: Reclaiming the Principles of Sportsmanship*. Champaign, IL: Human Kinetics.

Deford, Frank. 1976a. "Religion in Sport." *Sports Illustrated*, April 19, 1976. https://vault.si.com/vault/1976/04/19/religion-in-sport.

Deford, Frank. 1976b. "Reaching for the Stars." *Sports Illustrated*, May 3, 1976. https://vault.si.com/vault/1976/05/03/reaching-for-the-stars.

Deford, Frank. 1976c. "The Word According to Tom." *Sports Illustrated*, April 26, 1976. https://vault.si.com/vault/1976/04/26/the-word-according-to-tom.

Eitzen, D. Stanley. 2012. *Sport in Contemporary Society*, 9th ed. Boulder, CO: Paradigm.

Elwell, Walter, ed. 1989. *Evangelical Commentary on the Bible*. Grand Rapids, MI: Baker Book House.

Garner, John, ed. 2003. *Recreation and Sports Ministry: Impacting Postmodern Culture*. Nashville: Broadman & Holman.

Hoffman, Shirl. 2010. *Good Game: Christianity and the Culture of Sports*. Waco, TX: Baylor University Press.

Hoven, Matt, Andrew Parker, and Nick Watson. 2019. *Sport and Christianity: Practices for the Twenty-First Century*. New York: T&T Clark Bloomsbury.

Kerrigan, Michael. 2008. "Sports in the Christian Life." Center for Christian Ethics at Baylor University. Accessed June 17, 2012. www.baylor.edu/content/services/document.php/75229.pdf.

Kretschmann, Rolf, and Caroline Benz. 2012a. "God Has a Plan: Moral Values and Beliefs of Christian Athletes in Competitive Sport." *Journal of Human Sport and Exercise* 7, no. 2 (May 2012): https://doi.org/10.4100/jhse.2012.72.14.

Kretschmann, Rolf, and Caroline Benz. 2012b. "Morality of Christian Athletes in Competitive Sports—A Review." *Sport Science Review* 21, no. 1-2 (April 2012): https://doi.org/10.2478/v10237-012-0001-y.

Lay, Nancy. 1993. "Sport and Religion: An Unholy Alliance." Accessed May 15, 2021. Knoxville: University of Tennessee. eric.ed.gov/?id=ED358047.

Linville, Greg. 2014. *Christmanship: A Theology of Competition and Sport.* Canton, OH: Oliver House.

Martens, Rainer. 2012. *Successful Coaching.* Champaign, IL: Human Kinetics.

McCown, Lowrie, and Valerie Gin. 2003. *Focus on Sport in Ministry.* Marietta, GA: 360 Sports.

Neal, Wes. 1975. *Total Release Performance: A New Concept in Winning.* Branson, MO: Institute of Athletic Perfection.

Palmiter, Brian. n.d. "Cheating, Gamesmanship, and a Concept of Practice." Harvard University. Accessed July 1, 2021. https://scholar.harvard.edu/files/brianpalmiter/files/cheating_gamesmanship_and_practices.pdf.

Putz, Paul. n.d. "How Billy Graham Made Peace with Sunday Sports." Athletes in Action. Accessed June 29, 2021. https://athletesinaction.org/articles/how-billy-graham-made-peace-with-sunday-sports.

Quebedeaux, Richard. 1979. *I Found It: The Story of Bill Bright and Campus Crusade.* New York: Harper & Row.

Reich, Frank. 2002. "Competition and Creation." *IIIM Magazine Online* 4(6): www.yumpu.com/en/document/view/2280692/competition-and-creation-by-frank-reich.

Reinke, Tony. 2018. "Spring Sports and Sunday Church." Desiring God. April 17, 2018. www.desiringgod.org/articles/spring-sports-and-sunday-church.

Shafer, Michael. 2015. *Well Played: A Christian Theology of Sport and the Ethics of Doping.* Cambridge, UK: Lutterworth Press.

Tim Tebow Foundation. 2021. Accessed August 21, 2022. Timtebowfoundation.org/about/board/tim-tebow.

Treat, Jeremy. 2015. "More Than A Game: A Theology of Sport." *Themelios* 40(3): 392-403. www.thegospelcoalition.org/themelios/article/more-than-a-game-theology-of-sport.

Warner, Gary. 1979. *Competition.* Elgin, Illinois: David C. Cook Publishing.

Woods, Ronald. 2016. *Social Issues in Sport,* 3rd ed. Champaign, IL: Human Kinetics.

Chapter 8

Atcheson, Wayne. 1994. *Impact for Christ: How FCA Has Influenced the Sports World.* Kearney, NE: Cross Training Publications.

Bright, Bill. 2007. "How to Witness in the Spirit." Cru. Accessed December 2, 2021. www.cru.org/content/dam/cru/legacy/2012/04/brighthowtowitnessinthespirit.pdf.

Chambers, Oswald. 1963. "The Discipline of Spiritual Tenacity." In *My Utmost for His Highest.* Uhrichsville, OH: Barbour Publishing.

Chen, James. 2021. "Transparency." Investopedia. Accessed July 17, 2021. www.investopedia.com/terms/t/transparency.asp.

Compton, Ray. 2014. "Tom Abernethy's IBA: An Academy of Basketball and Life Lessons." *Carmel Monthly Magazine,* June 6, 2014.

Evangelical Council for Financial Accountability. n.d. "About ECFA." Evangelical Council for Financial Accountability. Accessed November 16, 2021. https://www.ecfa.org/About.aspx.

Evans, Tony. n.d. "A Spiritual Return on Investment." Tony Evans. Accessed January 7, 2022. https://tonyevans.org/blog/a-spiritual-return-on-investment.

Fellowship of Christian Athletes. n.d. "Vison and Mission." Fellowship of Christian Athletes. Accessed January 7, 2022. www.fac.org/aboutus/who-we-are/vision-mission.

Fried, Gil, Timothy DeSchriver, and Michael Mondello. 2020. *Sport Finance,* 4th ed. Champaign, IL Human Kinetics.

God's Chemistry Set. 2011. "As Iron Sharpens Iron." September 22, 2011. *God's Chemistry Set* (blog). https://godschemistryset.blogspot.com/2011/09/as-iron-sharpens-iron.html.

Gospel Patrons. n.d. "Our Story." Gospel Patrons. Accessed February 6, 2022. www.gospelpatrons.org/our_story.

Got Questions. n.d. "Why Is a Multitude of Counselors Valuable?" Got Questions. Accessed January 6, 2022. www.gotquestions.org/multitude-of-counselors.html.

Kay, Sarah. 2014. *No Matter the Wreckage, Poems by Sarah Kay.* Austin, TX. Write Bloody Publishing.

Leonard, Kimberly, Jane Haskins, and Cassie Bottorff. 2021. "501(c)(3) Application: Apply for Tax-Exempt Status Online." Forbes Advisor. Accessed December 10, 2021. www.forbes.com/advisor/business/501c3-application-online.

Lotich, Bob. 2022. "Tithing in the New Testament & Old." Seedtime. June 29, 2022. https://seedtime.com/tithing-in-the-new-testament.

MacArthur, John. n.d. "35 Christian Quotes on Stewardship." Viral Believer. Accessed January 7, 2022. https://viralbeliever.com/christian-quotes-on-stewardship.

Morwick, Rick. 2018. "Bigger Vision Links Basketball, Faith in Whitestown." Current Publishing. Accessed December 10, 2021. https://youarecurrent.com/2018/01/06/bigger-vision-links-basketball-faith-in-whitestown.

Nouwen, Henri J. 2010. *A Spirituality of Fundraising.* Nashville: Upper Room Books.

Qgiv. 2021. "Giving USA 2021 Report: Charitable Giving Trends." Qgiv. Accessed July 27, 2022. www.qgiv.com/blog/giving-usa-2021.

Packer, Michael. 2011. "Jesus Talked the Most About . . . Money?" Patch. July 23, 2011. https://patch.com/.../jesus-talked-the-most-aboutmoney.

Shadrach, Steve. 2013. *The God Ask.* Fayetteville, AR: CMM Press.

TEAM. 2020. "Ask TEAM: How Do Missionaries Get Paid?" TEAM. October 9, 2020. https://team.org/blog/how-missionaries-get-paid.

Von Gunten, McKenna. n.d. "8 Ways Missionaries Make Money Overseas." Bethany Global University. Accessed January 8, 2022. https://bethanygu.edu/blog/funding/8-ways-missionaries-make-money-overseas.

Zylstra, Sarah Eekhoff. 2016. "Southern Baptists Lose Almost 1,000 Missionaries as IMB Cuts Costs." *Christianity Today*, February 24, 2016. www.christianitytoday.com/news/2016/february/southern-baptists-lose-1132-missionaries-staff-imb-cuts.html.

Chapter 9

Baker, Dave. 2017. "7 Steps to Writing an RFP That Gets High-Quality Responses." Super Copy Editors. August 29, 2017. https://supercopyeditors.com/blog/writing/tips-for-writing-an-rfp.

Bragg, Steven. 2022. "Pro Forma Financial Statements Definition." AccountingTools. May 22, 2022. www.accountingtools.com/articles/what-are-pro-forma-financial-statements.html.

Conklin, Mike. 2002. "That Hang-Time Religion." *Chicago Tribune*, June 7, 2002. www.chicagotribune.com/news/ct-xpm-2002-06-07-0206070003-story.html.

De Pree, Max. 2004. "Excerpt From Leadership Is An Art." LeadershipNow. Accessed May 5, 2021. www.leadershipnow.com/leadershop/3024-8excerpt.html.

Derrick, J.C. 2020. "Moody Proposed Sale of 8 Acres, Including Prized Solheim Center, Moves Forward." The Roys Report. November 5, 2020. https://julieroys.com/moody-sale-solheim.

Earthnetworks. 2019. "8 Things to Consider When Building a Sports Complex." Earth Networks. February 22, 2019. www.earthnetworks.com/blog/8-things-consider-building-a-new-sports-complex.

Examples.com. n.d. "How To Write a Request For Proposal." Examples.com. Accessed February 18, 2022. www.examples.com/business/write-request-for-proposal.html.

Fellowship of Christian Athletes. n.d. "About Us." Central Maryland FCA. Accessed February 27, 2022. https://cmdfca.org/aboutus.

Fried, Gil. 2015. *Managing Sport Facilities*, 3rd ed. Champaign, IL: Human Kinetics.

Garner, John. n.d. "Sport Facilities: Maximizing What You Have." Recreation and Sports Ministry.com. Accessed February 18, 2022. https://recandsportsministry.wordpress.com/tag/church-facilities.

Garner, John, and Gary Nicholson. 2006. *Guidebook for Planning Church Recreation Facilities*, 2nd ed. Nashville: LifeWay Christian Resources.

Koehler, Sezin. 2020. "The Untold Truth of the Field of Dreams." Looper. January 14, 2020. www.looper.com/183254/the-untold-truth-of-field-of-dreams.

LetsBuild. 2019. "RFP in Construction: A Comprehensive Guide." LetsBuild. January 11, 2019. www.letbuild.com/blog/rfp-in-construction.

Mid America Specialty Services. n.d. "Score Big With Sports Facility Preventative Maintenance." Mid America Specialty Services. Accessed February 18, 2022. www.massus.com/blog/score-big-with-sports-facility-maintenance.

Moody Bible Institute. n.d. "History of the Solheim Center." Moody Bible Institute. Accessed January 21, 2022. www.moodyarchers.org/solheim-center/history/history_of_solheim_center.

Murray, Andrew. n.d. Christian History Institute. Famous Quotes from Famous People. "The world asks, 'What does a man own?' Christ asks, 'How does he use it?'" https://christianhistoryinstitute.org/magazine/article/famous-money-quotes-from-famous-people.

One7. n.d. "About Us." One7. Accessed February 19, 2022. https://one7.org/about-us.

Sadler Sports and Recreation Insurance. 2006. "Before You Sign the Sports Facility Lease Agreement." Sadler Sports and Recreation Insurance. March 10, 2006. www.sadler-sports.com/riskmanagement/sports-insurance-lease.php.

Scalisi, Tom. 2021. "The 6 Stages of a Construction Project & Why They Matter." LevelSet. December 30, 2021. www.levelset.com/blog/construction-project-phases-2.

Sports Facilities Companies. 2018. "Feasibility Study: Five Reasons Why You Need to Conduct One." Sports Facilities Companies. May 13, 2018. https://sportsfacilities.com/feasibility-study-five-reasons-need-conduct-one.

Tortschnekkel, Vanda. 2009. "Willa A. Foster: Quality Quote Perpetuates Idiotic Mistake." Tortschnekkel Today. May 8, 2009. http://tortschnekkel.blogspot.com/2009/05/willa-foster-quality-quote-perpetuates.html.

Chapter 10

Baptist Standard. 2010. "What Should Churches and Ministries Know About Employment Law." Baptist Standard. July 2, 2010. www.baptiststandard.com/news/faith-culture/what-should-churches-and-ministries-know-about-employment-law.

Better Coaching. 2022. "Emergency Action Plan." Better Coaching. Accessed June 6, 2022. www.betteryouthcoaching.com/emergency-action-plans.

Cachila, J.B. 2016. "5 Bible Verses on the Responsibilities of a Christian, the Ambassador of Christ." Christian Today. June 18, 2016. www.christiantoday.com/article/5-bible-verses-showing-the-responsibilities-of-a-christian-the-ambassador-of-christ/88518.htm.

Cam, Christine. 2019. "How to Stay Safe During a Lightning Storm." Sciencing. November 19, 2019. https://sciencing.com/stay-safe-during-lightning-storm-2313448.html.

Cameron, Courtney. 2017. "Death of Toddler Raises Goal Post Safety Concerns." Athletic Business. May 3, 2017. www.athleticbusiness.com/operations/safety/article/15150208/death-of-toddler-raises-goal-post-safety-concerns?eid=61623946&bid=1743975.

Church Law. 2020. "Which Federal Employment Laws Apply to Churches." Church Law. November 10, 2020. www.churchlawcenter.com/church-law/which-federal-employment-laws-apply-to-churches.

Congress.gov. n.d. "First Amendment." Constitution Annotated. Accessed June 2, 2022. https://constitution.congress.gov/constitution/amendment-1.

Corada. n.d. "Mission Statement." Corada. Accessed February 22, 2022. www.corada.com.

Cornell Law School. 2017. "Administrative Law." Cornell University. Last updated June 2022. www.law.cornell.edu/wex/administrative_law.

Cornell Law School. 2019. "Constitutional Law." Cornell University. Last updated June 10, 2019. www.law.cornell.edu/wex/constitutional_law.

Cornell Law School. 2020. "Common Law." Cornell University. Last updated May 2020. www.law.cornell.edu/wex/common_law.

Cotton, Doyice. 2017. "Soccer Goals: 40 Deaths and 59 Injuries in 38 Years." Sport Waiver. May 16, 2017. www.sportwaiver.com/soccer-goal-posts-40-deaths-59-serious-injuries-in-38-years.

Cwik, Paulina. 2016. "Lightning Victims All Have This in Common." NOAA, July 21, 2016. www.noaa.gov/news/lightning-victims-all-have-in-common.

DeLench, Brooke. 2015. "Emergency Action Plan: Essential for Youth Sports Safety." Moms Team. July 24, 2015. www.momsteam.com/health-safety/general-safety/emergency-medical-plan-essential-for-youth-sports-safety.

Federal Judicial Center. 2016. "The U.S. Legal System: A Short Description." Federal Judicial Center. March 26, 2016. https://ar.usembassy.gov/wp-content/uploads/sites/26/2016/03/U_S__Legal_System_English07.pdf.

Fried, Gil. 2015. Managing Sport Facilities, 3rd ed. Champaign, IL: Human Kinetics.

Gershom, Richard, and Kimberly Peer. 2008. "Program and Facility Emergencies in Youth Sports, Part II: Dealing With the Event." The Sport Journal 24 (July 7, 2008). https://thesportjournal.org/article/tag/volume_9_number_2/page/4.

Goodreads. n.d. "The Best Defense Is a Good Offense." Goodreads. Accessed February 26, 2022. www.goodreads.com/quotes/135817-the-best-defense-is-a-good-offense.

Green, Lee. 2015. "Top Ten Sports Law Issues Impacting School Athletic Programs." NFHS. May 20, 2015. www.nfhs.org/articles/top-ten-sports-law-issues-impacting-school-athletic-programs.

Green, Lee. 2016. "Sports Event Management and Security: Legal Issues, Strategies." NFHS. October 5, 2016. www.nfhs.org/articles/sports-event-management-and-security-legal-issues-strategies.

Hamilton, Marci C., and Michael McConnell. n.d. "The Establishment Clause." Interactive Constitution. Accessed June 3, 2022. https://constitutioncenter.org/interactive-constitution/interpretation/amendment-i/interps/264.

HG.org Legal Resources. n.d. "Statutory Law." HG.org Legal Resources. Accessed February 26, 2022. www.hg.org/statutory-law.html.

Indeed Editorial Team. 2022. "What Is Constitutional Law? Definition, Importance and Jobs." Indeed. April 14, 2022. www.indeed.com/career-advice/finding-a-job/what-is-constitutional-law.

Legal Career Path. n.d. "What is Contract Law?" Legal Career Path. Accessed February 26, 2022. https://legalcareerpath.com/what-is-contract-law.

Legal Dictionary. 2015. s.v. "Common Law." Legal Dictionary. October 15, 2015. https://legaldictionary.net/common-law.

Legal Knowledge Base. 2022. "What Is an Example of Common Law?" Legal Knowledge Base. Last updated February 19, 2022. https://legalknowledgebase.com/what-is-an-example-of-common-law.

Moorman, Anita, C. Reynolds, and S. Siegrist. 2019. Legal Considerations in Sport. In Paul Pedersen and Lucy Thibault (eds.), Contemporary Sport Management, 6th ed. (pp. 358-379). Champaign, IL: Human Kinetics.

Morrow, Angela. 2019. "When Your Fears About Dying Are Unhealthy." Verywell Mind. Last updated June 9, 2022. www.verywellmind.com/scared-to-death-of-death-1132501#:~:text=The%20fear%20of%20death%20and,an%20unhealthy%20fear%20of%20.

Office of Disability Employment Policy. n.d. "Employment Laws: Overview and Resources for Employers." U.S. Department of Labor. Accessed June 3, 2022. https://www.dol.gov/agencies/odep/publications/fact-sheets/employment-laws-overview-and-resources-for-employers.

Pedersen, Paul, and Lucie Thibault. 2019. Contemporary Sport Management, 6th ed. Champaign, IL: Human Kinetics.

Russo, Nick. 2020. "Why Are You Safe From Lightning in a Car?" NBC12 WWBT News. Last updated April 6, 2020. www.nbc12.com/2020/04/06/why-are-you-safe-lightning-car/#:~:text=Cars%20are%20safe%20from%20lightning%20because%20of%20the%20metal%20cage,and%20safely%20into%20the%20ground.

Spengler, John, Daniel Connaughton, and Andrew Pittman. 2006. Risk Management in Sport and Recreation. Champaign, IL: Human Kinetics.

Sports Field Management. 2018. "Limiting Liability for Your Sports Facility." Sports Field Management. February 27, 2018. https://sportsfieldmanagementonline.com/2018/02/27/limiting-liability-for-your-sports-facility-3/9334.

Stop Sport Injuries. 2019. "Heat Illness Prevention." American Orthopedic Society for Sports Medicine. Accessed February 26, 2022. www.stopsportsinjuries.org/STOP/STOP/Prevent_Injuries/Heat_Illness_prevention.aspx.

United States Courts. n.d. "First Amendment and Religion." United States Courts. Accessed May 27, 2022. www.uscourts.gov/educational-resources/educational-activities/first-amendment-and-religion.

USLegal. n.d. s.v. "Tort Law." USLegal. Accessed February 26, 2022. https://definitions.uslegal.com/t/tort-law.

Chapter 11

Drury, Linda. 2005. *Go, Ye: A Guide to Short Term Missions*. Greenwood Village, CO: Linda Drury.

Elmer, Duane. 2006. *Cross-Cultural Servanthood: Serving the World in Christlike Humility*. Downers Grove, IL: InterVarsity Press.

Lanier, Sarah. 2000. *Foreign to Familiar: A Guide to Understanding Hot- and Cold-Climate Cultures*. Hagerstown, MD: McDougal Publishing.

National Christian College Athletic Association. 2018. "PHED 305: Learning About Ministry By Doing Ministry." *The Pursuit* 29(3): 4-6 (July 2018).

Reichart, Richard. 2001. *Missions Is a Contact Sport: A Survival Manual for Short-Term Missions*. Richard Reichart: First Books Library. www.1stbooks.com.

World Health Organization. 2022. "Malaria." World Health Organization. July 26, 2022. www.who.int/news-room/fact-sheets/detail/malaria.

Chapter 12

Associated Press. 2013. "Bob Ladouceur Finishes 399-25-3." ESPN. January 4, 2013. www.espn.com/espn/story/_/id/8814474/bob-ladouceur-coaching-great-de-la-salle-high-school-retires-34years.

Athletes in Action. n.d. "Sports Complex and Retreat Center." Athletes in Action. Accessed December 20, 2021. www.athletesinaction.org/sports-complex/facilities.

Bird, Warren, and Scott Thumma. 2020. "Mega Church 2020: The Changing Reality in America's Largest Churches." Hartford Institute for Religion Research. Accessed December 29, 2021. www.hirr.hartsem.edu/megachurch/2020_megachurch_report.pdf.

Brotherhood Mutual. n.d. "NFL Copyright Guidelines: Hosting a Game Day Bash? Brush Up on Copyright Basics." Brotherhood Mutual. Accessed December 23, 2021. www.brotherhoodmutual.com/resources/safety-library/risk-management-articles/administrative-staff-and-finance/documents-and-data/nfl-copyright-guidelines.

Camp JYC. n.d. "Home." Camp JYC. Accessed December 29, 2021. www.campjyc.org.

CSRM. n.d. "Who We Are." CSRM. Accessed December 28, 2021. www.csrm.org.

Grace and Truth Sports. n.d. "What Is G&T?" Grace and Truth Sports. Accessed December 20, 2021. www.gandtathletics.info/about.

Leeman, Matthew. 2021. "The Movies That Best Demonstrate Christianity in Sports." April 28, 2021. The Roar. www.piedmontroar.com/9148/sliderposts/the-movies-that-best-demonstrate-christianity-in-sports.

Mason, Bryan. 2003. *Into the Stadium: An Active Guide to Sport and Recreation Ministry in the Local Church*. Bucks, UK: Spring Harvest Publishing.

Mount Pleasant Christian Church Community Life Center. n.d. "About the CLC." Mount Pleasant Christian Church Community Life Center. Accessed December 29, 2021. www.pcc.info/community-life-center/welcome/about-the-clc.

Naismith Memorial Basketball Hall of Fame. n.d. "Cathy Rush Induction." Accessed December 27, 2021. Naismith Memorial Basketball Hall of Fame. www.hoophall.com/hall-of-famers/cathy-rush.

On Goal. n.d. "Our History." On Goal. Accessed December 19, 2021. www.ongoal.org/history.

Pathway Community Church. n.d. "Sports Ministry." Pathway Community Church. Accessed December 14, 2021. www.pccfw.org/ministries/sports.

Pedersen, Paul, and Lucie Thibault, eds. 2019. *Contemporary Sport Management*, 6th ed. Champaign, IL: Human Kinetics.

Chapter 13

Baseball Chapel. n.d. "What is Baseball Chapel?" and "Baseball Chapel History." Baseball Chapel. Accessed February 12, 2022. www.baseballchapel.org/documents/presentation.pdf.

Chicago Eagles. n.d. "The Summer Academy." Chicago Eagles. Accessed January 28, 2022. https://play.chicagoeagles.com/page/show/5888391-sa-u23-sa-2021-.

Christians in Sport. n.d. "Christians in Sport." Accessed February 20, 2022. www.christiansinsport.org.uk.

Climbing for Christ. n.d. "Climbing for Christ." Accessed February 4, 2022. www.climbingforchrist.org.

Go. Serve. Love. 2019. "Meet an Agency: Push The Rock Sports Ministry." Go. Serve. Love. January 29, 2019. www.goservelove.net/push-rock.

Hauge, Sarah. 2019. "What Shredding Means." Out There Outdoors. December 25, 2019. www.outthereoutdoors.com/what-shredding-means.

Herd, Aimee. 2006. "God in the Game—How Baseball Chapel Helps Keep Players Spiritually in Tune." Breaking Christian News. September 29, 2006. www.breakingchristiannews.com/articles/display_art.html?ID=3086.

Kuhn, Bowie. 1997. *Hardball: The Education of a Baseball Commissioner*. Lincoln, NE: Bison Books.

Lausanne Movement. 1983. "Lausanne Occasional Paper: Cooperating in World Evangelism: A Handbook on Church/Para-Church Relationships." Lausanne Movement. Accessed February 3, 2022. www.lausanne.org/content/lop/lop-24.

Push The Rock. n.d. "Push The Rock." Accessed February 11, 2022. www.pushtherock.org.

ReadySetGO. n.d. "ReadySetGO." Accessed February 20, 2022. www.readysetgo.ec/en.

Saunders, Jon. 2015. "The Place and Purpose of Parachurch Ministries: Serving the Local Church and Fulfilling the Great Commission at Her Side." The Gospel Coalition. August 31, 2015. www.thegospelcoalition.org/article/parachurch-ministry.

SIM. n.d. "About Us." SIM. Accessed February 8, 2022. www.simusa.org/about.

Snowboarders and Skiers for Christ. n.d. "Snowboarders and Skiers for Christ." Accessed February 5, 2022. www.wearesfc.org.

Sports Friends. n.d. "Sports Friends." Accessed February 8, 2022. www.sports-friends.org.

Sports Outreach. 2021. "The Chess Academy." Sports Outreach. Accessed February 3, 2022. www.sportsoutreach.net/southern.uganda.

Stiles, J. Mack. 2011. "Nine Marks of a Healthy Parachurch Ministry." 9Marks. March 1, 2011. www.9marks.org/article/journalnine-marks-healthy-parachurch-ministry.

Summer's Best Two Weeks. n.d. "Summer's Best Two Weeks." Accessed February 4, 2022. www.sb2w.org.

Youth Dynamics. n.d. "Youth Dynamics." Accessed February 6, 2022. www.yd.org.

Chapter 14

Coleman, Timothy. n.d. "Disability in Kenya: Reaching Out to the Hidden and Forgotten." SIM. Accessed February 24, 2022. www.sim.org/w/disability-in-kenya-reaching-out-to-the-hidden-and-forgotten-1?Ministry_ID=&countries=Kenya.

Cook, Keelan. 2019. "Why Understanding Culture Helps Us Fulfill the Great Commission." Center for Faith & Culture. July 29, 2019. www.cfc.sebts.edu/faith-and-culture/understanding-culture-helps-fulfill-great-commission.

Cosper, Mike. 2014. "What's the Deal With Foot Washing?" Crossway. November 20, 2014. www.crossway.org/articles/whats-the-deal-with-footwashing.

Elmer, Duane. 2006. *Cross-Cultural Servanthood: Serving the World in Christlike Humility*. Downers Grove, IL: InterVarsity Press.

Geldenhuys, Norval. 1979. *The Gospel of Luke*. Grand Rapids, MI: Eerdmans Publishing.

Hiebert, Paul. 1986. *Anthropological Insights for Missionaries*. Ada, MI: Baker Academic.

Lane, William. 1974. *The Gospel of Mark*. Grand Rapids, MI: Eerdmans Publishing.

Morris, John. 1971. *The Gospel According to John*. Grand Rapids, MI: Eerdmans Publishing.

Tasker, R.V.G. 1960. *The Gospel According to St. John*. Grand Rapids, MI: Eerdmans Publishing.

United Nations Refugee Agency. n.d. "Europe." United Nations Refugee Agency. Accessed February 26, 2022. www.unhcr.org/en-us/europe.html.

INDEX

Note: The italicized *f* and *t* following page numbers refer to figures and tables, respectively.

David Lewis, DMin, is a sports ministry practitioner and educator, presently serving as associate professor at Huntington University in Indiana, where he oversees the sport management students. He is also an adjunct professor in the graduate program at Milligan University in Tennessee. Prior to Huntington, he created and directed the academic sports ministry minor at Houghton University in New York and developed and taught sports ministry courses.

His own sports ministry practice began as an undergraduate at The King's College in New York, where he and his college roommate organized an informal weightlifting ministry, combining strength demonstrations with Christian testimony and biblical instruction. A collegiate All-American soccer player, upon graduation Lewis moved to southern California and served full time with Athletes in Action Soccer, the sports ministry arm of CRU. Lewis has actively used sport, recreation, and camping as ministry tools in the local church. He has served as a youth pastor, associate pastor, and senior pastor at churches in Massachusetts and New York.

Since 1991, Lewis has coached women's soccer and is among a small group of collegiate women's coaches to achieve over 400 career wins. In 2015, he led the Houghton University women's soccer team to the National Christian College Athletic Association (NCCAA) Division I national championship, becoming the first and only NCAA Division III team to win the title. He was subsequently named the NSCAA/NCCAA Division I National Coach of the Year. Believing that one learns about ministry by doing ministry, he has led his soccer teams on multiple short-term soccer-specific sports ministry trips to 11 countries on five continents in partnership with ministries such as SCORE International, Missionary Athletes International, Sports Friends, Surge International, and Global Partners. An ordained minister, Lewis has performed the weddings of more than two dozen of his former soccer players.

After earning a bachelor's degree in religion and philosophy from The King's College, Lewis earned master of divinity and doctor of ministry degrees from Gordon-Conwell Theological Seminary in Massachusetts.

Courtesy of Ryan Irby

Dave Irby, MAT, is the founder of Surge International/Surge soccer, a 501(c)(3) nonprofit sports ministry that has virtual offices in the United States and Liberia. A native of southern California, Irby played soccer on the inaugural varsity team at Azusa Pacific University, which was his first time playing organized soccer. At the age of 23, he became the head coach of the Cougars, twice being named Coach of the Year, while playing with the Athletes in Action soccer team during the same time period.

A pioneer of the soccer ministry movement, Irby has criss-crossed the globe as a soccer player, coach, and speaker. He founded the Seahorse soccer team for Missionary Athletes International and was the first full-time staff member. This experience would provide the inspiration for the founding of Surge International in 1992. Irby and the soccer teams he has led have traveled to 32 countries to play in a variety of settings, including prisons, jungle villages, and national soccer stadiums. His multinational teams have helped with reconciliation in Uganda after that country's civil war, were on a peace tour to Sudan during their civil war, and traveled to Burundi to help with civil war prevention. More recently, from 2016 through 2019, Irby oversaw a soccer ministry project in Austria where he and his multinational colleagues used the platform of soccer to help refugees integrate into European society and to share Christ's love with them. Surge has extended their work to Liberia with the launching of Surge Soccer Liberia, an initiative that is training leaders, assisting in educational development, and shedding light on the great needs of the country. Surge Soccer and their mascot, Sammy Surge, have visited over 150,000 children in four states and four foreign countries.

Irby has self-published two books on Amazon: *Undefeated*, a compilation of four soccer-specific devotionals, now in five languages; and *Sammy Surge in Study Hard, Play Fair, Help Others*, a children's book featuring life principles taught by Sammy Surge, the world-traveling mascot of Surge Soccer.

Irby is a U.S. Soccer A-licensed coach. He has a master's degree in teaching from University of La Verne in California and has a bachelor's degree in social science and a bachelor's degree in physical education from Azusa Pacific University in California. He is a member of United Soccer Coaches and Toastmasters International.

Irby resides in Salem, Oregon, with his wife, Susan, and has three grown children and three grandchildren. He has attended five World Cups and enjoys hiking, reading, and travel, which has taken him to 47 countries and counting.

William Galipault, DMin, is the executive director for the Seahorse Soccer ministry, a division of Missionary Athletes International (MAI). Seahorse Soccer has youth camps and clinics, a youth league, an urban youth program in the Los Angeles area, and an under-23 team in the United Soccer League (USL2), and they do international trips each year to Japan, Cuba, and the Czech Republic. He is also active in education as an adjunct professor with The Master's University and Houghton University and as the director of the master's in sports outreach program at Barclay College.

Galipault's career in sports began at Nyack College (now Alliance University) in New York, where he was the men's head coach for seven years and earned coaching honors at the district and regional levels while completing a master of professional studies degree at Alliance Theological Seminary and a master of science in education for physical educators at Lehman College. Along the way, he added experience as an assistant athletic director and a PE instructor, ran soccer camps at the school, and took his players internationally, which is where he caught the attention of MAI and was recruited to join its staff.

Bringing his experience to MAI, Galipault was involved in all areas of the ministry while also helping oversee the mission's finances. He and his family spent six years in the Czech Republic, where he held ministry training conferences for Czech Christian athletes and led a small team from the United States and England in helping Czech churches learn how to use sports ministry as part of their work with their communities.

Throughout his career, Galipault's focus has been ministry training coupled with theoretical and philosophical underpinnings when working with young men and women coming into various ministries. His desire to make this same training available in universities is what prompted Galipault to obtain a doctor of ministry degree; his doctoral project was titled "Spiritual Formation in the Team Sport Environment and Its Application for Churches.'

Wayne Rasmussen, EdD, is the program director of the new sport management major and an associate professor in the School of Business and Communication at The Master's University. He plans to blend an academically challenging curriculum with valuable practical experiences that will prepare university students to serve in all levels of professional, collegiate, and youth sports in the areas of administration and management. He also serves as the faculty athletics representative. Prior to this, Rasmussen enjoyed a successful five-year run at Columbia International University in South Carolina, where he created, launched, and directed the school's undergraduate sport management program in their School of Business in the summer of 2015.

Rasmussen's career began at Southern Methodist University in Dallas, where he was an assistant soccer coach before leaving for a head coaching job at Creighton University in Omaha. He later held positions on the administrative staffs of the Olympic and U.S. men's national soccer teams as well as roles with three Major League Soccer clubs. Notably, he was the LA Galaxy's director of operations and player development during the team's inaugural MLS season in 1996 in the Rose Bowl. Rasmussen had a stint with the Tampa Bay Mutiny before becoming one of the founding members of the Philadelphia Union.

During his career, Rasmussen has also been an athletic director and head soccer coach at Eastern University in St. David's, Pennsylvania. He has organized sports ministry trips and has led multiple cycling tours and wilderness adventure trips.